FINANCIAL SERVICES MARKETING

We work with leading authors to develop the strongest educational materials in Marketing, bringing cutting-edge thinking and best learning practice to a global market.

Under a range of well-known imprints, including Financial Times Prentice Hall, we craft high-quality print and electronic publications which help readers to understand and apply their content, whether studying or at work.

To find out about the complete range of our publishing please visit us on the World Wide Web at:

www.pearsoneduc.com

FINANCIAL SERVICES MARKETING

Tina Harrison
University of Edinburgh Management School

An imprint of Pearson Education

Harlow, England · London · New York · Reading, Massachusetts · San Francisco · Toronto · Don Mills, Ontario · Sydney
Tokyo · Singapore · Hong Kong · Seoul · Taipei · Cape Town · Madrid · Mexico City · Amsterdam · Munich · Paris · Milan

Pearson Education Limited
Edinburgh Gate
Harlow
Essex CM20 2JE
England

and Associated Companies throughout the World.

Visit us on the World Wide Web at:
www.pearsoneduc.com

First published 2000

ISBN 0-273-63297-3

British Library Cataloging-in-Publication Data
A catalogue record for this book can be obtained from the British Library

Library of Congress Cataloguing-in-Publication Data
Harrison, Tina.
Financial services marketing/Tina Harrison.
p. cm
Includes bibliographical references and index.
ISBN 0-273-63297-3 (alk. paper)
1. Financial services industry – Marketing. 2. Bank marketing. 3. Marketing.
4. Information technology. I. Title

HG173 .H37 2000
332.1'068'8 – dc21 00-021794

10 9 8 7 6 5 4 3 2 1
05 04 03 02 01 00

Typeset by 3
Printed and bound in Great Britain by Redwood Books Ltd, Trowbridge, Wiltshire.

Contents

Financial Services Marketing in Practice

Chapter 1

Chapter 2

Chapter 3

Chapter 4

Chapter 5

Chapter 6

List of figures

List of tables

PREFACE

In the last thirty years or so, the financial services sector has experienced changes unprecedented in its history. Prior to this, the sector was characterised by functional demarcation and regulatory restrictions, which served to limit competition. Successive deregulation, advances in technology and a more sophisticated, cynical and mobile customer base have altered both the structure of the industry and the nature of competition within it.

In 1989, Brooks noted:

> 'Soon all that will remain of the old industries are the names of the founding institutions – and even those are changing.'

Indeed, many of the large building societies and life assurance offices have demutualised, or converted to public quoted companies. The boundaries between institutions have increasingly become blurred, to the point that most institutions now offer the same products to the same customers. A number of take-overs and mergers have taken place, which have altered even the names of institutions. The Midland Bank, has been renamed HSBC, following acquisition by the Hong Kong Shanghai Banking Corporation. Other potential mergers are a subject of constant debate in the press. Furthermore, alongside the traditional institutions in the marketplace are supermarkets, retailers, internet organisations and utilities companies all offering financial services, and many at competitive rates with higher customer service levels.

The result has been to heighten competition in the sector and place increased emphasis on marketing in an attempt to retain market shares and profitability. While marketing may be seen as crucial to the long-term success of financial organisations, the traditional institutions have been criticised in the past for their lack of attention to marketing and the customer – being accused of adopting merely some activities of marketing but failing to embrace a true marketing philosophy. The entry of more 'customer-focused' organisations to the competitive arena only serves to reinforce the importance of adopting a customer-centred philosophy.

Interest in the subject of financial services marketing has grown. There are a number of journals now devoted specifically to the publication of marketing research in the financial services sector, and there are a growing number of courses and, indeed, degree programmes on the subject. The growth in interest is both a function of the development and changes in the sector as well as a recognition of the importance of the financial services sector to global economies. While good books on the subject already exist, the pace of change within the sector means that most of them now pre-date many of the exciting new developments that have taken place recently. This book is important because it addresses these new developments.

In addition to attempting to provide a thorough coverage of the key issues that surround the marketing of financial services, it offers:

- An up-to-date account of regulatory developments, including the purpose and function of the Financial Services Authority and the Financial Services and Markets Bill.
- A whole chapter on technology-based delivery systems, including telephone and internet banking.
- Significant sections on the role of IT in segmenting and targeting customers and in relationship management and retention.
- A specific chapter on relationship marketing.
- A separate chapter on the tactical issues of customer retention and loyalty building.
- A whole chapter devoted to the marketing of financial services to corporate customers.

Outline of the book

The book is organised into twelve chapters. Chapter 1 presents an overview of the financial services environment, with particular emphasis on the socio-economic and regulatory environments. In addition to charting the main regulatory developments over the last thirty years, the chapter provides an up-to-date account of the proposed plans for financial regulation under the recently established Financial Services Authority.

The second chapter focuses on the financial services consumer. Financial institutions have been criticised in the past for their lack of attention to the customer. This chapter highlights some of the main social and economic trends affecting the demand for financial services and their impact on consumer behaviour. The chapter also highlights how the specific characteristics of intangibility, risk, uncertainty, longevity and complexity associated with many financial services may affect consumers' purchase decision processes.

Chapter 3 builds on the broader understanding of consumer behaviour and discusses the differences between consumer segments in respect of their financial services requirements. The chapter outlines ways of segmenting financial services consumers and discusses the relative merits of segmentation techniques available. It ends with a discussion of market fragmentation through increased use of direct marketing and information technology.

The fourth chapter focuses on the development and management of financial products, covering the product concept, new product development, management of products over the life cycle and the, often overlooked, topic of product elimination. The chapter highlights some of the problems associated with the application of product concepts and strategies to intangible financial services.

Chapter 5 is the first of two chapters on distribution and delivery of financial services. This chapter looks at the traditional channels of distribution such as branch networks, the direct sales force and independent financial advisers. The chapter outlines the trends in each of these areas and the changing roles and function of each mode of distribution.

Chapter 6 focuses on more recent developments in distribution made possible by technology. It begins by outlining the impact of technology on the delivery of financial services before going on to discuss trends in self-service technology, smartcards, telephone banking and the use of the internet. The chapter also discusses the role of IT in creating enhanced customer service.

The role of pricing is discussed in Chapter 7. The chapter outlines the changing role of price within the competitive environment and looks at how both price and non-price strategies have been used. The factors affecting pricing decisions are discussed and analysed in the context of mortgage pricing. The role of financial intermediation and its impact on pricing is outlined, and both overt and covert pricing methods are discussed.

Chapter 8 focuses on the communication and promotion of financial services. The role of promotion in financial organisations is outlined, as too are the communications tools and the factors that influence promotion of financial services. Given the difficulties of communicating intangible and often complex financial services, particular attention is given to the communication message and the use of fear appeals in advertising.

The focus of Chapter 9 is on building customer relationships. The chapter takes a holistic approach to the development of customer relationships, emphasising the strategic importance of relationships and the inter-functional dependencies within the organisation in the creation of relationships with customers. The chapter discusses the rationale for relationship development, the stages of relationship development and several key components of a relationship, including trust, the role of employees, service quality and the management of customer complaints.

Chapter 10 focuses on the tactical issues concerned with customer retention and loyalty. It provides a definition of retention and defection and discusses the motives for both retention and defection. A strategy for the retention of customers is outlined. In terms of customer loyalty, the chapter discusses the components of loyalty and critically evaluates the extent to which customer loyalty programmes in the financial services sector actually contribute to building loyal customers.

Chapter 11 discusses the corporate market for financial services. While the concept of marketing applies equally to both personal and corporate customers, corporate customers possess some distinct characteristics that make them different from personal customers and which affect the way in which marketing is applied in this context. The chapter highlights the key differences between the personal and corporate markets, discusses the nature of corporate buying behaviour, reviews some of the issues associated with corporate banking relationships and outlines the characteristics and requirements of small businesses and their relationships with financial services providers.

The final chapter presents a series of projects that build on the material contained in the other eleven chapters. The chapter includes projects on: investor education, the mortgage purchase process, flexible mortgage segmentation, changing distribution channels in the life assurance market, holes in the bucket, self-service banking, product bundling and loyalty building, the design and launch a bank's student package, long-term retention of graduating students and small business–bank relationships. The projects cover different types of financial institutions as well as different types of products and customers.

Pedagogic features

The book offers a number of pedagogic features, which distinguish it from other texts on the same subject, and make it particularly user-friendly:

- Key learning objectives at the start of each chapter – Each chapter begins with a set of objectives, which provide a focus to the chapter and serve as a reference point for learning.
- Mini-cases/vignettes – Each chapter contains mini-cases with some short discussion questions. The cases are strategically placed within the text to highlight examples of financial services marketing in practice. They are deliberately short, to enable them to be used in class to stimulate class discussion. They require limited preparation and all are based on well-known financial institutions, allowing students and tutors to bring additional material to the case.
- End-of-chapter review questions – At the end of each chapter there are ten discussion or review questions. The questions allow students to test their recall of material and, more importantly, to check their understanding of the issues covered. For this reason, many of the questions do not simply require students to recount concepts, activities and theories, but to use the material to solve problems. Consequently, some of the questions build on the material encountered in previous chapters.
- Projects – Chapter 12 contains ten multi-themed project assignments. The objectives of the projects are to highlight issues of key concern to financial institutions, to provide practical experience of financial services marketing, and to consolidate the material in the book. All of the projects represent actual problems or issues currently experienced by financial institutions. Each project comprises a short background to the problem, a number of research questions, suggested research method and some directional reading. The projects can be used in a number of ways: as assessed assignments, as the basis for class discussion, or for examinations (either closed or open book).

Ancillaries

An *Instructor's Manual* is available to adopters of the text. The *Instructor's Manual* offers suggestions for course design and support material for teaching each chapter. In particular it includes:

- a suggested lecture outline for each chapter;
- transparency masters of diagrams used in the text;
- outline answers to mini-case questions;
- guidelines for end-of-chapter discussions questions;
- suggestions for project analysis.

About the author

Tina Harrison, BA (Hons), Dip.M, Dip.MRS, Ph.D, is Lecturer in Marketing at the

University of Edinburgh Management School. She has been at Edinburgh since 1993 where she teaches Marketing, Financial Services Marketing and Business-to-Business Marketing at undergraduate and MBA level. Before coming to Edinburgh, she was a researcher at the *Financial Services Research Centre* at UMIST, Manchester. It was here that her interest and research in financial services began, working with David Yorke on a segmentation project funded by the Trustee Savings Bank. The research developed into her Ph.D. Since then, she has written and published a number of articles and papers on the subject of financial services marketing, and has conducted research for several financial institutions, including: Girobank, Co-operative Insurance Society, Homeowners Friendly Society, Dunfermline Building Society and Scottish Widows.

Acknowledgements

This book represents the culmination of several years of teaching and research experience in financial services. While the majority of effort has been mine, there are a number of people who have assisted in making the book possible. I am particularly grateful to David Yorke for providing me with the opportunity to embark on such an exciting field of study, and for his valuable contribution to my doctoral thesis. I am also indebted to Professor Christine Ennew and Professor Hugh Macmillan who both gave me the opportunity to contribute to their own books on financial services.

I would like to thank the anonymous reviewers who read and commented on every single chapter of the book. Their comments were very helpful to the development of the book and, as far as possible, their suggestions have been taken on board. Thanks also to the publishers and authors who gave their permission for the reproduction of copyright material in this book. They are mentioned throughout the book at the relevant place.

I am also grateful to Liz Sproat and Jane Powell, from Pearson Education, whose constant (but gentle) nudges ensured the timely production of the manuscript.

Finally, I would like to thank my fiancé, Stewart Skinner, who has encouraged, supported and put up with me while I was writing the book. This book is as much his as it is mine.

Tina Harrison
November 1999

1 The financial services environment

INTRODUCTION

The financial services sector has recently undergone changes unprecedented in its history. These changes have had an impact on both the structure of the industry and the nature of competition within it. A number of external forces have exerted influence on the sector, including socio-economic, regulatory and technological factors. Socio-economic factors play an important part in determining the demand for financial services. In recent years, there have been significant changes in the distribution of income and wealth and patterns of consumption.

Changes to the regulatory environment undoubtedly have had the greatest impact. Successive deregulation has broken down the traditional lines of demarcation that once served to limit competition, and have paved the way for non-financial institutions to enter the competitive arena. Regulation, in the form of the Financial Services Act, has also played a central role in shaping the behaviour of suppliers and offering increased protection to consumers. The changes proposed to take place under the Financial Services Authority, the industry's new single regulator, serve to strengthen the procedures and practices already set in place.

Technology has also taken on increased importance for financial institutions. Traditionally paper-based systems have become fully automated, providing greater flexibility and scope for expansion. Without a doubt, technology holds the key to future long-term success for financial institutions, from innovative distribution channels, which are both cost efficient and effective at delivering customer service, to customer databases, which enable better use of target marketing.

It is not surprising that, within a rapidly changing environment, financial institutions have been forced to change the way in which they respond to the marketplace, becoming less focused on products and more focused on customers and relationships, less focused on the short term and more focused on the longer term. This chapter discusses the key external influences on the financial services sector.

OBJECTIVES

After reading this chapter you should be able to:

- understand the key socio-economic factors and their impact on financial services consumption;
- chart the main regulatory developments of the last 30 years, and their impact on the competitive structure of the sector;
- debate the rationale and potential problems of financial regulation;

OBJECTIVES

- discuss the proposed plans for financial regulation under the Financial Services Authority;
- briefly discuss the changing role of technology for financial institutions;
- chart the evolution of the financial services sector and the entry of non-financial institutions;
- outline the trends in strategic responses of financial institutions towards an increasingly competitive marketplace.

The socio-economic environment

Changes to the socio-economic environment have an impact on the general demand for financial services. Perhaps the most important trends are in relation to personal income and wealth. In addition to these, this section also reviews consumption of selected savings and investments and credit and loans.

Personal income

Income is one of the key factors influencing demand for financial services. Disposable income, in particular, influences what people spend their money on. In relation to financial services, it has an impact on the amount people save, their ability to raise and pay credit and loans as well as their attitudes towards risk and

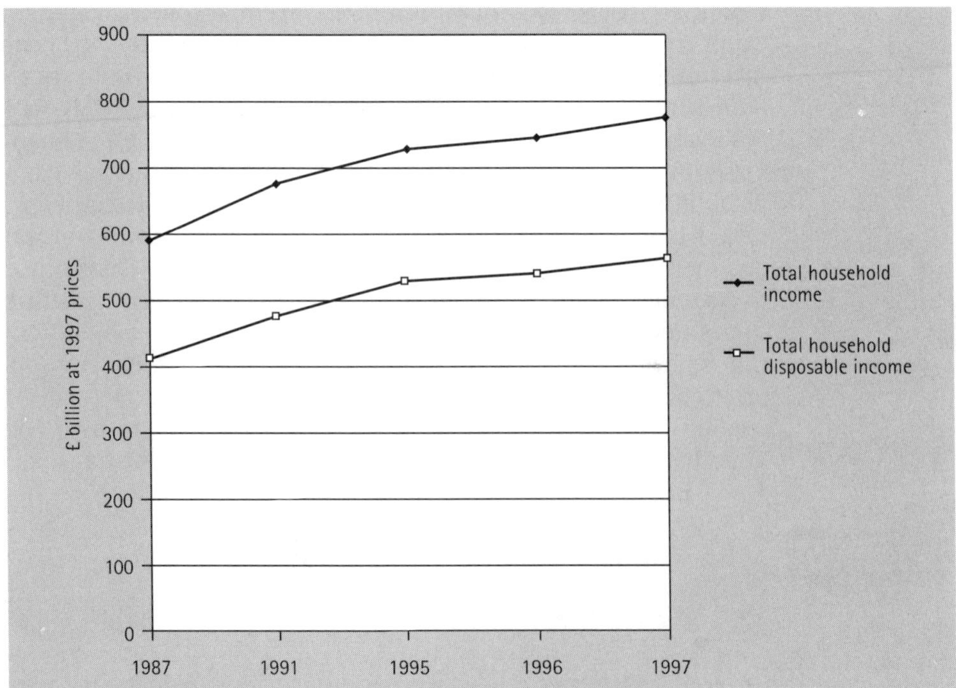

Fig. 1.1 Total household income and disposable income, 1987–1997

(*Source*: Adapted from *Social Trends*, Office for National Statistics, © Crown Copyright 1999, London: The Stationery Office, Table 5.2, p. 88)

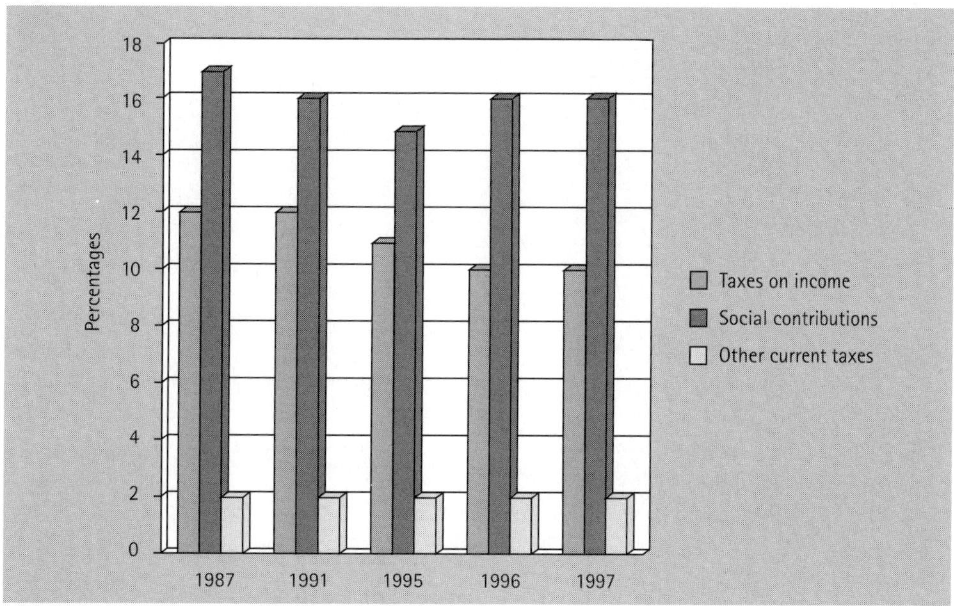

Fig. 1.2 Taxes as a percentage of total household income
(*Source*: Adapted from *Social Trends*, Office for National Statistics, © Crown Copyright 1999, London: The Stationery Office, Table 5.2, p. 88)

investments. These are also influenced by the broader economic environment. The population of the UK generally has become better off over the last few years. Figure 1.1 shows that in the period between 1987 and 1997, total household income increased by 30.5 per cent in real terms to reach £769 billion in 1997.

Income received by households is subject to taxation in the form of income tax, local taxes and contributions towards pensions and national insurance. Disposable income is that which is remaining after taxes and other social contributions have been deducted. Household disposable incomes have increased at a faster rate than total incomes (see figure 1.1). Over the ten-year period from 1987, total household disposable income increased by 36 per cent to reach £553 billion in 1997. This can be explained by the reduction in taxes and social contributions which occurred over the same period (see figure 1.2).

Rates of income tax, particularly those for higher incomes, have come down over the last twenty years. The higher rate hit a peak of 83 per cent from 1974–75 to 1978–79. The basic rate of tax fell steadily from 33 per cent in 1978 to 23 per cent from April 1997. The lower rate of 20 per cent was introduced in April 1992 (*Social Trends*, 1999).

Income comes from a number of sources: it is earned or derived from investments, benefits, pensions etc. Over the period of ten years from 1987 to 1997, the relative proportions of income from different sources have changed (see figure 1.3). While earned income still represents the largest proportion of income (accounting for just over half of all income in 1997), it has shown a steady decline over the period against an increase in income from social security benefits. Net property income has also risen slightly, while operating income has remained more or less stable.

For pensioners, benefits represent the largest component of income, accounting for over half of the total income on average. However, this has steadily declined

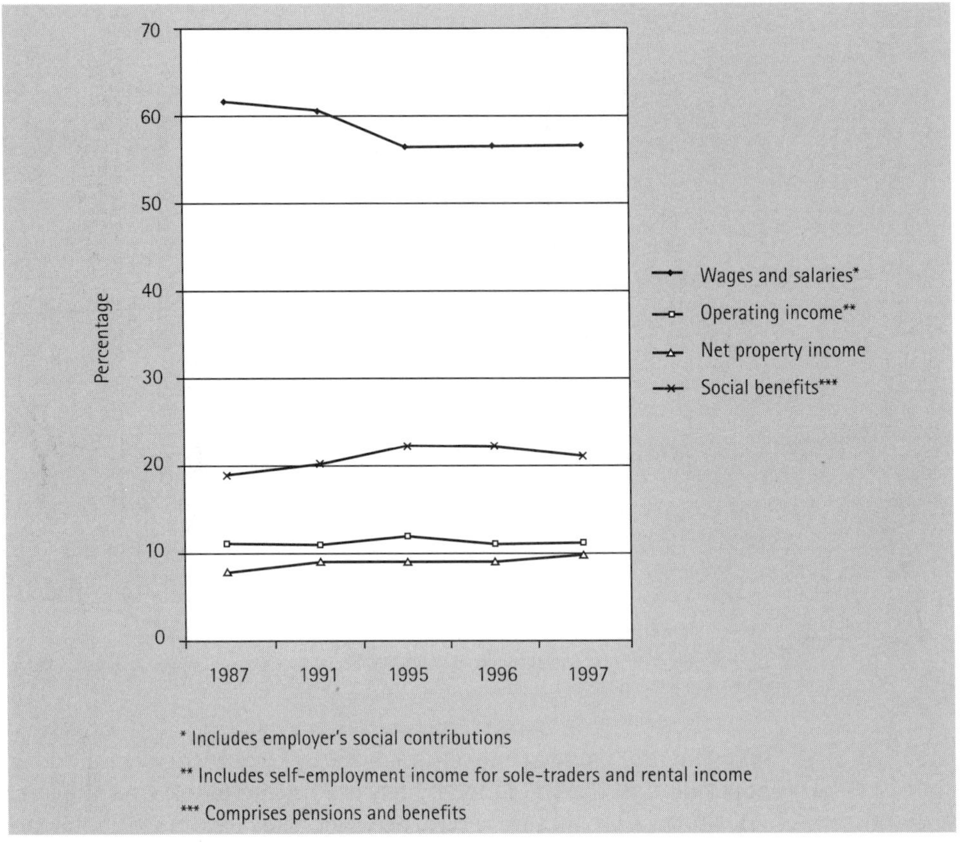

Fig. 1.3 Composition of household income
(*Source*: Adapted from *Social Trends*, Office for National Statistics, © Crown Copyright 1999, London: The Stationery Office, Table 5.2, p. 88)

over the last fifteen or so years. Other important sources of income are occupational pensions and investment. The picture is somewhat different for individuals that have just reached pensionable age compared with those who have been retired for longer. Benefits are less important as a source of income than occupational pensions and earnings for recently retired pensioners compared with other pensioners (see figure 1.4).

Although real disposable income has risen, the gap between the higher and lower incomes has widened. This was particularly so during the 1980s. One of the reasons for this is that the rich are benefiting from reduced taxes. In 1996–97 the average household income (after adjusting for taxes and benefits) was under £17,000. By 1999 it had risen to £20,265 (*Financial Times*, 5 July 1999). In the year 1996–97, 60 per cent of UK households received lower than the average income (see figure 1.5). Households in the bottom fifth of incomes had an original income of £2,310; after redistribution through taxes and benefits this amounted to £8,310.

For the highest fifth of incomes, redistribution reduced the original income from £44,780 to £31,790, leaving the lowest incomes almost £24,000 less than the highest incomes. Lone parents were more likely to be in the bottom fifth of incomes, with 42 per cent in the bottom fifth and only 3 per cent in the top fifth. Not sur-

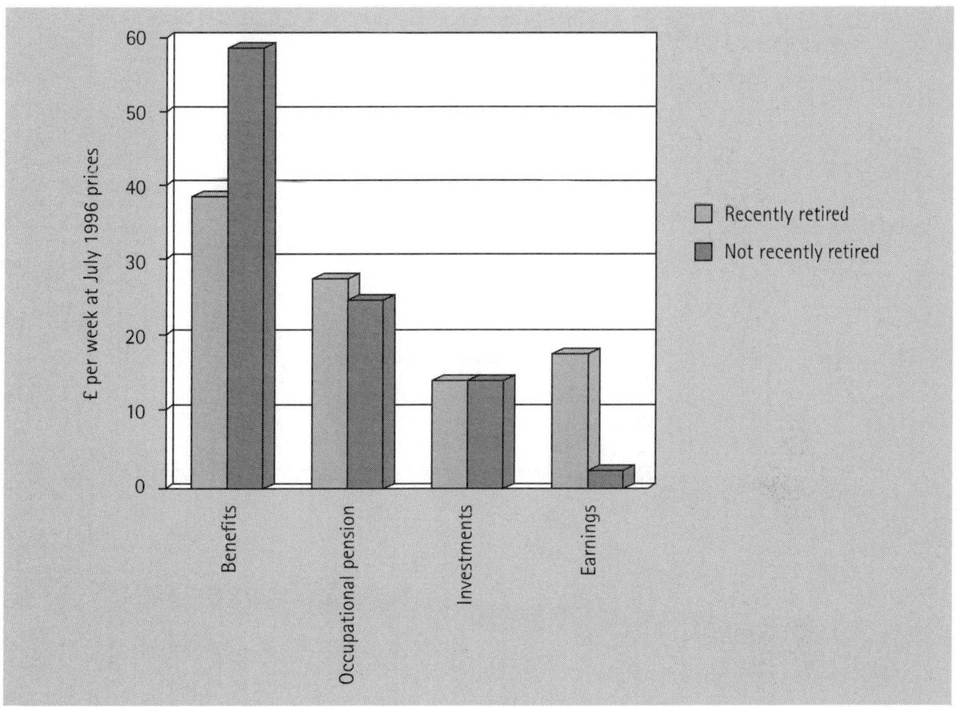

Fig. 1.4 Comparison of recently-retired and not-recently-retired pensioners' gross weekly incomes: comparison at 1996–97

(*Source*: Adapted from *Social Trends*, Office for National Statistics, © Crown Copyright 1999, London: The Stationery Office, Table 5.3, p. 88)

prisingly, couples without children are more likely to be in the top fifth of incomes (38 per cent of all couples without children were in this category in 1996–97) (*Social Trends*, 1999).

In the UK as a whole in 1998 over a quarter of all full-time employees had gross weekly wages under £250, and around a quarter received more than £460. The highest average earnings were in London, with the average for the South East generally higher than the average for the rest of the UK. Since 1981, overall full-time earnings have risen by nearly 7 per cent each year, although within this there are variations for different occupations (*Social Trends*, 1999).

The National Minimum Wage came into effect in the UK from April 1999. It is set at £3.60 an hour for employees aged 22 and over, and £3.00 an hour for those aged 18–21. The Bank of England estimated that the introduction of the minimum wage would add about 0.6 per cent to the wage bill of UK employers in its first year. The number of 18–21-year-olds estimated to be affected by the minimum wage is somewhere between 201 and 241 thousand, or approximately 14 per cent of employees in the age group. For those over the age of 21, about 8 per cent of the group are likely to be affected, although the absolute numbers are much larger at around 1.5–1.9 million (*Social Trends*, 1999). Among full-time workers, men have higher average earnings than women do in all age bands, with the greatest gap occurring for those aged 40–59 years.

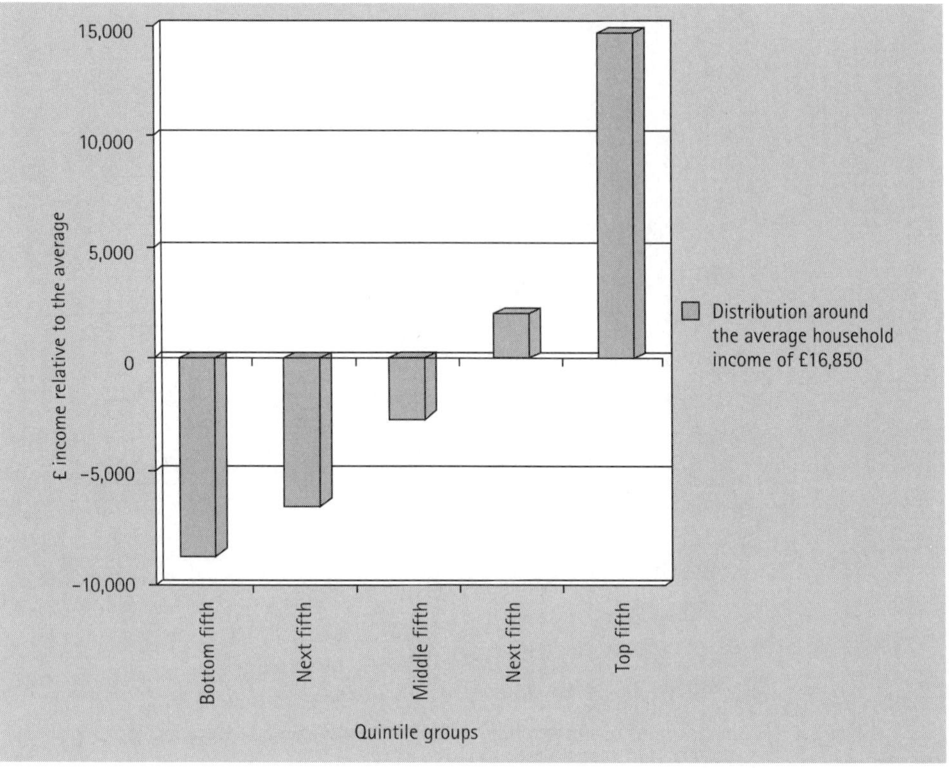

Fig. 1.5 Final household income (adjusted for taxes and benefits) relative to the average for the UK, 1996–97 (*Source*: Adapted from *Social Trends*, Office for National Statistics, © Crown Copyright 1999, London: The Stationery Office, Table 5.20, p. 97)

Personal wealth

Personal wealth is accumulated from saving part of income or through gains from existing investments. It also takes account of wealth associated with property. In the ten years between 1987 and 1997, the total wealth of the household sector increased in real terms by 42 per cent to reach £3,582 billion by the end of 1997 (*Social Trends*, 1999). This was made up of a slow rise in property values and a much larger increase in growth for financial wealth. The late 1980s saw large increases in property prices and owner-occupation. During the early 1990s property prices actually fell and many people found they were sitting on negative equity (the value of the property was less than the outstanding mortgage on it).

The composition of net wealth has changed over the period from 1987 to 1997 (see figure 1.6). In 1987 approximately one-quarter of wealth was held in the form of life assurance and pension funds; by the end of 1997 this had risen to account for over a third of total net wealth. The increase primarily reflects an increase in the take-up of personal pensions. Conversely, wealth in buildings has declined from approximately a third of wealth to a quarter in the same period. The proportion of wealth held in securities and shares has also increased.

In contrast to income, the distribution of wealth continues to be much more unequal. Marketable wealth consists of assets that can be sold or cashed in, such as shares and property. Since 1976, total marketable wealth has increased from £280 mil-

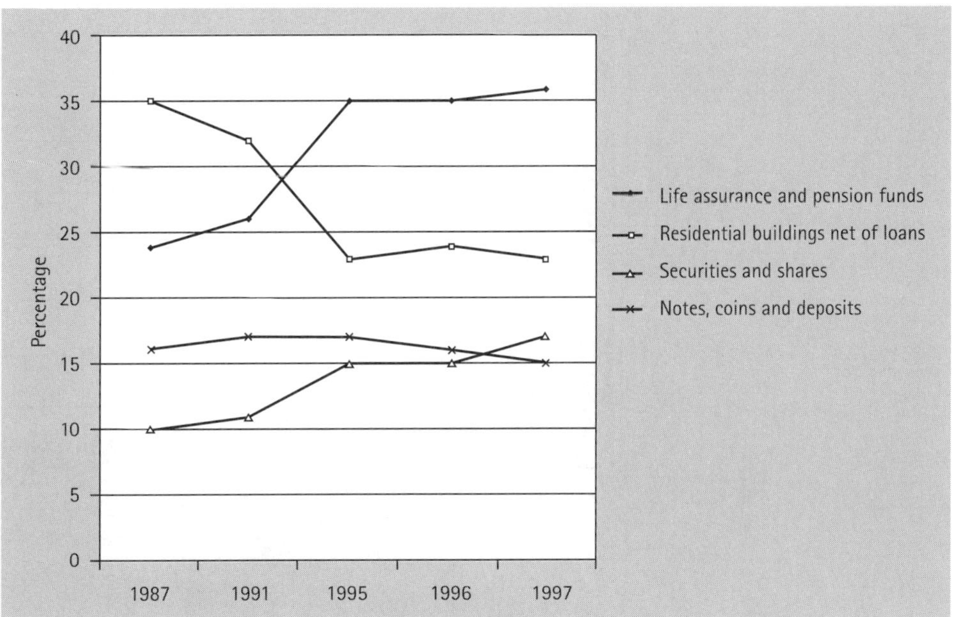

Fig. 1.6 Composition of the net wealth of the household sector
(*Source*: Adapted from *Social Trends*, Office for National Statistics, © Crown Copyright 1999, London: The Stationery Office, Table 5.24, p. 99)

lion to £2,033 million in 1995. The most wealthy 10 per cent of the population are estimated to own half the total wealth of the household sector and this is even higher (64 per cent) when the value of property is not taken into account (see figure 1.7).

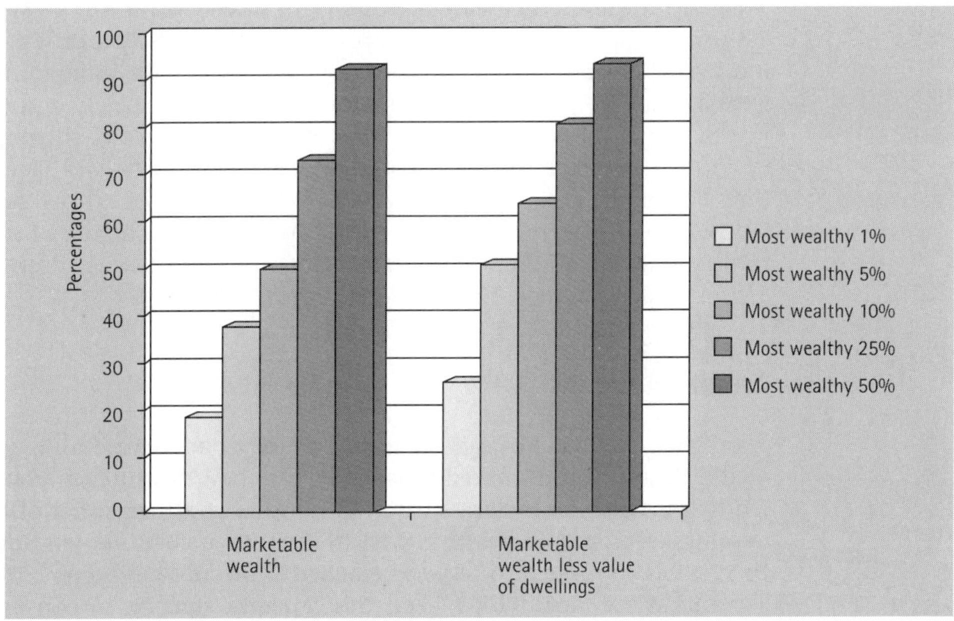

Fig. 1.7 Distribution of marketable wealth in the UK, 1995
(*Source*: Adapted from *Social Trends*, Office for National Statistics, © Crown Copyright 1999, London: The Stationery Office, Table 5.25, p. 100)

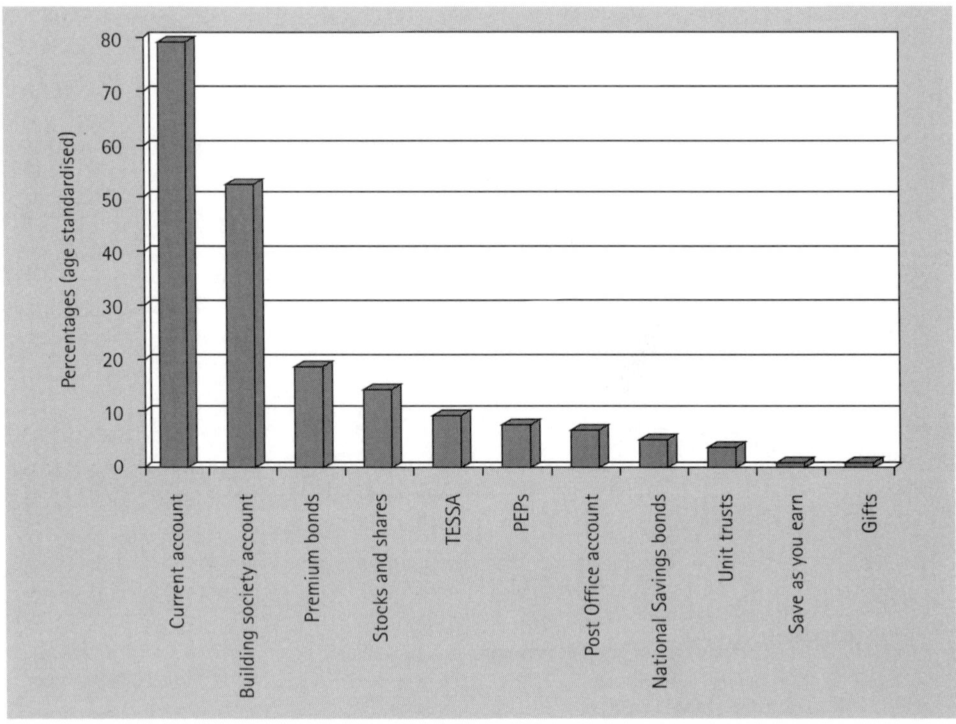

Fig. 1.8 UK adults holding selected forms of wealth, 1996–97
(*Source*: Adapted from *Social Trends*, Office for National Statistics, © Crown Copyright 1999, London: The Stationery Office, Table 5.27, p. 101)

Figure 1.8 shows the relative proportions of selected forms of wealth held by the UK population. Current accounts are held by almost 80 per cent of the population, indicating that the vast majority of the population have some form of relationship with a financial services provider. However, building society accounts are held by just over half the population, with less than 10 per cent of the population having investments in PEPs and unit trusts. Social and cultural factors have an influence on the consumption of financial services. Whereas almost 80 per cent of the population have a current account, ownership is highest among white adults (80 per cent) and lowest among Pakistani/Bangladeshi adults, while adults of Indian origin are more likely to have TESSAs (*Social Trends*, 1999).

Credit and loans

Many purchases are not paid for out of savings, but are paid for over time using one of the various forms of credit available. The best measure of growth in consumer lending is taken by looking at new lending to consumers, net of repayments. Net lending fell from around £2 billion in 1989 to a small net lending in 1992. Since then it has continued to rise and reached almost £4 billion in 1998 (*Social Trends*). The dip in the late 1980s reflects the general reduction in consumer expenditure during the last recession marked by high interest rates and unemployment. Figure 1.9 shows the composition of total indebtedness of consumers after allowing for inflation but excluding mortgages.

The amount of consumer credit outstanding increased rapidly in real terms by 56 per cent to reach £87.4 billion in 1997. The largest proportion was accounted for by bank loans, although this proportion has declined from 80 to 74 per cent over the period against an increase in the proportion of credit accounted for by other specialist lenders which has almost doubled. Retail credit accounts for a relatively small proportion, but that has also halved.

An increasing number of people are using credit, debit and charge cards to pay for goods and services. There were 37 million MasterCard and Visa credit cards and a similar number of Visa Delta and Switch debit cards in circulation at the end of 1997. In contrast to 1989, this represents just over a quarter more credit cards and two and a half times more debit cards (*Social Trends*, 1999). The number of transactions made using debit cards has increased over the period, exceeding the number of transactions made using credit cards for the first time in 1996.

Cheques have been in decline and automated payments now account for a larger proportion of payments than cheques did in 1985. In 1985 the rank order of payment methods was cheque first, followed by automated methods, then credit cards and charge cards. Debit cards were not around in 1985. Now the rank order is automated payments (including direct debits and standing orders), cheques, debit cards and credit cards. Payment methods tend to be used for different purposes. Credit cards tend to be used for larger purchases. In 1997, the average value of credit card transactions was £52 compared with £29 for debit cards. Hotels dominate credit card use, whereas food and drink dominate debit card use.

In relation to other forms of credit, credit cards have also increased at a slightly slower rate. In 1994, the value of credit card transactions amounted to £40,773 mil-

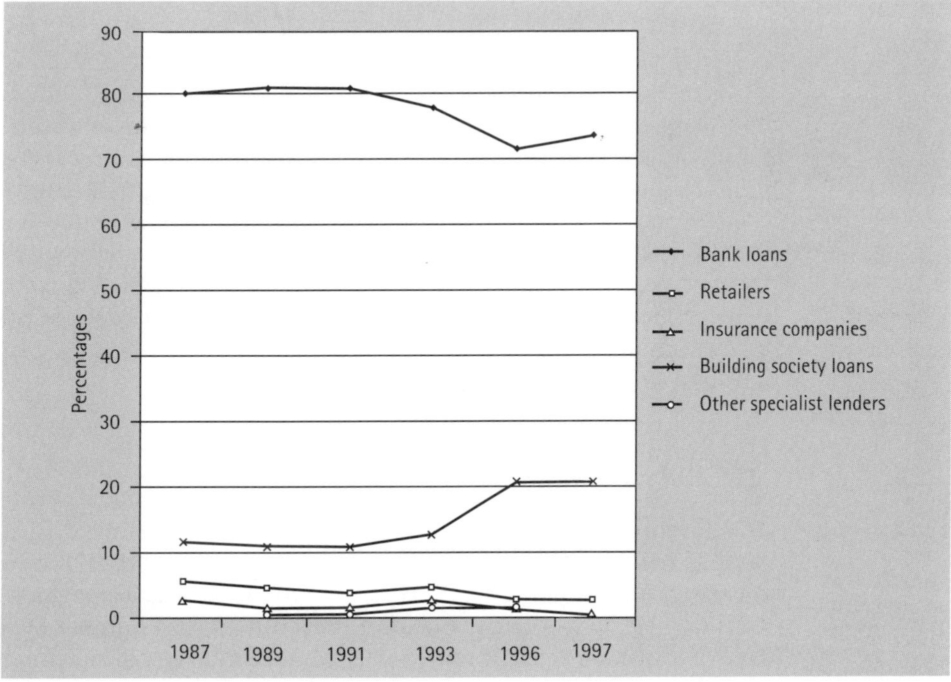

Fig. 1.9 Composition of consumer credit, 1987–1997

(*Source*: Adapted from *Social Trends*, Office for National Statistics, © Crown Copyright 1999, London: The Stationery Office, Table 6.18, p. 114)

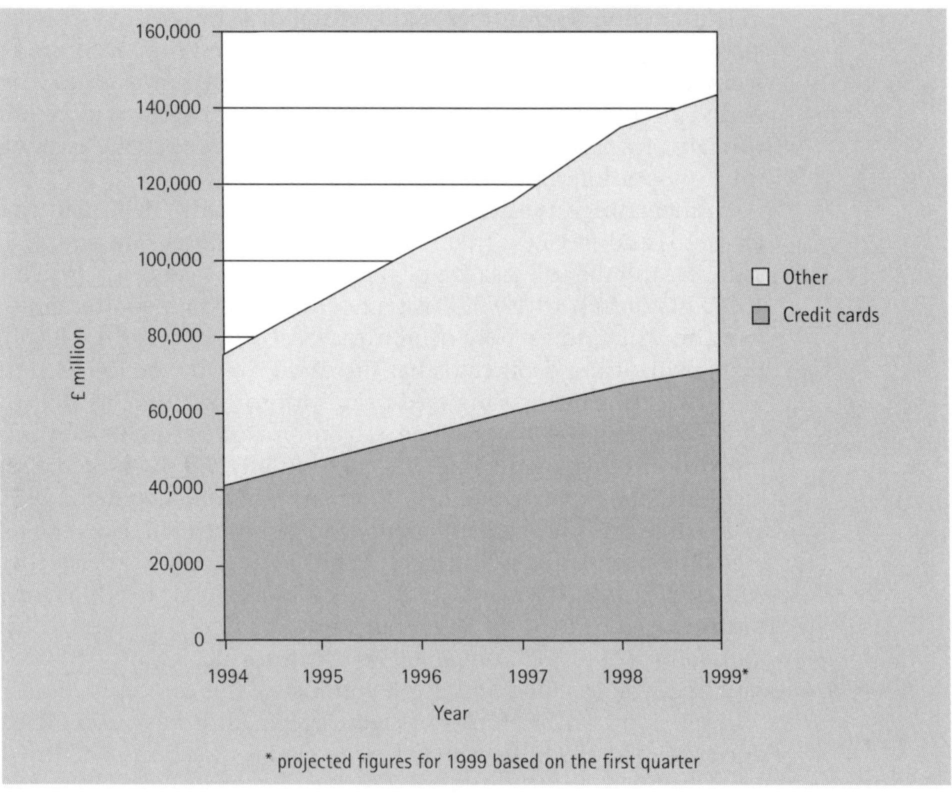

Fig. 1.10 Credit card lending as a proportion of total consumer credit
(*Source*: Adapted from *Financial Statistics*, Office for National Statistics, © Crown Copyright 1999, No. 445, May 1999, p. 62)

lion, compared with £34,114 million for all other forms of credit. By 1999, other forms of credit accounted for the larger proportion, having increased to £72,004 million against £70,996 million for credit cards (see figure 1.10).

Credit serves different needs such as affordability and convenience. The proportion of personal expenditure financed by credit declines with social class. Over one third of personal expenditure of the professional classes is financed by credit (see figure 1.11). This reflects credit card ownership: 87 per cent of professionals own a credit card against 26 per cent of unskilled social class and 14 per cent of individuals retired on a state pension.

Housing

The number of dwellings in the UK has grown steadily since 1961 to reach 24.8 million in 1997. In 1961, the number of owner-occupied dwellings was less than the number of rented dwellings. However, by 1997 the number of owner-occupied dwellings had more than doubled to reach twice the number of rented dwellings. One of the factors contributing to an increase in home ownership has been the sale of social-sector housing to tenants under the right-to-buy legislation. Sales in this category peaked in 1982 at over 200,000 properties, and then declined until 1986 when they began to increase again to reach another peak in 1989 at over 190,000

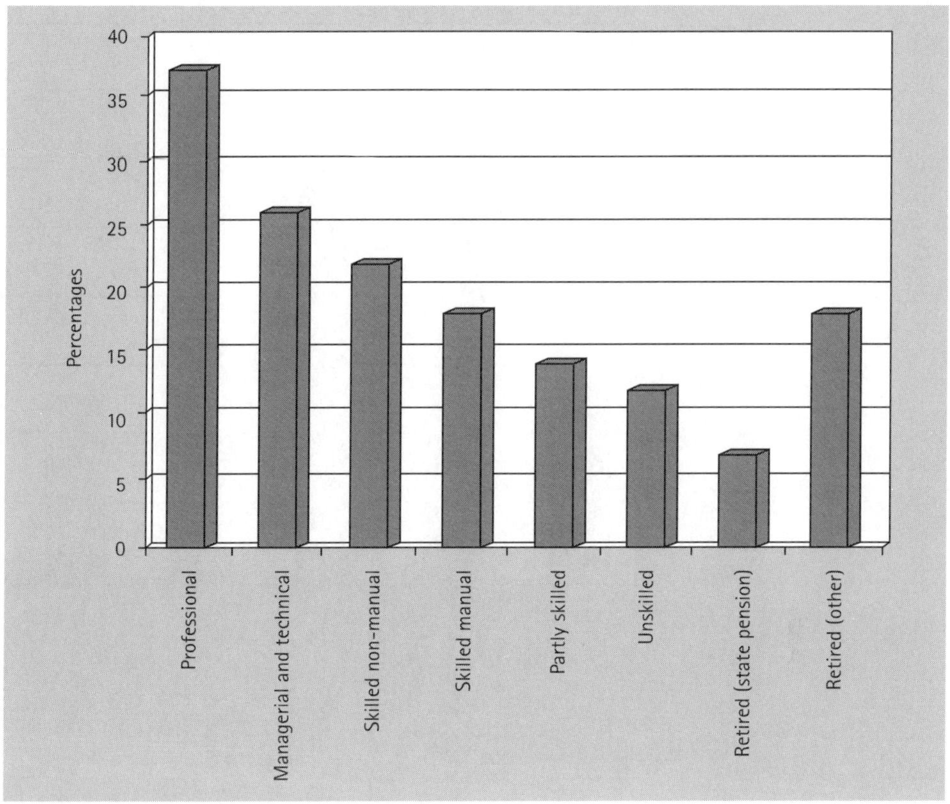

Fig. 1.11 Proportion of personal expenditure financed by credit: by social class, 1997–98
(*Source*: Adapted from *Social Trends*, Office for National Statistics, © Crown Copyright 1999, London: The Stationery Office, Table 6.20, p. 115)

properties. Since 1989 sales of social sector properties to tenants have stabilised at around 50–60,000 per year (*Social Trends*, 1999).

The average dwelling price in 1997 was £75,900 for all buyers, representing an increase of 8 per cent on the previous year. Highest property prices are in London, which were 39 per cent higher than the UK average in 1997, compared with the North East where property prices were on average 30 per cent lower than the average. The price of properties bought by first-time buyers (£52,500) are on average around half the price of properties purchased by former owner–occupiers (£96,200) (*Social Trends*, 1999).

Housing costs constitute a significant proportion of the household budget, regardless of whether it is in the form of a mortgage or rent. Owner–occupiers with mortgages face the highest average weekly household expenditure on housing costs. This drops dramatically on repayment of the loan, and is just above the cost of renting from the council (see figure 1.12). In 1990 moving owner–occupiers spent on average a third of their income on their mortgage repayments, while first-time buyers were spending roughly a quarter of income. These figures have now come down to 17 per cent and 13 per cent respectively. These are slightly higher than in 1996, but are otherwise lower than in any other year since 1978.

The increase in owner-occupation brought about an increase in the number of mortgages (see figure 1.13). There are a wide variety of mortgages. The most common

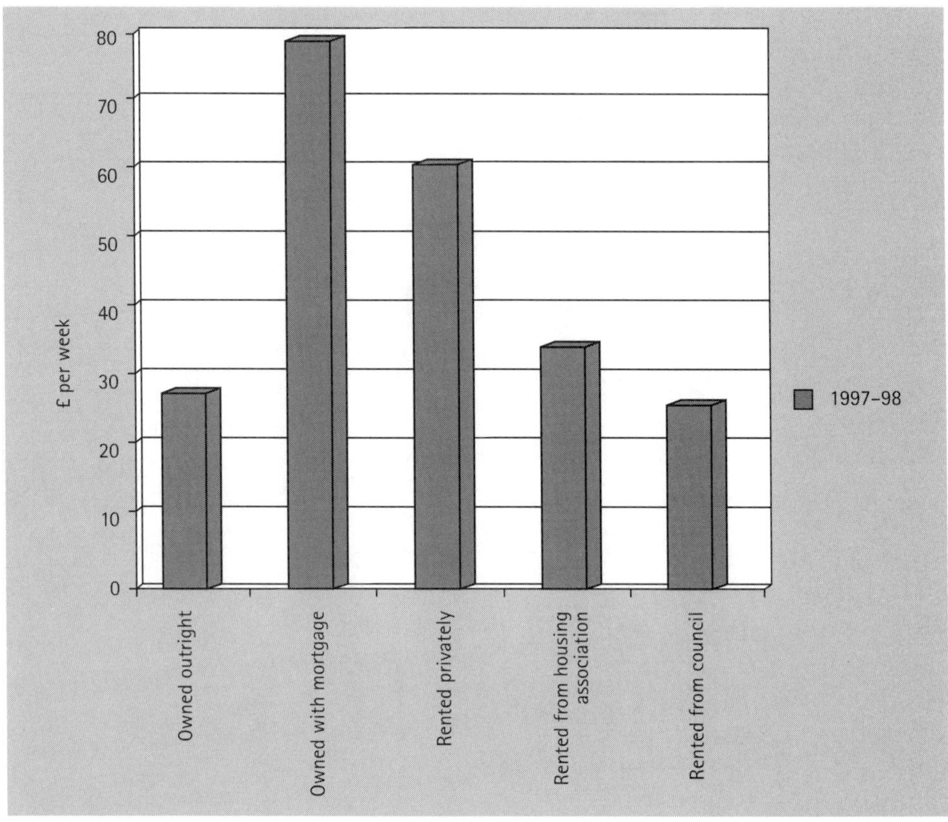

Fig. 1.12 Average weekly household costs by tenure, 1997–98

(*Source*: Adapted from *Social Trends*, Office for National Statistics, © Crown Copyright 1999, London: The Stationery Office, Table 10.24, p. 179)

types are repayment, endowment and interest only. During the mid-to-late 1980s endowment mortgages were the most popular of all types of mortgage, reaching a peak in 1988 when 83 per cent of new mortgages for house purchases were of this type (*Social Trends*, 1999). With an endowment mortgage, the individual pays only the interest on the loan. The capital is repaid at the end of the loan period from the proceeds of an endowment (savings) policy which runs concurrently to the loan.

Since 1989 the popularity of endowment mortgages has declined and the standard repayment mortgage now accounts for the majority of new mortgages. With a repayment mortgage, individuals pay both the interest and the capital, so the loan is progressively paid off over the mortgage term. Over the same period from 1980 to 1997, interest-only mortgages (such as PEP and pension mortgages) have also increased in popularity, although they still account for the smallest proportion of new mortgages. There has also been an increase in the take-up of fixed-rate mortgages and an increased willingness to remortgage to take advantage of the price differences between lenders.

With the increase in the number of mortgages has come an increase in the number of properties being repossessed as a result of non-payment of mortgage (see figure 1.14). Repossessions peaked in 1991 at 76,000 due to an increase in interest rates from mid-1988 leading to an increase in mortgage rates which went up from approximately 10 per cent in 1988 to over 13 per cent a year later. This led to an

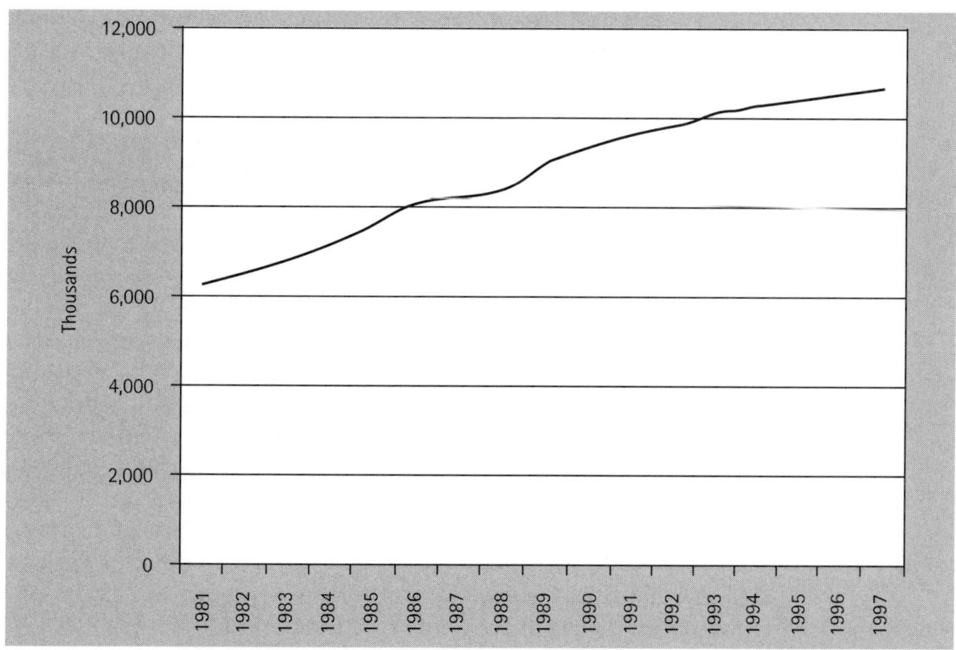

Fig. 1.13 Mortgages 1981–1997 in the UK
(*Source*: Adapted from *Social Trends*, Office for National Statistics, © Crown Copyright 1999, London: The Stationery Office, Table 10.27, p. 180)

increase in mortgage arrears and repossessions. Since 1991, the number of repossessions has more than halved against an increase in the number of mortgages. The number of repossessions remained a relatively low proportion of the total number

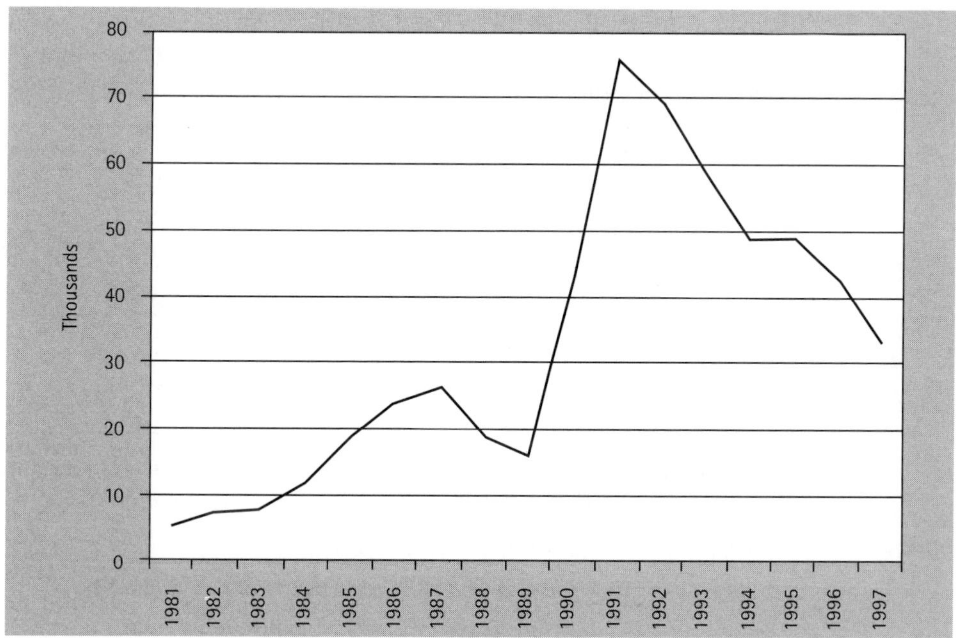

Fig. 1.14 Number of properties repossessed in the UK, 1981–1997
(*Source*: Adapted from *Social Trends*, Office for National Statistics, © Crown Copyright 1999, London: The Stationery Office, Table 10.27, p. 180)

of mortgages, and has not been more than 1 per cent of all mortgages even at its highest level, but has mostly been less than 0.5 per cent of mortgages.

The regulatory environment

Changes to the regulatory environment arguably have had the greatest impact on the financial services sector. Table 1.1 summarises some of the key developments that took place over the period from the early 1970s to the mid-1990s.

When the Bank of England dissolved the clearing banks' interest rate cartel, this marked what was to become the most significant period of regulatory change in the history of financial services. The big clearing banks (at that time Barclays, Midland, NatWest, Lloyds, TSB) had operated under a cartel agreement whereby interest rates were fixed. This essentially precluded price competition. Thus, abolition of the cartel signalled a general move towards price competition.

In 1979, the Supplementary Special Deposit Scheme, otherwise known as the 'Corset', was abolished. This meant that banks, and other financial institutions, were able to enter the mortgage market for the first time in history. Mortgages had previously been the exclusive domain of the building societies. This move opened up a threat to building societies who now saw the banks as direct competitors. Prior to this banks, building societies and insurance companies had operated in clearly distinct areas of the market. This move signalled a blurring of the traditional boundaries.

In response to this move, the building societies campaigned for greater freedom, arguing that the 1962 Building Societies Act constrained the activities of building societies. In 1986 the Building Societies Act was amended to allow a much wider range of activities and services to be offered by building societies under the newly created Building Societies Commission which was to oversee and supervise the activities of building societies. The changes provided the ability to extend their unsecured lending, to offer house buying packages, insurance brokerage, etc. It also allowed the building societies to convert to plc status. In doing so, they would cease to be regulated under the Building Societies Act and would be subject to banking regulation. Building societies were initially slow to convert (demutualise), the Abbey National being the first in 1989. Now, however, very few of the large building societies have retained their mutual status. The characteristics of mutuality are discussed later in this chapter.

Table 1.1 Key regulatory developments: 1970–1996

Time	Regulatory development
Early 1970s	Bank of England dissolves the clearing banks' interest rate cartel
1979	Abolition of the Supplementary Special Deposit Scheme – the 'Corset'
1986	Changes to the Building Societies' Act
1986	Reforms to the Stock Exchange Rulebook – the 'Big Bang'
1986	Establishment of the Financial Services Act
1995	Changes to the disclosure of commission and charges – 'Hard Disclosure' ruling

In the same year, reforms to the Stock Exchange Rulebook took place. These were brought about to foster competitiveness and essentially allowed banks and other financial institutions ownership of member firms. This move marked the end of the strict separation of principal and agent. Previously brokers conducted all their business through jobbers who did not deal directly with customers. As a result a number of high-street financial institutions set up 'share shops'.

Financial Services Act 1986 (FSAct)

In contrast to the previous changes which marked a period of deregulation, the FSAct marked a wave of re-regulation of the sector. The development of the FSAct was prompted by the desire to protect consumers from the adverse effects of financial deregulation. The Act was set up to cover all types of investments, the management of investments and the giving of advice related to investments. It had two primary objectives:

1 to regulate investment business affording greater protection to investors;

2 to promote competition in the savings industry.

The FSAct excludes all non-investment business, such as general insurance, short-term deposits, mortgages and loans, all of which are covered by other legislation (i.e. the Banking Act, the Insurance Companies Act and the Building Societies Act). Over 23,000 firms are authorised to conduct business in the UK. Most 'front-line' regulation is carried out by a number of specialist bodies, collectively known as 'Recognised Bodies'. A lead regulator, the Securities and Investments Board (SIB), set the standards for and monitored the activities of the Recognised Bodies. Its primary role was to oversee, although it was possible to be directly regulated by the SIB, and a number of large financial institutions applied to be so. This gave rise to some conflict of interest and caused unnecessary duplication. The implementation of the FSAct signalled an important move from institution-based regulation to market-based regulation which recognised the similarity between institutions as boundaries had become blurred by deregulation.

Recognised Bodies

The Recognised Bodies are shown in figure 1.15 and consist of three Self-Regulating Organisations, nine Recognised Professional Bodies, six Recognised Investment Exchanges and two Recognised Clearing Houses.

a) Self-Regulating Organisations (SROs) Most investment business is carried out by over 6,000 firms regulated by three SROs. An SRO has the power to authorise firms to conduct investment business in the UK, and under the Investment Services Directive, throughout the European Economic Area. The responsibilities of SROs include:

- vetting firms, checking whether they are 'fit and proper' to conduct investment business;
- prudential supervision and monitoring of the adequacy of financial resources;
- overseeing firms' dealings with investors, ensuring the provision of suitable information and advice;

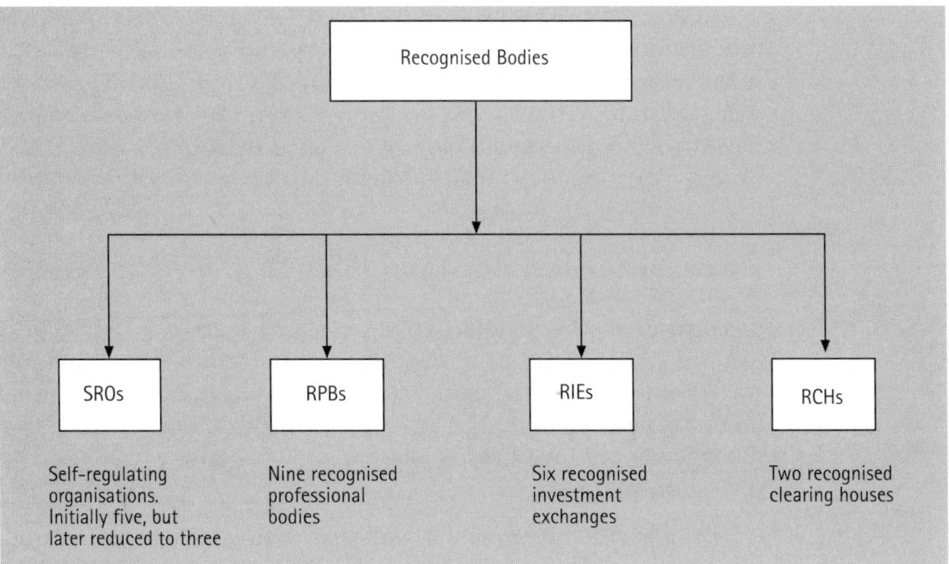

Fig. 1.15 The Recognised Bodies under the Financial Services Act

- making arrangements for the handling of investors' complaints;
- censuring or firing firms which have broken the rules, leading to compensation or expulsion from membership.

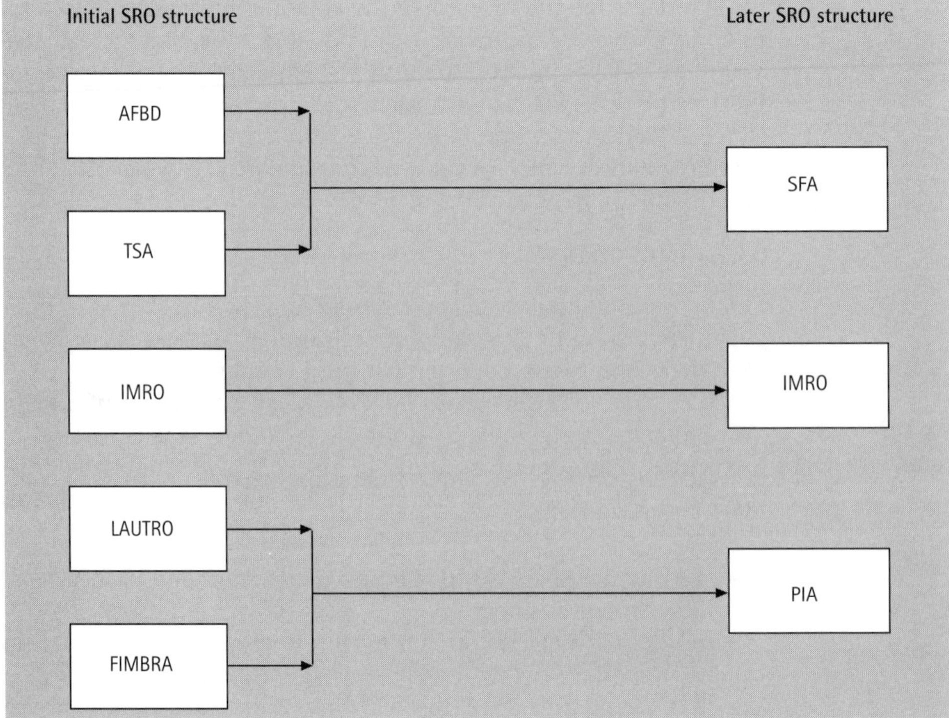

Fig. 1.16 Changes to the SRO structure

Initially, five SROs were established: the Association of Futures, Brokers and Dealers (AFBD), The Securities Association (TSA), the Investment Management Regulatory Organisation (IMRO), the Financial Intermediaries, Managers and Brokers Regulatory Organisation (FIMBRA) and the Life Assurance and Unit Trust Regulatory Organisation (LAUTRO) (see figure 1.16).

The AFBD was responsible for overseeing firms dealing in futures and options. The TSA replaced the Stock Exchange as the monitor of several hundred firms ranging from provincial stockbrokers and licensed securities traders to large international investment banks. However, the monitoring activities extended beyond those originally undertaken by the Stock Exchange. IMRO was concerned with the authorisation of investment managers and LAUTRO dealt with companies dealing in life assurance and unit trusts but only these products, the companies themselves continued to be regulated under the Insurance Companies Act 1982. FIMBRA regulated the provision of services by independent investment intermediaries. FIMBRA members were required to maintain independent status.

In 1991, the AFBD and the TSA merged to form the Securities and Futures Association (SFA). Thus, all Stock Exchange-related activities were brought together under one SRO to avoid duplication and reduce costs. In 1992 LAUTRO and FIMBRA merged to form the Personal Investment Authority (PIA) which was operating by 1994 and is primarily concerned with regulating retail investment business. The rationale behind the creation of the PIA was that it too would reduce duplication and increase consistency in standards and competence as well. It meant that a number of firms now only needed to be regulated by a single SRO instead of two or more. IMRO remained unchanged and continues to oversee investment managers.

b) Recognised Professional Bodies (RPBs) Members of certain professions, such as accountants and lawyers, who have some minor involvement in investment business may conduct investment business following 'certification' by their Recognised Professional Body (such as the Law Society or one of the three main Institutes of Chartered Accountants).

c) Recognised Investment Exchanges (RIEs) Investment exchanges are organised markets on which member firms can trade investments. There are six of these currently supervised under the FSAct. An RIE is responsible for ensuring that business conducted on the exchange is done in an orderly manner and so as to afford proper protection to investors.

d) Recognised Clearing Houses (RCHs) The UK clearing houses are bodies which organise the settlement of transactions on recognised investment exchanges. There are currently two – the London Clearing House (LCH) and CrestCo. The LCH guarantees and clears derivatives transactions on LIFFE, the LME and IPE, and guarantees securities transactions on Tradepoint. CrestCo clears and settles securities transactions on the LSE and Tradepoint, together with securities transactions on LIFFE resulting from equity options.

Other issues arising from the FSAct

- *Polarisation* – Under the FSAct, intermediaries who give advice on investments were required by law to choose, and to declare to customers, whether they were acting as a representative of one company (a tied agent) or whether they were fully independent and able to advise on the full range of products offered by different companies. This polarisation has caused some controversy and confusion amongst consumers. It has also raised doubts about the impartiality of advice provided by fully independent intermediaries. Due to the costs associated with maintaining a fully independent status, the majority of high-street banks and building societies are now tied to one particular company, prompting concerns over the extent to which such concentration at the retail level and limited consumer choice contributes towards the original objective of investor protection.

- *Commission disclosure* – Under the original LAUTRO proposals, the disclosure of commissions was covered by a 'maximum commissions agreement', resulting in the practice of 'soft disclosure'. This meant that there was no need to make customers explicitly aware of commissions and charges, provided they were within the maximum limits set, and the customer did not request to know. At the start of 1991, the Office of Fair Trading (OFT) objected that this practice was uncompetitive and amounted to an illegal price-fixing cartel. It was recommended that the industry move to a practice of 'hard disclosure'. Initially, this took the form of a percentage disclosure, not a strict monetary disclosure. But since January 1995 (with effect from August 1995), there has been a practice of hard disclosure of the monetary value of commissions, expenses, charges and early surrender value to customers at the point of purchase. Naturally, companies were worried that consumers' decisions in the choice of provider would be affected as price essentially became more transparent.

Criticisms of the Financial Services Act 1986

According to Simpson (1997), there exists a body of evidence to suggest that the FSAct has not been successful in meeting its objectives, particularly with regard to serving the interests of consumers. He outlines six key areas which indicate the failing of the FSAct:

- *Fraud* – One of the principal concerns of the FSAct was the reduction of fraud. However, incidents such as the Levitt and Maxwell cases, among others, have shown that the system has not been able to do this effectively. The drawbacks of the FSAct, in this respect, are further underlined by the fact that there were only seventeen prosecutions for insider dealing between 1990 and 1997, only twelve of which were successful.
- *Market misconduct* – More recently attention has focused from fraud to market misconduct, or malpractice or mis-selling. Market misconduct occurs in a grey area between fraud and incompetence and might be described as unfair trading in other industries. The mis-selling of personal pensions has received a great deal of press. The number of reported cases where consumers were sold products which did not meet their needs or where consumers were reportedly ill-advised bears testimony to the fact that the FSAct has not been effective at preventing malpractice.
- *Loss of confidence* – Largely as a result of the publicity of market misconduct, referred to above, consumers lost confidence in the market. This was further exacerbated by the fact that the SIB took three years to conclude compensation arrangements in cases of the mis-selling of personal pensions,

thus undermining the powers of the FSAct in protecting consumers. During this time the reputation of the industry was damaged. Consumers perceived all companies to be equally at fault. Consequently, all financial institutions became tarred with the same brush.

- *Restriction of competition* – Rather than increasing competition, Simpson argues that the FSAct actually served to restrict it in many ways. For example, the SIB and its subsidiaries fought for ten years actually to prevent commission disclosure, thus inhibiting the onset of price competition. Furthermore, Simpson argues that Gower, who was originally behind the introduction of the Financial Services Act, did not consider the relationship between regulation and the competitive market process, nor did he investigate the circumstances of the industry. If he had, he might have concluded that the interests of investors would have been served better by measures to promote greater competition rather than by greater regulation.
- *Costs* – It is argued that the imposition of regulation led to an increase in the cost burden disproportionate to the benefits derived from the regulation. These costs are borne initially by the companies, but ultimately are passed on to the customers whom the regulation was set up to protect. Peacock and Bannock (1995) estimated the total cost of regulation in 1994 to be in the region of £169–330 million, although this is a conservative estimate. As far as the life assurance industry is concerned, this represents roughly 9 per cent of turnover.
- *Bureaucracy* – The regulatory system under the FSAct has been criticised for being unnecessarily bureaucratic. The three-tier structure of the system essentially insulates the lower regulatory bodies from any accountability for their behaviour.

Simpson (1997) also criticises the term 'investor protection', as a regulatory objective, arguing that it is objectionable on at least three counts:

1 it suggests that consumers need protecting from market forces;

2 there is an implicit paternalism: i.e. it infers that decision-making can be removed from the consumer and transferred to some 'better-informed' body; and

3 it begs the question, protection from whom? In the case of mutual organisations this would suggest that members of the organisation (or policyholders) need protection from themselves, since members or policyholders are in effect the owners of the business.

Regulatory developments: 1997 onwards

Until the Labour government came into office in 1997, there were several financial regulators and supervisors overseeing different types of financial business under the FSAct 1986. One of the aims of the government was to form a single regulator, thereby simplifying the financial regulation system. There is widespread support for a unitary authority that will remove the scope for duplication, gaps and inconsistency that have dogged regulation under the FSAct.

Table 1.2 Regulatory developments since 'New Labour'

28 October 1997	SIB changed its name to Financial Services Authority
1 June 1998	FSA took over responsibility for the supervision of banks and the wholesale money market from the Bank of England under the Bank of England Act 1998
1998	Draft Financial Services and Markets Bill. This will supersede the FSAct, but is unlikely to become law until sometime during 2000
Beginning of 1999	FSA assumed responsibility for the supervision of building societies, mutuals and insurance companies

On 28 October 1997, the Securities and Investments Board (the lead regulator under the FSAct) changed its name to the Financial Services Authority (FSA). The FSA is to become the financial sector's sole regulator. The government is in the process of introducing new laws to merge the various financial regulators and supervisors under the auspices of the FSA. The first of the new laws, which came into effect on 1 June 1998, was the Bank of England Act 1998 which transferred responsibility for banking supervision in the UK from the Bank of England to the Financial Services Authority. The main objective of the FSA, in its role as supervisor of banks, is to fulfil the responsibilities contained in the Banking Act 1987. This means protecting depositors by ensuring that anyone wishing to set up a deposit-taking business is authorised to do so.

The second instalment took place when the government published a draft Financial Services and Markets Bill. The Bill will supersede the FSAct 1986, but is unlikely to become law until some time during 2000. Once the Bill has been passed in Parliament, the FSA will take on responsibility for all the sectors delegated by the FSAct 1986 to the SROs. In the meantime, the PIA, the SFA and IMRO will retain the powers that enable them to supervise and discipline firms. Since the beginning of 1999, the FSA has assumed responsibility for the supervision of building societies, mutuals and insurance companies.

The FSA will, thus, combine all the supervisory and punitive powers previously enjoyed by various regulatory and supervisory bodies, giving it unprecedented

Table 1.3 Organisations joining together to form the FSA

Organisation	Current responsibility
Building Societies Commission	Supervision of building societies
Friendly Societies Commission	Supervision of friendly societies
Insurance Directorate of HM Treasury	Supervision of insurance companies
Investment Management Regulatory Organisation (IMRO)	Regulation of investment management business
Personal Investment Authority (PIA)	Regulation of retail investment business (pensions, life assurance etc.)
Register of Friendly Societies	Supervision of credit unions, and registering mutual societies
Securities and Futures Authority (SFA)	Regulation of securities and derivatives business

(*Source*: Financial Services Authority)

responsibilities as the sole financial regulator with power over such areas as life assurance and derivatives in addition to overseeing banks and financial exchanges. Table 1.3 shows the organisations joining together to form the FSA.

According to Howard Davies (1999), Chairman of the FSA, the model of the FSA offers two key advantages in terms of efficiency and effectiveness:

1 From a market point of view there are many advantages and benefits from a one-stop regulatory shop. Under the FSAct there was a great deal of overlap: insurance companies, building societies and banks have gradually become to all look alike, offering the same services and products, yet continuing to be regulated by different bodies to a large extent. A single regulator would add to the efficiency of regulation.

2 The other advantage relates to the effectiveness of regulation. The new regulator is designed to be flexible enough to cope with changing financial services markets in the future. One of the key problems with the FSAct was that it was not adaptable to new markets and new products. The FSA

FINANCIAL SERVICES MARKETING IN PRACTICE

International financial regulation: a trend towards consolidation

With the exception of perhaps Sweden and Denmark, the recently established Financial Services Authority in the UK is one of the few examples, internationally speaking, of a single unified regulator. However, it is perhaps fair to say that regulatory consolidation is now occurring in a number of other countries.

In Canada, banking and insurance regulation was merged some time ago, outside the central bank. The Belgians and Swiss have banking and securities regulators, also outside the central bank. The Australians have a single prudential regulator covering all sectors of the financial services industry, but again outside the central bank.

In Japan, banking and securities regulation has been merged to form the Japanese Financial Supervisory Agency, known as the JFSA. The Japanese model owes a great deal to the observation of the formation of the FSA in the UK. Ireland has also decided to take the same route, although it is not yet clear whether it will be inside or outside the central Bank of Ireland.

The US operates quite a different model, and there is no evidence to suggest that a single regulator will be established there in the foreseeable future. In the US, there is the federal dimension to regulation, but at the same time there are fierce defenders of the different sectoral responsibilities. In this instance it seems fair to say that the US is not typical of international practice which is generally showing a trend towards regulatory consolidation.

However, not as many countries have gone quite so far down the road with consolidation as the UK has with the formation of the FSA.

Nevertheless, it seems that further consolidation is set to continue. The G7 Finance Ministers have agreed to set up a committee to bring together regulators and central bankers from around the world. It is proposed that each country should be represented by its finance ministry, central bank and 'leading national regulator'. It is easy to see that the FSA fits this position for the UK, however, it is less clear what body would fit that role from other countries. This factor alone may provide the impetus for further regulatory consolidation in order to meet the needs of the global financial marketplace.

Source: Adapted from Davies (1999) 'Building the Financial Services Authority: What's New?, 1999 Travers Lecture.

Questions:

1 Why is there currently a trend towards regulatory consolidation?

2 What are the advantages of a single unified regulator?

3 What comment would you make about the degree of regulatory consolidation in each of the countries mentioned?

provides the opportunity to update legislation, which is a key competitive advantage since financial markets, and the products traded within them, evolve rapidly and often unpredictably. Regulation needs to be able to adapt to new entrants and new products. The internet alone is creating new challenges, and for the marketplace to remain attractive it needs to renew its regulation constantly. The advantages of the FSA are obvious in this context, and there is a general trend towards financial consolidation in other countries as well (see Financial Services Marketing in Practice: 'International financial regulation: a trend towards consolidation').

The rationale for financial regulation

Criticisms of the FSAct have raised doubts about the effectiveness of financial regulation. Indeed, some may question the need to regulate a market at all, arguing that competitive forces alone would serve to protect consumers. Yet, Davies (1998) and Llewellyn (1999) argue that the financial services sector is quite unique in terms of the products and services provided and the nature of the business. For these reasons alone, the financial services sector requires regulation. Three key areas are identified which form a basis for regulating financial services markets:

1 *To sustain systemic stability* – Llewellyn (1999) posits: 'Regulation for systemic reasons is warranted when the social costs of failure of financial institutions (particularly banks) exceed private costs and such potential costs are not incorporated in the decision making of the firm' (p. 13). Systemic issues have been central to the regulation of banks, particularly because of their pivotal position in the financial system, especially with regard to the payments system.

2 *To maintain the safety and soundness of financial institutions* – Financial institutions perform a fiduciary role on behalf of the customer. For this reason it is necessary that the safety and soundness of the institution is supervised to ensure the welfare of the customer is safeguarded.

3 *To protect the consumer* – The consumer needs protecting from market imperfections or market failures which could compromise the welfare of the consumer. There are many market imperfections in financial services:

- inadequate information on the part of the consumer;
- asymmetric information (consumers are less well informed than suppliers);
- agency costs (asymmetric information can be used to exploit the consumer);
- potential principal–agent problems arising from issues related to conflicts of interest;
- problems of ascertaining quality at point of purchase;
- imprecise definitions of products and contracts;
- inability of retail consumers to assess safety and soundness of firms;
- consumer under-investment in information and resultant 'free-rider' problems – consumers assume that others have investigated the safety and integrity of suppliers;
- due to the technicalities of some products, consumers are not all equally equipped to assess quality etc. (Llewellyn, 1999).

A number of these points essentially mean that it is difficult for consumers to assess the risks and returns of transactions they undertake. The problem of asymmetric information is especially true for investors of long-term contracts where the expected returns may not appear for many years. Without regulation to provide some assurance to consumers about the terms on which contracts are offered, saving and investment would be discouraged with damaging economic consequences. Moreover, healthy competition will be enhanced by empowering consumers through education and disclosure of information on charges and other key features of financial products.

Financial Services and Markets Bill

The Financial Services and Markets Bill gives the FSA extensive powers to make its own rules, as well as to issue broad statements of principles and codes of conduct. It will be able to change these rules as it sees fit, or waive them in special cases. As mentioned above, the Financial Services and Markets Bill, when passed in Parliament, will replace the FSAct and will become the key piece of regulation for the sector.

One of the features of the Bill is that it is based on a set of statutory objectives which act as the core of the new legislation. These objectives include: maintaining confidence in the UK financial system, promoting public understanding of the financial system, securing the appropriate degree of protection for consumers, and reducing the extent to which it is possible for a business carried on by a regulated person to be used for a purpose connected with financial crime. Let us now take a look at how each of these objectives will be delivered.

1 *Maintaining confidence in the UK financial system* – Maintaining confidence is not easy to measure, although it is obvious when confidence is lacking, as has been discussed already. Maintaining confidence can be explained under two generic types of regulation and supervision: prudential regulation and conduct of business regulation.

   Prudential regulation focuses on the solvency, safety and soundness of financial institutions. The case for prudential supervision is that consumers are not in a position to judge for themselves the safety and soundness of financial institutions. It is necessary because of imperfect consumer information, information asymmetries, agency problems associated with the nature of the business, and because the behaviour of the firm after the consumer has dealt with it affects the value of the consumer's stake in the firm. According to Llewellyn (1999) there is a need for prudential regulation when:

   - the institution performs a fiduciary role;
   - consumers are unable to judge the safety and soundness of institutions at time of purchase or signing contract;
   - post-purchase behaviour of the institution affects the value of contracts;
   - there is a potential claim on an insurance fund or compensation scheme because the costs of hazardous behaviour of an individual firm can be passed on to others who eventually pay the compensation.

   Conduct of business regulation focuses on the ways and means by which financial institutions conduct business with their customers. It focuses on mandatory information disclosure, the honesty and integrity of firms and their employees, the level of competence, fair business practice, and the way products are marketed etc.

2 *Promoting public understanding* – This objective takes the financial system into new territory. For the first time in the history of financial services in the UK, a financial regulator has been given a specific objective in the area of consumer education. Consumers need appropriate information on which to base their decisions, and the ability to understand that information. Transparency is essential for financial markets to work effectively and can bring real benefits to consumer welfare. The overall aim of this objective is to improve the quality of decision-making by consumers. There has been a good deal of mis-selling in recent years, and the FSAct did not protect consumers enough in this respect. However, there has been, and continues to exist, a lot of mis-buying, and the regulatory authorities and financial institutions should not be expected to take responsibility for this. There could be a significant welfare gain if the FSA can assist consumers in becoming better purchasers of products. In the long run better educated and more demanding customers are better for the industry.

   The FSA is seen as having two key roles in enhancing financial literacy and providing generic advice. Generic advice is that which helps people to arrive at a more informed judgement but stops short of recommending a particular product. The best way of promoting financial literacy is through courses incorporated into the curriculum in schools and colleges. There are moves to include in the curriculum a citizenship component into which financial literacy can be included. On the advice side, the FSA has already been quite active in putting out publications helping people to think about the implications of their decisions. They have introduced helplines, both general and specific to the mis-selling of personal pensions. In addition, pilot town meetings have been held to get into direct contact with investors and answer specific questions.

3 *Protection of consumers* – This objective is closely linked to the other objectives and sits at the heart of the FSA. The aim is to put mechanisms in place for complaints handling and redress which will offer greater simplicity and ease of access to consumers. A single financial services ombudsman will be introduced and a unified compensation scheme within which there will be appropriate differentiation between different markets and types of customers. However, it is neither possible nor appropriate to offer complete protection to customers of financial institutions. No system can fully insulate customers from the responsibility of taking their own financial decisions. Thus, the aim is to protect consumers while keeping in mind their own responsibility to inform themselves and to take ultimate responsibility for their decisions.

4 *Financial crime* – The prime focus of this objective will be to ensure that financial institutions have systems and practices in place to protect themselves against being used as vehicles by financial criminals, especially by way of money laundering. In addition, like the Securities and Exchange Commission in the US, the FSA will have the power to impose civil sanctions, with unlimited fines for offences such as insider trading. This

particularly is to improve on the statutory framework, enshrined in the FSAct 1986 and the Criminal Justice Act, which has been criticised for being ineffective in combating fraud.

In addition, the Bill brings together the rules covering financial advertising and cold-calling into a single regime governing financial promotion. The borderline between an advertisement, which might be a recorded telephone message, and an unsolicited call, which could be a scripted conversation, has become blurred. The new regime is also expected to provide a clearer framework for financial services sold over the internet.

One of the controversial issues surrounding the formation of the FSA, is its accountability. There are outward manifestations of accountability in the form of a board appointed by the Treasury. The board consists of a large majority of non-executive members. There is a clear separation of duties between the Treasury and the FSA. Treasury ministers are responsible for the statutory framework while the FSA is responsible for acting effectively within that framework. The FSA is also accountable through Treasury ministers to Parliament. The FSA must submit an Annual Report on its performance against the statutory objectives, outlined earlier. In addition to these outward manifestations of accountability, the FSA is also proposing to build checks and balances into its internal procedures. In line with this, there will be a Consumer Panel which will report publicly on the performance of the FSA against the key consumer-related objectives of promoting consumer understanding and consumer protection, and a Practitioner Forum which will focus particular attention on whether the regulation is meeting the objectives set out in relation to providers.

The legislation also provides for appeals against decisions by the FSA to go to an independent financial services tribunal, and there will be an independent complaints commissioner to look into complaints against the way in which the FSA has managed its administrative procedures.

The technological environment

The use of technology in the financial services sector fills a number of different roles. Traditionally, financial institutions used paper-based systems for recording customer account details. The advent of computer technology provided institutions with the ability to automate many of the back-office tasks and essentially become more efficient. This meant that more time could be devoted to selling products in the branches rather than back-office processing of accounts and transactions. Not only did computerisation allow costs to be reduced, but it also reduced the degree of human error inherent in the paper-based approach. This led to an increase in both efficiency and effectiveness. Computerisation also made it possible for financial institutions to offer more products and to reach more customers. Customers were rewarded with an increase in the speed of transactions and an increase in the quality and consistency of administration.

As well as providing automation of services, technology has also enabled financial institutions to widen their access to customers, providing greater convenience. Automatic teller machines were first introduced in an attempt to increase the restricted branch opening times and enable customers to have access to cash with-

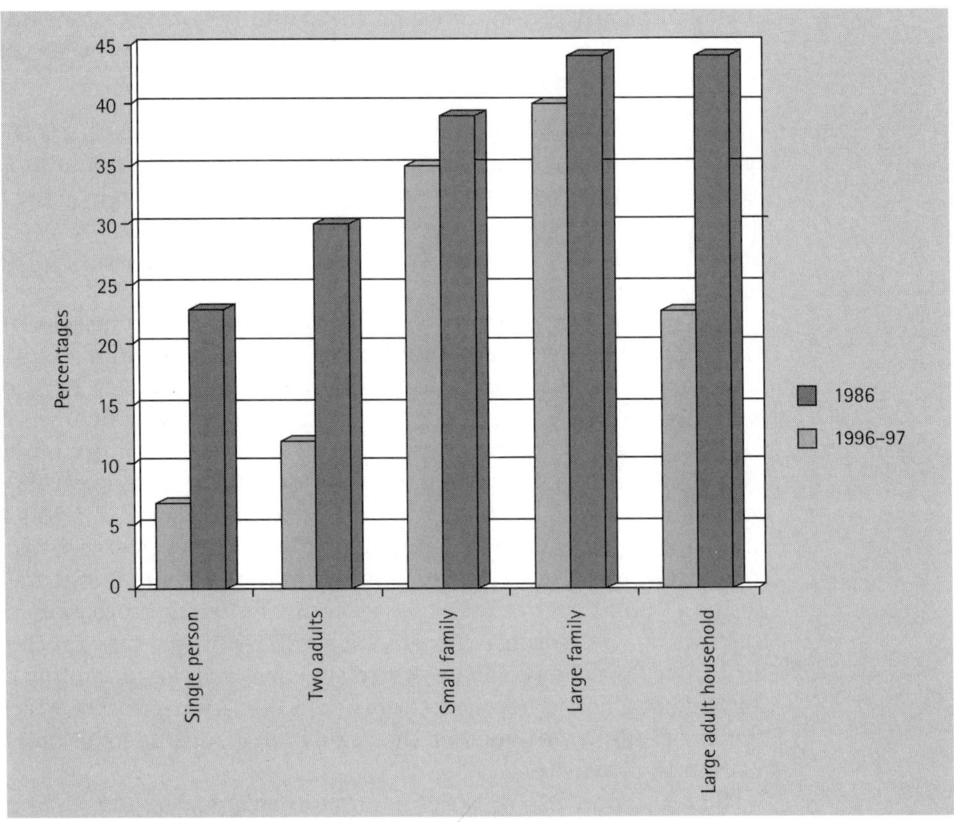

Fig. 1.17 Ownership of a home computer by type of household, 1986 and 1996–97
(*Source*: Adapted from *Social Trends*, Office for National Statistics, © Crown Copyright 1999, London: The Stationery Office, Table 13.6, p. 212)

drawals outwith banking hours. It soon became apparent that ATMs could also be used for a wider number of services, such as cash withdrawals, balance enquiries and statements, thus reducing the demand on branch staff time and reducing queues within the branches. ATMs paved the way for other forms of remote access such as telephone banking and PC banking. Indeed, the market for PC banking and internet banking has increased significantly in the last few years. The proportion of UK households owning a home computer almost doubled from 16 per cent in 1986 to 26 per cent in 1996–97 (*Social Trends*, 1999). Figure 1.17 shows that households comprising families with children are more likely to have a computer than single-person households. Ownership of home computers also varies by social class. Nearly two-thirds of households in the UK headed by professionals owned a personal computer in 1996-97, which is more than four times the proportion among households headed by unskilled manual workers.

As well as providing increased access to financial services, technology has also contributed to increasing customer service. Customers now have a range of methods by which they can access their financial services provider and conduct transactions. While some customers prefer to make use of one method predominantly, they may also choose to make use of other distribution methods for either complex or one-off transactions.

In addition to the distribution and customer service aspect, technology has also enabled marketing efforts to be used to greater effect and efficiency through database management. Traditionally, financial institutions arranged their administration systems around products and accounts, not customers. Furthermore, in many cases, customer details were not recorded in the same format across different products. This emphasises the traditional focus on products and not customers. However, as institutions became more focused on customers, they found that their systems were not adequate enough to allow them to build up a picture of the customer and the customer's consumption of financial services. Thus, during the early 1980s many financial institutions went through the process of reorganising customer information into databases or customer information files (CIFs).

The rationale behind a properly constructed customer database is that the institution can identify individual customers (or groups of customers) and describe what products they buy and how they use them. Institutions are, therefore, in a position to track patterns of behaviour and can identify opportunities to target products to specific individuals. Using a marketing database in this way allows the institution to set up an internal market of its own customers and identify cross-selling opportunities, and define the profiles of customer segments for further recruitment. It is argued that the long-term success of financial institutions lies in the effective use of customer databases.

Evolution of the financial services sector

The financial services sector, as we know it today, evolved from the convergence of several previously distinct and very separate sectors. Most notable amongst these are the banking, insurance and building society sectors. Going back almost two centuries, the banking sector was highly fragmented, consisting of a large number of small banks, none of which had a significant share of the market (see table 1.4). Just a century later, the sector had become concentrated in the hands of some 13 joint stock companies. In 1967, the Prices and Incomes Board promoted further amalgamation, resulting in a series of mergers throughout 1968. This produced several of the key clearing banks still in existence today, although the TSB and Lloyds have

Table 1.4 Development of the banking sector

1825	➧	Low concentration	=	554 small private banks with less than 2 branches per bank on average.
1925	➧	Concentration	=	13 joint stock companies with over 8,000 branches in total.
1967	➧	Prices and Incomes Board promotes further amalgamation	=	The number of branches expands to over 12,000.
1968	➧	Series of mergers takes place	=	This produces the large clearing banks: National Westminster Bank, Barclays, Lloyds, Midland, Royal Bank of Scotland, Trustee Savings Bank (TSB).
1999	➧	Further consolidation takes place	=	Midland acquired by the HSBC Group, Lloyds/TSB merger.

recently merged to produce the largest banking group in the UK, and the third largest financial institution, and the Midland Bank has been under the ownership of the Hong Kong Shanghai Banking Corporation for a few years. Taking into account the demutualised building societies, the Halifax, Alliance & Leicester/Girobank and Nationwide Anglia are now among the top UK 'banks'.

The building society sector has also experienced some dramatic consolidation. Back in 1900 there were some 2,000 building societies. Prior to deregulation in 1986 there were around 150, but today there are a little over 70. Only 20 building societies have assets of more than £1 billion, while 20 have assets of less than £100 million (*Financial Times*, 10 March 1998).

The life assurance sector is similarly experiencing patterns of concentration and rationalisation, although it remains a much more fragmented sector compared with banking and building societies. There are over 200 authorised life assurers in the UK, yet a little over 60 of these might be classified as 'substantial' life groups. The top 10 companies have roughly 46 per cent of new business and 52 per cent of assets. By comparison the top 10 banks (or building societies) control over 90 per cent of retail deposits. No one company in the life assurance sector has more than 10 per cent market share. Fragmentation essentially means a higher cost of doing business. Among the top life assurers in the UK are: Prudential, Standard Life, Norwich Union, Legal and General and Sun Life/Axa (Christophers and Macmillan, 1997).

Consolidation and rationalisation has been prominent in the sector for a number of reasons (see table 1.5). Prior to deregulation, the banking, building society and insurance sectors operated quite distinct from one another, with clear lines of demarcation. Competition was restricted to institutions of the same kind, since there were clear differences in the types of products and markets operated in by each of the sectors. Furthermore, the banks and the building societies operated price cartels which served to inhibit price competition and created a cosy operating environment which protected profit margins, and to a certain degree enabled less efficient institutions to survive. The institutions were, thus, protected from competition within the sector, but were also protected from competition from outside since the barriers to entry to the sectors were high. Any new entrant would have to invest significant resources, particularly in bricks and mortar, since the competitive norms relied on institutions having a significant high street presence through an extensive branch network.

Following deregulation, the clear lines of demarcation were broken down as different types of institutions were allowed to compete more directly with one another. More importantly, the different types of institutions brought with them quite different cost structures, which had a significant impact on the degree of price competition. Banks started to take business away from the building societies, being able to offer 100 per cent mortgages, and the building societies started offering interest on current accounts, placing the banks at a disadvantage.

The net result was that institutions started to become more focused on the costs of doing business and started to reduce the number of branches in order to control operating expenses. Technology, as discussed above, aided the reduction in branches as the number of ATMs increased the distribution network. As the barriers to entry came down new players started to enter the market, yet they showed that significant investment in branches was not required to be a successful contender. Direct Line and First Direct proved that customers were willing to conduct financial

Table 1.5 General competitive trends in the financial services sector

Pre-1980s		2000 onwards
Non-price competition	Basis of competition	Price competition
High barriers to entry	Barriers to entry	Low barriers to entry
High investment costs	Investment required	Relatively low investment required
Clear competitive boundaries	Lines of demarcation	No competitive boundaries
In-house production of services and skills requirement	Degree of specialisation	Out-sourcing of skills and services

transactions over the telephone without needing to come into face-to-face contact with bank personnel. Indeed, the advent of virtual banks on the internet showed that a high-street presence merely added to the cost burden of the institution. The entry of non-financial institutions such as retailers and utilities companies illustrated that the financial services sector was emerging as a sector any company could do business in. Consumers have also become more aware of the alternatives available and the entry of new players is having an impact on behaviour. Who would have thought twenty years ago that people would be taking money out of the long-established, tried and trusted banks and putting it into supermarkets and utilities companies?

New entrants

Deregulation of the financial services industry not only opened up competition between the different sectors of the industry but also provided the opportunity for a number of non-financial institutions to enter the financial arena. In the last few years a number of companies have started to offer financial services. Marks and Spencer started offering financial services in 1995 and now offers a range of savings, investment and credit and loan products. Following Tesco's lead in 1996, all the major UK food retailers, including Sainsbury, Safeway, Morrisons and ASDA, now provide some sort of financial services. Table 1.6 summarises some of the new entrants to the financial services sector and their approximate date of entry.

It could be argued that financial services are integral to any business. Indeed, many companies have offered some basic form of credit and/or saving services to their customers for many years through payment services and Christmas clubs. However, such services were related to specific purchases or specific retail outlets, were not generic financial services and, therefore, were not considered to be a threat to the mainstream financial institutions. The big difference now, is that retailers and other companies are offering generic savings, loans, credit cards and other financial services which can be used in place of those offered by traditional financial institutions and offer a real threat to them. One of the problems facing traditional financial institutions is that the supermarkets have long-established brand names which can be used to promote loyalty to their financial services.

In order for a company to provide financial services it must first be granted a banking licence from the Bank of England. Due to the difficulties associated with

Table 1.6 Summary of new entrants to the financial services sector

New entrant	Date of entry
Marks and Spencer	1995
Scottish Widows Bank plc	May 1995
Tesco Personal Finance	June 1996
Virgin Direct	October 1997
Sainsbury's Bank	February 1997
Safeway	February 1997
Midland at Morrisons	May 1997
ASDA	September 1997
Standard Life Bank Ltd.	January 1998
Egg (Prudential)	November 1998

this, and the fact that many new entrants have no previous financial services experience, a number of joint ventures have been established with traditional financial institutions. In the case of the supermarkets, this seems to have been the preferred route (see Financial Services Marketing in Practice: 'Supermarkets check out financial services'). As business environments have become more complex, joint ventures have become more popular. A joint venture helps to reduce the risk of failure by enabling companies to pool their resources and core competencies, thereby making them more effective.

The question remains, however, why banks such as the Bank of Scotland and the Royal Bank of Scotland would want to form joint ventures with the likes of Sainsbury and Tesco when competition is at its highest in the financial services sector. The answer surely must be that if they didn't, someone else would. Both the Bank of Scotland and the Royal Bank of Scotland are underrepresented in the English market, compared with the main English banks such as the NatWest and Barclays. Sainsbury and Tesco, on the other hand are very prominent supermarkets in England. Thus, these joint ventures allowed the Scottish banks to gain wider access to the market south of the border with the potential for expansion into Europe and further afield.

While joint ventures may reduce some of the risks of entry into a new market, they are not entirely without their risks themselves. In the case of the supermarket/bank joint ventures, the control is fairly evenly split, yet there is potentially the risk that the supermarkets may want to go it alone in the future, leaving the bank partner behind.

However, of more immediate concern perhaps is the reputational risk that both parties face in the joint venture. The Bank of Scotland recently suffered this as a result of the alliance with the American TV evangelist, Pat Robertson. Pat Robertson owns the Christian Broadcasting Network in the US with an estimated 55 million viewers each year. The purpose of the joint venture was to provide a telephone banking operation, named New Foundation Bank, aimed at building a solid customer base with the viewers. The venture was based on the Sainsbury's Bank model: the bank providing its expertise in telephone banking while Mr Robertson would market the direct

FINANCIAL SERVICES MARKETING IN PRACTICE

Supermarkets check out financial services

New entrants to the financial services sector have steadily taken business from the traditional institutions. Life assurers, such as Standard Life, Legal & General, Prudential and Scottish Widows have accumulated deposits of an estimated £6 billion. In less than one year of operating, Sainsbury's Bank attracted 650,000 accounts and £1.4 billion of deposits and claims to be opening 10,000 new accounts each week. Tesco Personal Finance has attracted over half a million savers and Safeway acquired around £200 million in deposits in just two months of the launch of its account.

For the life assurers, moving into banking represents a related form of diversification and not entry into a totally new business. Thus, it can be argued to be a natural progression from their core activities. For the supermarkets the move into banking does represent a move into a new business area, and one may question why all the supermarkets have entered.

One of the key factors prompting the supermarkets to look for new areas of business was the fact that future development and expansion in the retail grocery sector was becoming increasingly difficult. The 'golden age' of retailing, experienced during the 1980s, had come to an end.

Between 1982 and 1990, the share of the market held by the top five retailers in the UK had increased from 25 to 61 per cent of sales; the major food retailers were enjoying increased profits due to sales from new out-of-town superstores that had opened. However, by the mid-1990s, competition for superstore development sites had intensified.

By 1992, European 'deep discounters', such as Aldi and Netto, had entered the UK market, causing further unease and a threat to the comfortable profit margins previously enjoyed by the UK supermarkets.

Growth in the sector slowed down, and the retailers began to look elsewhere for their business. Consequently, in the early 1990s there was some foreign market activity as a means to expansion. Sainsbury entered the US market by buying into the Shaw's supermarket chain, and Tesco entered France through the purchase of the Chatteau chain of supermarkets and Hungary through a small investment in the Global chain.

Back in the UK, government policy on land use planning and retail development was also changing. In 1993, the Department for the Environment released a revised Planning Policy Guidance Note emphasising the government's position towards the town centre as the 'anchor of the retailing system'. The policy essentially aimed to restrict out-of-town development in areas where it threatened to undermine the economic stability of nearby towns. Since this time there has been some movement back into the town centre – Tesco began to open its Metro stores in city centres, and Sainsbury followed suit with its Sainsbury's Central stores.

With most areas covered and competition intense, the retailers decided to look at other areas. The deregulated financial services sector had opened up competition from non-financial institutions, creating an opportunity for companies like Sainsbury. ATMs were already established at supermarkets, and an increasing number of customers were making use of the 'cash-back' facility provided at the check-out – movement into mainstream financial services seemed the next step.

In order to provide a banking service, the company needs to be granted a banking licence from the Bank of England. Given the difficulties of obtaining such a licence, all the major UK supermarkets decided to enter the financial services arena in conjunction with an established financial institution. However, they have not all decided to take the same route.

Joint ventures seem to be the preferred method of entry; Sainsbury's Bank and Tesco Personal Finance were established through joint ventures with the Bank of Scotland and the Royal Bank of Scotland respectively. Sainsbury's Bank is 55 per cent owned by J. Sainsbury and 45 per cent owned by Bank of Scotland with the Board of Directors comprised of both grocers and bankers. Tesco Personal Finance is 50 per cent owned by Tesco and 50 per cent owned by the Royal Bank of Scotland.

Safeway entered the financial services sector via a partnership with Abbey National, though not as a joint venture. Abbey National provides the banking services for the supermarket and also

FINANCIAL SERVICES MARKETING IN PRACTICE

supplies the ABC Bonus Account. Morrisons takes the US model of supermarket banking which is akin to the 'shops-within-shops' concept, providing floor space for Midland branches within the store.

The Morrisons model differs from Sainsbury's and Tesco's in that the supermarket is actually used as a sales channel for financial services. Sainsbury's Bank and Tesco Personal Finance operate predominantly from call centres, offering access to the call centre via a telephone in the store. Apart from in-store advertising of financial services, the store itself is not used as a 'bank branch'. However, there are moves afoot to make more effective use of the floor space with the possibility of bringing banking representatives into the store to provide financial advice to customers.

Sources: Adapted from N. Wrigley, (1994), 'After the store wars: towards a new era of competition in UK food retailing', *Journal of Retailing and Consumer Services*, Vol. 1, No. 1, pp. 5–20; *Economist*, 'On the money: Britain's real financial supermarkets ... Supermarket banking', 28 March 1998

Questions:

1 Why do joint ventures seem to be the preferred mode of entry?

2 What advantages/disadvantages do supermarkets have in offering financial services?

3 What strategy would you suggest for the traditional financial institutions to compete effectively against the supermarkets?

banking operation to his millions of followers. The Bank would control 60 per cent of the joint venture, Robertson Financial Services 25 per cent, and Marshall & Ilsey (which would process the telephone bank's transactions) would hold 15 per cent.

Since its announcement in March 1999, the alliance had prompted a degree of unease among certain circles, particularly churches, trade unions and local authorities in Scotland. Pat Robertson was known to have strong views on homosexuality, among other things. The Bank defended criticism until Pat Robertson described Scotland as a 'dark land' that had lost its morals. By this time the Bank estimated it had lost between 400 and 500 accounts directly as a result of the alliance. The Bank had little choice but to end the relationship some three months after its announcement.

Developments in technology and customer preferences for alternative distribution channels meant that the new entrants have been able to take advantage of lower-cost forms of delivery. Most of the supermarkets have entered the market via direct telephone banking from call centres. In many cases the call centre services are out-sourced to the banks. The products initially offered by the supermarkets were straightforward in nature. Indeed, that was the key concept: to cut through the confusion and complexity surrounding the traditional financial institutions and to emphasise simplicity. Sainsbury's, for example, started with two savings accounts and two credit cards. In addition to these four accounts provided initially, it now offers a range of products covering personal loans, household insurance, fixed- and variable-rate mortgages, pet insurance, and a low-interest-rate credit card. Initially, Sainsbury's and Tesco's savings accounts offered competitive rates. However, later entrants, such as Standard Life Bank and Egg, have also used price as a competitive tool, emphasising higher savings rates. The rates have proven not to be sustainable in the long term and have since come down. The supermarkets have also introduced 'tiering' to their accounts which originally received the same interest rate irrespective of amount saved. This has prompted some criticisms.

Strategic responses to the challenges of the financial services environment

The previous sections of this chapter outline the main changes that have occurred to the financial services sector in terms of the socio-economic environment, regulatory changes and technological developments. Over the last few decades, the financial services sector has undergone unprecedented changes which have altered both the structure of the sector and the nature of competition within it. It is not surprising that over this time, financial institutions (particularly traditional financial institutions) have had to adapt in order to remain competitive. Figure 1.18 summarises some of the key areas in which financial institutions have had to rethink their strategy.

Focus on retaining customers

Following the early wave of deregulation in the sector, financial institutions began to expand their product portfolios. Banks started to offer mortgages and building societies moved into personal loans. Increased product proliferation meant that financial institutions focused their attention on acquiring new customers for the new products. Many of the financial institutions employed aggressive acquisition strategies to build a critical mass of customers. However, as competition increased, new customers became harder to attract and more costly to acquire.

Recently, financial institutions have started to focus more of their attention on their existing customers. The costs of retaining customers have been found to be more favourable than the costs of acquiring customers. Furthermore, rather than

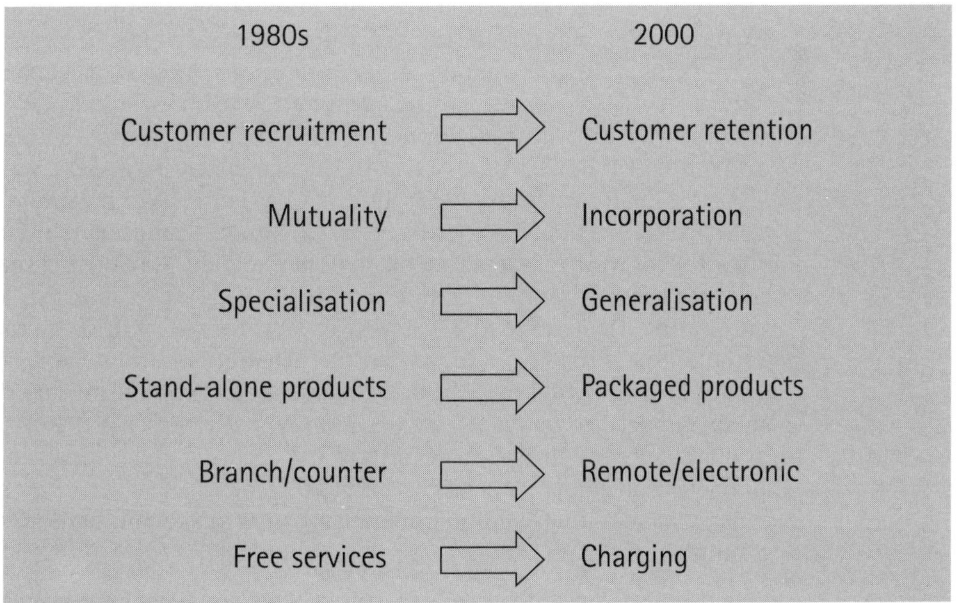

Fig. 1.18 Trends in strategic response

attempting to acquire new customers for new products, it became apparent that the range of financial services offered by the majority of large financial institutions fitted the broad needs of customers over their lifetimes and should, therefore, be targeted at them.

Focusing on existing customers is important. In their attempts to cross-sell products and services to existing customers and generate further business from them, financial institutions have set up databases to identify key cross-sell opportunities. Chapters 9 and 10 of the book focus specifically on customer relationships. Chapter 9 takes a more holistic view of relationship development, focusing on the philosophy of relationships. It encompasses the impact of relationship development on the whole of the organisation. Chapter 10 takes a look at the more tactical issues of customer retention and loyalty.

Demutualisation

Building societies, life assurance offices, friendly societies and credit unions traditionally are mutual organisations. A mutual organisation is one that is owned by its customers (members) and not shareholders. The traditional business of mutual organisations is to gather and invest members' funds. When the customers cease to be policyholders they cease to be members and lose all associated benefits (see Financial Services Marketing in Practice: 'The case for incorporation: successful conversions').

Mutuality has its roots in Roman times, and has thrived in its present form since the 18th century. The first UK mutual, Equitable Life, was founded in 1762 and is still going strong. Yet, changes to the Building Societies Act 1986 allowed building societies to demutualise or convert to plc status. Although building societies initially were slow to demutualise (the first demutualisation occurred in 1989), the last few years have witnessed the demutualisation of building societies and life offices on a vast scale to the extent that mutuals may all but disappear in the 21st century. Extinction is a real possibility; the mutuality pool is not being replenished (other than through the formation of credit unions) and it is equally unlikely that companies will be re-mutualising (although Scottish Life did in 1968). The year 1997 was a particularly busy one in the UK, providing one in three adults with a windfall, and brought Halifax, Woolwich and Alliance & Leicester to the stock market.

According to Armitage (1997) the aim of a mutual is to maximise the payouts and service to policyholders whereas the main aim of a proprietary office is to maximise shareholder wealth, not payments to policyholders. Maximising shareholder wealth requires the organisation to offer competitive products, but this is a means to an end rather than an end in itself, as is the case with a mutual organisation. Essentially a different person is put first. Demutualisation, thus, changes the ownership and the aims of a mutual organisation. When a mutual demutualises the members need to be paid compensation which represents the loss of voting rights and arguably the loss of ownership of the accumulated reserves to which they and previous policyholders have contributed.

Why have so many mutual financial institutions demutualised? There have been a number of drivers:

- *Competition* – Financial services markets are oversupplied and margins are being depressed in highly competitive markets. The situation has been exacerbated by new entrants that are perceived as innovative and flexible by customers.

- *Lack of understanding* – For many people there is a general lack of understanding of the concept of mutuality. Few people understand what it means and what the benefits are to them.
- *Short-termism* – Many consumers have been attracted by the short-term windfalls achieved through demutualisation.
- *Lack of control of external events* – Mutuals are not in control of external events. It is impossible to know when a predator might pounce or when members might be tempted by the prospect of sudden gains and vote for demutualisation.
- *Increased access to capital* – Perhaps one of the key drivers of demutualisation is that mutuals are unable to increase capital by issuing shares; they are dependent on retained earnings. This limits growth in many cases, especially the rate of growth, and can prevent them from making take-overs of significant size.
- *Management control* – One argument is that managers of mutuals have less of an incentive to promote efficiency compared with those in an incorporated company. In a mutual organisation, ownership and voting power is widely dispersed among policyholders or members, the vast majority of whom may not be particularly well informed about the affairs of the organisation, or interested in them, resulting in voter apathy. In other companies, where the ownership is more clearly and narrowly defined, managers are able to exercise greater control. Another reason is that it is impossible to reward managers of mutuals through share options.

Recently there has been a slowdown in the number of demutualisations. Labour's re-election and a more pro-mutual tone in the press have helped the mutual cause. But, at the same time, there are very few mutuals of significant size remaining. This naturally puts a strain on the small mutual organisation. If they cannot outperform shareholder-owned companies they will not survive any more than poorly performing quoted companies. Some critics believe that small mutuals face a bleak future due to intense market competition and higher unit costs by volume operations. Costs are a key concern. Yet, despite higher costs smaller building societies argue that they can survive on smaller margins than the banks. Furthermore, one of the advantages of a mutual is that it does not have to pay shareholder dividends. This means a saving of up to 40 per cent on costs compared with a shareholder-owned company.

Trend towards generalisation

Prior to deregulation of the financial services sector, banks, building societies and insurance companies operated in distinct and specialist product areas and in clearly defined competitive arenas. However, since the competitive boundaries have come down and the lines of demarcation have been eroded, all financial institutions have begun to look alike. Indeed, financial institutions have been forced to offer a wider range of products in order to compete effectively.

Thus, in comparison to specialisation prior to and during the 1980s, there has been an increasing trend towards generalisation with most financial institutions offering banking, savings and insurance products to their customers. The trend towards generalisation is also consistent with the focus on customer retention. If financial institutions wish to retain their customers and build long-term satisfying relationships with them, they need to be able to offer a range of products which meet customers' needs over their lifetime. This has an impact on the firm's understanding of the consumer and his or her behaviour. Chapter 2 of the book discusses consumer behaviour issues for financial services and details the buying process and the factors influencing it. Chapter 3 focuses on market segmentation and understanding differences in customer needs and requirements. It emphasises the need to track segments as they migrate and to continually update and revisit customer requirements throughout their financial lives.

Packaged products and bundling

The trend towards generalisation has also meant that financial institutions are now in a position to offer packaged products and not just single products. Indeed, packaged products, or product bundles, offer several advantages from the point of view of the financial institution. Product bundles essentially amount to cross-selling since the customer is sold a number of products at the same time to meet a range of needs. For example, mortgages are usually accompanied by house insurance and possibly life assurance. The customer may also be required to open a current account if they are not already a customer of the institution providing the mortgage.

From the customer's point of view this does simplify the process, since all products can be purchased at the same time. The financial institution hopes that this bundle of products will strengthen the ties with the customer. Packaged products or bundles are most effective when they are meaningful to the customer, and also when the value of the bundle is more than the total value of the individual products. However, in many cases it is difficult for the customer to weigh up the relative value of each of the component parts of the bundle. Chapter 4 is devoted to a discussion of the issues associated with financial services product policy, including the development of new financial services, the management of them over the life cycle, and the elimination of products from the product range.

'Arm's-length' distribution

Over the last few decades the distribution of financial products has moved steadily from branches to more remote methods such as telephone and internet banking. Branches traditionally have been the main delivery vehicle for banks and building societies. One of the reasons for this was that many financial products were thought to be complex and required a face-to-face interview with the customer. The other reason was that personal contact with the customer enabled a relationship to be developed and cross-selling to take place. It is true that bank managers may have got to know their customers very well in small branches or rural locations. However, the number of customers served by large city-centre branches would be too great to allow personal relationships to be developed with many customers.

More recently, there has been a growth in remote distribution methods. There are a number of reasons for this. One of the key drivers has been the desire of financial institutions to streamline the branch network and reduce its cost. Since the early 1980s, the number of bank branches in the UK has steadily declined, and the number of building society branches has declined rapidly since 1988. Another reason for the move to remote distribution is that financial institutions wanted to provide customers with greater access to them. It seems now that many customers actually prefer to have an arm's-length relationship with their financial services provider and are making use of the telephone and, increasingly, the internet to conduct their financial transactions. Many of the new entrants to the financial services sector operate entirely by direct means, providing no face-to-face contact with the customer. Chapters 5 and 6 are devoted to a discussion of distribution and channel issues. Chapter 5 focuses on the traditional methods of distribution: the branch network, the direct sales force and independent financial advisors. Chapter 6 looks at technology-based delivery methods, including telephone banking, the internet and smart cards.

Charging

In the 1980s and earlier, the concept of free banking reigned. However, as will be discussed later in Chapter 7, there is no such thing as free banking: services incur a cost which needs to be recovered somewhere, either from another customer or through the purchase of another product. However, free banking essentially meant that current accounts, for example, could be operated free of charge to the customer providing the account was kept in credit or did not go beyond an agreed overdraft limit. The customer was implicitly charged by not receiving interest on credit balances. This provided an important source of income for the banks which were able to use interest-free deposited funds to furnish short-term borrowing which would be charged at the current interest rate.

When building societies began to offer current accounts, they started to provide interest on credit balances, prompting the banks to follow in order to remain competitive. However, this move created a squeeze on the interest margin for banks and effectively reduced their income. New entrants have entered the market offering savings at higher rates and loans at lower rates than the banks. They have been able to do this due to the different cost structures and, in many cases, not having to support a costly current account product. In order to compete on price, banks have been forced to introduce charges on such products as current accounts. This has reduced the need for current accounts to be subsidised by other products and has allowed their prices to be reduced in line with the competition.

Charges have also been introduced in relation to distribution channels in an attempt to change the behaviour of customers so that more efficient use of channels is made. On 2 August 1999, Abbey National introduced a £5 charge for customers paying utility bills and other third-party credits in its high-street branches. The aim is to encourage customers to use other methods which are free of charge, such as the telephone, post, direct debit or cash machine, thus allowing customers to conduct such transactions more quickly and easily and at the same time reduce queues in bank branches.

FINANCIAL SERVICES MARKETING IN PRACTICE **FT**

The case for incorporation: successful conversions

Customers are demanding more products and services and these require capital. Abbey National, Halifax, Alliance & Leicester, Woolwich, Clerical & Medical, Cheltenham & Gloucester, Norwich Union, Scottish Mutual, Scottish Equitable, Provident Mutual and others have one thing in common – they were all mutual institutions 10 years ago. Now they are either quoted companies or have been acquired by quoted companies.

They are reputable, successful and have many millions of customers. They were all established 100 years ago, or longer, with the object of promoting home ownership. What has happened to make them shed mutuality?

First, some facts. Home ownership was less than 10 per cent of tenure at the turn of the century versus about 70 per cent today. To encourage home ownership most governments this century have offered tax breaks to mortgaging borrowers. But as home ownership has grown, the value of the tax breaks has declined whether for endowment policies or for mortgage income tax relief, to such an extent, that they are now marginal.

Customers of former building societies and mutual life companies are demanding more products and services and these, in turn, demand investment and therefore capital.

Neither building societies nor mutual life companies have the same access to capital as quoted companies and are constrained.

Ten years ago about eight out of 10 mortgages were provided by building societies. Today eight out of 10 mortgages are provided by quoted companies – banks. This is a dramatic change. What is the reason for this?

The first new radical building societies legislation in more than 100 years was the Building Societies Act. This allowed building societies to offer limited unsecured loans, own a life company, expand overseas and own a minority share in a general insurance company, and so on. But before building societies could adopt these new powers they had to get permission from the regulators – the Building Societies Commissioner – and this took so long that by the time they adopted new powers the market opportunity had gone. The new act also had a clause, which enabled building societies to convert, but the hurdles for conversion were so high that they were considered to be almost impossible.

In 1986 Abbey National had 7m customers all with either a mortgage or a savings product. Deregulation was in its infancy but banks and some new lenders were becoming more active in the mortgage market knowing that they were able to offer a fuller range of personal financial services.

Abbey National's choice was either to see its traditional and only market erode or test the conversion hurdles. It chose to convert in 1989 since when its customers have doubled to 14m and its share price has increased from £1.30 to £11 plus. Other former mutuals such as the Halifax and Norwich Union have since followed suit.

The former building societies, now known as mortgage banks, have access to capital and are free from the prescriptive Building Societies Act. They are able to diversify and offer their customers a full range of services. For example, Abbey National is no longer just a mortgage and saving company. About half of its income is derived from life and pensions, general insurance, consumer finance and from treasury and wholesale banking. It is no longer so dependent on the vagaries of the housing market. Moreover, these mortgage banks are now able to attract talented personnel, from graduates to senior managers.

Since 1986 the Building Societies Act has been modified to enable building societies to offer more services. But they still do not have access to capital and they are constrained by a prescriptive act. This may change under the new regulator, the Financial Services Authority, for banks, building societies and life companies later this year.

Whatever happens building societies and mutual life companies will not have the same access to capital as quoted companies.

Building societies and mutual life companies must take all the credit for the growth that has taken place this century in home ownership and through thrift. But change is inexorable and those that challenge change and identify opportunity will in the longer term be the most successful. Peter Birch was chief executive Abbey National from 1984 to 1998.

FINANCIAL SERVICES MARKETING IN PRACTICE FT

Source: Peter G. Birch, *Financial Times*, 10 March 1998. Reprinted with permission.

Questions:

1 What strategies have mutual organisations adopted to cope with regulatory restrictions?

2 What are the drivers of demutualisation?

3 What are the advantages of conversion?

SUMMARY

This chapter has provided an overview of the financial services environment. The chapter began by outlining the key socio-economic changes that have occurred and their impact on the demand for financial services. General trends indicate that the UK population has generally become better off, but the distribution of incomes and wealth shows some interesting segmentation issues. There are also interesting social and cultural factors influencing the take-up and ownership of particular financial services.

The regulatory environment undoubtedly has had the greatest impact on the sector in terms of changing its structure and the nature of competition. Competitive boundaries have been eroded and new players have entered the market, offering a real threat to the traditional institutions. Recognising the similarity between different financial services providers, the newly created Financial Services Authority aims to consolidate financial regulation in the UK under one single regulator. Key issues are concerned not only with the prudential regulation of financial institutions themselves, but with protecting and educating the consumer and combating fraud.

Whereas changes to the regulatory structure have had the greatest impact on the sector in the past, technology is likely to bring about the greatest changes in the future, and hold the key to long-term success. Technology has enabled financial institutions to achieve greater speed and accuracy of operations and is increasingly being used to widen access to consumers. Indeed, many of the developments in delivery are now perceived as suitable alternatives to the traditional branch network, putting the traditional institutions under even greater strain.

It is not surprising that, during a period of immense changes, financial institutions have had to change the way in which they respond to the marketplace. The emphasis has switched from products to customers, and from short-term gains to longer-term relationships. This has meant a focus on customer retention, loyalty, product bundles and the use of innovative technology-driven distribution channels.

DISCUSSION QUESTIONS

1 Outline the challenges facing financial institutions in the 21st century and discuss how they can best respond to them.

2 Discuss the key regulatory developments in the financial services sector and their impact on financial institutions.

3 What are the objectives of the FSAct? How far do you think the objectives have been achieved?

4 What is the rationale for regulation? Why is there a particular justification for regulation in the financial services sector?

5 To what extent has deregulation of the financial services sector benefited the consumer?

6 Outline the key objectives of the Financial Services and Markets Bill. How achievable are the objectives, and to what extent do they offer an improvement on the FSAct?

7 What role has technology played in the nature and scope of competition in the financial services sector?

8 To what extent do the supermarket banks pose a real threat to traditional financial institutions?

9 How has the nature of competition in the financial services sector changed over the last 30 years?

10 In what ways have financial institutions been forced to respond to the challenges of the financial services environment?

2 The financial services consumer

INTRODUCTION

Understanding consumers and consumer needs and requirements is the guiding philosophy of marketing. A marketing orientation requires the organisation to view its business from the point of view of its customers. This demands an insight into the wider aspects of consumer psychology and behaviour, including what motivates consumers, what their attitudes and perceptions of the company and its products are, as well as an understanding of their decision processes. Some of these phenomena can be understood simply by observing the consumer in action, yet many can only be uncovered through in-depth research. The intangible and sometimes complex nature of financial services only serves to compound the difficulties usually associated with consumer research.

Financial institutions have been criticised in the past for their lack of attention to the consumer, and have been slow to adopt the philosophy of the marketing concept. Yet, they have discovered that understanding the consumer is no longer just a marketing requirement, it has become a legal requirement. The Financial Services Act, discussed in the previous chapter, brought with it an obligation for financial institutions to 'know their customer'. This requirement is being further reinforced by the Financial Services Authority, which is putting measures in place to educate the financial consumer and enable better decision-making.

The need for financial institutions to understand what makes their customers tick is greater now than ever before, not only because of legal requirements but also because of the changes and trends in the consumer market culminating in a more knowledgeable, more sceptical and more mobile customer than they have been used to previously. Furthermore, the proportion of consumer spending on financial services is set to increase into the future. Financial institutions which continue to ignore their customers, do so at their peril.

OBJECTIVES

After reading this chapter you should be able to:

- discuss the social and economic trends affecting the demand for financial services;
- outline the characteristics of financial services products and their implications for buyer behaviour;
- examine financial needs and motives;
- critically evaluate the traditional models of consumer behaviour and their applicability to financial services;
- present a conceptual model of financial services buyer behaviour.

Social and economic factors affecting the demand for financial services

Over the past couple of decades a number of important social and economic trends have occurred which have influenced (and indeed continue to influence) the market for personal financial services. Indeed, over this period financial institutions have seen the 'traditional' financial services customer change. This section builds on the general trends outlined in the previous chapter and discusses the specific marketing implications. Into the new millennium, these issues need to be addressed. Financial institutions need to understand with whom it is they are doing business. Generally, the trends can be summarised as in figure 2.1.

A more mature customer

The traditional targets of financial institutions were predominately younger (under the age of 40) males. However, changes to the age structure of the UK population have shifted the emphasis to a slightly older customer. Figure 2.2 shows that the population of Great Britain is ageing. McKechnie and Harrison (1995) note that between 1990 and 2020 it is projected that the number of individuals aged 15 to 29 and 30 to 44 will fall by 3.8 and 2.9 per cent respectively, while the proportion of people aged 45 to 64 is expected to rise by 5 per cent and those over the age of 64 by 3.4 per cent. More recent estimates suggest, however, that the proportion of older individuals will outnumber younger individuals long before the year 2020. (See Financial Services Marketing in Practice 'Pensioners set to outnumber the under-16s within a decade'.)

The net result of these demographic changes is that there will be fewer workers in the future to support the same number of retired people. Gerdes (1996) notes

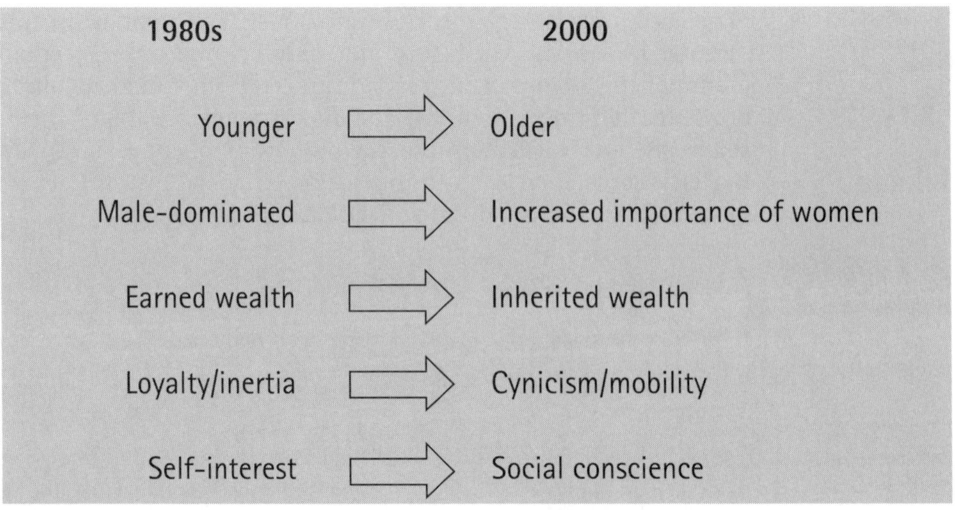

Fig. 2.1 Forces of social and economic change

that there are currently 10 working people to support every 3 retired individuals. In approximately 50 years, the same number of working people will have around 6 retired individuals to support. Thus, government will find it increasingly difficult to meet state pension needs. For financial institutions this presents opportunities in the area of personal pensions and other income-generating investments, although, these may have little appeal to many potential consumers.

FINANCIAL SERVICES MARKETING IN PRACTICE **FT**

Pensioners set to outnumber the under-16s within a decade

A picture of Britain with an ageing population, where those aged over 65 are now expected to outnumber those under 16 for the first time, is presented in Social Trends, the annual snapshot of life in the UK.

It is a country where more women work, where men in their late 50s continue to fall out of the workforce, where a divorce takes place every three minutes, and where attitudes towards benefits for lone parents and the unemployed are hardening.

It is also, however a country where divorce rates have stabilised over the past five years, the rate of growth in the number of lone parents has slowed, and where more than a quarter of households consist of only one person. In the 35 years since 1961, Social Trends records, the numbers aged over 65 rose by nearly half to reach 9.3m. Between now and 2007, however, there will be only a small increase before the numbers rise rapidly again to 12m people by 2021.

The number past retirement age is expected finally to peak at over 15m in the 2030s.

The increase has implications for pension provision and health care, and will occur alongside an anticipated decline in births, down from around 750,000 a year in the past decade to 723,000 annually between now and 2001 and to below 700,000 in the succeeding two decades.

The changed projections mean Social Trends anticipates that the numbers past the state pension age of 65 will now outnumber those aged under 16 by 2008 – eight years earlier than the projection made in last year's report.

The figures come as the Labour government reviews welfare state provision amid signs that public support for greater spending on pensions and benefits for the disabled remains high. Pension spending is rated by 71 per cent of the population and disabled benefits by 54 per cent as their top priorities for higher social security spending.

Support for increased benefits for lone parents and the unemployed has declined, however, an attitude which may have informed the government's recent decisions to cut benefits for lone parents and to introduce more coercion into the benefit system for the jobless. Only a quarter of the population now believes higher spending on the unemployed should be a top social security priority, a figure down by a fifth on the level a decade ago, while a mere 12 per cent rate higher benefits for lone parents as a top priority – a third fewer than did so in 1986.

Social Trends also charts a sharp rise in education at both ends of the age range. Almost 60 per cent of three-year-olds and four-year-olds now attend school, three times the percentage in 1970, while the numbers entering higher education have more than trebled over the same period.

Girls are now comfortably outperforming boys at school, and by 1995/96 there were more female than male students in higher education – reversing the situation found five years earlier. In 1970 there were twice as many male students as female.

The number of women working continues to rise, reaching almost 45 per cent of the workforce. Increasing numbers of married mothers are returning to work or never leaving it. Both partners work in just over 60 per cent of married couples with dependent children, against half in 1980.

Social Trends also charts the latest research on adults' movement on the income ladder. Just over half of those who were in the bottom fifth of the income distribution in 1991 were also there in 1995. There was considerable movement in the middle – only a third in the middle fifth staying there over the four-year period, slightly more seeing their income fall than seeing it rise.

FINANCIAL SERVICES MARKETING IN PRACTICE FT

Despite the changes the UK has seen in the past 20 years, the most wealthy 1 per cent of adults still own about 20 per cent of total marketable wealth, while over the same period the least wealthy half have consistently owned less than 10 per cent of total wealth.

The housing slump of the early 1990s, combined with increased private pension investment and more individual ownership of stocks and shares has produced a change in the wealth picture.

The value of financial investments almost doubled between 1989 and 1996. And while housing accounted for 36 per cent of net personal wealth in 1986, it now accounts for only 26 per cent. The share taken by life assurance and pensions has risen rapidly from 26 to 36 per cent – a reflection of private pension provision replacing state pensions. Holdings of stocks and shares have increased in a rising market so that they now account for 14 per cent of net personal worth, against 10 per cent a decade earlier.

Source: *Financial Times*, 29 January 1998, p. 12

Questions:

1 What is the impact of these trends on consumers of financial services?

2 What are the opportunities and threats for financial institutions?

3 How might consumers respond to the opportunities available to financial institutions?

The impact of an ageing population will also be felt by the already over-stretched Health Service. While many people still believe that the state should provide for health care arrangements, the harsh reality is that increasingly people will have to make their own provisions for old age. While the prospect of this seems far from attractive to many people, financial institutions are already anticipating the opportunities for long-term care products.

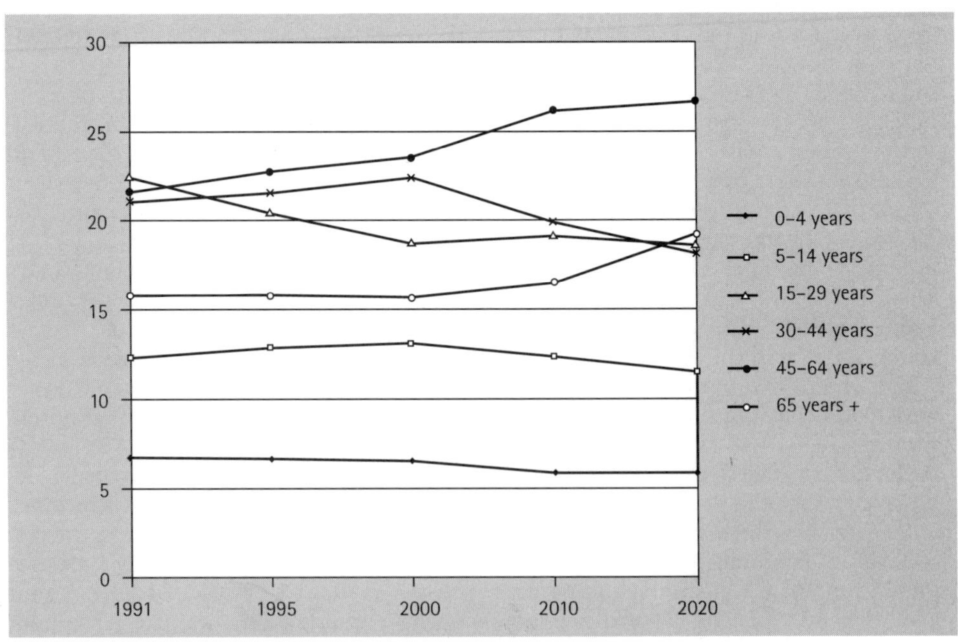

Fig. 2.2 Projected population of Great Britain at mid-year by age (percentages)
(*Source*: Adapted from Advertising Association, 1994)

Increased importance of female customers

An important social trend which is having an impact on the targeting of financial services, is the increase of working women. Arising from economic necessity, the desire to increase one's standard of living or purely for personal achievement, an increasing number of women are in paid employment and have their own independent sources of income. In fact, the proportions of working women have shown a rising trend compared with a decline in the proportions of working males. Furthermore, over half the females in paid employment are working full-time.

In addition, the economic activity of working mothers has also increased. Sly (1994) notes that between 1984 and 1994 the proportion of working mothers with children under the age of 16 rose from 55 per cent to 64 per cent compared with an increase from 66 per cent to 71 per cent for all women of working age in the same time period. However, the greatest increase in labour market participation has been among women with children aged under 5 years, up from 37 per cent in 1984 to 52 per cent in 1994. These issues are also important when considered alongside other life cycle changes.

Alternative sources of income

According to Vittas and Frazer (1982), the level of consumer income and wealth is seen to be one of the most important influences on the extent of financial services consumption. Over the past couple of decades consumers have generally become better off. Yet, employment trends are having various effects on consumer financial services consumption. These trends include: the shift to self-employment and part-time work (particularly among males), the increase in temporary employment and the fall in job stability (Gerdes, 1996) which mean that traditional life-cycle cash flows are changing. Table 2.1 compares the traditional and emerging life-cycle cash flows. The stages of the traditional family life cycle and its modern variants are explained more fully in the next chapter. Basically, factors such as divorce, periods of unemployment, inheritance and the demands of caring for the elderly drastically alter the cash flow. While increased job uncertainty and employment gaps do not bode well for long-term mortgage commitments, they may provide a boost to the savings market.

Inheritance is becoming increasingly important as a source of wealth compared with purely earned income. Inherited wealth causes the windfall effect, a relatively recent phenomenon, which essentially describes the situation in which people who already own their own homes, usually on a mortgage, inherit mortgage-free property from parents. These beneficiaries are mostly at the height of their earning power and may also be 'empty-nesters'. The windfall effect has been brought about by the growth since the Second World War in home ownership which now impacts on two generations. It means that there are increasingly numerous lump sums of money injected into the economy, either as consumer expenditure or seeking investment channels. This will undoubtedly have implications for financial services, particularly the need for advice and inheritance planning and investment.

In addition to the increased inter-generational transfers of wealth, many consumers in the past couple of years have also been the beneficiaries of windfalls from the demutualisation of a number of building societies. This has injected some considerable sums into the economy with a resultant impact on consumer spending and saving.

A more mobile customer

An old adage notes that people were more likely to change their spouse than their bank, indicating that customers of financial institutions were generally thought to be loyal to their bank or building society. However, financial institutions should be wary of assuming that their customers are loyal simply because they are long-standing customers of the institution. Loyalty is discussed more fully in Chapter 10, but basically is composed of two primary factors: a behavioural component and an attitudinal component. The attitudinal component requires that the consumer has a favourable attitude towards the financial institution, is satisfied and generally chooses to remain a customer of that institution because they perceive it to be better than other institutions. Loyalty of a purely behavioural kind may result from a rather less appealing process of habit or inertia.

Indeed, much of what was thought to be customer loyalty in the past largely amounted to inertia and the lack of suitable alternatives. Two reasons can be highlighted for this. The first reason amounts to 'better the devil you know'. Having invested time and effort into seeking out a suitable financial services provider, filling out the necessary forms and waiting for accounts to be set up, consumers may be discouraged from going through the process again in order to switch provider. Thus, while at least a mild degree of satisfaction is experienced, many consumers may just be content to maintain the status quo. Some even perceived it was too difficult or even impossible to change accounts with worries over standing orders and direct debits being lost. In addition to this, it may be difficult to compare alternative financial institutions and their different services on offer to obtain an informed idea of what is available. Thus, many consumers will automatically renew insurance policies, for example, without contemplating an alternative provider.

The second issue is that for many financial services there is no decision. Take for example a current account, a savings account or a credit card. These are essentially continuous services. Writing another cheque, making another deposit or paying off the credit card balance do not amount to decisions as such, but are one-off transactions in a continuous process. The lack of decision presents limited opportunity for switching.

Recently, however, patterns of loyalty or inertia have been replaced by increasing customer mobility. The propensity of individuals to switch financial service providers has increased commensurably. There are a number of factors which have contributed to this. First, consumers have become more sophisticated and knowledgeable about financial services which has given many the confidence to switch financial services provider. The Financial Services Act, discussed in the previous chapter, has been responsible for making increasing amounts of information on financial services available to consumers. The Financial Services Authority also aims to educate consumers, further enhancing decision-making. In addition, the popular Sunday newspapers regularly contain information on investment opportunities and 'best buys'. Increasing amounts of information and improved financial sophistication have also brought about a heightened level of cynicism among financial services consumers. This has also been fuelled by reports of mis-selling.

The financial institutions themselves have been partly responsible for the footloose behaviour of their customers. While many financial institutions are acknowledging the importance of loyalty and customer retention, they are at the same time actively encouraging switching through aggressive customer acquisition strategies.

Table 2.1 Comparison of traditional and emerging life-cycle cash flows

Life-cycle stages defined by age	Traditional life-cycle cash flows	Emerging life-cycle cash flows
Twenties to early thirties 'The Early Years'	**Financial independence** The majority of people expected to enter a lifetime of stable employment. Income rises steadily, outweighing expenditure in the early (single) years but is then outweighed by expenditure during the family formation years	**Financial responsibility** Income rises steadily in line with expenditure. Expenditure outweighs income in the later years but this is likely to be due to house purchases by single individuals rather than family formation
Mid-thirties to mid-forties 'The Family Years'	**Financial freedom** Income and expenditure stabilise and are fairly evenly balanced. Expenditure continues to be relatively high due to dependants	**Financial fluctuation** Income fluctuates, possibly due to job changes, redundancies and relocations. Expenditure rises dramatically, possibly due to divorce of early marriages or family formation of later marriages
Mid-forties to mid-fifties 'The Mid-Life Years'	**Financial freedom** Children leave home, bringing about a sharp fall in expenditure. Income remains constant	**Financial injection** Children leave home or start full-time education, resulting in a dramatic fall in expenditure. Income continues to be unpredictable, due to redundancies and early retirements. Possible injected sums of money from inheritance
Mid-fifties to mid-sixties 'The Golden Years'	**Financial prosperity** A short, but enjoyable period of unprecedented financial freedom with high disposable income before retirement	**Financial uncertainty** An unsettling period in which incomes continue to fluctuate in the early part of this stage and then fall sharply, after which they remain constant. Expenditure in the early stage is relatively low providing a very brief period of disposable income. However, over the course of this stage expenditure rises due to the provision of care for elderly relatives, leaving expenditure outweighing income by the end of this life stage
Mid-sixties and beyond 'The Twilight Years'	**Financial survival** A sharp fall in income brought about by retirement, resulting in a fall in living standards	**Financial deficiency** Expenditure falls as older dependent relatives die and then rises again as individuals themselves are being cared for. Income remains constant

(*Source*: Adapted from Gerdes, 1996)

Particular examples are in the mortgage market where discounts, cash-back offers and low interest rates are used to entice customers away from their existing mortgage provider (see Financial Services Marketing in Practice: 'Trends in the UK mortgage market'). First Direct attempts to dispel the misconception that changing one's bank account is difficult or problematic by arranging everything on behalf of the customer and offering a financial guarantee should any mistakes be made.

In addition to this, the current economic climate has made customers more aware of the cost of doing business with different financial institutions. The hard disclosure ruling on financial intermediaries' commissions and charges, discussed in the previous chapter, has made the price of financial products more transparent and more important as a decision variable in the choice of financial service provider.

FINANCIAL SERVICES MARKETING IN PRACTICE

Trends in the UK mortgage market

The UK mortgage market was traditionally dominated by the building societies. However, progressive deregulation throughout the 1970s and 1980s created opportunities for other financial institutions to enter the mortgage market. Recently the sector has witnessed further cross-over of activity between the banks, building societies and insurance companies. The result has been that building societies are finding that their traditional business is coming under pressure.

In addition to this, the mortgage market has recently been attacked by new entrants to the market (such as Direct Line and Virgin Direct), customer-oriented companies with strong brands and effective marketing. Furthermore, the consumer is becoming increasingly price-sensitive and is focusing more on lending rates as a basis for comparing mortgage lenders. Not surprisingly, financial institutions are finding that their profit margins are being squeezed.

Thus, the situation facing the mortgage lenders is quite different from the booming market of the 1980s which saw a growth in the size and number of mortgage suppliers, as well as an increase in the choice of mortgages available. A number of factors (political, economic and social) are affecting the general demand for mortgages, with important implications in terms of marketing to potential and existing mortgagees.

Political

Aside from the changes to regulation which have brought about an oversupply of mortgage products, the reduction and eventual withdrawal of MIRAS (Mortgage Interest Relief At Source) introduced by the Conservative government has had some significant impact on mortgage repayments.

Economic

Economic factors affecting the market include: employment, interest rates and wider macroeconomic factors.

Social

Arguably some of the most important trends have been due to social and demographic changes.

For example, shifts in the age structure of the UK population have meant that there is now a decline in the traditional first-time-buyer market and an increase in the second-time-buyer market. In addition to this, the reduction in the size of the family and an increase in the age at which individuals settle down and get married has meant that the demand is moving to smaller houses of lower cost.

Consumer attitudes towards home ownership have also changed. During the boom period of almost two decades ago, the perception of consumers was that home ownership was a source of financial appreciation as well as personal security. Yet, with the slowdown of the market and the rise in negative equity, consumers have lost confidence in the housing market.

A further factor which impacts on the older generations is the increase in inherited property. The post-war generation of home-owners are now bequeathing property to relatives. The value of inherited property is set to increase.

FINANCIAL SERVICES MARKETING IN PRACTICE

A switch in emphasis

The combined effects of a depressed economy and demographic shifts have meant that the traditional focus on the first-time-buyer has been reduced. While the first-time-buyer market is still important, emphasis is being placed to an increasing amount on the second-time-buyer market and the remortgage market.

The market has, thus, become increasingly competitive, with lenders offering discounts, cash-backs, fixed, capped and variable loans, making up a plethora of marginally different products derived from the basic mortgage loan. The market has recently moved towards a more flexible approach to mortgages, for example in terms of payments, accelerated payments, deferred payments, menu-type selection of products, continuous discount and cash-back at the choice of the customer.

A more flexible product may be seen as a means of attracting second-time buyers and retaining existing customers, as it provides for changes within the customer's life cycle, or possibly encourages loyalty by future incentives. It is necessary to understand what are the characteristics of customers who are most interested in such features, when in their mortgage-buying life the product would be most applicable, and to what extent this may encourage loyalty, so that financial institutions can target customers for a flexible product more efficiently and effectively.

Questions:

1. What impact have the trends had on the demand for mortgages?
2. How have financial institutions responded to the trends?
3. Where are the opportunities in the mortgage market, and why?

A more socially conscious customer

The 1980s was a period which focused on and promoted individuals and individualism. Thus, many of the activities promoted by the Thatcher Government were founded on self-interest: for example, the right-to-buy legislation, further promoting home-ownership, the introduction of personal pensions and private health care. However, somewhat of a reversal of the trend towards self-interest has been evident in the 1990s and is likely to continue in the new millennium. Thus, consumers are displaying much more of a social conscience which is having an impact on purchase decisions and consumption. Consumers not only want to invest money but they want to make sure that their money is invested in an appropriate manner. This has presented product opportunities for many institutions. An example of this has been the development of so-called 'ethical' investments. The Co-operative Bank uses this selling point as a primary feature of its advertising, asking people: 'Why bank with one that isn't?'

Financial services characteristics and their implications for buyer behaviour

The financial services sector forms part of the wider service sector. Thus, it is necessary to take into account some of the factors that affect services in a broader context. In terms of the marketing of services, this has tended to start with an appreciation of the characteristics that set services apart from goods. These are widely recognised as being: intangibility, inseparability, heterogeneity and perishability. McKechnie (1992) adds a further two characteristics which are specific to financial services: fiduciary responsibility and two-way information flows.

It has long been established in the services marketing literature that services are different from goods. Goods and services are not polar extremes (Shostack, 1977), yet, it has been argued, the characteristics outlined tend to dominate in services and create unique challenges for marketing. Despite this, much of what has been written about such differences has tended to be approached from the point of view of the seller, leaving little indication as to the impact of such differences on the buyer. Such differences are only important in so much as they affect and change consumers' behaviour towards services and bring about differences in evaluation and decision-making processes. Indeed, some are sceptical about whether services marketing is in fact different at all, Foxall (1985) argues that 'marketing *is* services marketing'.

Even if it is accepted that services are in some way different from goods, it is nonetheless difficult to generalise; not all services are the same, varying enormously within the broad category of services let alone within the more narrowly defined area of financial services. In the area of financial services alone it is possible to find a great variety in the levels of complexity of the products, varying levels of consumer participation, varying degrees of product uniformity from highly standardised to completely customised, as well as high and low levels of involvement. Thus, while these characteristics are offered it should be remembered that there are exceptions to the general rules. The following paragraphs will critically evaluate the characteristics in relation to financial services.

Intangibility

The most fundamental difference between services and goods cited in the literature is that of intangibility; essentially it is argued that services possess no physical dimension. According to Berry (1980) a good is 'an object, a device, a thing' whereas a service is 'a deed, a performance, an effort'. As a result of this it has been argued that services are impalpable: they cannot be seen, felt, tasted or touched in the same way as physical goods can. Thus, they are difficult to grasp mentally and therefore difficult to evaluate (Bateson, 1977).

Intangibility, however, is a matter of degrees (Shostack, 1977). Not all services are entirely intangible, neither are all goods entirely tangible. Even though the essence of what is being purchased in a service product is a performance, most services are in fact supported by tangibles. Many financial services, for example, contain tangible elements on which the service can be judged or evaluated, such as the branches, ATMs, account statements, so-called examples of 'physical evidence'.

Intangibility as a characteristic creates two special problems for financial service providers. First, in making the product difficult to grasp mentally, it compounds the already complex consumer decision process in the purchase of financial services. Second, it means that the products themselves often cannot be displayed or physically demonstrated to customers, posing problems in the advertising and trial of products.

Inseparability

Inseparability results from services being processes or experiences. Thus, the service becomes a performance occurring in real time (Gabbott and Hogg, 1994) in which the consumer co-operates with the provider. Regan (1963) compared the stages of production, marketing and consumption between goods and services and noted that tangible goods are produced, then sold, then consumed. Thus, the process consists of several discrete stages occurring at different time periods and often in different locations. In contrast, services are sold, then produced and consumed simultaneously. Thus, production and marketing become interactive processes. Front-line service employees play an important 'boundary-spanning' role as do consumers themselves in their capacity as 'partial employees' (Bowen and Schneider, 1988).

In some respects, the characteristics of inseparability may only apply to a few financial products. McGoldrick and Greenland (1992) question at what point an insurance policy or a savings account is actually consumed. In the case of financial advice it may be argued the advice is 'produced' and 'consumed' simultaneously. However, the recommendations of the advice (the real reason for receiving the advice) – which may be a recommendation to invest in a personal pension scheme or a unit trust – cannot fully be consumed or evaluated until the point of maturity which may be some years later.

Heterogeneity

The characteristic of inseparability in production and consumption leads to services being more prone to variation in quality. This has two consequences: from the supplier's perspective it raises the issue of how to deal with non-standardisation; from the buyer's perspective it increases the uncertainty of the purchase outcome.

Some services have greater potential than others for variation from highly customised to highly standardised services. There has been a tendency to view variations in quality or the inability to supply a consistent performance over time as a problem. The degree of variation is affected by the extent to which the service organisation is 'people-based' or 'equipment-based' (Thomas, 1978). The greater the human involvement, the greater the potential for variations in service quality. Financial institutions traditionally are predominantly 'people-based' organisations; most customers would traditionally interact face-to-face with tellers in the branches. Yet, technology has enabled the service to become more 'equipment-based' and has enabled the service-offering to become more standardised through the use of ATMs, telephone banking and on-line home banking.

From the buyer's perspective, variations in service quality and inconsistent performance only increase the risk of purchase as uncertainty over the purchase outcome becomes greater. Even though the marketing and delivery of an investment product may be able to be standardised, the final outcome may still be uncertain as a result of factors outside the control of the financial institution. For example, two people may invest the same amount of money in the same investment product for the same length of time, but because they started the investment at different times they may be affected by different economic conditions, hence the returns may be different for each investor. A person experiencing a good return may be satisfied with the 'quality' of the investment. However, a person experiencing a poor return may conclude that the product was of inferior 'quality'. This may have an impact on future purchasing behaviour.

Perishability

The characteristic of perishability describes the real-time nature of the product which occurs as a result of simultaneous production and consumption. The problem of perishability for the supplier is that it presents an inability to build and maintain stocks. Thus, it is argued, fluctuations in demand cannot be accommodated in the same way as for goods. Unused capacity has been described as a running tap with no plug: the flow is wasted unless customers are present to receive it (Lovelock, 1984). Similarly, when demand exceeds capacity customers are likely to be sent away disappointed, since there will be no inventory available for back-up. Thus, an important task for service marketers is to find ways of smoothing demand levels to match capacity.

However, Foxall (1985) argues that these problems are no more specific to services than they are for products in general. Unused capacity can also create problems for goods marketers, and stockouts can also be a cause for dissatisfaction.

Fiduciary responsibility

Fiduciary responsibility refers to 'the implicit responsibility of financial service organisations for the management of their customers' funds and the nature of financial advice supplied to their customers' (McKechnie and Harrison, 1995). In a financial services marketing exchange the consumer is essentially buying a set of promises: the financial institution promises to take responsibility for looking after the buyer's funds and their financial welfare. Thus, trust and confidence in the financial institution and its personnel are imperative. However, trust and confidence may only be established as a result of experience with the company and its personnel, which is why consumers rely on other cues (such as the size of the financial institution, its image and the longevity of business) to provide an indication prior to purchase of the extent to which promises are likely to be honoured.

The development of trust may be a factor contributing to the development of inertia in the financial institution–consumer relationship, since supplier selection carries with it many risks and effort for the consumer with few guarantees.

Two-way information flows

Financial services are not simply concerned with one-off purchases but involve a series of regular two-way transactions over an extended time period. Examples of these two-way transactions include: the issuing of statements, account handling, branch visits, use of ATMs, etc. This type of interaction provides the potential for a wealth of information to be gathered on consumers with regard to account balances, account use, saving and borrowing behaviour, credit card purchases, stores frequented, etc. However, as discussed in the next chapter, not all financial institutions use this opportunity to their best advantage.

Implications for consumer evaluation processes

As a result of the characteristics presented above, services have been noted to possess three distinct qualities which are argued to have an impact on consumer evaluation processes in the selection and purchase of services and service providers. The first two, search and experience qualities, were noted by Nelson (1970). Darby and Karni (1973) added the third category of credence qualities which have particular relevance to financial services.

- *Search qualities* describe the attributes of a service which can be determined prior to purchase of the product. Therefore, they affect the ability of consumers to gather and evaluate information on the service prior to purchase. For many financial services, search qualities relate to the tangibles that the customer can draw information from, such as the branch network, or technology, which provide an indication of the level of service the consumer can expect from the provider.
- *Experience qualities* relate to the attributes which are only discernible either during consumption or after purchase, thus not prior to the purchase. These may include experience of the technology, such as using telephone banking or using ATMs. It can also include experience of interactions with staff and advice or information received, and the subsequent quality of it.
- *Credence qualities* are characteristics which the consumer may find impossible to evaluate even after purchase and consumption. For financial services there may be many of these. For complex products, such as pensions and investments, it may be difficult for the consumer to evaluate whether the fund performed optimally, or to evaluate whether advice received was the best that could have been given. Thus, in such circumstances the consumer is forced to trust the financial services provider.

Zeithaml (1981) argued that search, experience and credence qualities occur in a continuum along which goods and services can be arranged. Thus, the continuum moves from high in search to high in experience to high in credence-type products, indicating the difference between easy-to-evaluate and more-difficult-to-evaluate products. It is argued because experience and credence qualities dominate in financial services that consumers may employ different evaluation processes compared with other products where search qualities may dominate. These ideas are developed in the later sections of this chapter after taking a look first at some of the factors motivating financial services consumers.

Financial needs and motives for buyer behaviour

Consumer needs and motives are at the heart of marketing. It is important to address what basic financial needs consumers have and what motivates or drives consumers to acquire financial services.

Motivation describes the forces which initiate and drive behaviour towards the

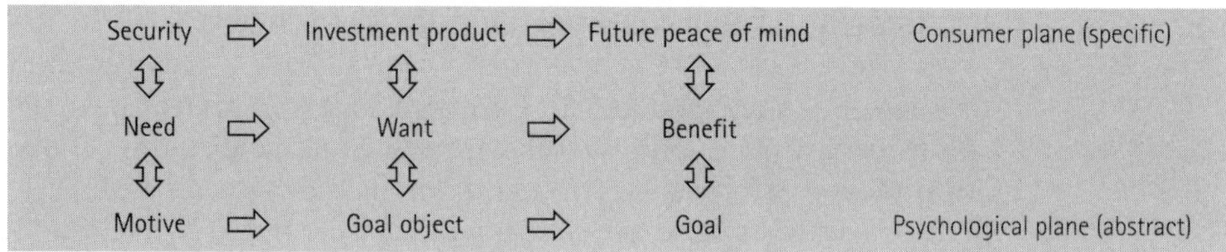

Fig. 2.3 Elements in a motivating situation
(*Source*: Adapted from Foxall and Goldsmith, 1994)

attainment of specific goals or objectives (Markin 1977). Goals are the result of needs which cause a state of tension in an individual. Thus, two important aspects are necessary in a motivating situation. First, there must be a goal or an objective that acts as an incentive. Second, there must be a state or condition within the person that stimulates action. The attainment of goals is frequently achieved by acquiring 'goal objects' which represent the goal attainment. This process is illustrated in figure 2.3. The diagram also applies the motivating situation to financial services. For example, the individual may have a desire to achieve a comfortable standard of living during retirement (the goal) which may be stimulated by a feeling of insecurity about the future financially (the motive). The way in which this goal may be achieved could be through a savings account or a personal pension or other investment activity (the goal object).

According to Chisnall (1995), human needs and motives are inextricably linked: the relationship between them is so close that it is difficult to identify the precise differences that may categorise them. Thus, the terms tend to be used interchangeably. Foxall and Goldsmith (1994) imply that motives operate on a more abstract psychological plane compared with needs and wants which operate on a more specific consumer plane. They make a useful distinction between the often interchangeable terms 'needs' and 'wants'. A need is, thus, a felt manifestation of a physiological, personal or social motive which essentially arises from a discrepancy between an actual and a desired state. A want refers to a specific manifestation of a need: it is the expression of abstract motives. Benefits are what the consumer derives from the product: consumers do not buy products for themselves, but for the benefits they provide. Thus, many products are but a means to an end, whereas financial services largely provide a means to a means to an end.

Needs drive motives in a specific direction. Individuals are generally motivated to experience pleasure and to avoid pain (Hilgard *et al.*, 1975). Thus, positive goals provide the attainment of pleasure whereas negative goals provide the avoidance of pain. Lewin (1935) referred to these as 'approach' and 'avoidance' objects. According to Betts (1994), avoidance objects would seem to be the *raison d'être* of most financial services. The 'fear appeal' is used widely in messages to communicate the necessity of protecting oneself against the unpleasant financial consequences of theft, ill-health, impoverished old-age, car accidents, unemployment, home repossessions, etc. Particularly strong messages on this theme are found in literature on critical illness benefit products, mortgages and other major loan protection plans, life assurance policies and pensions, to name but a few, and are discussed more fully in relation to promotion in Chapter 8.

Bayton (1958) noted that it is difficult to derive a basic list of human needs and suggested two general categories of needs: biogenic and psychogenic. Biogenic, or primary, needs are largely related to bodily functions and the need for food, drink and survival. Psychogenic needs embody the emotional or psychological sphere and reflect the complexity of human behaviour. Bayton suggests the various formulations of psychogenic needs could be classified into the following three categories:

1 affectional needs which refer to the building and maintaining of relationships with others;

2 ego-bolstering needs which refer to the need to enhance or promote one's personality;

3 ego-defensive needs which refer to the need to protect one's personality from physical and psychological harm.

Individuals may be moved by one or any combination of needs. Maslow (1970), however, pointed out that people are perpetually wanting creatures and that generally their wants are only partially satisfied and partially unsatisfied. As soon as one need is satisfied another appears in its place. The process, according to Maslow, is unending. This led him to develop a hierarchy of needs which proposes that human needs develop in a sequence ordered from 'lower' wants to 'higher' wants.

In addition to this, Maslow (1970) also admitted the existence of a smaller hierarchy of needs related to the desire to know and to understand. These are referred to as 'cognitive needs'. However, Maslow urged that they should not be considered as separate from the other needs since the desire to know and understand is also conative. This is more commonly known as the 'curiosity' need and, in relation to financial services, is perhaps particularly relevant to the self-actualisation stage of the hierarchy where individuals may invest time and effort in familarising themselves with the intricasies of the stock market. This is important in marketing since it can relate to information-seeking behaviour.

Yorke (1982) identified a set of basic needs that financial consumers have, and these have also been echoed by Stevenson (1989). The needs are:

- *Cash accessibility*: Customers need to have frequent access to cash. Thus, there are a range of money transmission services that cater for this need, such as ATMs, credit cards and cheques as well as telephone banking which enables quick and easy movement of funds.

- *Asset security*: This relates to two sub-needs, the first is the need for physical security of one's assets (i.e. protection from theft). One of the most basic functions of banks is that of safe-keeping. The other sub-need is to protect one's assets from depreciation. Thus, consumers have a need to earn a return on their money.

- *Money transfer*: This refers to the need to be able to move money around. Significant technological developments have made this possible and also reduced our reliance on cash.

- *Deferred payment*: The need to delay payment of goods and services at a reasonable cost is increasingly important as a means to acquiring goods and services. The range of credit cards, loans and mortgages cater to this need.

- *Financial advice*: As financial products increase in number and complexity, consumers have a greater need for information and advice in order to make appropriate purchase decisions. Financial advice in itself is not necessarily a solution, but may be instrumental in finding one.

It is argued that financial needs or objectives form a hierarchy which evolve over time. Financial needs are also related to the stages of the family life cycle. This is discussed again in the next chapter in relation to segmentation. Thus, individuals and households have a financial life cycle which is reflective of the needs and objectives which are important at particular stages in the family life cycle. For example, consider two groups of financial services (credit and loans, and savings and investments) which individuals and households acquire. Savings products can be viewed as a means of financing future consumption based on current earnings, whereas credit and loans products are viewed as methods of financing current consumption based on future earnings. Both take-up and ownership of these products have been hypothesised to depend on financial needs and the ability to acquire (Kantona, 1960). For example, such objectives could be to save (borrow) for the sake of emergencies, maintaining liquidity, making major purchases, children's education, retirement, growth in capital value or generating future income (Kamakura *et al*, 1991).

Certain financial needs or objectives assume that other needs have already been (or are capable of being) met. Figure 2.4 illustrates the hierarchy of financial needs/objectives. Thus, the diagram shows the movement of financial services consumers from the base of the pyramid to the tip. The assumption is that over time individuals move from higher-liquidity, lower-risk products to those requiring greater resources and with lower liquidity. This enables both financial services and users to be positioned along a 'latent' difficulty/ability dimension which assumes that the more 'difficult' financial products require higher levels of investment 'ability' or maturity. Thus, according to this concept the ability (in financial terms)

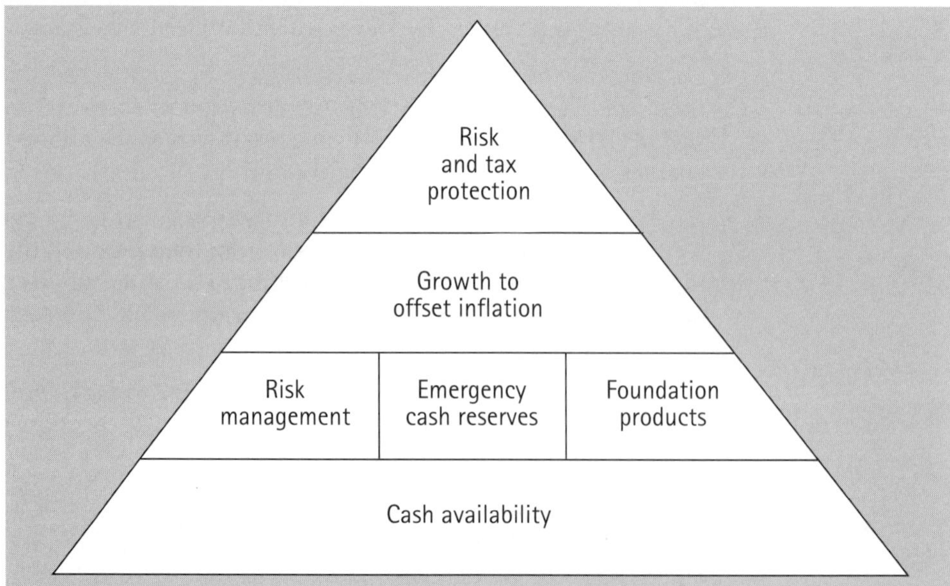

Fig. 2.4 Hierarchy of financial needs
(*Source*: Adapted from Kamakura *et al.*, 1991)

to become involved with any of the basic foundation products (such as current accounts, savings and deposit accounts and loans) is necessary before the more 'complex' products involving longer-term commitment, resources and risk can be considered. This hierarchical movement between financial services is referred to as 'financial maturity'.

The hierarchy of financial objectives is very similar to the hierarchy of needs proposed by Maslow (1970) which states that the lower, basic needs pertaining to human survival must be met before the higher needs, which are not directly related to human survival but relate to life enhancement and quality of life. In terms of financial services consumption the question of resource allocation is of importance. It is, therefore, expected that basic objectives such as liquidity, cash reserves and insurance are satisfied before allocating funds to higher-order products. However, similar to Maslow's hierarchy of needs, the extent and rapidity of the upward movement varies from individual to individual as a result of a number of factors.

Financial services decision-making

The majority of literature on consumer–buyer behaviour is centred around consumer behaviour models which were developed in the late 1960s. 'The reigning model became that of consumer-as-information-processor. Much like a computer, the consumer was seen as acquiring and processing information to assist in making decisions about which brand to acquire in a particular product or service category' (Belk, 1995, p. 59). One of the frequently cited models is the Engel–Kollat–Blackwell model (Engel *et al.*, 1968) which breaks decision-making down into five discrete but interlinked stages: problem recognition, information search, evaluation of alternatives, purchase decision and post-purchase evaluation. A common feature of this and other response-hierarchy models is that they are built around the information processing model or the AIDA model (Awareness, Interest, Desire and Action) which assumes that buyers pass through a cognitive, affective and behavioural stage when there is a high degree of involvement in a product category which is perceived to have a high degree of differentiation of products within it (McKechnie and Harrison, 1995). Thus, the models imply that consumers first search for information about possible alternatives and their attributes, they then compare a number of selected alternatives and evaluate them on their attributes, and once the purchase decision is made the product is re-evaluated to assess whether the correct decision was made.

Although the models were largely framed in terms of information processing, they did attempt to incorporate other issues such as culture, subculture, group processes, social class, family influences, learning and personality (see for example, Nicosia, 1966 and Howard and Sheth, 1969).

McKechnie (1992) notes that similar approaches are also evident in the field of organisational behaviour. For example, the 'buy grid' framework, presented by Robinson *et al.* (1967), is built on eight decision stages around the same AIDA theme, and also incorporates 'buy phases' which take into account the novelty and complexity of the purchase as an indication of the degree of buyer involvement.

The general approach adopted by the traditional models outlined above has been criticised in the literature. These criticisms are levelled at the models generally, and not at their capacity to explain buyer behaviour in any particular product field. McKechnie (1992) summarises the criticisms, noting that they: assume an all-too-rational consumer and decision-making process; are too rigid, indicating that evidence exists to suggest that the orderly discrete stages can in fact take place both out of sequence and overlap in some buying situations; are not empirically testable; and only consider one-off purchases rather than ongoing, repeat purchases.

The following sections examine the traditional consumer behaviour model in more detail in relation to financial services. A simplified version of the model is used which breaks the process down into three stages: pre-purchase information search, evaluation of alternatives and post-purchase evaluation. These stages broadly take into account the cognitive, affective and behavioural dimensions encompassed in the models described above.

Pre-purchase information search

Prior to making a purchase decision, consumers can gather information from a variety of sources. For example, they can engage in pre-purchase trial of the product, they can observe the product's characteristics and qualities, they can rely on the experience of others who have already used the product. Thus, pre-purchase information can be broadly categorised as being from an internal or an external source. Internal sources of information have been referred to as 'memory scanning' (Bettman, 1979). When faced with a new purchase decision it is argued that consumers first examine their memory for information on the product in question. Such information may constitute an attitude about the product or knowledge of the product formulated through past experience.

Where internal information is not available or is insufficient, the consumer may be motivated to search externally for information. External sources of information can be either personal in nature (such as a recommendation from friends or relatives and positive, or negative, word-of-mouth) or non-personal (such as marketer-generated advertising, or non-marketer-generated publicity). The extent of external search which the consumer engages in is argued to be dependent on a number of factors. These include previous experience of the product category, the complexity of the product and the degree of uncertainty felt by the consumer. Since product complexity and buyer uncertainty are almost certain to exist in the case of many financial services purchases, the need for external sources of information would seem to be important in reducing the risk associated with the purchase.

However, while both personal and non-personal sources of information can be used quite successfully in the marketing of a broad range of physical goods, there can be difficulties in communicating experience qualities through conventional forms of promotion. As a consequence of this, it has been argued that internal sources of information and external sources of a personal nature are the most appropriate in situations where experience qualities dominate and when objective standards by which to evaluate the product decrease (Murray, 1991; Robertson, 1971). The importance of word-of-mouth communication in the consumer decision process in financial services has been noted by File and Prince (1992). In these situations, information is based on the second-hand experience of others who are trusted as a credible source of information.

In considering the role of external sources of information, Murray (1991) argues that it is not enough to simply analyse the absolute number of sources, but is more productive to assess the effectiveness of the source of information. This is particularly relevant to financial services where high-credence qualities dominate which often make it difficult for consumers to judge for themselves the likely outcome of the decision.

As a result of lack of pre-purchase information for many financial services, one might argue that the whole pre-purchase stage in the consumer decision process is of less importance to consumers compared with the post-purchase stage with particular regard to the evaluation of products and providers. According to Zeithaml (1981) services are generally in contrast with the learning-response model and the low-involvement model (Ray, 1973) on this point. Where these models generally assert that consumers seek information and evaluate products prior to purchase, services buyer behaviour fits more closely with the dissonance response (reducing) model where most evaluation occurs after purchase. This takes the following route:

1 the consumer selects the service from a set of virtually indistinguishable alternatives;

2 through experience of the service an attitude is developed towards the service and the service provider as to how they both perform;

3 later the consumer learns more about the service by paying attention to messages which support the consumer's choice.

Consumers of services are, therefore, argued to engage more in post-purchase than pre-purchase evaluation. This notion would also seem to sit well with financial services where consumers have an extended relationship with the financial services provider after the initial contact and purchase of the product. It is this extended relationship and the series of discrete contacts which take place within it which provide the opportunities for continued evaluation of both the product and the financial institution. Thus, evaluation is likely to occur at each subsequent point of contact with the institution providing the consumer with important information in determining whether to continue or terminate the relationship.

Evaluation of alternatives

In traditional consumer behaviour models the process of information search leads to the comparison between alternative products and suppliers. From the information gathered it is argued that the consumer develops an 'evoked set', a small number of products and/or suppliers from which the final choice will be made. Thus, the decision is assumed to be based on a rational and informed choice.

In services, the difficulty of obtaining pre-purchase information is likely to result in a smaller evoked set than for physical goods. With regard to financial services, the evoked set may consist of only one financial institution, particularly if the information gathered was from personal sources. In addition to this, there are a number of other reasons why the evoked set may be smaller. Many physical goods can be displayed in retail outlets or in catalogues for consumers to see and compare. In fact, a retailer of physical goods will normally stock and display a number of different products in the same product category from different manufacturers, enabling easier alternative evaluation for consumers, all under the same roof.

Although a number of the high-street banks have attempted to adopt many of the mainstream retail concepts, it is nonetheless very difficult to display financial products and their features for consumers to compare. Despite recent attempts at branch refurbishments and the attention to atmospherics, it is debatable whether financial institutions can ever hope to achieve the same sort of 'shopping environment' as many other high street retailers. In addition to this, the majority of financial institutions offer only one 'brand'. Fully independent institutions can offer a much wider range of products to their customers, yet all the main clearing banks and the vast majority of building societies have tied status; thus their product portfolios consist of a limited range of brands. As mentioned in the previous chapter, the move to tied status by the main financial institutions has only served to increase concentration at the retail level and limit consumer choice.

Another factor affecting the size of the evoked set is that there are still consumers who perceive certain types of financial institution for certain types of products. For example, many still perceive that building societies are largely for mortgages and banks are for loans and current accounts, thus limiting their possibilities. Furthermore, the process of applying for many financial products (for example, loans and mortgages) can be quite lengthy, requiring considerable time commitment from the consumer. The relief of discovering that one's application for a loan has been accepted may be enough simply to make the consumer sign the contract without fully comparing the alternatives. Thus, in such situations it may be that consumers satisfice by selecting the first acceptable alternative rather than optimise by considering all the available alternatives.

In situations where products are compared, evaluations of product quality occur on the basis of product attributes. With physical goods there are normally many cues that can be used to judge the quality of the product. For services the cues are generally more limited. Since services are largely intangible, peripheral cues are often used to make an assumption about the level of service quality. Generally consumers are looking for cues which will give an indication of the likelihood that the financial institution will honour its promises. The physical facilities housing the service can be particularly useful in providing an indication of the professionalism of the organisation, as too can the size, reputation and history of the company. The customer contact staff are also important in enabling the consumer to establish a level of trust in the organisation.

Following the hard disclosure ruling on commission charges, the price of financial products is becoming increasingly transparent to consumers, thus providing them with another attribute on which to base purchase decisions. It is, therefore, not surprising that a number of life assurance companies were so opposed to the move towards hard disclosure claiming that other important factors, such as the fund's performance, were far more important attributes. Fund performance is, however, far less easy to evaluate, particularly prior to purchase.

Another important factor is the issue of branding and brand loyalty. As a result of limited pre-purchase information available on financial services and the greater risk associated with the purchase, it might be expected that brand loyalty be prominent among financial services consumers. Bauer (1967) stated that brand loyalty is a 'means of economizing decision effort by substituting habit for repeated, deliberate decisions' which basically reduces the risks associated with the purchase. The degree of commitment to a brand depends on the costs of switching (often perceived to be high among financial services consumers, but really depends on the product), the availability of substitutes, the perceived risk associated with the purchase and the degree of satisfaction obtained in the past from the same supplier.

As mentioned earlier, what was previously believed to be loyalty among financial services consumers has in fact turned out to be a level of inertia towards the financial service provider. Thus, it would seem that the 'brand' has contributed little in the past to the retention of financial services consumers. Long-standing customers may just be the result of the need for repeat patronage. For example, in the case of many regular premium investment products it may not be in the customer's interests to switch financial service provider.

Post-purchase evaluation

The post-purchase evaluation stage is necessary to consumers as a means of building experience and knowledge. Consumers evaluate products on the basis of whether they have fulfilled predetermined needs or met expectations. This in itself may pose some problems with financial services since there may not have been a perceived need to begin with but simply a legal obligation to buy, as in the case of car insurance for example. It is questionable, then, to what extent this builds in unavoidable dissatisfaction. Alternatively, the 'need' for the financial product may have been generated from a financial advisor. Thus, the consumer may find it difficult to evaluate the product in the absence of any of their own predetermined needs or specifications. Furthermore, as many financial products are high in credence qualities, it might be argued that for many consumers it is simply impossible to fully evaluate the quality of the product outcome.

For many financial services the process of evaluating is more complex because the consumer is evaluating the product before it has actually been consumed. For example, when a consumer begins an investment plan, they cannot really evaluate the quality of the outcome until its maturity. They may, however, be forced to make some evaluation of the decision made.

The problem also comes when consumers do not have the knowledge or the experience to evaluate what they have received. Maybe their expectations of what they wanted from the financial institution are not clear. It may be difficult for the consumer to evaluate whether the investment product has performed optimally so they make their evaluation on other attributes which are discernible to them. It is argued that the delivery mechanism of the service (including the physical process of delivery, any systems involved and personnel) becomes one of the key attributes against which it is evaluated. This holds true for financial services. Customers are more likely to focus on the 'functional quality' of the product; for example such factors associated with the delivery of financial services are: the willingness of counter and telephone staff, the knowledge and courtesy of staff, the empathy of staff towards the customer's needs and any signs, symbols and artefacts of service delivery.

When consumers are disappointed with their purchase they may attribute their dissatisfaction to a number of different sources. In the case of physical goods dissatisfaction is likely to be attributed to the product, the company or the service, for example. With services, because the consumer participates in the service process more they may feel more responsible for any dissatisfaction caused in the purchase of services compared with physical goods. Thus, the way in which the consumer participates in the production of the service can influence the consumer's evaluation of the service received. With regard to financial advice, the success of the outcome depends to a large extent on the information provided by the consumer and how the consumer expresses their needs. If the consumer cannot or does not clearly articulate or communicate their requirements they may, if they become disappointed with the outcome, attribute part of the blame to themselves as well as to the advisor for giving the wrong advice. Thus, the quality of financial advice received does depend on the consumer's input. It is also argued that as a result of the attribution of dissatisfaction, consumers are more likely to complain less. However, the complaints about financial institutions continue to rise.

A model of financial services behaviour

To date there has been little attempt to develop a model of consumer behaviour specifically to explain financial services consumer decision processes. As a subject of academic enquiry, the area is significantly lacking in theoretical development. This may have less to do with the specific product category but more to do with the relatively limited amount of information available on services buyer behaviour in general.

While a considerable amount of conceptual and empirical material exists relating to how consumers make decisions, the vast majority of it was developed in the context of purchase decisions for goods rather than for services, leaving the literature on services and financial services buyer behaviour far less developed. There are possibly several reasons for this. First, as mentioned previously, the general buyer behaviour models have been criticised for not lending themselves to empirical testing. Secondly, they may not necessarily be the most appropriate models, in either a general or a specific context. Third, there has tended to be a lack of appropriate measures specifically related to services for testing behaviour. Finally, there has been little conceptual work on how consumers buy services, let alone financial services.

One model which was developed specifically for financial services (Guirdham, 1987), bases the decision process on the AIDA framework but adds the variables of knowledge and 'know-how' at several points in the process. The model, thus, recognises that knowledge, or 'know-how', is a critical factor for the first-time buyer of complex financial services such as unit trusts. The model also suggests that 'awareness' comes in two stages, first in relation to the general product category and later on in the decision regarding which particular brand or offer. Knowledge and 'know-how' would seem to be important variables as the reliance on internal sources of information increases for financial services purchases.

The lack of a theoretical framework, however, has otherwise not inhibited empirical work in financial services. McKechnie and Harrison (1995) summarise a variety of studies in the area of consumer behaviour in financial services. Not surprisingly, empirical work has tended to avoid testing empirical frameworks. The focus has tended to be on specific issues relating to the whole decision process or customer–financial institution relationships, such as: bank (financial institution) selection criteria; factors affecting financial services consumption; customer loyalty and customer satisfaction. The importance of factors such as confidence and trust have been highlighted in several studies. These findings tie in with what was said earlier. Some common choice criteria in the selection of a financial institution have been found to be: dependability of the institution, institutional size, location, convenience, ease of transactions, professionalism of personnel and availability of loans. It would appear that the consumer of financial services is thus more concerned with the 'functional' quality of the service (i.e. how the service is delivered) rather than the 'technical' quality (the outcome of the process). This is consistent with the discussion earlier on the effect of high-credence qualities and the lack of pre-purchase information on consumer evaluation processes.

Thus, the development of a model to explain financial services consumer behaviour should take account of the following:

- Financial services, unlike many physical goods, are not simply one-off purchases, but involve a series of interactions within the context of an extended relationship.
- As a result of the above point, interaction between the consumer and the financial institution is an important influence on behaviour.
- There is a difference in the nature of information used prior to the purchase decision, after purchase and during consumption in the evaluation of the decision outcome.
- Thus, internal information sources, experiential information and personal sources of information, possibly in the form of word-of-mouth, take on increased importance.
- The post-purchase phase is arguably the most important in the whole process.
- As a result of the above point, dissonance-reducing measures are important in strengthening the consumer–financial institution ties and lengthening the relationship.
- Evaluation of both the financial services offered and the financial services provider increases in importance and intensity throughout the purchase process (i.e. it is cumulative). The role of post-purchase evaluation is particularly important in enabling the consumer to decide whether to continue or terminate the relationship.

Figure 2.5 illustrates a conceptual model of the financial services purchase decision process. While the model takes account of the above-mentioned points, it is nonetheless still a general model within the specific area of financial services. It aims to describe the process consumers go through in the purchase or take-up of a new product or contract with a financial institution, for example opening a new current account or savings account or starting a personal pension. It focuses mainly on situations where the ultimate decision to take or reject the product rests with the consumer. This is in contrast with situations concerning loans and other forms of credit where the financial institution decides whether the consumer is eligible for the product. Furthermore, the model is mainly applicable to high-involvement and complex financial services and does not apply to situations where there is essentially no decision, as when the consumer writes another cheque or makes another deposit into a savings account.

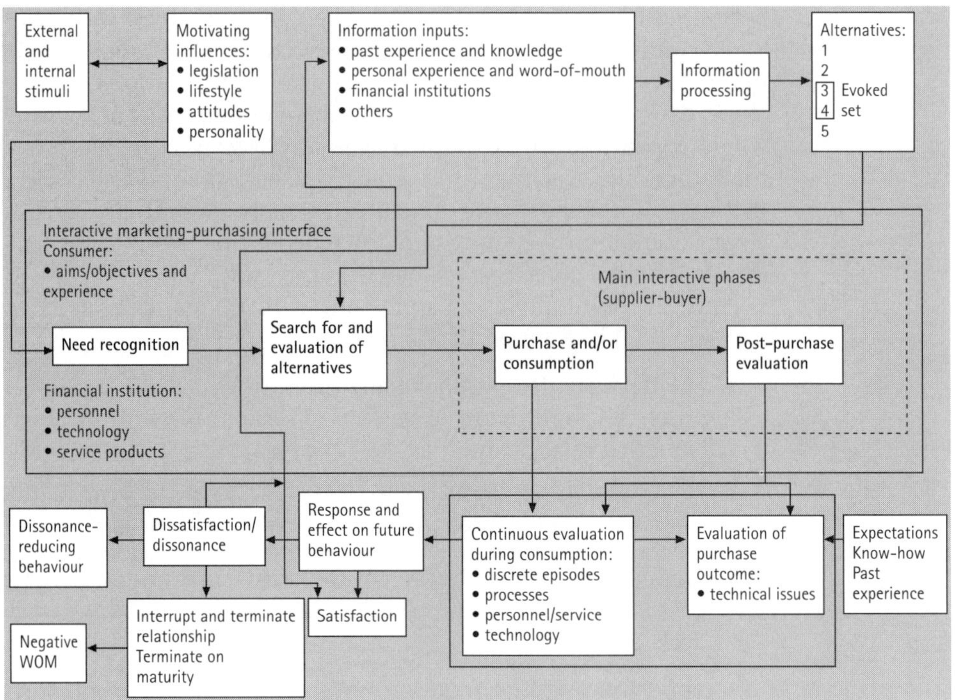

Fig. 2.5 A conceptual model of the financial services purchase decision process

SUMMARY

Recent social and economic trends have had an impact on the 'traditional' financial services consumer, the wider ramifications of which are being felt in the changes to consumer demand for various financial products. The result of this has been that getting to know the consumer and understanding what influences decisions to purchase financial services are of paramount importance to financial institutions if they are to attract new customers and retain existing ones. The proportion of consumers' budgets taken up by financial services will continue to increase, not only due to the withdrawal of the state in the provision of pensions and health care but also due to contracting earning periods for many consumers. However, financial institutions should not allow themselves to get overly focused on product proliferation, since consumers are becoming more demanding of the service they receive; they may want more, but they also want it better.

This chapter has attempted to cover a number of issues under the heading of the financial services consumer, beginning with the impact of social and economic trends on the demand for financial services. Financial needs and motives were discussed, as too were the characteristics of financial service products and their implications for buyer behaviour. Having critically evaluated the suitability of traditional consumer behaviour models for financial services decision-making, a conceptual model of financial services buyer behaviour was presented which took into account a number of factors specific to financial services.

DISCUSSION QUESTIONS

1 Forces of social change are having an impact on the future needs and requirements of financial services consumers. Outline how and why consumer financial needs are changing and suggest ways in which financial institutions can meet the challenges.

2 Evaluate the trends in financial services consumption over the last couple of decades and provide an indication of what you believe future trends might be. Justify your prediction.

3 How does the specific nature of complex financial services affect the suitability of 'response hierarchy' models in understanding behaviour of financial services consumers?

4 To what extent has the consumer of financial services changed over the last twenty to thirty years? In view of this, how relevant will the traditional models of consumer behaviour be in researching the financial services consumer in the 21st century?

5 Outline and discuss the implications of changes to traditional life-cycle cash flows and recommend ways in which financial institutions can address the changes.

6 How different are financial services from other services and physical goods? What impact might any differences have on consumer decision-making in the purchase of financial services?

7 Using the hierarchy of financial needs pyramid, identify specific consumer situations and product requirements for each level of the hierarchy.

8 The 'fear appeal' is a frequently used motivator in the communication of financial products. Evaluate how effective you think this is. Are there any other appeals that might be used to greater effect?

9 For a recent financial services purchase, evaluate the stages and decisions that you went through. How does your purchase decision process relate to the conceptual model presented in this chapter?

10 Why do you think past research into the financial services consumer has tended to shy away from testing conceptual frameworks? What impact has this had on our understanding of financial services buyer behaviour?

3 Identifying and targeting financial prospects

INTRODUCTION

The previous chapter discussed financial services consumer behaviour, the decisions that financial services consumers go through and the factors that influence or motivate the purchase of financial services and products. Thus, Chapter 2 provided an understanding of the broad patterns of financial services consumer behaviour. However, the development of an effective marketing strategy by financial institutions also necessitates an understanding of the differences between consumers in respect of their financial services requirements. This is the subject of market segmentation and the focus of this chapter.

Market segmentation consists of viewing a heterogeneous market (one characterised by divergent demand) as a number of smaller, more homogeneous, markets. In its ultimate form segmentation could result in each customer being treated as a potential individual market to be served uniquely. Customised marketing can, though, prove expensive and tends to be rare generally in consumer market situations. However, with improved efficiency in delivery systems and the support of information technology, customised marketing is a possibility for financial institutions. These issues are discussed later in the chapter. Despite this, a feasible approach is to group or segment individuals on the basis of some similar need or requirement.

OBJECTIVES

After reading this chapter you should be able to:

- build on the broad understanding of financial services consumer behaviour by specifically focusing on the factors which differentiate consumers' financial services requirements;
- categorise and define various bases for market segmentation;
- critically review a selection of bases used to segment financial services consumers from both an academic and a practitioner perspective;
- discuss the relative merits of the strategies and techniques available for segmenting markets;
- comment on the issue of market fragmentation through increased use of direct marketing and information technology.

Benefits of market segmentation

The following benefits of segmentation have been outlined in relation to the segmentation of insurance markets (Harrison, 1997b). However, they are generic benefits having applicability to the wider financial services market.

- Market segmentation enables costs to be reduced via a closer matching of company resources with market requirements;
- customer satisfaction can be enhanced by meeting customer requirements more accurately;
- certain groups can be selected to the exclusion of others, enabling the company to focus its efforts on a narrower target, thus, gaining a specialist knowledge of the needs and requirements of that group of customers;
- new customer requirements can be anticipated by projecting known segment characteristics onto new/potential customers;
- customer retention can be improved via increased customer satisfaction and anticipation of customer needs through segment migration.

Despite the benefits offered from a segmented approach, many financial institutions have been slow to realise its full potential. As new customers become harder to acquire and existing customers prove as difficult to retain, financial institutions cannot afford to ignore the benefits of segmentation and getting to know their customers.

Bases for segmenting financial services consumers

Definition and categorisation of bases

The purpose of market segmentation is to group individuals into segments according to their differences/similarities in product needs. Since needs are not explicitly actionable, behavioural scientists have turned to the use of proxy variables. These are variables which are assumed to have a correlation or association with behaviour; they may even be the determinants of behaviour. Such variables are known as 'segmentation bases'.

A segmentation basis has been defined as 'the characteristic or groups of characteristics of consumers used to assign consumers to segments' (Wedel, 1990, p. 22). Although there are an almost infinite number of variables in existence which can be used as segmentation bases, this does not necessarily mean that they are all equally applicable to all segments and markets. Wind (1978) suggests that there are a number of 'preferred' bases for segmentation which have been shown to offer better outcomes than other variables for a number of marketing decisions. These include: benefits sought, needs and product usage patterns. The explanation for the success of these variables could be that benefits and needs relate more closely to the anticipated or derived satisfaction from the product and that usage patterns add a behavioural dimension.

Due to the vast number of variables which can be used for segmenting markets, efforts have been made to classify them into groups according to their properties

	Customer-specific	Situation-specific
Observable	Cultural, geographic, demographic and socio-economic variables	User status, usage, frequency, brand-loyalty, store-loyalty and patronage, usage situation
Unobservable	Psychographics: personality and lifestyle	Psychographics, benefits, perceptions, attitudes, preferences and intentions

Fig. 3.1 Classification of segmentation bases
(*Source*: Adapted from Frank *et al*., 1972)

and their ease of application and interpretation. Thus, segmentation bases can be broadly divided into two groups: 'customer-specific' bases and 'situation-specific' bases. These two groups can be classified further according to whether they can be measured objectively (observable bases) or whether they must be inferred (unobservable bases). The classification, showing examples within each category, is illustrated in figure 3.1.

Certain variables, such as demographics and socio-economics, clearly belong to the category of customer-specific observable characteristics since details of individuals' ages, locations, etc. are indisputable. However, as well as belonging to a particular chronological age category, or an identified social class grouping, an individual's self-perception may place them in quite a different category. For example, a middle-aged person may perceive themselves to be quite a number of years younger, may in fact look younger, and may possibly exhibit the behaviour of a younger person. Similarly, an individual categorised as belonging to social class C_2 may, in fact, have aspirations to belong to social class B and may exhibit all the purchasing behaviour and lifestyle expected of someone from this social class. These differences are important since they shift the emphasis from the demographic domain to the psychographic one.

Psychographic variables, whilst largely unobservable in nature, can be either customer-specific (such as an attitude towards corporal punishment, or a gregarious personality; such factors which remain with the individual usually regardless of the situation) or product-specific (such as attitudes towards credit). However, even this distinction can also become blurred, since factors which might be considered to be customer-specific (such as an attitude towards risk) might assume increased importance in relation to certain product situations (i.e. certain types of financial products) and, in such an instance, might be considered to be product-specific. It is, therefore, important to identify all factors which are likely to have an impact on the area of investigation, whether they be customer- or product-specific, observable or unobservable.

While this type of categorisation may have its weaknesses, it does offer some guidance in terms of research methodology (observable data may be acquired from secondary data sources or through the use of observational techniques whereas unobservable data will require the use of interview or questionnaire techniques, for example). The following sections review several segmentation bases which have been used in segmenting financial services consumers.

Geographic bases

Haley (1968) notes that historically geography was perhaps first used as a segmentation variable. It was a basis by which small companies, unable to supply the entire country, could limit their distribution of goods since it enabled markets to be analysed nationally, regionally or locally. Prior to the turn of the century, the UK was geographically fragmented, not, however, as a result of marketing strategy, but as a result of an inadequate logistical infrastructure to support national distribution. Today geographic concentration of industries is evident, and is a feature of industrial market segmentation (Gross *et al.*, 1993). Many regionally situated building societies segmented geographically by default. However, advances in technology, distribution and delivery systems have achieved a broadening of the customer base outside the local geographic area for many small institutions.

Demographic bases

Demographic segmentation consists of grouping people according to gender, age, family size, family life cycle, etc. Demography also offers a straightforward form of segmentation: consumers are placed on definite scales of measurement which are easily understood. The information is easily interpreted, relatively easily gathered and easily transferable from one study to another. Demographics are useful in providing measurability of and accessibility to markets. These are primary reasons why demographics continue to be the mainstay of market research.

Gender

Traditionally men were the targets of financial institutions; women were viewed as having far less importance in such matters. A number of reasons, including the status of women as society's homemakers rather than breadwinners (Betts, 1994), contributed to this. However, the trends outlined in Chapter 2 have resulted in working women making greater use of financial services compared with those in unpaid employment in the home (Burton, 1994). Furthermore, with the demise of the nuclear family, as discussed later in relation to the family life cycle, a number of women are heads of households with all the associated financial responsibilities.

Despite this, research indicates that there has been a tendency for women to feel less confident than men in dealing with financial services. A Key Note report (1992) investigating awareness of investments revealed that while 17 per cent of men surveyed were aware of personal equity plans only 5 per cent of women in the survey were. Similarly, only 9 per cent of women were aware of unit trusts compared with 19 per cent of men.

More recent research (Harrison, 1997a) identifies four segments of financial services consumers according to their perceived knowledge of financial services (discussed more fully in relation to psychographics). Gender distributions for three of the four clusters were found to be fairly even. However, one segment, the 'Capital Accumulators', was found to comprise 40 per cent more males than the other segments. Interestingly, it was this cluster which had been identified as the most knowledgeable, confident and interested in financial services and the most financially active. These results might suggest that the most financially astute and financially active are most likely to be, although they are not always, male.

Aside from this it is open to question whether women are actually less knowledgeable than men in dealing with financial services. A number of factors could contribute to such results. For example, men may be less willing than women to admit their lack of knowledge due to cultural pressures contending that it is the man's role to take care of family financial matters. Indeed, women may know as much as their male counterparts but may feel that their knowledge is insufficient to make a wise decision. While both the above research sources show that there are some gender differences the results are insufficiently discriminatory for gender to be of value as a segmentation basis alone.

Despite this, financial institutions can make use of these findings in gaining a better understanding of how to communicate with women and understand that perceived lack of knowledge may have some bearing on a reluctance to make financial decisions.

Age

The age of the consumer is one of the simplest methods of segmenting a market. The process is relatively easy, requiring individuals to be grouped according to their age, and the assumptions made are that individuals with similar ages have similar needs and requirements. The age of a person has been shown to have important meaning for financial services, discriminating between different age groups in terms of their use of financial services (Stanley *et al.*, 1985). Results show that younger customers generally have a larger demand for loan facilities than their older counterparts who are more likely to deposit rather than borrow funds.

Not surprisingly, financial institutions have developed a number of different accounts to respond to various age segments. One of the important developments occurred in the 1970s with the introduction of student accounts aimed at school leavers going into further education (Lewis, 1982a). The key factor driving the introduction was that, at the time, almost all students received local education authority (LEA) grants which were paid by cheque, requiring the student to have a bank account. In addition to this, the banks were also attracted by the potential earning-power of the segment as they excelled in their future careers. Marx (1995) reports that students are very loyal and brand-conscious, noting that brand loyalties formed while at college often last a lifetime. Although loyalty may be strong while at college, particularly for those products which are visible to others and, hence, susceptible to peer pressure, students are, nonetheless, in a transitory phase of their lives and one might question the longevity of many loyalty patterns beyond graduation. It is precisely this high mobility of students on graduation, and also the recent reduction in LEA grants, which has rendered this segment a more challenging prospect for many institutions. At the same time, school leavers entering full-time employment have received the attention of other institutions. For example, The Trustee Savings Bank (TSB) attempts to benefit from this segment through its Youth and Independent Accounts which it targets at young, single individuals in full-time employment with no dependants. This group is particularly attractive compared with students and other individuals of the same age with young families, as a result of significantly larger discretionary incomes.

In an attempt to catch them young, financial institutions have also identified school children as an important segment, partly because they constitute a significant proportion of the population but also because they possess significant discretionary purchasing power through pocket money, monetary gifts and earned income (Lewis, 1982b). They have also been found to save extensively (Lewis, 1982c). Many financial institutions have responded to this segment through the introduction of young savers accounts which are supported by gifts (incentives). The primary aim seems to be to instil the importance of saving in the youngsters, particularly with that institution.

At the other end of the age spectrum, demographic shifts towards an ageing population (Johnson, 1990a, 1990b) have focused the attentions of financial institutions on the older age groups, the so-called 'Greys' or 'Third Agers' (Kreitzman, 1994). As outlined in the previous chapter, the greatest increase is predicted to occur among those over 50 but under pensionable age. Aside from the volume increase in the older segments, important economic and lifestyle factors also contribute to their appeal. In the United States it was found that many individuals between the ages of 50 and 75 are income-rich (83 per cent are not solely dependent on state benefits), asset-rich (8 million own their homes outright), and the recipients of substantial windfalls largely in the form of inheritance (Silman and Poustie, 1994). A report by Mintel (1990) on inherited wealth in the UK estimated that the average inter-generational transfer per beneficiary in 1985–86 was £8,430 rising to £10,125 in 1990/91 and was estimated to be £23,875 (£18,020 at constant prices) by the end of the century. In terms of how inherited money is used, a survey of 45–54-year-old beneficiaries shows that 64 per cent either saved or invested some of the money, 44 per cent used the money to buy either a car or a holiday or for other general consumption. With regard to inherited property, two thirds of beneficiaries reported selling it almost immediately, 22 per cent reported living in it and 3 per cent allowed someone else to do so (Housing Research Foundation, cited in Mintel, 1990). Thus, from the point of view of financial institutions, these individuals represent a valuable target for savings products.

In addition, changes to patterns of behaviour and lifestyle through the generations have brought about differences in attitudes to the extent that tomorrow's 'Greys' are likely to think and feel quite differently from the 'senior citizens' of yesterday. Thus, many older individuals may be unwilling to compromise their lifestyles beyond retirement, in the way that they might have done in the past. However, financial institutions should avoid viewing 'the old' as a single homogeneous segment. Buck (1990) notes that polarisation of wealth among the older age groups is greater than among any other age group. The over-55s in the ABC_1 social classes have a greater propensity to save than their counterparts in the C_2DE social classes particularly in relation to building society savings. 'The old' are also far from homogeneous in terms of their attitudes. Silman and Poustie (1994) identified the following five attitudinal segments among the 50–75-year-old segment: Astute Cosmopolitans, Thrifty Traditionals, Temperate Xenophobes, Apathetic Spenders and Outgoing Funlovers. Each segment presents different marketing challenges; however, the Astute Cosmopolitans seem to be the most lucrative for financial institutions since they are more likely to belong to the upper social classes, exhibit greater investment behaviour and show an interest in financial services. The challenge for financial institutions is to identify the wealthy few.

Life cycle

While the age of a person would seem to offer some guidance in terms of describing financial services requirements, it is important to achieve a balance of age seg-

FINANCIAL SERVICES MARKETING IN PRACTICE

The meaning of life cycles: marketing savings

In their efforts to remain competitive in the personal savings market, financial institutions have undergone changes unprecedented in their history. Customers, too, have changed. Thanks to increased access to information, they have become more sophisticated in their personal financial dealings. But as they read reports of bad financial advice and the mis-selling of personal pensions, they have also become more cynical about the motives of financial institutions. The result is that financial institutions now have a customer base that is far more likely to switch its business than it was a few decades ago.

Customer fickleness is therefore a problem, particularly for retail financial institutions whose lending portfolios depend on a healthy deposit account base. What's more, there are now fewer new customers, and the costs of acquiring them have increased with competition. The result is that customers are being lost faster than they can be replaced.

This 'leaking bucket' effect presents a number of challenges. Historically, the focus of banks' and building societies' marketing has been on acquiring customers. Today, however, the emphasis needs to be on retaining customers – finding ways to stop the bucket from leaking.

To retain customers, financial institutions must meet their needs not merely once but throughout their lives. This means building continual relationships with them and understanding their needs at every stage of their life cycle.

Banks and building societies that offer savings accounts need to be aware of customers' motives for saving and how these may change in the course of their life. People may have several savings objectives and these will be affected by a number of factors, including the state of the economy (interest rates and inflation), level of income, perception of risk and stage in the life cycle.

Some people save to be able to spend in the near future. For them, the purpose of saving is to accumulate enough money to buy something (a holiday, a household item, a car), although the growing availability of interest-free credit has diminished the need to do this. These customers look for simple deposit accounts with easy access.

Others save for emergencies or the unexpected. These customers also require relatively easy access to their funds. Customers with longer-term objectives, such as saving for retirement, or for their children's education, will need longer-term savings products of a lower liquidity. These could include personal pensions, tax exempt special savings accounts (Tessas), or notice accounts. People who want to accumulate capital, on the other hand, will look for higher risk, equity-based investments.

These savings objectives can be viewed as a hierarchy of savings motives: the lower objectives of saving to spend must be met before the higher objectives of saving for capital accumulation can be achieved. In practice, however, people have both long and short-term goals for their saving, depending on which stage of life they are at. The basic family life cycle consists of five stages: 'youth', 'independent', 'family', 'empty nester', 'retired'.

Youth

The youth market, while not particularly profitable, is important for the income it may generate in the future. This is why many financial institutions target their savings accounts at young people. Their intention is to capture customers while they are young, instil in them the importance of saving, and keep their custom throughout their financial lives.

However, financial institutions should also consider targeting members of these young customers' families. Market research by Mintel, for example, has found that the single most important factor influencing a young person's choice of bank or building society (*Personal Financial Intelligence*, Vol. 2, 1995) is their parents' choice. Thus, it makes sense to offer parents and grandparents information about young people's savings accounts.

Opportunities for targeting young customers are growing, too. So while young people are becoming more critical of the media and advertising, they are also more likely to accept new technology, particularly home and 'virtual' banking. Financial institutions therefore need to take advantage of growing levels of personal computer ownership.

FINANCIAL SERVICES MARKETING IN PRACTICE

In addition, they could promote more school-based activities designed to make young people more financially aware. Such promotions need to be supported by a range of current and savings accounts.

Independent

While the student market is adequately provided for, other members of the 'independent' market are less well served. Yet potentially they represent a far more profitable market for savings. These include school leavers who are entering employment or undertaking training.

'Independents are at the transitional stage between 'youth' and 'family'. Their savings objectives are likely to be short-term, such as getting together the deposit on a house, buying a car or getting married.

Family

At the 'family' stage, most people are unable to put money aside for the future. If they save at all, it will be to pay for short-term needs. However, the birth of more children during the family stage may prompt parents to open children's accounts or save for their education.

Empty nester

At this stage, banks and building societies have a chance to renew their savings activity of customers whose children have recently left home. These 'empty nesters' are likely to have more disposable income and be looking for ways to put it to work. They are also likely to be thinking about the financial implications of retirement and are therefore likely to be in the market for lower liquidity and possibly higher risk savings instruments.

Retired

In this, the final stage of the life cycle, customers savings objectives will change from building savings to using them as a source of income. Customers will be keen to retain an achieved level of savings and to secure a rate of return that will provide them with the quality of life they want.

By looking at the life cycles of their customers, banks and building societies can prepare for the ways in which their savings objectives are likely to change over time. This is essential if they are to retain the loyalty of their customers, who are becoming increasingly footloose.

Know your customer

The life cycle concept is a useful marketing tool that enables banks and building societies to offer their customers the right savings products at the right time, before they start shopping around for alternative providers. As with the direct marketing of any product, however, the accuracy of the information used to target potential savers is paramount.

Source: T. Harrison (1996). Reprinted with permission of *Chartered Banker*, May 1996.

Questions:

1 Why is life stage important?

2 How can financial institutions use the life cycle concept to build customer relationships?

3 Suggest ways in which financial institutions can keep track of movements between life stages

ments, particularly in financial services. If, for example, only younger customers are targeted, they may be lost as they age if the company does not meet their changing requirements as they move into more 'mature' segments. The life cycle is, thus, becoming important because of its potential for relationship development (see Financial Services Marketing in Practice, 'The meaning of life cycles: marketing savings'). Indeed, a key aspect of the life cycle approach is that it enables financial institutions to develop a relationship with their customers and also retain them by offering the right product at the right time as and when the customer requires it. In mature markets the opportunities for gaining new-to-the-business customers are limited. Thus, the retention of existing customers is crucial to the long-term prosperity of the organisation. Astute financial institutions will guide their customers through the various life stages from young savers accounts to school leavers, to student and to graduate accounts from where the full range of mortgage, loan and investment products will be made available.

The importance of the life cycle or life stages for financial institutions is that research has shown that different life-stage segments exhibit different requirements in terms of financial services. Wilson (1992) notes that the youth market primarily demands money transmission services, overdraft and loan facilities, simple savings accounts and travel facilities, whereas the family segment require mortgages and home improvement loans, longer-term savings for children, insurance and wills, pensions and loans.

Despite the popularity of the family life cycle (FLC), it has received considerable criticism. There is disagreement in the literature with regard to the definition of stages; no uniform classification has been developed and a number of different variations are in existence. It is based largely around the presence of children in the family and their ages, particularly the age of the youngest child – while this may be important in determining income patterns the oldest child may be most important in determining expenditure patterns. It has also been criticised for obscuring both family size and the age/sex structure of the family.

Perhaps one of the major criticisms of the family life cycle has been its inability to keep pace with sociological trends. Over the last few decades, the UK has experienced the following trends: an overall decline in the size of the family – for example, in 1967 30-year-old women had an average of 1.9 children compared with only 1.3 children for 30-year-old women in 1997 (*Social Trends*, 1999); an increase in the average age of individuals before first marriage, with individuals choosing to lead longer single lives before marriage (but not necessarily as one-person households as is assumed in the FLC); shorter childbearing cycles as women choose to have children both later in life and closer together to return to work quicker; rising divorce rates; remarriage; increasing numbers of lone parents; and greater longevity.

Despite the apparent criticisms, the life cycle and life stages have become popular bases for financial institutions. For example, the Trustee Savings Bank has segmented its customer base into Youth, Independent, Family, Empty Nester and Retired segments, using an adaptation of the classic Wells and Gubar (1966) life cycle. Other banks are perhaps less explicit about the life cycle stages, but nonetheless emphasise the 'whole-of-life' service or product range on offer. For example, Allied Dunbar talks about 'the life you don't yet know' and Bank of Scotland emphasises its lifetime relationship with its customers through its 'Friend for Life' slogan.

More recently, however, the notion of the financial life cycle has become important. Similarly to the family life cycle it recognises that individuals have different financial needs and objectives at various stages of life. However, the financial life cycle focuses primarily on existing and emerging financial needs, particularly the order in which financial needs arise. Thus, while financial needs may evolve over the life cycle they are not necessarily life-cycle-dependent. A more detailed discussion of financial needs and objectives was provided in the previous chapter.

Socio-economic bases

Social class

Social class retains an important place in consumer behaviour texts. The preoccupation with social class in Britain may owe something to the well-defined hierarchical social class structure which dominated before the expansion of the mass middle class. Social class is a measurement of the type of educational background, occupation, income level that a person has. It also has a historical element in that individuals are assessed according to the social-class backgrounds from which they come. Although traditionally an individual's belonging to a particular social class may have been determined by parentage, in modern society it is relatively easy to upscale as well as downscale. The social class premise implies that individuals in a certain class will behave like and exhibit similar preferences and values to the other members in that class.

A popular social class classification, which is widely used commercially, is that presented by the National Readership Survey. It consists of six scales from A to E. Groups A to C_1 are non-manual (white-collar) occupations. Groups C_2 to E are manual (blue-collar) occupations. Figure 3.2 shows the relative proportions of the UK population belonging to each social class group.

A number of problems are associated with social class, due to its theoretical underpinnings and its measurement (Leach, 1987; Cornish and Denny, 1989), which might be argued to render it a less than optimal basis for segmentation. For example, it is predominately focused on occupation and does not take into account enough variables. Furthermore, it does not reflect income. In terms of measurement, the precise classification of an individual depends on details of occupation,

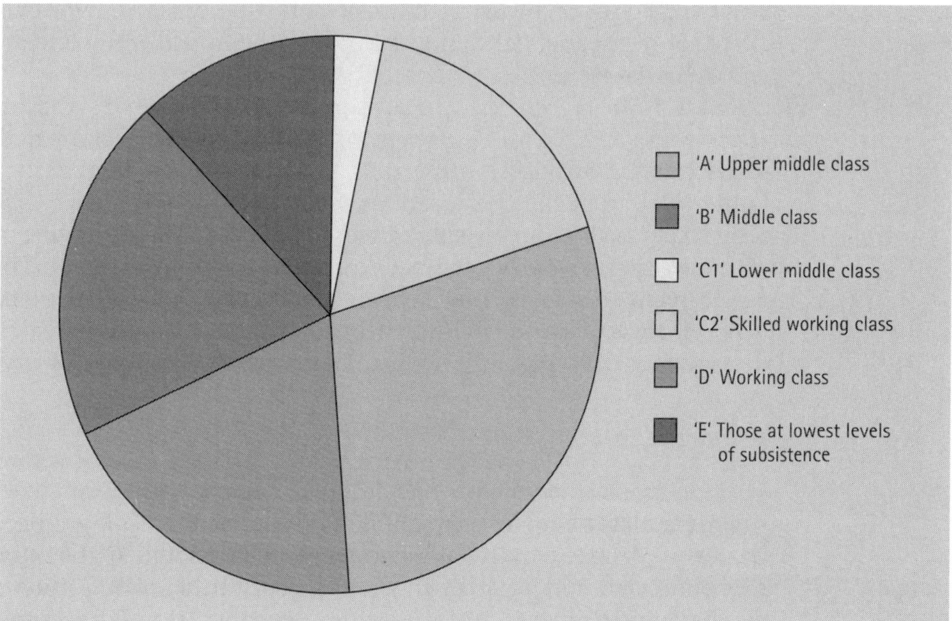

Fig. 3.2 The UK population by social class
(*Source*: Adapted from *Marketing Pocket Book* (1994), The Advertising Association/NTC Publications Ltd)

qualifications, responsibilities and the establishment where he/she works or used to work, all of which are difficult and time consuming to collect. In practice, individuals are often graded on the basis of a shorter and subjective version of the measure, leaving it insufficiently robust and reliable enough to take the weight that is often placed on it.

Despite this, research in the financial services sector has shown that social class offers discriminatory power with regard to savings and investments. Meidan (1984) notes, in relation to savings and investment of funds, that it has been generally thought that the lower social classes tend to opt for an account which they perceive as being more tangible, such as a savings account which has a pass-book, a tangible representation of the product. Members of the lower social classes have tended to take fewer risks where financial matters have been concerned and have preferred accounts which can be quickly converted into cash. Conversely, the higher a social class the person belongs to, the more likely it will be that he (or she) will take risks in financial matters. According to general belief his savings will take the form of investments and he will involve himself in longer-term commitments and possibly look for higher returns in less tangible savings such as bonds and debentures. The save–spend behaviour of the higher versus the lower social classes has been summarised by Meidan as consisting of generally more savings aspirations for the upper social classes compared with a tendency towards more spending aspirations for the lower social classes. However, it is debatable whether this is a true representation, since the combination of increased wealth for the lower social classes coupled with increased sophistication may cause individuals to view savings differently.

With respect to unit trusts, Cornish and Denny (1989) found that ownership was determined more by social class than income, which also appears to be true of other more complex financial products including ownership of equities and credit cards. The explanation proposed was that individuals of ABC_1 occupations will often be brought into contact with such financial instruments through their work and their choice of newspaper. It would, thus, seem that a person's working environment is an influential factor.

Results from a recent study (Harrison, 1997a) indicate that the lower social classes are showing an increasing propensity to invest in shares compared with the upper social classes. On closer inspection, the shares most frequently purchased were found to be from the privatisations made under the Thatcher Government. It has been recognised that these share issues introduced to share buying many individuals who had not previously been active in this type of investment. Thus, the evidence would seem to suggest that social class alone is not sufficient in discriminating between investors and non-investors of shares. However, it may still be useful in determining the type of share purchased by different groups of customers.

Income

The traditional hierarchical and triangular-shaped arrangement of British society (the richest at the tip of the pyramid and the majority poorest occupying the base) has evolved into a mass middle-class. This development has been partly due to rising incomes and changes in the distribution of wealth and also partly due to demographic shifts causing an ageing population. In addition to this, continuing polarisation of income is expected to occur at the edges, further contributing to the unequal distribution of consumer spending power.

As social class distinctions are increasingly being obscured by rising incomes, income itself may be a more reliable measure of segment behaviour. However, researchers must be careful about how they define income – disposable income should not be confused with discretionary income; as Bowles (1985) notes: 'High income families often have high financial commitments for housing costs, school fees and support for dependents, that they have little discretionary income to spend' (p. 38). Furthermore, income alone does not give any indication of what people actually need and want, only what they may be able to afford!

Traditionally, income taken as a measure of purchasing power for the family unit has been referred to as that of the head of the household (typically the husband or male partner). In view of the trends discussed in relation to gender, financial institutions should be looking not only at the man's income in the family but also at the woman's income as well – she may in many cases be earning more. Indeed, women are reported to be the main breadwinners in about 30 per cent of all households worldwide and in Europe 59 per cent of women provide at least half of the family income (*Financial Times*, 17 February 1998).

Associated with income is the affluence or 'worth' of the person. This moves beyond merely income and considers a number of factors. Such variables have been investigated as possibilities for segmenting markets; however, the problem is one of definition and measurement. Wealth can be either liquid or illiquid (i.e. in the form of property) which may not yield an income for expenditure purposes. Also important to consider is inherited wealth. As well as the actual affluent segments there are also the pseudo-affluent groups, whose aim it is to appear as if they were affluent.

Geodemographic bases

Attempts to overcome some of the inabilities of single variable bases and social class groupings to sufficiently differentiate consumer requirements have led to the development of geodemographics – multivariate systems combining geographic with demographic information, and more recently also including consumption patterns of a wide range of products and services and lifestyles. The main benefits are that they say more about lifestyle than traditional demographics (Whitehead, 1987).

The early development of geodemographic research can be traced back to a study in 1959 referred to as 'urban typology' (Moser and Scott, 1961). The study consisted of an analysis of British towns according to demographic, economic, social and political dimensions in order to 'type' towns and regions into fairly distinct groups. The first commercial system to be developed, ACORN (A Classification Of Residential Neighbourhoods) pioneered by Richard Webber and initially based on the 1971 census of population data, worked on this basis. The census provides a collection of some 40 variables on housing, demographic, social and economic factors enabling people and households to be classified according to the neighbourhood type in which they live. The system is based on the premise that individuals living in neighbourhoods with similar social and economic characteristics will exhibit similar lifestyle features and patterns of behaviour. According to McKechnie and Harrison (1995), it simply quantifies what burglars already know – the areas in which people live tell something about the products they buy and the things they own.

The current ACORN classification is based on the 1991 census and classifies the population into 17 groups and 54 ACORN types. The number of ACORN types has increased with successive revisions of census data (as a result of housing and economic developments) from 36 in 1971 to 38 in 1981 to 54 in 1991. Until 1985 CACI was the only supplier of such geodemographic systems. However, a number of other suppliers have since entered the market offering similar services. The most common among these are: MOSAIC (by CCN Systems, also set up by Richard Webber after ACORN) which classifies individuals into 12 lifestyle groups which are an amalgamation of 52 MOSAIC types; Superprofiles (NRS) an 11-group classification based on an individual classification of adults; CACI Change ACORN which profiles customers in trading areas or on a database into 6 groups and 44 types as an aid to understanding changing customer demographics; Pin (from Pinpoint Analysis, subsequently acquired by CACI) which uses both census enumeration districts and postcodes to 'pinpoint' customers into 60 different neighbourhood types (*Lifestyle Pocket Book*, 1996).

In addition to the general classifications, a number of developments have been made in the specific product/market areas, notably financial services. Pinpoint in 1986 launched FinPin, a classification of individuals and households according to financial activity. In 1992 CACI launched the Mortgage Market Database, in 1993 the Savings Market Database and in 1994 Financial ACORN (similar to FinPin which was later acquired by CACI) which is based on a combination of census data and NOP's Financial Research Survey which provides data on actual financial services consumption across the full range of financial services. The current Financial ACORN classification is shown in table 3.1.

The basic collection unit for geodemographic information is the enumeration district (ED), which is both the building brick for census statistics and the foundation of census fieldwork (Rhind, 1983). There are currently estimated to be over 130,000 EDs covering an average of 170 households each. Matching the data with postcodes (one postcode for approximately 15 households), allows the identification of indi-

Table 3.1 Financial ACORN

Financial ACORN consumer classifications	% GB population
CATEGORY A – FINANCIALLY SOPHISTICATED	19.5
Wealthy equity-holders	11.1
Affluent mortgage-holders	8.4
CATEGORY B – FINANCIALLY INVOLVED	31.3
Comfortable investors	6.2
Better-off borrowers	13.1
Prosperous savers	11.9
CATEGORY C – FINANCIALLY MODERATE	24.1
Younger spenders	2.5
Settled pensioners	9.0
Working families	8.6
Thrifty singles	4.0
CATEGORY D – FINANCIALLY INACTIVE	24.7
Middle aged assured	6.1
Older cash users	10.0
Low income unemployed	9.4

(*Source*: CACI Limited (1999).

vidual households and their characteristics. However, some debate has ensued over the accuracy of geodemographic systems with respect to the use of EDs and postcodes; the boundaries of census EDs and postcodes differ. Douglas (1985) notes that under the earlier ACORN system many postcodes were allocated to the wrong ED, meaning that ACORN could have been targeting the wrong groups! These problems have, no doubt, been rectified since then.

Psychographic bases

Wells (1975) notes that marketing researchers collect demographics as a matter of routine, and marketers feel comfortable using them. However, demographics as a segmentation basis have been the subject of considerable criticism. The main reason for this is that it is assumed that differences in buying behaviour occur as a result of differences in demographics such as: age, gender, income, etc. Yet, it has been shown that demographics are poor predictors of behaviour (Haley, 1968; Frank *et al.*, 1972). The explanation is that demographics are descriptive and not causal and that individuals with the same external characteristics (such as age, occupation, income, etc.) can exhibit very different behaviours and lifestyles. The psychographic premise argues that this results from different internal characteristics such as attitudes, beliefs, preferences, motives, etc. Thus, in order to identify the factors influencing buying behaviour, marketers need to gain an understanding of the consumer that goes beneath the skin.

The core of psychographic segmentation hinges entirely on the way the consumer thinks (Wills, 1985); it pinpoints thinking, not just being. Although many researchers understand the general concept of psychographics, a common definition of what it entails is difficult to find. Wells (1975) surveyed twenty-four articles on psychographics to find no less than thirty-two definitions all with some sort of difference. Yet, within this diversity, some common elements are identifiable. Psychographics mean something more than demographic information, including a wide range of variables such as activities, interests, values, personality, etc. and they are quantitative and qualitative, involving the use of precoded, objective questionnaires and multivariate statistical analysis.

Psychographics have perhaps not reached their full potential as a segmentation basis, particularly among financial institutions. Thompson (1986) notes: 'Banks really didn't have to understand customer thinking or lifestyle characteristics to enquire about check design or color schemes. But that was yesterday. Today's selling culture demands a more precise and less intuitive insight into those factors contributing to a customer's mind set'. The following sections look at some of the specific psychographic applications in financial services.

Attitude segmentation

The Midland Bank used attitude segmentation to group its customer base. The basis for the segmentation was two attitudinal dimensions: 'confidence' and 'respect for the banking authority' (Gavaghan, 1991). Broadly speaking, younger individuals are lower in confidence than older individuals. In addition, individuals differ according to whether they have high or low respect for the authority of the banking system.

The research identified four segments (New Bankers; Traditionalists; Minimalists and Opportunists) each differing in terms of the two dimensions. New customers were identified as 'New Bankers' who tend to exhibit low levels of confidence and a high respect for the authority of the banking system. As these individuals become more established customers of the bank they may migrate into one of two segments: 'Traditionalists' who use the full range of banking services or 'Minimalists' who develop a low respect for the authority of the banking system and make only infrequent use of the services on offer, preferring to operate a cash-type economy. The final segment 'Opportunists' exhibit a high level of confidence and are the most likely to take the opportunity to avail themselves of the best offers, willing to switch financial institutions to obtain them.

Midland Bank used the findings to develop and position three new multi-service accounts including chequeing and saving facilities. The first of these, the Vector account, was targeted at the 'Opportunists', young, upwardly mobile individuals. The second account, Orchard, was aimed at the home-owning and family formation segments which comprised both 'Opportunists' and 'Traditionalists'. The third account, Meridian, catered for the Empty Nesters with larger amounts of disposable income as a result of paid-up mortgages, savings and inheritance. This segment comprised largely 'Traditionalists'.

Awareness, knowledge and understanding

Recent research (Harrison, 1994, 1997a) considers the dimensions of individual perceived knowledge of financial services, attitudes towards financial services and level of involvement (interest) in financial services in the segmentation of financial consumers. Knowledge would seem important for a number of reasons. First, the intangibility of financial services (as outlined in the previous chapter) affects the ability of the consumer to conceptualise and formulate the service, such that it becomes difficult to grasp mentally (Bateson, 1977). This has posed problems for both marketers and consumers. For the marketer it presents problems in the area of communication since intangible 'entities' are more difficult to display visually. Consequently the consumer is faced with a lack of external pre-purchase information on which to base product choice, forcing the consumer to seek alternative information sources possibly placing greater emphasis on past experience, learning and knowledge. Perceived knowledge, compared to actual or 'real' knowledge, has been identified as this assumes the effects of confidence discussed above. These ideas originate from Bandura's Social Learning Theory (SLT) (Bandura, 1977a and 1977b) and the concept of self-efficacy. According to SLT, people who possess the ability to perform optimally may not do so because they have doubts about their ability to perform. Similarly, individuals who perceive their knowledge and understanding of financial services to be poor compared to others may avoid certain financial products as they feel they lack the ability to deal with them. Hence, the individuals' actual knowledge is of less importance compared to their perceptions of themselves and their ability.

Segmentation along this basis produced four segments (see figure 3.3) differing in terms of knowledge of financial services, level of involvement, attitudes and use of various financial services. Use of financial services was measured in terms of the degree of financial maturity (Kamakura *et al.*, 1991) exhibited by the individual which is based on the complexity of the product, the relative liquidity and the risk associated with it (discussed in more detail in the previous chapter). The

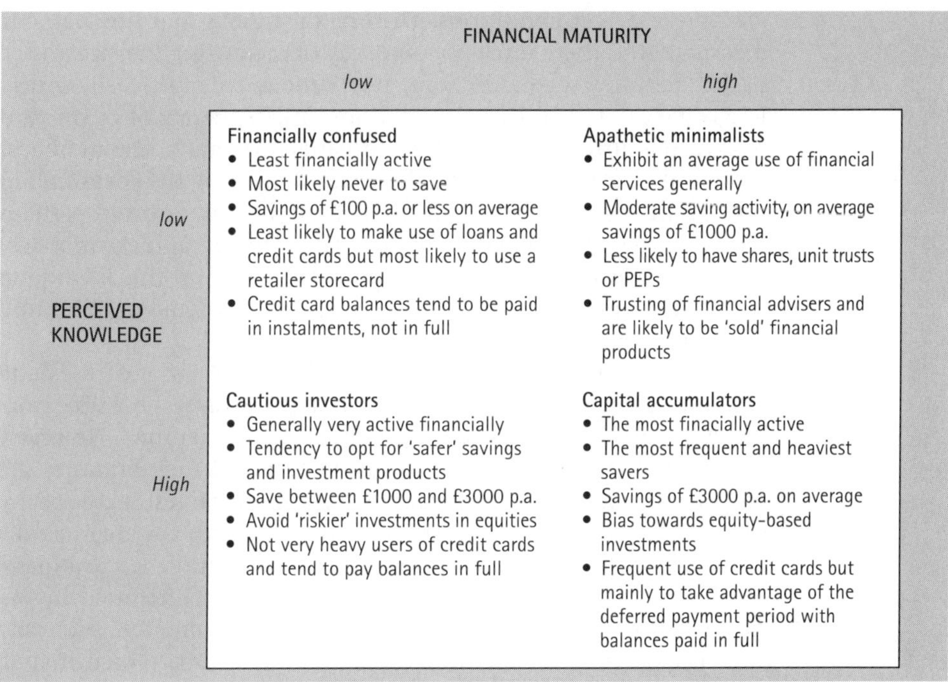

Fig. 3.3 Summary of the key knowledge segment differences in terms of their use of financial services (*Source*: Adapted from Harrison, 1997a)

'Financially Confused' and the 'Apathetic Minimalists' are perhaps the least interesting from the point of view of the financial institution since they do not consider themselves to be very knowledgeable about financial services, have very short-term planning horizons and are the least financially active. In addition, they are the least interested in financial services and financial institutions. The higher financial maturity exhibited by the 'Apathetic Minimalists' seems to be largely as a result of financial institutions' successful sales efforts. The 'Cautious Investors' and the 'Capital Accumulators' are the more knowledgeable and sophisticated financial users, both are very future-oriented, have longer-term financial objectives and are very interested in financial services. The major difference between the two segments is that the Cautious Investors are more risk-averse than the Capital Accumulators, preferring to avoid products which they perceive as being high-risk (such as stocks and shares, unit trusts and PEPs) and opting for 'safer' investment items (including pensions and regular savings plans). A summary of the main differences in terms of each segment's use of financial services is shown in figure 3.3.

Requirements for effective market segmentation

The accuracy of a financial institution's identification of market segments contributes to its competitive advantage since it is a prerequisite to the development of market segmentation strategies. A number of conditions have been noted to affect the effectiveness and potential profitability of the marketing strategy. Kotler (1997) identifies five key conditions. The first of these is that the segments should exhibit measurability: there must be some way of measuring the size and purchasing power of the identified segments. Some phenomena are more easily measured than others. For example, it is far easier to measure the frequency of credit card usage than it is to measure attitudes towards credit cards. Generally, the more qualitative and the more interpretative the data, the more difficult is the measurability. In this sense, one might argue that the measurability of a segment could perhaps be expressed in terms of the quantifiability of the data. Demographic variables are, thus, much easier to measure than psychographic variables and this is undoubtedly one factor which has contributed to the predominance of demographics in financial services research.

A second condition proffered in the literature is that of substantiality. In Kotler's (1984, p. 298) words: 'A segment should be the largest possible homogeneous group worth going after with a tailored marketing programme'. However, this view seems to suggest that only large segments, in terms of their volume, should be targeted. Not all companies are in a position to target the largest segments in the marketplace and segments should represent a strategic fit with the financial institution to provide the greatest benefit to both the company and the customer. Successful niche marketers have shown that some small segments (defined in volume terms) can generate high returns. The high net worth segment is such an example in the financial services sector, and companies like Coutts which manages private banking, may, in some cases, be focusing on a segment of one.

Thus, the condition of substantiality should not only be viewed in volume terms but also in value terms, and these should be considered within the context of the organisation's offering and competitors' actions. However, with the importance of relationship marketing and the need to build long-term relationships with customers it is important not only to consider the current status of the segments but also to consider their future status. Thus, financial institutions should ask: is the segment currently substantial in volume and value terms, and will it continue to be of sufficient size and generate returns? Some segments may not be considered as currently substantial, but may offer returns at some future (predictable) date. For this reason it might be worth targeting them in order to build a relationship with them to benefit from future returns. This is the approach taken by many UK banks with regard to the student segment. Students require only a limited range of banking services (primarily current accounts and loans). However, after graduating and embarking on a career they become potential customers for a whole range of services.

A third requirement suggested is that of accessibility. Having identified the segments it should be possible to reach them effectively and serve them. This means that it should be possible to locate and communicate with the segments via currently available channels of communication. In some respects, the advent of telephone banking, which has contributed somewhat to the reduction in customer visits to branches, has enabled increased access to the customer via a medium which the customer feels more comfortable with.

A fourth requirement proposed is that of actionability. This is the degree to which effective marketing programmes can be designed and implemented to attract and serve the segments. One of the main reasons for segmentation studies not being actionable is undue consideration to the marketing and operational environments and the competitive structure before applying segmentation. The Midland Bank failed to account for the actionability of its segmentation programme in identifying segments for its Vector, Orchard and Meridian accounts discussed previously. The segments were largely based on attitudinal data and, although on computer customers were easily identified within their segment, the branch staff were unable to identify to which segment customers belonged when they walked through the doors of the bank.

The final requirement proposed by Kotler is differentiability. This means that the segments should be conceptually distinguishable and should respond differently to the different marketing variables. Baker (1992) also highlights this as an important condition, maintaining that segments should be unique in their responses to marketing stimuli. This indicates that the segments are in fact different and do warrant tailored marketing programmes.

Thomas (1980) adds the property of stability and argues that although segments are not static they should possess a certain degree of stability over time in order that marketing programmes can be designed and implemented before the segment has shifted. The stability of the segments is dependent upon a number of factors including the segmentation basis chosen, the volatility of the marketplace and consumer characteristics. Certain bases, such as demographics, allow the prediction of segment membership and segment migration. Life cycle is useful, since it has been identified that financial needs have a life cycle which can be predicted on a broad level (as indicated above in Financial Services Marketing in Practice, 'The meaning of life cycles: marketing savings').

Segmentation strategies

Financial institutions may perceive different degrees of segmentation in the marketplace from completely aggregate to completely disaggregate. This section addresses the issue of which and how many segments to target and what to offer each segment in terms of the marketing mix. Abell (1980) and Kotler (1997) identify five different strategies for the selection and targeting of market segments.

- *Single-segment concentration* occurs when the organisation targets just one segment to the exclusion of all others; the total marketing effort is aimed solely at this one segment. The firm may do this because of limited resources, or because the segment represents a natural match between the firm's offering and the segment's requirements, or it could be a logical launching pad for further segment expansion. However, there are also the risks of 'putting all one's eggs in one basket'. Successful niche marketers have shown that focusing on a small segment can reap good returns. A single-segment strategy is feasible for targeting commercial or private banking segments, yet it is unlikely to bring long-term success to most retail banks catering for the personal market.

- *Selective specialisation*, or multi-segment coverage, occurs when a firm chooses a number of segments. This may be as a result of a variety of product offerings or an attempt to minimise the effects of competition. However, the appeal of this type of strategy is the ability to diversify one's risks. To a certain extent banks have traditionally adopted this approach, certainly from a product perspective. The need to balance deposits with loans in order to generate revenue streams has meant a focus on both different products and different customer groups to achieve this.

- *Product specialisation* occurs when a firm concentrates on marketing a certain product to several segments. Product modifications will normally be made to allow for the differences in the segments and their preferences etc. However, no different product groups are offered. It is a strategy which bears some resemblance to that of product differentiation which focuses primarily on the needs of the seller and not the buyer. Reliance on one product can prove to be a risky strategy, particularly in view of shortening product life cycles. There are few situations in financial services where companies have been successful selling only one product. Credit card companies are possibly an exception. Insurance companies have achieved success, not in selling one type of insurance necessarily but in selling a product group, general and/or life assurance. For banks and building societies such a strategy is not feasible since it would not allow deposits and loans to be balanced if the financial institution focused only on either savings or lending products.
- *Market specialisation* is when a firm concentrates on serving the many needs of a particular customer group. Firms operating this strategy typically carry an array of products to satisfy the needs of their target markets. Thus, firms become specialists in serving a particular group and are possible channel agents for any new products that the group may need. This strategy is similar to that described under single-segment concentration; however, where the former deals with a single product/market combination, this deals with many products for one market. Single-segment concentration can develop into market specialisation. Direct Line started out with a single-segment strategy selling general insurance to the over-45s. Over time the product range has been extended to meet a variety of needs of this customer group, including savings and mortgages to the extent that Direct Line now operates a market specialisation strategy.
- *Full market coverage* is when a firm attempts to serve all customer groups with all the products that they might need within the range of the company. The strategy is usually only feasible for large companies which have the capability of producing for such a large audience. Full market coverage can be in one of two ways: undifferentiated market coverage or differentiated market coverage. Undifferentiated market coverage has been described by others as 'mass marketing' (Tedlow and Jones, 1993). It is a strategy defended on the grounds of cost economies. The firm focuses on common customer needs and not differences and attempts to reach the greatest number of customers. Banks have tended to pursue this strategy in the past. There are, however, strong doubts about the success of the strategy. As markets become more competitive and customers become more sophisticated the need for a strategy which recognises customer differences becomes more important. Firms which operate a differentiated marketing strategy will usually serve many segments but design different marketing programmes for each of the segments to account for the differences in customer requirements.

Approaches to segmentation

The ability of segmentation to identify causal relationships or associations between variables depends to some extent on the methods used to classify or partition the data. The methods of segmentation fall into two broad categories: *a priori* and *post hoc* (Green, 1977; Wind, 1978).

- *A priori* segmentation is 'planned' in that the researcher chooses some segment-defining characteristic in advance, such as age or income, and respondents are classified into segments. The segments are then further examined regarding their differences on other characteristics such as investment activity, credit card usage, etc. Thus, *a priori* segmentation is driven by theoretical expectations developed before examining the data.
- *Post hoc* segmentation, by contrast, is driven by empirical concerns and occurs after seeing the data. Hence, respondents are grouped according to the similarity of their multivariate profiles regarding such characteristics as purchasing behaviour or attitudes. Subsequent to this, the segments may then be examined for differences in other characteristics which may not have been used in the original analysis (Green and Krieger, 1995). Only the set of variables by which consumers are to be clustered is prespecified.

In addition to deciding on the general approach to be taken, one must also consider the type of statistical method to be used. The methods can be either *descriptive* or *predictive*.

- *Descriptive methods* – Hair *et al.* (1987) refer to these as 'structural, interdependence methods' since they analyse the mutual association across a set of segmentation variables, with no distinction between dependent and independent variables.
- *Predictive methods* – These are referred to as 'functional dependence techniques' since they analyse the relationships between two sets of variables, where one consists of dependent variables, such as purchase behaviour, and the other consists of a set of independent (or explanatory) variables, such as consumer attitudes.

Figure 3.4 provides an illustration of the various statistical techniques which fall into each of the categories outlined.

	a priori	*post hoc*
Descriptive	Contingency tables	Clustering methods Factor analysis
Predictive	Regression Discriminant analysis Conjoint analysis	Automatic interaction detector (AID) Canonical analysis

Fig. 3.4 Classification of segmentation techniques

A distinction between the two types of segmentation approaches (*a priori* and *post hoc*) and the segmentation techniques (descriptive and predictive) is important since it poses implications in terms of the outcome of the analysis and the assumptions which the segmentation model makes about the relationship between variables. These issues are discussed in the sections below in relation to some of the segmentation applications already discussed.

A priori segmentation

Under *a priori* segmentation individuals are allocated to segments on the basis of characteristics chosen by the researcher. As a result of this, *a priori* segmentation methods rely on prior knowledge of the market or phenomenon under investigation since assumptions are made about expected relationships between the variables; it is these assumptions which lead to the choice of certain segmentation variables.

According to Speed and Smith (1991) most of the segmentation conducted in the context of financial services has been *a priori* in nature. Examples of this would be segmentation by age, such as the student segment, school leavers, school children, the 'Greys'. Age would be chosen on the assumption that financial services product requirements differ with age. The segmenting variable (i.e. age) and the number of categories (i.e. five age groups) are chosen and individuals are assigned to a group accordingly.

- *A priori descriptive methods* – A simple way of displaying the associations between different segmentation bases is by cross-classifying the variables in contingency tables. An example of this would be to take the five age categories outlined above and to cross-classify them with information on each individual regarding their use of financial products. Representation of the data is simple and associations can be tested. However, the problem with this type of segmentation is that there is not necessarily a link between the segments identified and buyer behaviour; the analysis merely describes behaviour, it does not predict it.
- *A priori predictive methods* – In order to determine the predictive ability of age, stage in the family life cycle and gender as segmentation variables for financial services a suitable technique would have to be chosen, such as regression or discriminant analysis. These techniques require the prior specification of dependent variables (use of financial services) and independent variables (age, stage in the family life cycle, gender).

Post hoc segmentation

In contrast to *a priori* segmentation, *post hoc* segmentation is more exploratory in nature. It does not make assumptions about relationships in the data and, therefore, it is more conducive to the identification of previously unknown phenomena and subsequent explanations. In *post hoc* analyses cases are not allocated into previously defined segments but are grouped on the basis of a similarity identified by a technique chosen by the researcher. Thus, the identification of segments is dependent on the data collected and the methods applied. The segmentation discussed under the heading of psychographics employs largely *post hoc* methods to group financial services consumers.

- *Post hoc descriptive methods* – Examples of methods in this category are factor analysis and cluster analysis. Such techniques have been described as 'structural interdependence techniques' since they analyse the mutual associations across a set of segmentation variables. In the research by Harrison (1997a) outlined earlier, consumers were classified according to similarities in their responses to attitude scales and scales which measured their level of awareness, knowledge and understanding of financial services. The number of segments is not always known, and four segments emerged from this analysis.
- *Post hoc predictive methods* – *Post hoc* predictive methods combine the *post hoc* grouping of individuals mentioned above with predictive ability. Dependent variables are mostly measures of purchase behaviour or purchase predisposition. Techniques which fall into this category are Automatic Interaction Detector (AID) and canonical analysis. Some of the data-mining software is built on these techniques.

Do segments exist or are they created?

This question arises since it is possible to segment a market (i.e. divide up a population into smaller groups) without producing any meaningful understanding of how this may relate to differences in behaviour or behavioural intent. For example, there will always be some characteristic which can be identified which some consumers have in common with one group of consumers but not in common with yet another set of consumers. This allows groups of consumers to be formed. Indeed, much of the work discussed with respect to the use of demographics in segmenting financial services markets could be argued to fall into this category since segments were created based on some predetermined external consumer characteristic and not on the basis of some behavioural difference or any factor which is either closely related or assumed to determine behavioural differences.

In addition, many of the statistical techniques outlined in the preceding section can 'create' segments. Cluster analysis, it has been argued (Punj and Stewart, 1983), will reach a cluster solution even when there are no 'natural' groupings in the data. According to Wells (1975), unless there are very different relatively homogeneous groups of consumers actually in the population, the analysis would only be reflecting 'adventitious bleeps' which in no way justify the development of tailored marketing programmes. In such instances it is necessary to perform some statistical tests to ascertain the validity of the segments. Yet, the real test of validity might be in terms of how the segments relate conceptually and theoretically to our understanding of consumer behaviour.

If partitioning a market does not bear any relationship to behavioural differences or to marketing phenomena, it provides little insight. In order to ascertain whether a segment is representative of real marketing phenomena or is merely a construct, it is necessary to return to the original notion and purpose of market segmentation and, indeed, consumer behaviour in attempting to understand behavioural differences. The understanding of consumer behaviour is inherent to the implementation of the marketing concept which Kotler (1994, p. 18) defines as 'determining the needs and wants of target markets and delivering the desired satisfactions more effectively and efficiently than competitors'. Drucker (1985, p. 233) argues: 'to start out with the customer's utility, with what the customer buys, with what the realities of the customers are and what the customer's values are – this is what marketing is all about'. Yet, Foxall and Goldsmith (1994, p. 9) argue that the job of the marketing manager is complicated and diverse – it is concerned with creating 'marketing mixes that reflect consumers' subjective, perceptual and cognitive processing of information about such matters, their personal lifestyles, values and motivations'. In attempting to understand consumers, it is apparent that not all consumers behave or think in the same way. Effective market segmentation cannot work without thorough research which leads to an incisive understanding of the consumer. Thus, it might be argued that the more closely segmentation is related to an understanding of the behavioural differences between consumers and the factors which determine such differences, the less likely are the resulting segments to be artificial constructs but representations of real phenomena.

Segmentation versus fragmentation

Some may argue that the process of identifying customer groups was predominately the view of companies in the 1980s and that an approach advocated for the 1990s and into the 21st century is a more personalised approach based on direct marketing and relational databases. Tedlow and Jones (1993) suggest that developments in information technology are currently prompting a move to what they call the 'fourth phase of marketing' – micromarketing or hyper-segmentation, with a vision of customisation, a segment of one.

In the financial services sector such technological developments have paved the way for direct selling techniques and have created opportunities for large and small institutions to widen their distribution networks. With the direct-sell market now accounting for £927m of the car and motor insurance market alone (*Marketing*, June 1995), this is big business. The pioneer, Direct Line, has also shown that in addition to motor insurance, home insurance, mortgages and life assurance can all be sold direct over the telephone.

With increased attention to direct marketing and database marketing in catering for individual requirements, one may question the continued role of market segmentation in financial services. Market segmentation is undoubtedly important and still has its place alongside direct marketing techniques; the two techniques actually complement one another. At a macro or strategic level it is important that a company understands the broad set of characteristics which make up various customer segments. Strategic decisions must also be taken as to which and how many segments to target. At a micro or operational level direct marketing can be used to reach the individuals within the identified segments. Working on the general information provided by the segmentation analysis, and combined with the specific circumstances of the individual, a picture of the individual consumer's product requirements can be obtained and a suitable marketing communication programme developed. A further argument for the continued importance of market segmentation to financial institutions is that they have generally been slow to adopt the marketing concept and segmentation; hence many institutions are still at the point of realising its full potential. While evidence would suggest that many banks have segmented their customer base and are targeting certain customer segments for cross-selling, insurance companies still tend to view customers through 'product eyes'. Thus, target marketing in many insurance companies still tends to be rather rudimentary.

Direct marketing of financial services

Direct marketing has been described as an interactive system of marketing which uses one or more media, such as mail, telephone, fax, email, World Wide Web and other non-personal contact tools to communicate directly with or solicit a direct response from specific customers and prospects.

It has a number of benefits which have been outlined by Betts and Yorke (1994): it

- offers targeting precision;
- enables testing of markets, products, services, etc.;
- is measurable and accountable;
- provides a new distribution channel and support for existing channels;
- allows control over timing;
- provides advertising cost-effectiveness;
- offers more precise segmentation;
- is invisible to competitors.

From the point of view of the financial institutions, the popularity of direct marketing is easy to understand since it offers a means of increasing both the efficiency and the effectiveness of marketing effort. Yet, it is also becoming more popular among consumers who are increasingly willing to deal with financial institutions over the telephone, not only to organise their motor insurance but also for more complex transactions like arranging a mortgage. For the customer the direct route offers speed and convenience. This is particularly, although not exclusively, appealing to the young. It also puts the customer in greater control of the relationship with the financial institution by avoiding any intrusive physical presence. The customer also controls when to start and terminate the relationship. In addition, the direct method makes it easier for the customer to contact a greater number of financial institutions and investigate alternative options when deciding to choose a new product. The effect of this is that some customers can become very focused on price as a primary decision factor. This is particularly a feature of motor insurance purchasing. Very few customers, however, seem to be aware of the differences between a direct insurer and a direct seller and the impact that this may have on the eventual price of the insurance.

The direct financial services industry has been driven largely by the general insurers, particularly motor insurance. Direct Line was the first to offer insurance direct in 1985. Stone and Woodcock (1997) forecast that by the year 2000 it will have taken the direct motor insurance industry 15 years to penetrate 25 per cent of the market. The issue facing most suppliers is whether the curve will continue to grow or whether it will turn out to be an S-shaped curve. Opinion seems to favour the continued growth of the industry. One of the features of the industry is that it has shown little sociodemographic bias with all income levels and ages of motorists equally responsive to the direct route. This could be because most general insurance is required by law and is not 'sought' by the consumer. Hence, the direct route would be equally appealing to a wide variety of consumers as a means of controlling their cost of general insurance.

The success of First Direct, the pioneer of direct banking, seems to have been built largely on its customer service and customer retention. Since a large proportion of First Direct's customer base were Midland customers who switched to direct banking, the other major banks have not tended to perceive First Direct as a serious threat to their business. Thus, the other banks have not rushed to build their own direct banks but have tackled the issue by establishing a direct banking service as a service defence for existing customers.

Not all financial institutions have had the same level of success with direct marketing, a significant proportion of direct mail used merely amounts to direct mass marketing where all consumers receive the same indiscriminate messages. Financial institutions need to understand the difference between 'direct-order' marketing and 'direct-relationship' marketing. Direct-order marketing takes on the traditional role of generating sales leads and securing business. This is where a lot of financial institutions are currently with their direct mail. Direct-relationship marketing is more concerned with retention of customers and targeting customers with products which meet their needs as they change.

It may be possible to improve customer retention by better direct mail; however, what is required to support this is good quality information to ensure that individuals are being mailed information on products which they do not already have and which are appropriate for their life stage and financial resources. Most customers are aware that banks hold data on them, some even overestimate the amount of data held, but unfortunately few believe that this data is used effectively. The next section looks at the value of information and data management.

Database marketing

According to Kotler (1997) database marketing is the process of building, maintaining and using customer databases and other databases (e.g. product, supplier and reseller databases) for the purposes of contacting and transacting. The premise of database marketing is that the database becomes central to the company strategy of customer management and is not just a tactical tool for launching the occasional direct marketing campaign. Companies which fall into this trap believe that a customer mailing list can act as a suitable customer database. The result is the mailing of indiscriminate mail messages or product offerings, so-called 'junk mail'.

Within any company there may be a number of different types of databases, serving different purposes. Stone and Woodcock (1997) identified the following types of databases in their investigations in the financial services sector.

- *The master customer file* – This is a database which holds basic customer identifying details such as name, address, telephone number, etc. In banks it is usually held within the transactions database.

- *The operational or transactions database* – This database is used to manage sales and service transactions with customers. There are usually several of these in a financial institution and they are used to manage transactions for different product types.
- *The customer database* – The customer database is an organised collection of comprehensive data about individual customers or prospects. It provides a single view of the customer in terms of the products bought, policies held, transactions, etc. It is built from operational data which has been cleaned and deduplicated. It is an interactive database and is accessed by all 'customer-facing' staff. Although financial institutions have been gathering customer data for years, there are still some which have not constructed proper customer databases. Data was, and for some still is, held as several product files. The banks and building societies are generally ahead of the insurance companies in the development of customer databases, but this is not necessarily an advantage since there are high costs associated with being a pioneer. One of the problems with the customer database is that cleaning and deduplicating is very expensive and is rarely totally effective, yet the impact of mailing the same client twice can be serious. One of the biggest obstacles is identifying effective deduplicating criteria. Furthermore, even if the database is clean, it may not take 'customer-facing' staff very long to create duplicates.
- *The marketing database* – The marketing database supports both business and marketing planning. It provides a view of the business over time. It is used to drive campaigns and assists the tracking of prospects and proposals. In addition, it tracks and supports the development of customer relationships over time and may include data from external sources such as lifestyles, psychographics, demographics, segmentation codes and questionnaire responses. Some of these will be written back into the customer database and used at point of sale to determine into which segment customers belong and how they should be handled. The database is usually accessed in batch mode for campaign selections, analyses and so on.
- *The data warehouse* – The data warehouse contains data from many of the above-mentioned databases and possibly others besides these. It is used for analysis or simply to provide a master standardised data set which other applications can use. Datamining is a technique which is increasingly being applied to large data sets or databases to analyse the data and identify key patterns of behaviour. High-street banks can generate hundreds of millions of transactions a week. Tracking and understanding this behaviour involves building complex and sophisticated systems. Credit card companies make use of such techniques to identify factors which determine revolvers, defaulters and those most likely to pay their balances in full.

  Although datamining is potentially a very powerful tool, it is not a miracle science. Before being able to mine data one needs to be able to predefine what general things are being looked for. Datamining can be done on a one-off basis or as a routine activity in which case provision must be made for automatic updating of data. Marketers rarely need data warehouses that are constantly updated because in general they are looking for well-established patterns of behaviour; it is only useful in continuous activity if new patterns of behaviour emerge.

Customer demand for on-line access, not just for banking transactions but also for obtaining details of products and for buying them, is also driving the move towards professional database management. Customers expect their financial institutions to make it easy for them to buy products and manage their data well enough to continue to offer relevant products (and not ones which they have just been sold). Thus, on-line access brings with it the need for improved customer database management.

Customer retention through database marketing

It is now being recognised that databases offer a potentially powerful means to re-activating and deepening customer loyalty. If financial institutions are to use their databases effectively to this end they must ensure that the information driving the database is accurate, current and relevant. Customer and marketing information is the cornerstone of any marketing activity, and it is particularly relevant to understanding customers' product requirements. If financial institutions are to seriously embrace the concept of segmentation and use their databases to track and identify segments' needs over time, then their information support systems should be adequate to allow them to do so.

Retention of customers means not only satisfying the needs and requirements of market segments and individual customers once but throughout their lives. From the point of view of the financial institution this means effectively cross-selling to the consumer. For cross-selling to be effective it should be rooted in a deep understanding of customers' needs and their buying cycles. For some financial institutions this may pose a problem since they may find that the responsibility for marketing a particular product rests with a particular product area. Thus, many financial institutions have a poor understanding of a complete customer life cycle.

In order to maximise the success of their databases in cross-selling and retaining customers financial institutions need to include data on purchasing cycles in their customer databases. The sale of a product depends on achieving access to the customer at the time the customer is 'ready to buy'. This represents the period in which the customer is actively looking for a product and is receptive to product information and direct mail shots. This period is, however, limited and varies from one type of financial product to another; some can be predicted and some cannot. In the case of motor insurance (and most other general insurance) the 'ready to buy' period is predictable for existing customers. This period may amount to between four and six weeks prior to the renewal date of the policy. What this means is that the consumer is only 'ready to buy' approximately seven to eleven per cent of the time. In the case of mortgages the 'ready to buy' period is much less predictable. A person may move house every seven to ten years on average. The consumer may be 'ready to buy' up to six months prior to needing a new mortgage. Predicting these six months on a seven-to-ten-year cycle can be almost impossible.

In order to achieve high cross-selling ratios these periods of 'ready to buy' must be identified and made use of. Most financial institutions unfortunately do not have enough data for this. Simply targeting the customer base in an attempt to cross-sell without having this information is no better than untargeted marketing. There are several points in the financial institution–customer relationship where information can be gathered and customer information files updated. The most obvious point is the initial contact when the individual first becomes a customer. At this point there is the opportunity to gather much data about the products currently held and an indication of future needs. Subsequent points occur when the customer purchases another product or interacts with the company in some other way. Many of the high-street financial institutions now organise annual financial health checks or financial reviews with their customers as a means to identifying potential 'ready to buy' windows. A third option for data collection is to conduct some periodic survey to gather data and update customer files on a large scale. Regardless of how the information is gathered, the deployment of new information technologies is the key to successful customer management in the future.

SUMMARY

In addition to understanding the broader patterns of behaviour, the development of an effective marketing strategy also requires that financial institutions understand the differences between customers and their financial service requirements. This chapter has addressed the issue of customer differences through market segmentation. Having outlined the benefits of a segmented approach to the marketplace, various bases for segmenting financial services consumers were discussed and evaluated. Although most of the segmentation employed in the financial services sector appears to be largely based on demographic or sociographic information and descriptive in nature, there is vast scope for the application of psychographically based segmentation and predictive techniques.

The advent of direct marketing is putting increasing pressure on information technology. Databases will continue to grow in importance as a means to segmenting, targeting and tracking customers and their requirements and will serve as a source of competitive advantage in building and maintaining long-term customer relationships. Financial institutions need to understand the data they have on their customers and understand the value of the data in driving marketing information and strategy. It is essential that databases are kept up-to-date in order that current customer details are available. Many financial institutions already capture significant customer data, yet success will be determined not by the amount of data gathered, but by how the data is used to create targeted marketing programmes.

DISCUSSION QUESTIONS

1 Demographics continue to be the mainstay of market segmentation research in the financial services sector. How valid are demographics in aiding a bank's understanding of consumer financial services requirements?

2 Using the life cycle concept, as applied in 'The meaning of life cycles: marketing savings' (pp. 72–3), show how it can be used to understand consumer requirements for credit and loan products at each stage of the life cycle.

3 How might you target each of the four segments identified by Harrison (1997a)? Suggest marketing communication themes for each of the segments.

4 Show how financial institutions can make better use of psychographics in segmenting their customer bases. What approach would you recommend?

5 Discuss the implications for using either *a priori* or *post hoc* segmentation approaches. What would your findings tell you?

6 Discuss the future of segmentation within the context of the direct revolution.

7 Having segmented a market, how can a financial institution be sure that it has identified relevant and valid customer groups?

8 You have been given the task of setting up a customer database to enable a direct insurer to segment and target its customer base. Outline what information should be held on each customer and for what purpose.

9 How would you gather the information for the database described above and how would you keep the information up-to-date?

10 How would you use market segmentation to retain customers? Outline the strategy you would employ.

4 Development and management of financial products

INTRODUCTION

The product is usually the basis on which customer satisfaction is created. As such, it is a vital component of the marketing mix. Indeed, for many organisations it is the most direct link the customer has to the organisation. The product provides the basis for competition, it enables the company to generate income and it can provide a tangible indication of the strategic direction of the company. The effective management of the product is recognised as being fundamental to the long-term success of the organisation. All these factors are as true for financial institutions as they are for many other organisations. While many financial institutions may not have placed much importance on the development of the product range in the past, the increase in competitive pressure has focused attention more closely on the product and service delivered as a means of creating and sustaining a competitive advantage.

Thus, financial institutions have become increasingly concerned with a number of issues surrounding product strategy, including: the processes and procedures involved in the development of new financial services; the factors which contribute towards the successful adoption of the new product; how to manage the product over its life to protect it from competition; how to use branding to differentiate the product from very similar alternatives; when to withdraw an unprofitable product from the range; and how to best implement the withdrawal process with minimal adverse effects for the financial institution as well as the customer.

With these issues in mind, this chapter covers three broad areas of product strategy: the development of new financial services, the management of existing financial services and the elimination of financial services from the product range.

OBJECTIVES

After reading this chapter you should be able to:

- define the concept of the financial services product;
- identify and discuss the factors affecting financial services product strategy;
- critically evaluate the theoretical process of new product development in relation to financial services practice;
- comment on the factors which have been identified as contributing to the successful introduction of new financial services in the marketplace;

OBJECTIVES

- discuss the importance of the product life cycle concept in identifying appropriate strategies at each stage of the financial product's life;
- highlight the role and increased importance of branding to financial services;
- review and discuss the rationale for and process of deleting financial services from the product range.

The product concept

Before embarking on the issues concerned with product management and development, it is necessary to first clarify what is meant by a product and how the theoretical notion of the product fits with our understanding and experience of financial products. Throughout this chapter the terms 'product' and 'service' will be used interchangeably to refer to the offering that the financial institution makes available to customers. Many definitions of what constitutes a product have been offered, yet they tend to have a central theme. For example, Kotler and Armstrong (1997) argue that 'A product is anything that can be offered to a market for attention, acquisition, use or consumption that might satisfy a want or a need'. Similarly, Dibb *et al.* (1997) maintain that 'A product is everything, both favourable and unfavourable, that one receives in an exchange. It is a complexity of tangible and intangible attributes, including functional, social and psychological utilities or benefits.' Doyle (1991) simply states that a product is 'anything which meets the needs of customers'.

For financial services, the definition of the scope and form of the financial services product is less than straightforward since it relates to a combination of prices, practices, promises and people. Thus, the 'product' is more deeply entwined with the other marketing mix variables. This will become apparent throughout the discussion. However, this chapter does attempt to focus more narrowly on the 'product' concerns leaving other chapters to devote more attention to the remaining marketing mix variables. According to the product concept, the product is comprised of several levels, each level adding more customer value and serving as a means of differentiation from competing products and brands. At its simplest, the product consists of three levels: the core product, the actual product and the augmented product. However, Kotler (1997) identifies five levels. An adapted version of this, taking note of both the three and the five levels, is depicted in figure 4.1.

- The *core benefit* or service is the most fundamental level which the product provides. This relates to a core need which the product is either perceived to fulfil or, indeed, actually fulfils. In Chapter 2 a set of basic financial needs was presented: cash accessibility, asset security, money transfer, deferred payment, financial advice. All financial products can be traced back to catering to at least one of these core needs.
- The *actual product* is the second level, and refers to the basic product and its features. In addition, this takes into account the capabilities of the product, its quality and durability, design and styling, etc.
- The *expected product* refers to the set of attributes and conditions that buyers

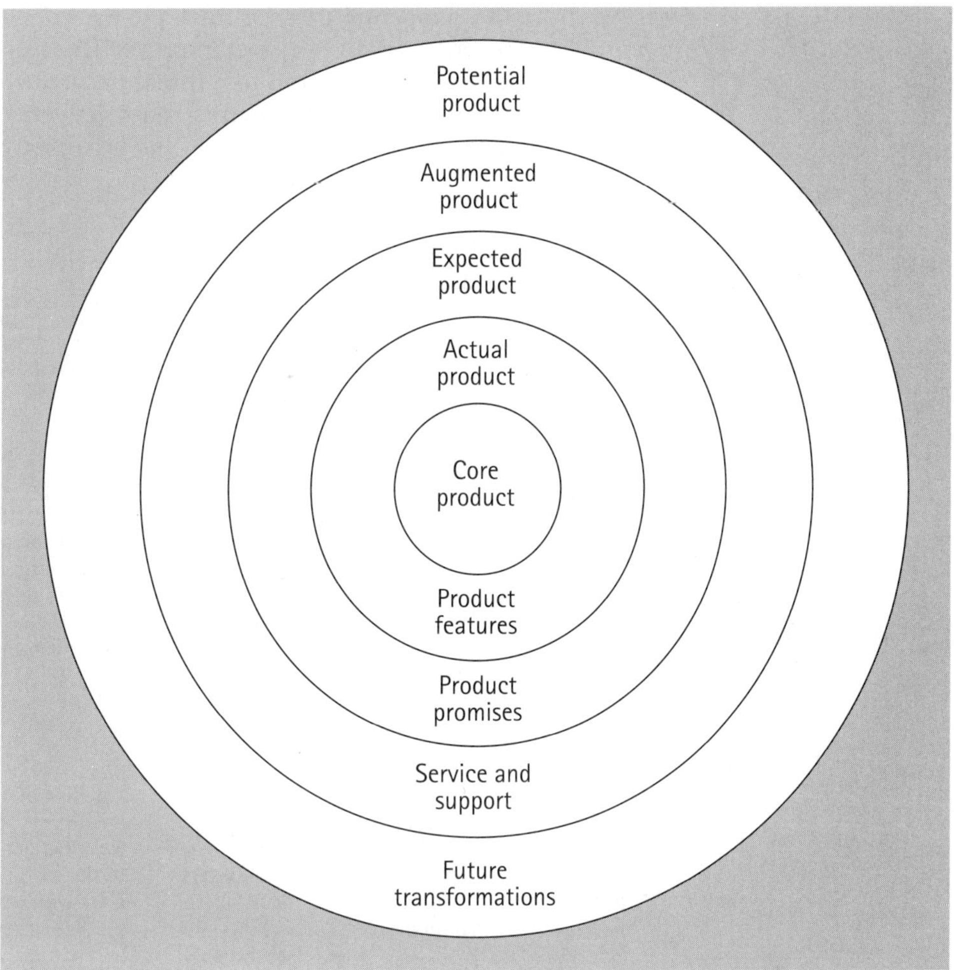

Fig. 4.1 Five levels of a product

would normally expect from the product. For financial services, what the customer can expect from the institution is usually outlined in the terms and conditions of the contract. These tend to form the so-called 'hygiene' factors which determine the minimum level of service that the customer expects to receive. They comprise a set of promises which may be written into the contract or unwritten in the implicit fiduciary responsibility of the institution.

- The *augmented product* aims to meet customers' needs beyond their expectations and usually refers to the 'support' systems which are put into place to serve the customer. These may include the assistance of salespersons, delivery and payment terms, warranties, after-sales support, etc. Most competition takes place at the augmented product level; it is where differentiation beyond the basic product features is possible. However, augmentation requires resources and the augmented benefits soon become expected benefits. All the major financial institutions implemented customer care programmes in the early-to-mid 1990s in an effort to differentiate themselves from the competition. But as these programmes became commonplace, customers began to expect improved levels of service as the standard, forcing financial institutions to rethink the augmentation of their products. Another reason why augmentation is not very effective is due to the ease and speed at which financial services can be copied.

Table 4.1 Application of the product concept to financial services

Core benefit	Actual product	Expected product	Augmented product	Potential product	Example
Cash accessibility	Cash card or withdrawal book, ATMs, branches and cash-back through retail outlets	ATMs to be in working order and serviced. Branches open and accessible at times stated	Additional services via ATMs and branches	Wider access, more distribution, e-cash	Halifax CardCash
Asset security	May be many products from simple savings to investments. Basic attributes provide a vehicle for keeping and growing funds	Safe-keeping and protection from theft. Protection from the effects of inflation. Access to funds at times stated	Additional services, tiered interest rates, penalty-free withdrawals	Individually set interest rates/ penalties based on individual saving behaviour	Bank of Scotland 90-day Notice Account
Money transfer	Provides the ability to move money around between accounts and pay bills	Secure and accurate systems which protect the transaction from mistakes	Insurance and guarantees for mistakes made in the system. The ability to check recent transactions	Provision of greater control over transactions to the customer. Links with other people's accounts and not just your own	Mondex, Bank of Scotland, HOBS
Deferred payment	Provides money now based on future earning potential	Level of interest rate and repayment term agreed at start. Penalties for defaulting	Payment protection insurance, preferential rates for early repayment, or penalties. Preferential rates for subsequent loans	Flexible repayment terms linked to personal circumstances, lump sum or regular payments	NatWest Personal Loan. Mortgage
Financial advice	Receiving advice on products and services to meet current and future needs	Impartial advice from a trustworthy and reliable source	Financial health check, to keep up-to-date with developments. Periodic reviews and the mailing of magazines/ product information to customers	Anticipate customers' needs, be proactive and provide for needs before they arise	Woolwich Independent Advisory Service

- The *potential product* encompasses all the product augmentations and transformations that the product may undergo in the future. Thus, it refers to the possible evolution of the product. Companies are attempting to surprise their customers by not just meeting their expectations, but by exceeding their satisfaction levels and delighting them. Table 4.1 shows the application of the product concept to the financial services core benefits. It highlights the meaning of each level to the product and provides an example of a product for each case.

Factors affecting product strategy

Whether the decision is to develop a new financial product, modify an existing one or withdraw one from the product range, it is likely to be affected by external as well as internal factors. Scanning the environment is, thus, important to financial institutions in order that they take advantage of any opportunities created by external trends, and, at the same time, are in a position to minimise the impact of any threats on the business. The external environment potentially can consist of numerous factors, many of which can have an impact on financial institutions. The financial services environment has been discussed in detail in Chapter 1; however, this section will consider just four factors which have the greatest impact on product decisions generally for financial institutions.

- *Customers*. A financial institution may have several different types of customers, including personal and business consumers and intermediaries such as brokers. It was established in Chapter 2 that consumers are at the heart of marketing. Understanding what consumers want and how to deliver products and services that meet their needs is (or should be) fundamental to any product strategy. Thus, decisions to develop new products, make changes to existing ones and kill off old ones should be driven, at least in part, by consumer needs and trends. One problem associated with this is that for many financial services, consumers may not feel that they have an actual need for the product, but there may exist a legal obligation to buy. This is particularly true of many insurance products. Thus, while it may not always be relevant to identify needs for a product, it is relevant to assess consumer requirements for various products. Chapter 3 clearly showed that consumers do differ in their requirements for financial services, and that there is significant value to be gained from analysing the differences between consumers in terms of financial services consumption. Similar analyses can be conducted for the business markets (which are discussed in Chapter 11), although the requirements and needs of businesses are likely to differ.

  In addition to the consumer markets, other customers might include a variety of intermediaries as well as a number of internal customers. It is important that the needs and requirements of these customers are also taken into account in making product decisions. This may involve additional communication and training to ensure that they are well versed in the developments and changes made so that they can be relayed to the final consumer.

- *Competitors* are a valuable source of information which can be used for a variety of decisions, not only for product decisions. Their actions provide an indication of how they perceive trends in the environment. This can serve to confirm the institution's own assumptions about how the market is changing, or alternatively can suggest that the institution has omitted to notice an important trend. As mentioned later in the chapter, a significant proportion of new product ideas come from competitors in the form of 'copy-cat' products. Thus, while consumers might be at the heart of marketing, they do not seem to be at the heart of financial institutions' new product development decisions. Copying competitors assumes that the competition have got it right. If they have, the imitator can benefit from significantly reduced research and development costs. Yet, if the competitor has misjudged the situation, the mistake can be as costly for the imitator as a full research and development programme might have been.
- *Technology* has a significant impact on the running of financial institutions from the customer databases to the support of back-office staff to providing the delivery of services through automatic teller machines and on-line home banking. Technological developments also have provided products in their own right, such as the Mondex smart card. Changes and developments to products can be facilitated both by advances in new technology and also led by them. It is important to ensure that technology does not become the driving force to the extent that customer needs take a back seat. Many new developments require that the appropriate infrastructures are in place so that customers can make use of the service offered. Furthermore, for technological advances to be implemented successfully they require that the customer keeps pace with developments and is comfortable with the changes to established patterns of behaviour that may be necessitated. Indeed, this was one of the main barriers to the successful adoption of the Bank of Scotland's HOBS (Home and Office Banking Service) which was developed more than 20 years before consumers were ready (on a large enough scale) to use on-line banking.
- *Government and legislation*. The unprecedented legislative change which has occurred in the sector over the last 25 years was documented in Chapter 1. Many financial products are controlled by legal contracts or affected by the tax system. It is, therefore, not surprising that changes to legislation provide a major impetus to product decisions. A range of new product opportunities have been opened up through legislation, but at the same time threats have been posed to some existing products, rendering them less attractive. Financial Services Marketing in Practice: 'One scheme too many: Britain's latest savings plan, ISA, is both unfair and unattractive' discusses the controversial replacement of PEPs and TESSAs by ISAs in April 1999.

  According to a report in the *Financial Times* (Tuesday 19 May 1998), ISAs that meet the proposed voluntary 'CAT standards' for cost, access and terms and conditions (see table 4.2) will be lightly regulated, allowing them to be sold cheaply and direct to the public. Philip Warland, director general of the Association of Unit Trusts and Investment Funds, criticised the proposals, saying that it 'will be economically illiterate, politically inept and lethal for some consumers', perhaps suggesting that products developed entirely as a result of changes to legislation might not be a good thing.

Table 4.2 Key standards for ISAs

	Cash ISA	Insurance ISA	Stocks and shares ISA
Cost	Promise of minimum interest rate	Controlled charges	Controlled charges
Access	Ceiling on minimum subscription; limit on withdrawal penalties	Controlled minimum premium	Controlled minimum subscription
Terms	No other requirements, e.g. no penalties for more than a certain number of withdrawals	Surrender values at least equal to return of premiums after a period of years	Must be unit trust or Open-Ended Investment Companies (OEIC); must track a general UK-based index; shares or units to be single-priced
Common themes	• Clear straightforward advertising • No bundling, no limitation to existing customers • Undertaking to keep to benchmark standards		

(*Source*: Treasury, cited in *Financial Times*, Tuesday 19 May 1998)

FINANCIAL SERVICES MARKETING IN PRACTICE **FT**

One scheme too many: Britain's latest savings plan, ISA, is both unfair and unattractive

Governments love new schemes for savings. In the past 15 years, Britain has seen the introduction of the personal pension, the Business Expansion Scheme (BES), The Enterprise Zone Trust, The Tax Efficient Special Savings Account (TESSA) and the Personal Equity Plan (PEP) to name but a few.

And just as much as they enjoy inventing new schemes, they love tinkering with old ones. PEPs have had their annual limit changed several times, their geographical basis changed and their rules altered to reward, rather than discourage unit trust investment.

This complexity has only tended to confuse investors and increase administrative costs. Complexity can also lead to fraud; part of the reason for the personal pension mis-selling scandal is that so few people have any idea how pensions work.

The government's new savings initiative – the Individual Savings Account – seems like another example of bureaucracy gone mad. The administration's stated aim is to encourage low income families to save. To that end there will be no minimum holding period – instant access to your savings, in other words – and the scheme will be available through consumer-friendly outlets such as supermarkets.

But this aim could have been easily achieved by changing TESSA rules for new applicants. TESSAs, interest bearing accounts, which are fairly easy to understand, previously had a five year holding period; that could have been abolished and the rules changed to allow the likes of supermarkets to offer them.

Instead, the government has set up a new system, with new rules, including a £1,000 annual limit on the total amount that can be put in interest-bearing deposits. Quite apart from the complexity involved (there is also a £1,000 limit on life assurance-related products, a £5,000 ceiling for all ISA savings and a £50,000 lifetime limit), this forces a small saver with just over £1,000 to his or her name to venture into the high-risk equity market, something few experts would advise.

The real reason for the scheme appears to be an attempt to limit the cost. The £50,000 lifetime ceiling is designed to penalise those who have accumulated more than that sum in PEPs and TESSAs. The aim is to spread tax relief more fairly between low and high earners.

However, the new rules will force all PEP and TESSA holders to convert their holdings into ISAs.

FINANCIAL SERVICES MARKETING IN PRACTICE **FT**

This will represent extra paperwork for the individuals and companies concerned (over the decade that PEPs have existed, many people will have taken out plans with several providers), and will require a centralised bureaucracy to ensure investors do not exceed the £50,000 ceiling.

Second, the new scheme represents a form of retrospective taxation on those who have accumulated more than the £50,000 limit.

These are not tax dodgers who have moved their money offshore, but individuals who have put money into schemes deliberately created by the government to encourage them to save. And £50,000 is not a huge amount, if that is the capital sum accumulated to fund a couple's retirement; drawing down a 5 per cent income would bring in only £2,500 a year.

In the past, when tax reliefs have been abolished, old privileges have been allowed to wither on the vine rather than being withdrawn on a particular date.

The government's arbitrary action is not only unfair, it will discourage saving by making investors suspicious; a government that changes the rules once is likely to do so again.

Closing PEPs and TESSAs to new investors – rather than ending them – would not have been an ideal solution (it would have still left those using PEPs to repay their mortgage with a problem, for example) but it would have been in keeping with the tradition of UK tax changes.

A more fundamental point is whether any economic purpose is served by such schemes. Many investors have merely used such tax breaks to move their existing savings into a more tax-efficient form, adding no net saving to the economy.

And the existence of such schemes can create a vast distortion in the savings market ... Nor is it easy to believe that the government will attract new savers from the lower-paid. The main reason the low paid do not save is that they have no money; there is little, except for accessibility, in the ISA to encourage them to cut back their spending and take up the scheme.

A much more radical scheme, with perhaps special bonuses for low income savers, would have been needed; and that would have been too costly.

There is a fairness case for giving tax breaks to savers; most are saving income out of salaries that have already been taxed ... But the Institute for Fiscal Studies believes the case for encouraging savings via tax incentives is pretty weak ... setting up elaborate schemes, with rules and disclosure requirements, the government may merely be creating a giant subsidy to the accountancy, legal and financial services professions who get to administer them. And that is surely not the idea.

Source: Philip Coggan, *Financial Times*, 6 December 1997

Questions:

1 What were the key factors influencing the introduction of ISAs?

2 What strategies were employed for the removal or modification of existing products?

3 To what extent do you think ISAs will encourage greater saving activity among the lower-income households?

Development of new financial services

The development of new products or services is accepted as a requirement for the continual growth and prosperity of all companies, not just for financial institutions. Yet, due to the changes which have occurred in the financial services sector, it might be argued that the development of new financial services is paramount in order to remain competitive. The reasons and opportunities for the development of new financial services have been brought about by deregulation, shifting industry boundaries, technological advances and increasingly dynamic and demanding markets. While there may be some general agreement that a 'new product/service' is something that essentially meets consumers' needs which are not currently being met by the organisation, it is interesting to note that a significant proportion (if not majority) of new financial services recently developed have been aimed primarily at capitalising on the new opportunities of markets made accessible as a result of the Building Societies Act and the Financial Services Act. It might, therefore, not seem surprising that since the vast proliferation of new financial services throughout the second half of the 1980s, the sector has witnessed some degree of rationalisation of its product/market scope.

Strategies for the development of new financial services

Financial institutions which aim to be the leaders in their field might be expected to take the initiative in the development of new products. Equally, there are other financial institutions for whom the risk of innovation failure may be perceived to be too great; they may opt for a strategy of copying successful innovations. Thus, the strategies for developing new products are many and may depend on a number of reasons including the corporate mission and goals, the size of the institution as well as the type of new product innovation.

At a broad level, financial institutions may be classified according to whether they are proactive or reactive in their new product development strategy. Proactive institutions initiate the major change. Cowell (1988) notes that this may involve the institution in actually creating the product or service or obtaining the rights to it (by either acquisition or licence). Acquiring the rights to the product avoids the risk of failure and any associated financial loss and overcomes any disadvantages of lead times. First-movers usually have strong research and development and marketing. Furthermore, a strong customer orientation is also essential in order to pre-empt needs and requirements, yet this need not necessarily be manifest through the marketing function.

A reactive strategy may involve the institution in attempting parallel entry whereby it simply imitates the first-mover and launches a 'me-too/copy-cat'-type product, or it may attempt late entry to the market with a 'second-but-better' product. In this scenario the institution employs a reactive yet sophisticated strategy of 'wait-and-see' which attempts to note and improve on any of the pioneer's failings. Alternatively, the institution may choose not to follow the pioneer in any way and may attempt a defensive strategy which aims to seek damage limitation through focusing on an aspect of differentiation to detract from the competitor's new product offering.

Edgett (1993) adds to this that new product orientation among financial institutions can be either technology-driven (resulting from the utilisation of new technology such as ATMs or smart cards), market-driven (where new products are designed to meet customer needs, such as flexible mortgages), or competitive-driven (where new products ideas are driven by competitor actions). In a sense, the market-driven and technology-driven orientations can be either proactive or reactive. Financial institutions can either develop new technologies or pre-empt new customer needs as well as react and respond to developments in both areas. Edgett (1993) noted in a study of building societies that size affected new product orientation: small societies are more likely to be competitively driven whereas large societies are more likely to be technology-driven in comparison to other societies, but more market-oriented than competitor-oriented in general.

The majority of new financial services developed in recent years have been 'me-too' in nature, suggesting that financial institutions are tending to react more to the competition than to the market. This would seem to suggest that the advantages normally associated with first entry do not apply to financial institutions. Indeed, Tufano's (1989) study of investment banks revealed that innovators did not appear to enjoy pricing advantages, in the form of premium prices, in the brief period of 'monopoly' before imitative products appeared. In fact, it was found that, over the long run, innovators charged prices that were below, and not above, those charged by rivals offering imitative products. It was, however, noted that innovating banks enjoyed quantity advantages, underwriting significantly more deals than imitating banks. Generally, it was found that rivals either quickly imitated the product (within 78 days of the pioneering issue) or it failed to be used extensively. In cases where five banks offered a given product, the innovators captured almost 40 per cent of the total market over the product's life.

Copy-cat strategies would seem attractive not only because of the ability to reduce the risk of failure but also because of the costs associated with being an innovator. According to Tufano (1989) investment bankers estimate that developing a new financial product requires an investment of as much as $5 million. This includes payment for legal fees and accounting, regulatory, and tax advice; time spent educating issuers, investors and traders; investments in computer systems for pricing and trading; and capital and personnel commitments to support market-making. Yet, imitators typically invest 50–70 per cent less than innovators to create imitative or 'knock-off' products. Thus, the lower costs coupled with greater likelihood of success would seem prudent reasons for following rather than taking the lead. However, the danger of imitating too closely is that there is little room for differentiation. This may be one of the reasons why financial institutions have found it difficult to retain customers recently.

Types of new products

Only 10 per cent of all new products are truly innovative and new-to-the-world. Booz, Allen and Hamilton (1982) identified six categories of new products in terms of their newness to the company and the marketplace:

- new-to-the-world products (such as Mondex and Barclay's Screenphone, totally new product innovations);
- new product lines (such as when banks and building societies moved into offering mortgages and current accounts respectively – not totally new products to the market, but a new product line for the institution);
- additions to existing product lines (such as Royal Bank of Scotland's Royalties account, a current account 'with frills'). The problem with introducing products similar to existing products in the line is that they quite often don't generate new business, they just shift it around. A significant number of applications for the Royalties account were from existing RBS standard current-account holders and not from competitors, resulting in an expensive customer upgrading);
- improvements to and revisions of existing products (this happens on a

continual basis with most products and might include revisions to safety procedures for credit cards issues or the automatic issuing of new cheque books);

- repositionings (such as the reconfiguring of PEPs and TESSAs into ISAs, enabling an existing product to be targeted at new segments);
- cost reductions (such as the low-cost credit card offered by Royal Bank of Scotland and Advanta, which is lower in price than the standard RBS credit card and is aimed at encouraging non-RBS credit card customers to switch from competitors).

Most of what is generally referred to as new product activity tends to be directed at improving and modifying existing products. Major innovations are new both to the financial institution and the market. Consequently, they tend to be rare, carry high risks, but at the same time hold the potential to generate high returns. McGoldrick and Greenland (1994) identify three different types of innovations. Continuous innovations involve a gradual change, such as paying the insurance company by direct debit rather than paying the representative in the home, and they have the least disruptive effect on established patterns of behaviour. Dynamically continuous innovations have some disrupting influence on established patterns of behaviour. This type of change has been witnessed in the move from cash payment to cheque payment to debit card payment methods. Discontinuous innovations have the greatest impact on behaviour, requiring the establishment of new patterns. Examples of such innovations have been in the area of home banking and in the use of Mondex and other smart cards.

New product development process

The development of any new product is usually the outcome of an iterative process, involving several people, perhaps from different departments within the organisation and involving individuals from outside the organisation. A structured and systematic process can contribute significantly to the success of a financial institution in the development of new financial products. Reidenbach and Moak (1986) bear testimony to this in their research, noting that top-performing banks have a more structured and formal new product development programme than average or below-average financial institutions.

A number of frameworks have been proposed for the development of new products. Most of them have been general frameworks, but perhaps more specifically aimed at the development of physical products. Some have also been developed specifically with services in mind (see, for example, Donnelly *et al.*, 1985; Cowell, 1984; Scheuning and Johnson, 1989). Yet, most of the frameworks are variations on a similar theme, suggesting that the process begins with the generation of ideas for new products, these are then screened to identify those with potential, then follows some form of testing and feasibility analysis, ending in the launch of the new product. The amount of time spent at each stage and the extent to which all stages are actually experienced, depends on a number of factors, including the characteristics of the product, the target market, competitive pressures, time and resources available, amongst other things.

The following eight-stage new product development process is used as the basis

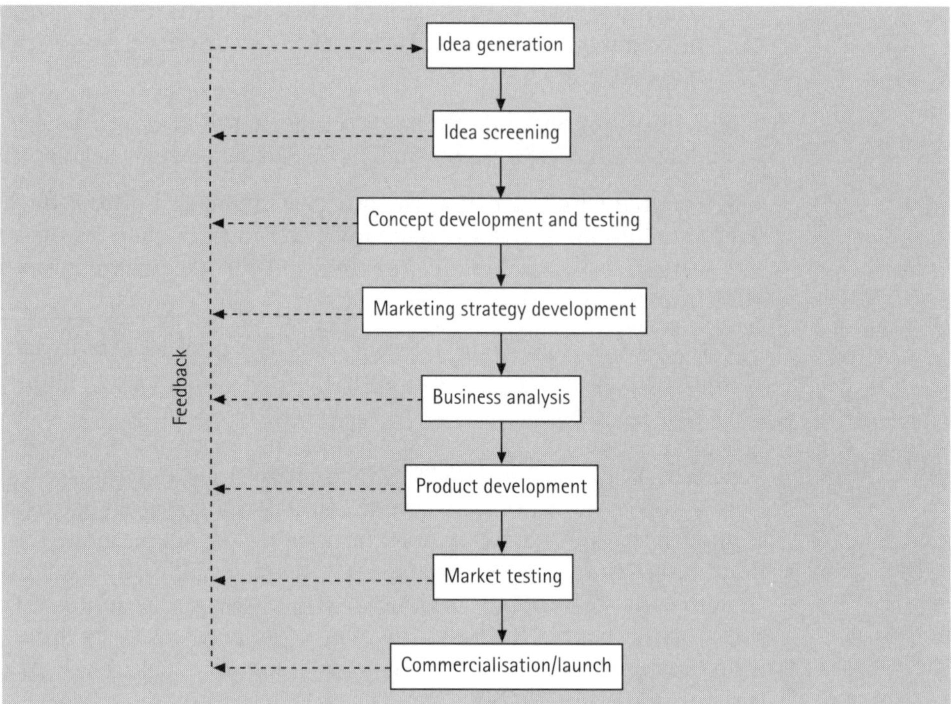

Fig. 4.2 The new product development process

for discussion (see figure 4.2). Particular attention is given to the unique characteristics of financial services and the extent to which such a framework can be applied to the development of new financial services.

Idea generation

Ideas for new products rarely come from just one source and will be influenced by competitor, technical and customer concerns. Generally, sources of ideas can be categorised as those which are internally generated and those which are generated by organisations and individuals external to the financial institution. Internal sources of information may be generated from research and development, through formal new product development procedures, from sales representatives (who act as the eyes and ears of the company), from marketing research and marketing departments, and from customer complaint data. Marketing and marketing research play a vital role in terms of the contact they provide with the customer through surveys and opinion analyses etc. In a survey of service businesses, Easingwood (1986) found that marketing and marketing research accounted for over 40 per cent of new product ideas compared with only 13.5 per cent generated by operations.

External sources of information are more diverse and can include outside agencies (such as advertising and marketing research agencies), competitors, channel members and intermediaries (such as Independent Financial Advisers, brokers etc.), universities, consultancies and publications. In the same study by Easingwood (1986) it was found that agencies, competitors, customers, overseas markets and suppliers generated ideas in 36 per cent of cases. Opinion seems to suggest that financial institutions use competitors and other external agencies as a primary source of new product ideas (Davison *et al.*, 1989). This has been attributed to the ease of copying the ideas and the potential to lower risks and costs in the process.

Ideas can be unsolicited or 'engineered' and there are a number of techniques which can be used to generate ideas for new products. These can involve need/problem identification, the listing of current attributes which are in need of improving and brainstorming. All of these can be performed internally (among staff members) or externally with the use of customers and/or intermediaries.

Sources of ideas for new financial services have tended to go in waves. Following the wave of deregulation, there was a major regulatory impetus to the development of new products as financial institutions were, for the first time, able to offer products outside their traditional domain. Advances in technology have also provided the means of developing new products and a number of innovations in the delivery of financial services have been driven by such developments. Now that competition has greatly increased, it can be noticed that much current new product development is competitively driven, based on copying and the development of 'me-too' products. Perhaps the wave of market-driven developments has yet to be fully realised.

Idea screening

Soliciting new product ideas may not present any problems, indeed the problem may be that too many ideas are generated which cannot all be taken through to development. Thus, the ideas must be evaluated and screened. Screening serves several functions but basically involves checking out the ideas which will justify the time, expense and management commitment of further investigation. First, the ideas are checked to ensure consistency with organisational strategy and to ensure that there is a fit with the capabilities and image of the organisation. Second, it means evaluating the ideas to single out the promising ones (which have potential) from the not-so-promising ones. The screening process should ensure that good ideas are not dropped, yet poor ideas should be dropped as soon as possible.

According to Cowell (1988) screening involves either establishing or using previously agreed evaluative criteria to enable the ideas to be compared. Ideas are then weighted, ranked and rated against the criteria identified. An investigation into the processes of new service development (Easingwood, 1986) revealed that 26 per cent of screening processes were found to be formal and 23 per cent informal, suggesting a balance between the two. Some of the criteria used to screen ideas were: compatibility with company objectives such as profit, market share, sales volume or customer goodwill; compatibility with company resources including capital, production, marketing, distribution, systems and salespeople.

By contrast, Edgett's study (1993) revealed that financial institutions favoured group decision-making formats. Informal rather than formal screening procedures tended to be used by the majority of financial institutions surveyed. Thus, it was concluded that while most financial institutions used a group procedure to screen new financial product ideas, the procedure was not formalised.

Concept development and testing

The approved ideas from the screening process are translated into service concepts for further development and testing. The service concept is the company's idea of the product expressed in meaningful terms to consumers which includes the set of features and attributes associated with the product and its positioning.

A product idea can be turned into several product concepts, depending on the target users and perceived benefits. For example, the flexible mortgage (a home loan with the option of adjusting repayments to suit the mortgagee) can appeal to several target groups. For example, it might appeal to those in the family formation stages of the life cycle where cash is limited and expenses outweigh incomes. The benefit of the flexible mortgage to these customers might be that it allows breaks from paying the mortgage during periods of high expenditure. Similarly, it may appeal to those who may experience job insecurity or who anticipate career breaks. Furthermore, it may be of benefit to the empty-nester segment which may be interested in paying off the mortgage quicker with the higher amounts of disposable income available.

Having developed a concept which relates the benefits and features to the target group, it then needs to be tested in order to gain a reaction from it. Word and/or picture descriptions can often be enough to get the concept across, yet for some financial services it may be difficult to get across the final product experience. It may be for this reason that Edgett (1993) notes that these early development stages are not very sophisticated in the development of new financial services. In terms of preliminary market assessment, it was found that use of discussions with either customer contact staff or customers themselves (i.e. external forms of research) tended to be used much less than internal research. In fact, Edgett (1993) discovered that a high proportion of building societies generally tended not to contact customers at all in the initial market assessment stage. Those that did adopt a more formal approach were among the largest of societies.

Marketing strategy development

Having tested the concept, a preliminary marketing strategy plan needs to be developed for the purpose of introducing the new product to the market. This may include the following:

1. a description of the target market, its size, structure and behaviour, planned positioning, sales, market share and profit goals for the first few years;
2. planned pricing, distribution strategy and marketing budget including advertising etc.;
3. long-run sales and profit goals and marketing mix strategy over time, taking into account not just the introduction of the product but how it is to be maintained and managed.

Business analysis

Having identified the appropriate strategy, the idea needs to be translated into a firm business proposal which details the attractiveness of the idea and its likelihood of success or failure. The proposal should consider the manpower resources, customer reactions, marketing and technical research requirements. It will also contain details of estimated costs and sales and profit projections.

In estimating sales of the new product, it is also important to take into account repeat purchasing and replacement cycles for the product. These were discussed in Chapter 3 in relation to the retention of market segments, where it was noted that replacement cycles (ready-to-(re)buy opportunities) not only vary enormously between products, from annual replacement cycles in the case of car insurance to 7–10-year cycles perhaps for a mortgage, and a perhaps once-in-a-lifetime purchase in the case of a pension, but they also vary in terms of whether they can be predicted with any degree of certainty. Thus, in estimating the sales of a new product, there should be some estimate of first-time sales and replacement sales.

While some financial products may have extremely long replacement cycles, such as a 10- or 20-year endowment policy, there are nonetheless opportunities for repeat purchase (of an additional product) to occur. There may be a predictable repeat purchase cycle for such products which occurs every 4–5 years. Marketing research should enable such data to be gathered.

Product development

Having established the viability and feasibility of the new product idea, the next stage involves translating the idea into an actual product or service. Up until this point the product or service has only existed as a word, a drawing or a description in the minds of both the developers and the customers. In the case of physical products this is where a prototype product would be developed in order to put it through rigorous functional and consumer tests. For technologically bound products which have an obvious physical dimension to them, such as Barclays Bank's screenphone service, it can be possible to develop a prototype for testing. Barclays ran a pilot scheme for six months involving 2,000 customers. However, in the case of many other financial services (such as a pension or an investment instrument) it is not possible to build a prototype. This has a number of implications for market testing.

Market testing

If satisfied with the functional performance and customer ratings, the next move is towards market testing. This is where the full product/service complete with brand name, packaging and other peripheral and augmented aspects of the product are offered to the market. The amount of market testing conducted is influenced on the one hand by the time pressure and research costs associated with the development and the investment costs and risk of failure on the other hand. A balance needs to be struck.

The disadvantages of testing the product are that it gives advance warning to competitors of the new product. In a sector where a significant proportion of new product introductions are 'me-too', it is important to reduce this advance warning which competitors can take advantage of. Due to the inseparability and longevity of many financial services, market testing among financial institutions tends to take the form of full introduction of the new product with limited promotion to restrict the initial demand and attention to the product. This allows time for the product to be tested out in preparation for a full national launch supported by the appropriate advertising.

Commercialisation/product launch

Market testing will normally provide enough information to decide whether to move to the full launch of the product, or whether changes need to be made. In moving to commercialisation of the product, a key decision is the timing of market entry. Financial institutions may take one of several decisions. They can aim for first entry into the market, capitalising on any first-mover advantages that may exist (as previously discussed), they can attempt parallel entry in which they wait and watch the competition and bring out a 'me-too' product, or they can go for late entry into the market which enables them to learn from any mistakes which the competition may have encountered and to launch a 'new improved' version of the product. In the financial services sector this may be an advantage since many products are long-term in nature and the true customer benefits or satisfactions are not recognised until some future date. In waiting to see this, the competitor can improve on the product.

Actual commercialisation can be considered as the true test of the product. It is generally hoped by this stage that the product will not fail, yet many still do. Despite this, it is argued that the financial loss from the failure of new financial services is low compared with other types of products due to the use of shared delivery and management systems. Yet, there are also hidden costs of failure which should also be noted, such as the cost of managerial effort wasted on weak products, the reduced ability to introduce other new products, and the adverse effect of unsuccessful new products on the corporate image. The following sections explore ways in which the success rate of new financial services can be improved.

Factors affecting the adoption of new financial services

The rate at which a new financial service will be accepted and adopted in the market depends on a number of factors, some of which can be attributed to the customer and some of which can be attributed to the product or service itself. Financial institutions need to make sure that they are aware of the reasons why some people may be quick to try the new product while others may wait a while, and they should attempt to identify and understand the barriers to non-acceptance of new products. Rogers (1962, 1983) classified people into 'adopter categories' based on the rate at which they adopted new innovations (innovators, early adopters, early majority, late majority, laggards). The early and late majority account for over two-thirds of the market. Rogers saw the five adopter groups as differing in their value orientations. For example, the innovators were seen as risk-takers and venturesome, the laggards seen as tradition-bound who adopted when the innovation was no longer 'new' but had taken on a tradition of its own. The early adopters and innovators should be identified so that communication is directed at them initially.

While the behaviour of customers is somewhat outside the control of the financial institution, it does have control over its products. There are a number of issues which can be addressed which affect both the likelihood of adoption and rate of adoption of a new product. Rogers (1962, 1983) noted that a successful new innovation should exhibit the following characteristics.

- *Relative advantage.* The product should, first, possess something which expresses unique benefits or superiority to the customer. First-movers into the market may be able to generate this, yet with so many copy-cat products the scope of relative advantage may be argued to be limited between the various features of financial products. Yet, the very nature of many financial services means that each time the service is rendered it differs. Heterogeneity can have a very positive impact in terms of customisation and the creation of a relative advantage, yet it can also have a negative impact in terms of variability in quality if it is not harnessed appropriately. For this to create a relative advantage financial institutions must pay meticulous attention to the design process in order to identify the tolerable levels of variability, as well as monitoring the new service after the launch to ensure customer satisfaction.

- *Compatibility* with the values and experiences of its target markets is the second characteristic that the innovation should exhibit. This comes back to some points made earlier about the extent to which products are market-, competitor-, technology- or regulation-driven. Market-driven products which are developed in response to market demand might reasonably be assumed to exhibit compatibility with customers' needs and values. However, there is a danger that products developed in response to the competition, advances in technology and changes to regulation may not cater to an actual need.
- *Complexity* relates to the relative ease consumers have in understanding the product. It has already been mentioned in Chapters 2 and 3 that the intangibility of financial services can cause some difficulty in mentally conceptualising the product, with knock-on effects in terms of information search and processing behaviour. De Bretani (1993) warns that there can be a danger of assuming that financial services are easier to develop because they are largely intangible. In reality, however, they can be highly complex processes, conceptual in nature, definitions can be vague and perceptions variable. Thus, it is recommended that in the development of new financial services a multi-phase iterative process is employed to ensure that key personnel from different departments are involved in progressively defining the service concept in terms that make it unique to the specific operational requirements. A detailed 'drawing board' or 'blueprinting' approach should be used to document the systems and subsystems that will eventually be used in the development of the financial service. De Bretani (1993) notes that making slight adjustments to a service after its launch may be easy in the general sense because it is intangible, yet this may not always be possible in the case of many financial services which often require the consumer to enter into a contract.
- *Divisibility* refers to the ability to try the product on a limited basis and generally covers the aspect of test marketing. This can be very difficult for financial services, as discussed previously. Divisibility is also affected by the inseparability of production and consumption of the product. This can have multiple effects on the processes used for developing and launching the service. There needs to be a focus on the outcome as well as the production experience the consumer will have. What this means is that financial institutions need to be both production- and marketing-oriented when they are producing new financial services. This means that operations and customer contact personnel will need to be involved in the later developmental stages to ensure that the process is efficient and in line with customer expectations.
- *Communicability* refers to the degree to which the new product can be communicated (i.e. advertised and promoted) to others. The lack of a

physical domain may present some problems and compound the difficulty already associated with conceptually grasping the nature of the product. The promotion and advertising of financial services is also regulated by law, which inhibits the communicability of the new product. These issues are explored further in Chapter 8.

Success factors

The development of any new product or service carries the risk of failure, which is likely to be even greater if it is not designed with the specific needs and requirements of target customers in mind. The rate of success of new products tends to be unfortunately low. In manufacturing, only one in every four products becomes a success, and it is estimated that almost 50 per cent of the resources devoted to innovation are spent on products which become commercial failures (Booz, Allen and Hamilton, 1982). De Bretani (1993) notes that evidence from managers in the business service sector would seem to suggest that new service products are not too dissimilar in this respect. Some of the specific services factors which account for their failure are that services are integrated, intangible and variable processes, often difficult to conceptualise, sometimes complex, dynamic, and are at risk from competition of substitutes and near-substitutes, as outlined above.

Companies are probably quite clear on how to evaluate a successful new product: it generates revenue and profit. In a study of banks, building societies and insurance companies, Johne and Vermaak (1993) utilised the following six measures of success:

- actual sales achieved
- increase in sales achieved
- actual market share achieved
- increase in market share achieved
- actual profit achieved
- increase in profit achieved

Thus, it would seem that financial institutions employ growth, in both volume and value terms, as a measure or outcome of the success of the new product. While it might be quite straightforward to identify whether the new product has been a success, financial institutions need to be able to identify what specific factors have contributed to or even determined the success of the new product. Several studies have been conducted, specific to the development of new financial services, which identify the factors associated with the success or failure of the new product (see de Bretani, 1993; Easingwood and Storey, 1991; Edgett and Jones, 1991; Storey and Easingwood, 1993). These can be categorised broadly into two groups: technical and environmental factors. Technical factors describe the steps and activities usually proposed by new product experts as being necessary for successful new products. Environmental factors refer to the corporate culture in which the new product development process operates. A summary of factors under each of these headings is provided below.

Technical factors

Formal up-front design and evaluation

- The formal planning, design and evaluation of activities are carried out prior to the launch of the new product, including generating and screening ideas, testing and assessing the market potential. A more formalised procedure might be ensured by securing the commitment of senior management to the project.

Formal and extensive launch programme

- Promotion needs to be planned to be effective, and supported by sufficient funding. An image must be created for the product. Effectiveness of the communication strategy has been found to be linked to technology leadership, suggesting that technology provides the competitive advantage around which to build an effective communication strategy – it acts as a point of differentiation.
- Internal marketing including the training of staff, provision of training material and a promotional programme aimed at them contributes towards the success of the product. Furthermore, an attempt should be made to match new products to the expertise of staff. Easingwood and Storey (1991) note that Nationwide Anglia tried to increase its staff's comprehension of the FlexAccount by inviting them to open an account prior to the launch. Midland has been noted to space its new product launches to allow staff time to familarise themselves with the new product and to avoid overloading them with information.
- Operational branch procedures could be enhanced by more testing of branch procedures prior to the launch coupled with training of branch staff so that they have a better understanding of the new product. Better communications need to be established with the branch staff selling the product.
- Intermediary support needs to be provided, in the form of helplines for example. Companies using intermediaries do not have direct control over the support given to their products. Giving intermediaries support is more likely to have an impact on the success of the new product.
- Attention should be paid to the overall quality of the product itself, the delivery and after-sales service.
- Product fit – Storey and Easingwood (1993) note that a typical high-street bank offers between 200 and 300 services to its personal customers. It is important that the new product complements rather than competes with existing products.
- Testing in the early stages of the launch can help to solve any teething problems before they become too widespread.
- Customers need to be clearly identified and targeted in order to make the most efficient use of communication. Better efficiency is gained with direct mail.

Environment factors

- Supportive and high involvement environment includes commitment from senior management as well as commitment early on from different functional groups. A high level of enthusiasm throughout the process from the product development manager and a high level of personal contact maintained with all the people involved with the product are essential. A product champion who is prepared to push the product through the system and overcome delays and difficulties greatly affects the success of the product.

- Strong marketing orientation is essential, although the marketing department does not necessarily have to be at the centre of the process. A link with marketing research and the monitoring of customer needs is crucial.
- Customer orientation ensures that ideas come from the customer.
- In-house experts provide a key role in generating new product ideas and planning the new product process.
- Product should be sufficiently differentiated from others on the market. Technology is used partly as a tool to manage the account and also to give value to the customer by providing an individual service. It can be used as a point of differentiation and to aid the development of long-term relationships. Technology is not just a cost control tool but a value adding tool. It can provide a competitive advantage.
- Control of costs is essential to copy-cat institutions since there is possibly little else to distinguish them from the pioneer. In addition, responsiveness and the speed of response are important. When a market opportunity occurs it is important to act quickly. Some financial products, such as unit trusts, can be conceived and launched in a week; this is particularly important when copying competitors or responding to regulatory changes.

Thus, the success of a new financial service is rarely down to one single factor. Easingwood and Storey (1991) note that four factors were found to be highly correlated with success. These were identified as: overall quality, differentiated product, product fit and internal marketing, and use of technology. In a later study, Storey and Easingwood (1993) noted different success rates between different financial institutions. Banks appeared to be the most successful, being particularly strong on market research and responsiveness; building societies were found to be slightly less successful but were good on internal marketing and synergy but had weaknesses in technological advantage and market research. Life companies were found to have no notable strengths and were generally less successful than banks or building societies. There was also a difference found between the relative successes of different products; interest accounts of various types were found to be the most successful, perhaps because they are easier to understand than some other products and familiarity with the product type reduces the need for market testing.

Management of existing products

The significance of new product development to the continued competitiveness of the financial institution has been acknowledged. Important though it may be, financial institutions still need to consider the many established products which they have in their product range and how to manage them to their best advantage. Managing the product range involves the constant re-evaluation of the products in order to decide whether modifications or repositions are necessary, or even deletion from the range. Modifications are usually performed in order to improve the performance of the product in line with changing customer requirements or competitor action. They could involve changes to the product itself, such as improvements to statements or interest paid monthly instead of annually on a savings account, or changes to the delivery of the product or access to the service. Modifications to the product are mostly pursued for mature products. It is also at this stage of a product's life that branding also takes on increased importance as a means of differentiating the product from many similar competing products. This section considers the management of existing products over their life cycle, taking into account key changes at each stage of the product's life, and the role of branding.

The product life cycle (PLC)

Products, like humans, have a finite life. This was perhaps not appreciated in financial services where longevity and permanence have been key characteristics. Yet, product proliferation, brought about by changes to legislation and the entry of new players to the sector, has brought with it a greater need to manage the product range and pay attention to appropriate strategies for products at various stages of their life.

The product life cycle is a biological metaphor that charts the life of a product. A number of variations on the same general theme exist, but all recognise that a new product is introduced to the market, if it is successful it grows, it then matures, and eventually (and this may occur within a very short space of time, such as months, or after many decades) the product loses appeal, sales decline and it is terminated. Each stage of the product's life brings with it different market conditions, different marketing objectives and a different set of appropriate marketing strategies for the marketing mix variables. Earlier sections discussed the process involved in the development of new financial products. This section focuses on the product's life at and beyond introduction to the market, and the successful management of it throughout the remainder of its life.

- *Introduction* – During the initial introduction of the product to the market costs usually outweigh the income derived from the product. This is particularly true for pioneers of new products, but perhaps less so for imitators. Growth during this stage is slow as the first customers adopt the product. A primary task is to raise awareness of the new product and to stimulate an interest in it. If the product is a totally new concept, it may also require some market education. Prices in the introduction stage may be set high to skim the market (as with on-line home banking) or low to penetrate the market (as with current accounts which provided 'free banking' initially, but now they are in the maturity stage fees have started to be introduced)
- *Growth* – As the product takes off, the appeal widens to other segments of the market. Competitors, attracted by the customer interest, quickly produce their own versions of the product and start to compete. Competition forces each company to re-evaluate its own offerings. Additional features and services begin to be offered. This was evident when most of the high street

financial institutions started to offer PEPs and TESSAs. Financial institutions attempted to differentiate on such features and services as type of company to invest in. The growth stage is the most profitable stage of the product's life, and a key objective is to build market share.

- *Maturity* – As more customers acquire the product and more financial institutions supply it, the market begins to reach saturation. Competition becomes very intense as each player attempts to hold on to its share of the market, defend its territory and protect it from the attack of competition. It is this stage that most financial services are currently at. This is evident from the marketing strategies which are being used. There is a strong emphasis on retaining the existing customer base, new customers are won by encouraging switching from competitors (for example, in the mortgage market this includes cash-back incentives, in the credit card market it is low APRs and in the savings market it is preferential interest rates), heavy use of advertising and sales promotion, and increased use of branding.
- *Decline* – The decline of products can occur for a number of reasons. The product may lose its appeal to customers whose needs may have changed, it could be made obsolete by the introduction of new technology, or it could be displaced by changes to legislation. Legislative changes are responsible for much of the new product development, product modifications and decline of financial services products. PEPs and TESSAs have been displaced by ISAs. One might view this as the untimely death of a product, or merely its re-

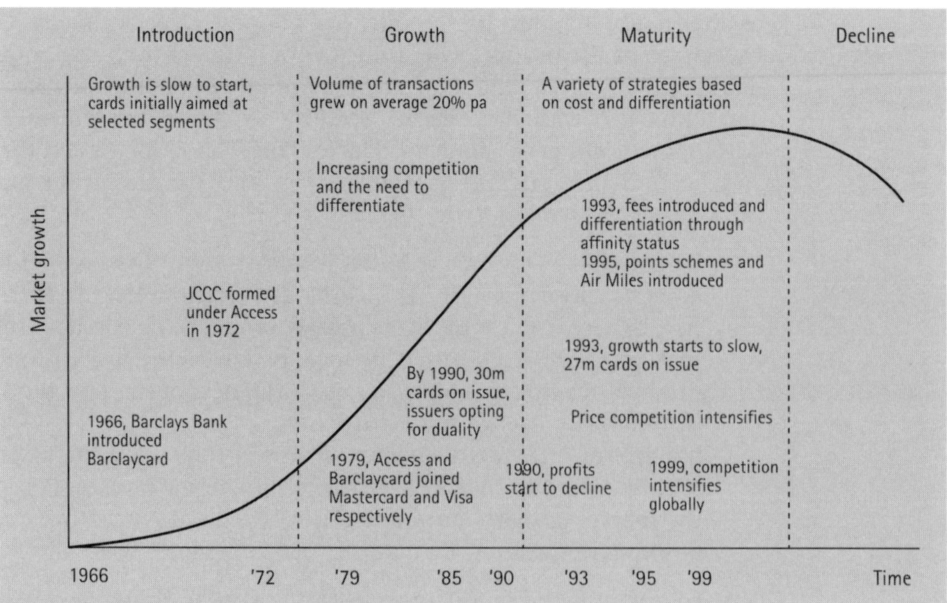

Fig. 4.3 The life cycle of the credit card
JCCC – Joint Credit Card Company formed by National Westminster, Lloyds, Midland and Royal Bank of Scotland under the brand name Access.
(*Source*: Adapted from information contained in Worthington, 1995)

Table 4.3 Marketing strategies at each stage of the credit card's life

	Life cycle stages Introduction	Growth	Maturity
Market conditions	Few players, limited competition. Sales slow to take off, limited to certain segments	Competition increases as other institutions issue credit cards. Sales increase as the mass market adopts	Intense competition, oversupply of credit cards. Heavy advertising and promotion
Marketing objectives	Awareness and comprehension of the new product concept and trial	Adoption and increase in volume and value growth	Holding market share – customer retention and relationship building
Marketing mix strategies			
Product	Basic product, limited features	Product proliferation. Increase in features including services, warranties. Product differentiation and market segmentation (silver, gold and platinum cards)	Affinity association, loyalty building, points schemes and branding and co-branding
Price	Low price, no fees, interest rate determines price	Introduction of some fees to curb multiple card holdership	Fees commonplace, some reduction of interest-free period. But at the same time intense price competition
Promotion	Selected promotion aimed at initial adopting segments. Message to raise awareness and highlight benefits of convenience	Mass advertising, especially TV, still focused on the benefits and convenience – the 'flexible friend'	As consumers become more price-sensitive, promotion changes to direct mail to encourage switching behaviour based on preferential 'targeted' interest rates
Place	Limited distribution and opportunity for use	Rapid increase in outlets available to use credit cards. More intensive distribution via duality	Further increase in outlets accepting credit cards. Credit card is commonplace

birth under another name. The important issue to consider when a product goes into decline, is how to manage the decline effectively. The later sections of this chapter consider various strategies for the deletion of products from the product range.

The product life cycle is illustrated in figure 4.3 in the context of the life of the credit card. Table 4.3 summarises the marketing mix strategies employed for the introduction, growth and maturity stages of the credit card's life. The credit card, in the UK market, is currently at the mature stage of its life cycle. The question is, how long can it remain in this stage of the life cycle? Financial Services Marketing in

FINANCIAL SERVICES MARKETING IN PRACTICE

The credit card: halting the decline

The credit card is currently in the mature stage of its life. From its introduction to the UK in the late 1960s the credit card has changed the face of payment methods. There are currently around 27 million credit cards on issue, although this number has declined over the last decade. Competition between credit card issuers has increased in intensity during the 1990s as profits have been attacked, first by the recession in the early 1990s and more recently by the entry of additional players to the market.

Competitive strategies have included the introduction of fees to alleviate some of the burden of costs, the introduction of branding, affinity status, points schemes and bonus points aimed at encouraging greater use of the card and building customer loyalty, and low-interest promotions aimed at encouraging switching.

It seems that a number of tactics have already been employed to keep the credit card where it currently is. The question is, how long can the credit card remain in maturity and how far off is decline?

In one respect, it seems that the credit card will go on for ever. It has become an established and convenient method of payment. The UK has witnessed the entry of international players to the credit card market, and it seems likely that this could prove to be a viable strategy for expansion for UK financial institutions: to branch out into international markets and segments.

Furthermore, developments in technology, specifically in relation to internet banking and other forms of on-line banking have taken off. The internet is also finding extensive use as a retail distribution channel. Shoppers by this method find that the credit card is one of the few accepted currencies. Thus, such developments can ensure the continued use of the credit card.

Yet, in a mature industry, one of the key issues is the problem of controlling costs under such competitive pressures. The issue was addressed somewhat in the late 1980s when fees were introduced by most credit card issuers. This meant that everyone made at least some contribution to the costs. Yet, some issuers made the decision not to introduce fees, or have since taken the decision to waive fees providing the card is in regular use. Thus, the whole pricing system for credit cards has become confused.

Credit card customers fall into one of two broad segments: revolvers and full-payers. Full-payers basically take advantage of the deferred payment period and pay up in full when the statement arrives. Revolvers, on the other hand, tend to have an outstanding balance accruing interest. Revolvers essentially subsidise the interest-free period enjoyed by full-payers.

One strategy to overcome this would be to move to costing and charging for the services and facilities used. This might involve a fee for holding the card plus a transaction fee. Furthermore, the interest rate or the interest-free period might be set according to the frequency with which the card is used or according to whether the customer is a revolver or full-payer. Such a strategy would be consistent with the general trends occurring in the pricing of financial services.

Yet, a dramatic alteration to the pricing structure could have an equally dramatic impact on credit card behaviour, signalling not the re-birth but possible decline of the credit card. Increasing the cost of the service for some customers may make the credit card a less attractive option vis-à-vis other payment methods and may encourage a preference for, for example, debit cards which are currently free to use.

Thus, it would seem that the appropriate strategy needs to be carefully contemplated, alongside a full appreciation of the implications. While the fate of the credit card is, as yet, unknown, it remains to be seen how financial institutions will resolve the issues.

Questions:

1. What major developments and modifications have occurred to the credit card over the product life cycle?
2. How can full-payers be encouraged to make greater 'income-generating' use of the card?
3. How could the credit card life cycle be extended?

Practice: 'The credit card: halting the decline' discusses some of the issues surrounding the future fate of the credit card.

Branding

The financial services sector is traditionally a commodity-based industry. The question arises as to whether branding serves a purpose for financial institutions. The answer is undoubtedly that it does. The justifications are found in the increasingly competitive environment that institutions are facing: competition from both traditional and new financial services providers. The diversification of established consumer brands, such as Marks and Spencer and Virgin, into the financial services sphere and the rise of merger and acquisition activity have created the need for financial institutions to manage customer perceptions of who they are and what they offer.

Financial institutions came to branding late. Thus, it may be necessary to revisit the notion of branding. According to Doyle (1991), 'A successful brand is a name, symbol, design or some combination, which identifies the "product" of a particular organisation as having a sustainable differential advantage'. However, Saunders and Watters (1993) warn that it 'is more than giving a product, like a current account, a name (Vector account). It is about identifying a target market and then developing a product and a brand personality that the target market will identify and prefer.' They go on to distinguish between products and brands, noting that: a product is made, a brand is bought; a product can be copied, a brand is unique; a product can become outdated, a brand is timeless.

The benefits of branding are many, and are experienced by both the seller and the buyer. Strongly branded products can command a premium price of 30 per cent or more. Moreover, successful brands can be 'stretched' to promote new products, as Richard Branson has successfully done by extending the Virgin label from recorded music to transport to financial services. Perrier (1997) notes that the brand establishes an emotional 'pact' between the supplier and the buyer which creates the basis for an ongoing relationship. This ongoing relationship is of paramount importance to financial services which are typically long-term in nature and rely on a continued customer commitment. Other benefits are summarised in table 4.4.

Specifically in relation to financial services, it might be expected that the brand has relevance to consumers in aiding search for and selection of potential products,

Table 4.4 A summary of branding benefits

To the buyer	To the seller
• Product identification	• Product awareness
• Shorthand cue of product features and benefits	• Helps introduce a new product
• Distinguishes products of similar type	• Secures demand
• Reduces buyer search time	• Enables repeat purchase
• Increases buyer assurance	• Fosters brand loyalty
• Assists in quality evaluation	• Enables premium pricing
• Offers psychological reward	• Provides equity value
• Brand association	• Offers proprietary brand assets

FINANCIAL SERVICES MARKETING IN PRACTICE

FT

Financial brands 'fail to catch on'

Financial services companies have failed to build any significant value for their brands, according to research by Dresdner Kleinwort Benson, the stockbroker, and Interbrand, the London-based brand strategy consultants.

In a review of some leading businesses in the financial sector, Kleinwort and Interbrand found that only Barclaycard had succeeded in building up brand name value – as opposed to simple name recognition – similar to consumer product groups such as Levi's, Michelin or Kodak.

Barclaycard, the credit card arm of Barclays bank, has maintained its dominant share of the UK credit card market without competing on price with cheaper card issuers. KB and Interbrand calculate that the brand it has built up is now worth £1.33 billion, 5.4 times its 1995 profits.

Halifax Building Society, the leader in the UK mortgage market, has a brand worth £956 million, but that is only 1.3 times profits. Abbey National's estimated brand value is £518 million, just 0.8 times profits.

There is only meagre value in the brand names of three building societies, all of which are planning to convert to banks and float on the stock market this year. Woolwich's brand was worth £113 million, Northern Rock's £24 million and Alliance & Leicester's just £16 million.

'Brands are important. They help to secure repeat business and sometimes they allow the brand owner to charge premium prices', said Mr Simon Samuels, analyst at KB. 'But historically, financial service companies have been dismissive of branding and almost cavalier in their treatment of brands when they acquire new businesses.'

'Banks and building societies have devalued their brands by competing on price and even giving away services such as current accounts,' he said. In the past, the main factor in winning market share was the size of the branch network, but as direct distribution channels such as the Internet become more important, banks may regret not having paid more attention to their brands.'

KB and Interbrand were unable to value the brands of the main high street banks since it proved impossible to separate the different elements of their business. Direct Line, the telephone unit of Royal Bank of Scotland, was given a £24 million brand value.

Source: George Graham, *Financial Times*, 15 January 1997

Questions:

1 Why have financial institutions paid such little attention to the brand in the past?

2 Why is the brand important for financial institutions?

3 How can financial institutions build brand value?

particularly in the absence of much pre-purchase information as with many financial products. Yet, as mentioned in Chapter 2, it would seem that the brand has contributed little in the past to the retention of customers. A possible explanation for this could be that branding has tended to be used rather differently by financial institutions, compared with its use for fast-moving consumer goods. Saunders and Watters (1993) note that there has been a tendency in the past for financial institutions to treat brands like products: many have been developed and expensively launched, only to be replaced a few years later. It is not surprising, then, that this lack of continuity has a similar impact on the interface with the customer.

One of the key benefits which branding can offer financial institutions is the contribution to the balance sheet. Perrier (1997) argues that brand value has become important to financial institutions and that they should measure the value of their brands. One way of doing this is based on an economic value approach which assesses the value of the brand according to its future brand earnings which are discounted to a net present value using a discount rate which reflects the risk of the

Table 4.5 Financial services branding strategies

Generic brand strategy	Brand hierarchy	Examples
Corporate dominant	• **Corporate** (corporate names used)	Halifax, Royal Bank of Scotland.
	• **Divisional** (subsidiary names used)	Coutts (from NatWest) Direct Line (from Midland)
Dual brands	• **Mixed** (two or more names given equal prominence)	Lloyds TSB (as a result of merger)
	• **Endorsed** (brand endorsed by corporate identify)	RBS Advanta (corporate and credit card mix)
Brand dominant	• **Branded** (single brand name used)	Liquid Gold, Vector, Orchard
	• **Furtive** (single brand name used and corporate identity undisclosed)	Girobank (banking service of the Alliance & Leicester). Midland (HSBC)

(*Source*: Adapted from Saunders and Watters, 1993)

future brand earnings being realised. This approach is based on the premise that brands create security of demand and future earnings which the unbranded product would otherwise not enjoy. Yet, as indicated in Financial Services Marketing in Practice: 'Financial brands "fail to catch on"', it seems that the majority of financial institutions have failed to build any significant value for their brand names.

Table 4.5 outlines some of the strategies which have been used in the branding of financial services. Corporate dominant strategies are applicable to all types of financial institutions, large and small. They can be an efficient means of promoting many products. The advantage of a corporate identify can be beneficial to the promotion of financial services which often lack a tangible dimension. Thus, the corporate brand provides some means of identifying with the physical 'bricks and mortar' of the branch network. Divisional branding can provide the financial institution with a means of serving a separate segment of customers who may need (and want) to be treated differently from the mainstream customer base.

Dual branding strategies have increased recently along with the increase in mergers and acquisitions. A justification for promoting more than one name is that it does not alienate the customers of the former pre-merged organisations. Some dual branding may, in time, be replaced by the use of one dominant name. This was a strategy pursued by the Alliance & Leicester and Girobank when they merged. Initially the Girobank brand was promoted as 'the banking service of the Alliance & Leicester', but this was subsequently dropped. Brand-dominant strategies focus on the product-level brand in contrast to the focus on the organisation-level brand mentioned so far. As a strategy among financial institutions, they have received less attention than corporate branding. The lack of a physical dimension may also be an explanation: as the association with the corporate identify is removed significant tangible cues also disappear. However, there may be an attempt to increase product-level branding in the future in response to the entry of well-known consumer brands to the competitive arena.

Product elimination

A product generally cannot satisfy the needs of target customers and make a contribution to organisational objectives indefinitely. Thus, when a product ceases to fulfil these criteria, several options can be considered. For example, an ailing product may benefit from some enhancement or modification to 'fine-tune' it to the changing needs of the target market, thus resulting in some form of product repositioning. If this fails to rejuvenate the product, its deletion or elimination from the product range may need to be considered. This can be effected by a process of organisational neglect in which the market essentially withdraws itself from the product, or by a managed process of elimination which attempts to achieve a desired outcome in terms of perhaps income generation and minimum adverse effects on customers.

Just as the development of new financial services is hampered by the specific characteristics of financial services, including intangibility, inseparability, longevity and contractual and legal obligations, so too is the elimination process. The types of elimination possible for financial institutions differ from those employed by manufacturing organisations, mainly due to the separation of production, marketing and consumption which is typically experienced for manufactured goods but not for services. Harness and Mackay (1997) suggest that two broad types of elimination are evident in financial services:

1 the elimination process takes the product out of existence for new customers (and possibly existing customers);

2 the product endures some form of (external) elimination, but retains a presence in the financial institution (because of continued contractual obligations).

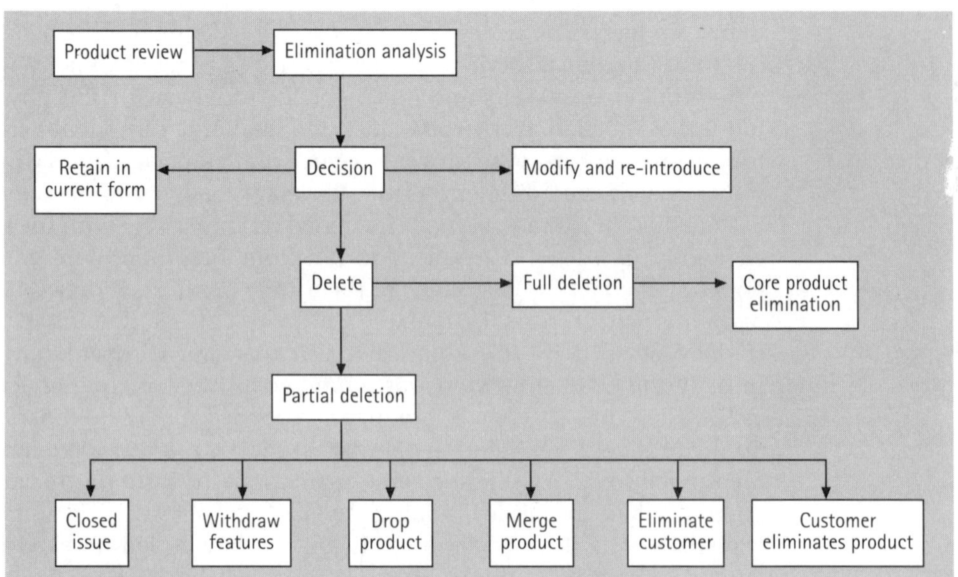

Fig. 4.4 The financial product elimination process
(*Source*: Adapted from Harness and Mackay, 1997 and Dibb *et al* 1997)

Table 4.6 Product elimination strategies for financial services

Strategy	Characteristics	Implications
Make a product a closed issue	• product not offered to new customers, existing customers unaffected • existing customers cannot make further use of facility • product kept open for specific segments only (to retain 'valued' customers)	The product is essentially 'put on hold', allowing the institution time to decide what to do with it. This does not remove the burden on management, however, since the product continues to consume a degree of admin. support. Customers may decide to choose an alternative product, given the restrictions imposed. Alternatively, the product will die a death as natural customer mortality occurs
Withdraw features	• removing the non-essential features and options of a product to essentially simplify the core product function • product features can be removed simultaneously, or alternatively phased out separately	Removing features is a way of reducing the cost of maintaining the product and its literature and admin. as well as training and sales force use. It may also be viewed as a step towards full elimination; the product may be less attractive to customers, hence, starting off a process of natural elimination. For certain products controlled by contractual obligations, it will not be possible to withdraw features after having issued the product to customers
Drop the product, keep its name, change the nature and function of the product	• drop the product's features and core attributes • keep the brand name and existing support systems • introduce a new product under the existing brand name	This is a strategy which is used to protect the investment of an established brand name. The brand-named product no longer meets customer needs, so the brand name is kept and used for a new product aimed at an unfulfilled need. The process involves moving existing customers to the new product as well as training the sales force and promotion. It can be used as both an acquisition and a retention strategy
Multi-product amalgamation	• a number of products are amalgamated (merged) to create a new product • similar or duplicate products must exist which can be amalgamated without infringing contractual obligations	Merging several products to create a new product can be used as part of a product enhancement strategy or a product withdrawal strategy. All customers of existing products must be transferred to the new product. The advantages are: product range simplification, service-level improvement, cost reduction, improved penetration levels, creation of spare capacity in operational and IT systems
Core product elimination	• the core product is withdrawn from the market • the product no longer exists in any form in the institution • full elimination and final activity of the elimination process	The strategy is not appropriate to all products at the same level. Care must be taken to avoid breaching contractual obligations. It can occur at the product level (the institution removes the product from its range), at the market level (the institution withdraws from a segment of the market), or at the organisation level (the institution ceases trading)

Strategy	Characteristics	Implications
Elimination of customer	• find a buyer for the customer if still generating business • close the product down if use is low (i.e. dormant accounts) • increase the price to make it too expensive for the customer, who will choose to leave	The objective of this strategy is to stop the customer from continuing to be a customer. The advantages are it enables the institution to concentrate on its core business, it reduces the costs involved in maintaining closed products, and it allows the removal of unprofitable customers. Finding another buyer for a customer is not simple, contractual obligations must be adhered to and the effect on retained customers must also be considered
Customer eliminates product	• customer breaches the terms and conditions of the product • the product ceases to function (i.e. insurance cover no longer provided), or its original intention is altered (e.g. repossessed house due to mortgage default)	The use of the product is outlined in its terms and conditions; these form a legal contract between the institution and the customer. When the customer breaks this contract the institution can either terminate the use of the product entirely or it can remove certain features from use

(*Source*: Adapted from Harness and Mackay, 1997)

Thus, product elimination in financial services can be either full or partial elimination. Partial elimination may be a first step towards the full and complete withdrawal of a product from the institution's portfolio. Irrespective of whether the elimination is full or partial, it is advised that a systematic elimination programme be set up. As illustrated in figure 4.4, this takes into account a regular review of the product and any decisions to modify or delete it from the product range. The elimination strategies are outlined in table 4.6.

Research by Harness and Mackay (1997) noted that, out of a total of 18 financial institutions contacted, the most commonly cited strategy was to make the product a closed issue and not offer it to new customers. This is perhaps not surprising given the contractual obligation and longevity of many financial services. The strategies taking second and third place were found to be the withdrawal of non-essential features of the product and the amalgamation of similar or duplicate products. These are perhaps the most popular means of limiting or withdrawing products from existing customers since they ensure some means of providing a continued service to customers and are unlikely to be in breach of the original terms and conditions of the contract. Core product elimination emerged as the least used strategy among the financial institutions contacted. One barrier is undoubtedly the contractual obligations which financial institutions face, yet financial services cater to a small number of core needs, and removal of a core product which caters to one of these needs, for example savings or loans, could place the financial institution at a serious disadvantage vis-à-vis its competitors.

SUMMARY

The product is a vital element of the marketing mix. It is the basis on which customer satisfaction is created and, for many organisations, it provides the most direct link a customer has to the organisation. The product also provides the basis for competition, enabling the organisation to generate cash. Although the concept of the product may be relatively easy to understand: 'it is anything which meets the needs of customers', the nature and scope of the financial services product is more difficult to define since it involves a combination of prices, practices, promises and people. Hence, the financial services product is less easily separated from the other marketing mix variables than are many physical goods.

Regulatory changes have provided the stimulus for much new product development and product proliferation, yet as the sector has become increasingly competitive financial institutions have been forced to rethink their product strategies, resulting in some rationalisation and modification of product ranges. The entry of established retail brands to the sector (such as Virgin, Sainsbury and Tesco) has also placed increased attention on the need to develop and build a brand image and brand value. Many of these product decisions have received little strategic attention in the past. Thus, this chapter aimed to cover the product decisions which are of prime importance to financial institutions, including the process for the development of new products and strategies to ensure their success, the management of existing products throughout their lives and the role of product modifications and branding, and the decision to delete products from the product range, outlining specific strategies and their implications.

DISCUSSION QUESTIONS

1 Discuss the major socio-demographic trends and their impact on consumer financial services requirements. What new product opportunities, if any, do these changes present?

2 Comment on the important features of product strategy in financial service organisations. What are the implications in a wider marketing context?

3 Discuss the relevance of the product concept to understanding the development, modification and deletion of financial services.

4 To what extent do financial institutions adhere to the stages of new product development, as outlined in this chapter, in the development of new financial services. What are the major points of departure, if any, and why do they occur?

5 What recommendations would you make to a financial institution that wants to ensure the success of its new products?

6 Discuss the reasons why many financial institutions have failed to achieve first-mover advantages in the development of new financial products. How do you explain that Barclays Bank has maintained market leader status with its Barclaycard as a first-mover in the credit card market?

7 To what extent does the classic product life cycle (PLC) concept apply to financial services marketing specifically in relation to product management and pricing policies?

8 Apply the PLC concept to the introduction, growth and maturity of PEPs and TESSAs and their replacement by ISAs.

9 Why have financial institutions failed to build any significant value for their brands. How can brand value be achieved?

10 To what extent is product elimination in the financial services sector actually an elimination of products?

5 Traditional channels of distribution

INTRODUCTION

Financial institutions need to make their products and services available to customers in order that they will adopt them. Thus, they need to employ effective distribution strategies. Distribution involves a wide variety of activities culminating in the creation of three types of utility: time, place and possession. In terms of time, distribution allows the customer to gain access to financial services when it is convenient for them to buy. In terms of place, distribution makes products and services available to customers in locations which are accessible and convenient to them. With regard to possession, distribution provides the customer with access to the product for consumption or future use. In addition to this, the distribution function also provides a means of effectively communicating with customers, and for customers to communicate with financial institutions.

Over the past few decades the distribution of financial services has rapidly altered. Changes to legislation, competitive pressures and customer demands have all influenced the evolution of distribution. What was convenient to the customer around thirty or forty years ago, no longer is. Similarly, what traditionally provided a cost-effective means of distribution, no longer does. Deregulation of the financial services market has enabled new competitors to enter the market, bringing with them innovative distribution methods.

The traditional method of distribution, for banks and building societies, has been via the branch network. Yet, new channels are beginning to emerge not merely as auxiliaries to the branch network but as suitable alternatives, creating a threat to the future role of branch networks and undermining the competitive position of banks in using the branch network as a competitive advantage. This chapter reviews some of these changes. It begins by outlining various types of distribution channel used by financial institutions and then focuses on three of the most used channels: branch networks, independent financial advisers and the direct sales force.

OBJECTIVES

After reading this chapter you should be able to:

- review various distribution channels used by financial institutions;
- chart the development of branch networks in the UK;
- outline the developments in branch refurbishments and comment on their impact on branch security and the role of branch personnel;
- discuss the characteristics and functions of the direct sales force;

OBJECTIVES

- account for the increase in independent financial advisers and comment on the controversy surrounding their roles and responsibilities.

Types of distribution channels

A channel of distribution, or a marketing channel, describes the groups of individuals and companies which are involved in directing the flow and sale of products and services from the provider to the eventual customer. Channels can be broadly defined as 'direct' or 'indirect'. Direct channels involve the movement and sale of products directly between the provider and the customer as in the traditional branch network, whereas in the case of indirect channels products flow via intermediaries or middlemen. Figures 5.1 and 5.2 provide some examples of direct and indirect channels used to distribute financial services.

Direct marketing includes direct mail and direct response advertising. Each method or tool can be used to achieve different objectives and to reach different segments. In the insurance sector, direct writers are increasing in number. Some of the most successful direct writers are integrating their direct marketing activities with other activities, such as face-to-face sales, to provide customers with a variety of means of dealing with the company. Direct marketing has given many direct writers a considerable cost advantage over traditional life companies and bancassurers with costs up to 70 per cent below the market average (Shelton, 1995)

The branch network is the traditional channel employed by banks and building societies. In contrast with direct marketing it offers a much more passive form of distribution, since it relies on the customer approaching the financial institution through the branch visit. Banks and building societies have attempted to overcome the passivity of their branches by adopting retail marketing concepts designed to encourage customers to enter the branches. Bancassurance reflects the shake-out in the high street following recent deregulation. It has blurred the distinction between banks, building societies and insurance companies as banks and building societies have established their own life companies. This channel is likely to play a major part in the distribution of insurance products by the turn of the century.

Direct sales forces traditionally have been used by the insurance industry which believes that insurance is not a sought product and has to be 'sold'. The direct sales force actively approaches customers, often in their own homes or places of work and conducts a face-to-face exchange with them. Although expensive, direct selling is valued because it provides direct access to specific customers, allowing precise targeting.

Intermediaries are third parties such as brokers, independent financial advisers, solicitors, accountants and estate agents who sell another company's financial products. A channel can employ one or more intermediaries. Traditionally, insurance companies made use of intermediaries, such as brokers, in the sale of their products, such as car insurance. However, in recent years, legislation has made it possible for banks and building societies to act as intermediaries for insurance companies and investment houses, taking business from the traditional intermediaries in these markets. While intermediaries perform several useful functions, allowing the company to widen its distribution coverage, selling via intermediaries requires that marketing effort is directed at both the intermediaries and the end customer.

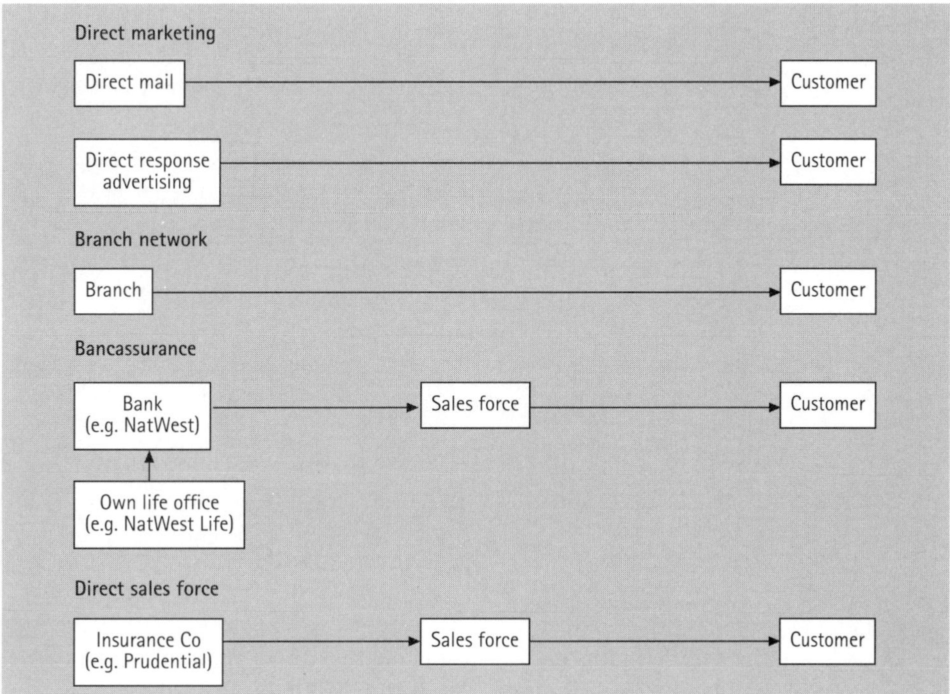

Fig. 5.1 Direct distribution channels

The Financial Services Act 1986 dictated that intermediaries advising on investments had to conform to one of two categories, forcing them to polarise. Either they could operate as a fully independent intermediary (opting for 'independent' status) or they could act as a representative or agent of one company (opting for 'tied' status). Independent intermediaries sell products from a number of companies while tied representatives are restricted to selling investment products from one particular company. While the polarisation rule applies to financial conglomerates (such as banks), separate parts of the business can polarise in different ways. For example, the Woolwich Building Society opted for tied status, but offers independent advice under the Woolwich Independent Advisory Service. This allows the building society to control its costs while at the same time making customers out of individuals for whom the building society does not offer suitable products.

In order to function as a fully independent intermediary a vast amount of training is required. Many financial institutions initially opted for tied status in order to save on training costs, prompting the criticism that greater concentration at the retail level was being created, thus limiting customer choice. In fact, the importance of tied status, in the early 1990s, was that it provided a transitory strategy for many banks and building societies as the large ties turned into life-office joint ventures to be replaced later by in-house life offices (bancassurance). In the future, the tied agency channel will not be so important.

The branch network and intermediaries are relatively passive forms of distribution compared with direct mail, direct response advertising and the direct sales force which seek to stimulate interest and response from the customer. In addition, the overlap between communication/promotion and distribution is the greatest for

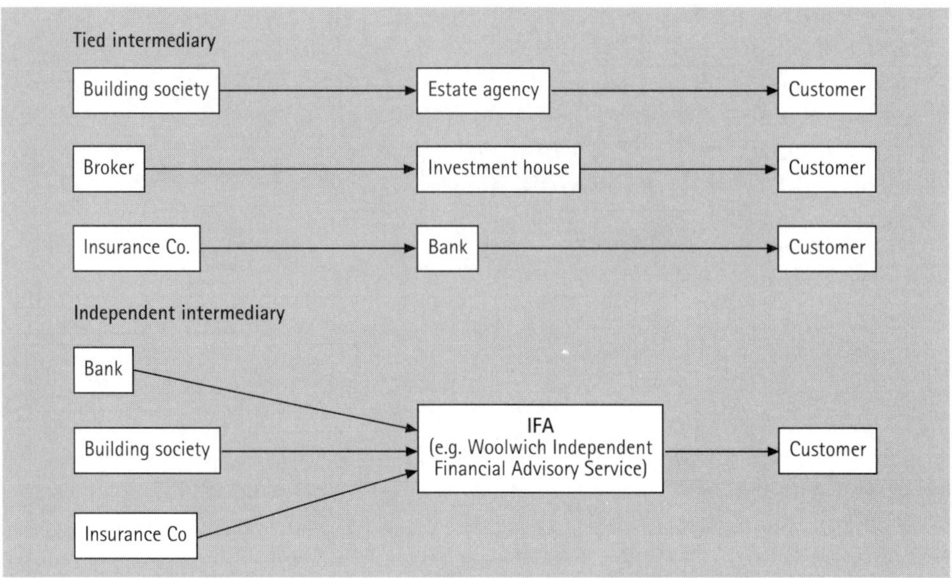

Fig. 5.2 Indirect distribution channels

the direct methods. As a result of this, direct mail and direct response advertising will be discussed in more detail in Chapter 8.

In terms of the extent to which various channels are used in the distribution of financial services, research by Easingwood and Storey (1997), involving a survey of 153 managers, revealed that the intermediary and branch network channels receive the most emphasis, accounting for 39 per cent and 26 per cent of total distribution effort respectively. The direct sales force and direct marketing were found to account for 10 per cent of effort available. More interesting, however, is the mix of channels employed by financial institutions. Four channel strategies were revealed and these are outlined in table 5.1. Significant differences were found between the type of financial institution and the mix of strategies employed by them. Banks, building societies and insurance companies were found to make more use of the

Table 5.1 A classification of distribution network strategies

Strategy	Extent of use*	Characteristics
Intermediary	14% of products	Almost a single-channel strategy focused mostly on the use of intermediaries with occasional support from direct-response advertising
Balanced	44% of products	The most widely used strategy, drawing on all methods of distribution, and the only method to make significant use of the direct selling route
Arm's length	12% of products	Emphasises the three methods of direct-response advertising, direct mail and intermediaries and does not involve direct person-to-person contact
Network	20% of products	The second most widely used strategy, making heavy use of branch networks, either own networks or via intermediaries

*Based on the proportion of products sold via the channel in the survey of 153 managers
(*Source*: Adapted from Easingwood and Storey, 1997)

'balanced' and 'network' strategies. For example, Lloyds Abbey Life, the life assurer now wholly owned by the Lloyds TSB banking group, sells unit-linked policies through a direct sales force. Black Horse Financial Services, however, sells life products through Lloyds bank branches. By contrast, investment companies were found to make more use of the 'arm's length' and 'intermediary' channels.

Whichever channel is used, it should be remembered that it is no longer appropriate to treat the distribution channel as a short-term tactical issue: the cost of acquiring customers is increasing and distribution is inextricably linked to longer-term customer retention policies.

Branch networks

Development of branch networks

The development and growth of branch networks, in the UK, owes perhaps more to the prevailing competition than to planned distribution strategies (see figure 5.3). Indeed, much of branch network expansion has been largely a consequence of evolutionary and unplanned growth. As mentioned in Chapter 1, the main clearing banks operated under a cartelised oligopoly until 1971. This was essentially an interest-rate-fixing cartel which precluded price competition. Hence, one of the few means by which banks could expand and compete effectively against one another was along functional lines: by growing their distribution networks and attempting to compete on market coverage and greater market presence. As a consequence of this, there was an expansion of branch networks during the 1950s and 1960s (Howcroft and Beckett, 1993).

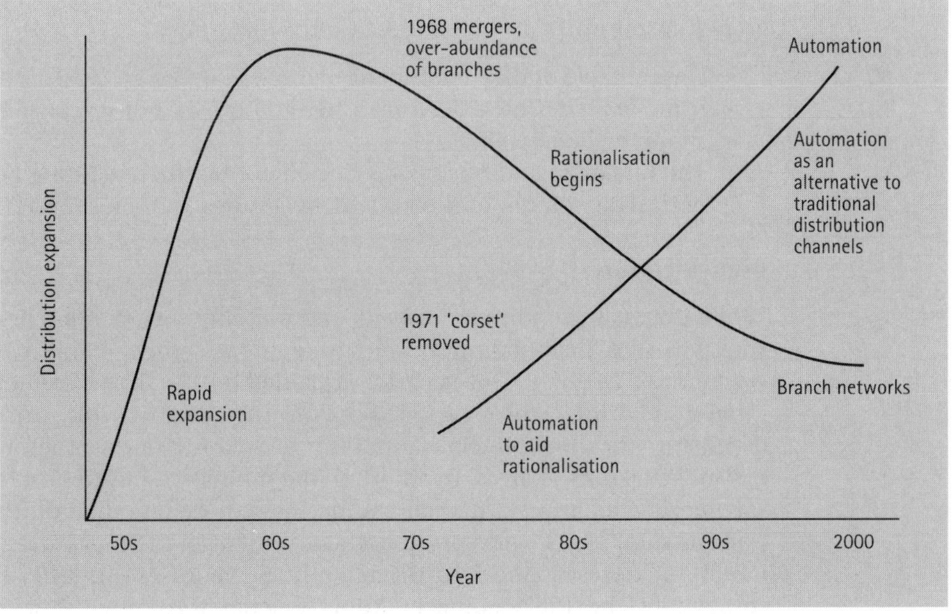

Fig. 5.3 Schematic representation of branch network development

At about the same time, the clearing banks were also starting to recognise the value of the personal market. Banks historically served the needs of businesses rather than individual customers and the lack of widespread distribution reflected this. However, as the importance of the personal market increased, so too did the need for numerous branches in convenient locations in order to attract relatively cheap retail deposits from individuals. Thus, in the personal sector, branch networks traditionally provided a very effective means of processing numerous transactions resulting from a largely cash-based and cheque-based society. Furthermore, extensive branch networks have provided an effective barrier to potential new entrants as well as facilitating the provision of an extended range of deposit and lending services.

In 1968, when a series of mergers took place, producing the main clearing banks which are still in existence, many banks found that they were overbranched in certain locations. Following this, a process of reduction in the number of branches began. With the dissolution of the interest rate cartel in 1971, the emphasis shifted from one of implicit price competition (manifested by the investment in and expansion of branch networks) to explicit price competition which focused on the interest rate. Consequently, financial institutions wanted to control costs as much as possible in an effort to offer keener interest rates. The problem was that the earlier means of competition by expansion had left many institutions with extremely costly branch networks. Furthermore, the arrangement and locations of existing branches were becoming increasingly less effective at providing customers with a convenient means of access to their cash. The growth in out-of-town and edge-of-town shopping centres in the 1980s and 1990s meant that many individuals were following the large retail outlets out of the high street, leaving banks occupying less-than-optimum positions in the centres of towns.

As a result of these changes, there has been a general trend towards the rationalisation of branch networks in terms of both the number of branches and their geographical spread. Three broad areas can be identified:

- Unprofitable and/or redundant branches have been closed down.
- Some branches have been relocated to new sites in response to trends in shopping behaviour.
- The functions and operations carried out by the remaining branches have been redistributed to accommodate closures and relocations.

Branch closures

While the main trend now for bank and building society branches is one of widespread closure, the building societies were, in fact, still expanding their branch networks into the 1970s. This is partly explained in that they were not affected by the interest rate cartel, since it applied only to the clearing banks, and they had a predominantly regional presence and, thus, needed to improve their representation in certain geographical areas. In addition, the traditional business of building societies was more straightforward than the business of banks; they did not offer money transmission, hence widespread and convenient branch location was not such an important issue. Changes to the Building Societies Act in 1986 altered this, and throughout the 1980s some building societies were buying up redundant bank branches in order to extend their access to the customer.

FINANCIAL SERVICES MARKETING IN PRACTICE

When is a bank branch not a bank branch?

The answer is, when it is an 'in-store' financial centre. This is the name which Tesco has given to the part of the supermarket which takes deposits, and dispenses cash, statements and advice to its banking customers. The reason for this is that the supermarket wants to avoid the negative connotations of traditional high-street bank branches.

All the major food retailers in the UK have established a banking operation, mostly through joint ventures with major high-street banks. However, the distribution of the service is handled by the supermarket concerned. Initially, distribution was via telephone and postal contact, although supermarkets are increasingly making use of their in-store floor space for financial services.

The first of Tesco's in-store financial centres was opened in an outlet during October 1997. It is planned that all 600 Tesco stores will eventually have one. Most financial transactions are handled by machine, but staff are on hand to give simple advice. Anything complicated is handled via the in-store freephone helpline or via video link to a call centre.

A recent survey by Bossard Consultants shows that the public like the idea of banking at a supermarket. This is good news for Tesco, Safeway and Morrisons, in the UK, which all deal in-store. But the findings are not so encouraging for Sainsbury which deals mainly with its banking customers by phone, since this came out poorer in the survey.

In the US, there is also a growing trend of 'supermarket banking', however, of a slightly different nature. Whereas in the UK supermarkets have established their own banking operations, in the US the supermarkets merely provide the distribution for existing banks through their in-store floor space.

Indeed, for some time, several large US banks have been closing traditional large free-standing retail branches in favour of smaller outlets inside large retail stores. It is estimated that there are around 4,000 in-store bank branches in the US, all of which pay rent to their host supermarkets.

The arrangement can be profitable for banks because it allows them to reduce staff (in-store branches are usually much more lightly staffed than a normal branch) and property rental costs, while at the same time increasing convenience to the customer. It also enables the bank to improve service to the customer through the provision of cheaper loans facilitated by the bank's lower overheads.

First Market Bank, a subsidiary of National Commerce Bancorporation, a $4.5bn bank based in Memphis, Tennessee, has taken the concept of in-store banking a step further. The bank's deal with Ukrop's, a Virginian supermarket chain, marks the first time that a retailer has taken a direct stake in an in-store bank. The supermarket wanted an ownership stake in the venture so that it could share in the profits and capitalise on the recent wave of banking acquisitions in Virginia. This signals the first active involvement of a supermarket in retail banking in the US and may lead to supermarkets taking more of a lead in in-store banking as they have done in the UK. This could leave some US banks in a vulnerable position.

Ninety-five of National Commerce Bancorporation's 114 branches are now in supermarkets, mostly branches of Wal-Mart, the largest US retailer. The San Francisco-based bank, Wells Fargo, has 772 of its 1,899 branches in retail stores across 10 western states.

Source: Adapted from *Financial Times*, 8 and 14 October 1997

Questions:

1. Why do customers like banking at supermarkets?
2. What are the differences in distribution between the UK and US supermarket banks?
3. What advantages do supermarkets have over traditional banks as retail environments?

The number of branch closures has increased and it is likely that further reductions will take place. Greenland (1995) estimates further reductions of around 20 per cent in the next five-to-ten years. One of the primary benefits of branch closure is the capital which it releases. Yet, as the property market has declined, the benefits of branch sales have also been reduced.

The decision to close branches tends to be made on the basis of sales efficiency data, cost-to-income ratios and the relative percentage of accounts lost compared with those gained in a specific period. This activity, known as 'red-lining', has come under attack, since it can result in institutions pulling out of poorer and rural regions altogether. However, in such circumstances an unprofitable branch may be retained purely for reasons of public relations, although it may be downgraded to cut costs. Closing branches can have serious adverse effects on customers. It was noted in Chapter 2 that customers are becoming increasingly mobile and are more prone to switching. If a customer's branch is closed, or even downgraded, it is likely to contribute even more to customer switching. In a mature market lost customers will be lost to the competition. Even customers who are not directly affected by a branch closure may perceive a lack of stability in the institution and may even switch institutions as a result.

Branch relocations

One of the key requirements of branch location is that it provides convenient access for customers. The branch must be in a customer catchment area in order to sustain business and profitability levels. In addition, the location must provide premises at a reasonable cost and size to allow the business to function. As town centres have changed over the last couple of decades, banks and building societies have found that their high-street locations have not only become increasingly expensive but increasingly inconvenient for many customers who are shopping out-of-town.

As a result of this, there have been a number of relocations of existing branches to other sites, particularly in shopping centres and supermarkets (see Financial Services Marketing in Practice: 'When is a bank branch not a bank branch?'). Many of these are not strictly relocations. More frequently 'relocations' involve the closing down of a, typically full-scale, town-centre branch and the opening up of a reduced-service branch in the form of either a semi-automated or a fully automated outlet. These outlets mainly serve the cash accessibility need of customers while at the same time creating a presence for the institution in the new location.

One of the problems associated with this type of relocation is that empty premises are being left behind in the primary and secondary retail cores of many towns and cities. As town centre locations increase in expense, suitable buyers for these redundant bank branches become harder to find. Many of these branches are vast buildings, traditional in style and limited in terms of their range of application. A considerable number of branches have been transformed into restaurants. In London, former NatWest bank branches have provided homes for 'Bank', a fashionable restaurant, and Pizza Express. Large banking halls can seat a substantial number of customers, often more than 200 at any one time. The imposing fronts allow restaurateurs easily to stamp their individuality on the premises and their locations make them ideal for a night on the town.

Changes to the role and function of branches

As well as changes to the number and location of branches, the roles and functions of branches have also changed. Traditionally, bank branches were function-driven, transactional-processing, service outlets. One of the main roles was the safe-keeping of funds and the impressive architecture and forbidding ambiences of many branches projected images of reliability, security and stability. By contrast, building societies have generally been associated with a friendlier image and less stern environments. However, a series of complex developments, driven by the need to create more revenue and make more cost-effective use of facilities and operations, has resulted in the role and functions of branches changing.

Technology has enabled costs to be cut in branches and economies of scale to be gained by removing processing and telephone enquiry functions from the branches to a centralised processing and enquiry centre. This has resulted in a large proportion of staff being made redundant, thus providing further savings. The remaining staff and premises have been reoriented from primarily account-based activities to a more retail function. Banks and building societies alike have begun to view themselves as retailers and branches have become more like shops with all the mainstream retail concepts. Whereas the goals previously were to process accounts, they are now focused on attracting, selling to and serving the customer. Traditional branches and sites were not conducive to this activity and did not present the right kind of image or create an effective cross-selling environment. Thus, old branch designs have been replaced by more open-plan layouts that have large glass frontages and more of a retail appearance about them.

Retail branch environments

Branch environments are among the most complex of designed environments: they are multi-function facilities incorporating both selling and working activities, as well as providing an important vehicle for communication with customers. Traditional branch environments bear little resemblance to today's modern branches; they were divided into the front office, the back office and public space and were characterised by a low customer-area to staff-area ratio (see figure 5.4). Consequently during busy times customers often had to wait in a crowded banking hall.

In addition, traditional branches made extensive use of bandit screens which not only made communication difficult and reduced the amount of privacy, but also gave customers a view into the back office. Being able to see staff at work during busy times when queues are long, is not conducive to the creation of customer satisfaction. Furthermore, the design of traditional branch environments was operationally driven and dictated by local management which meant that designs were often influenced by management's own preferences and convenience with little thought given to the customer.

As a result of trends in the role and function of branches, traditional branch layouts are no longer appropriate for modern banking objectives. In order to remain competitive, branches needed to be reorganised and retail concepts have been adopted allowing the branch to maximise selling opportunities while at the same time minimising operational and maintenance costs. A number of changes to the traditional branch environment have been witnessed, many of which have been made with the concept of 'atmospherics' in mind.

'Atmospherics' refers to the careful and planned design of environments in order to create a specific behaviour from those who experience the environment. According to Kotler (1973), an atmosphere or environment is experienced through four of the five main sensory channels: visual, aural, olfactory and tactile. The physical environment created in a retail setting (in a bank branch or retail store) can have a strong psychological impact on customers, often occurring below the level of consciousness (Mehrabian and Russell, 1974). Emotional reactions can be triggered which directly influence the following shopping behaviour:

- shopping in the outlet with enjoyment;
- spending time browsing and exploring the outlet's offerings;
- spending time engaging in conversation with sales personnel;
- spending more money;
- returning to the outlet.

Both the exterior and the interior of a branch can have an impact on its perceived atmosphere. Exterior characteristics of a branch include the general external appearance, windows and window displays, signs and entrances. Interior characteristics include lighting, wall and floor coverings, fixtures and fittings, layout and displays. Table 5.2 highlights some of the changes to the retail branch design.

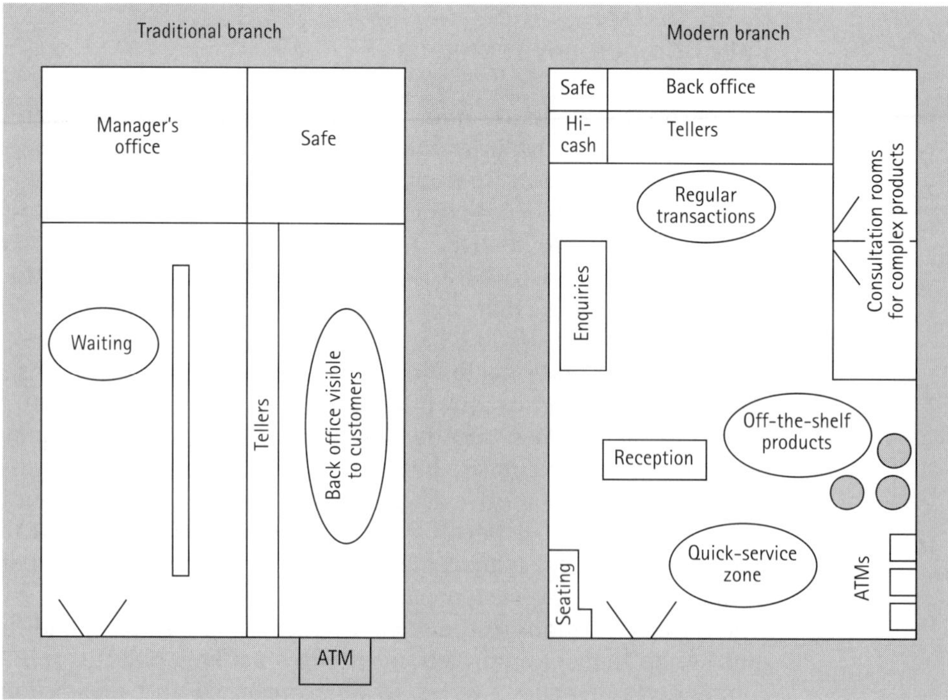

Fig. 5.4 Traditional versus modern retail bank branch layouts
(*Source*: Adapted from Howcroft, 1991 and Greenland 1994)

Table 5.2 A comparison of traditional and modern bank branch environments

Traditional branches	Modern branches
• Low customer area to staff-area ratio	• High-customer area to staff-area ratio
• Extensive use of bandit screens	• Fewer intrusive security measures
• Lack of privacy	• More private interview areas
• Primarily banking concepts	• Adoption of retail concepts such as merchandising
• Foreboding environment, customers not encouraged to stay	• Customers encouraged to spend more time in the branch and browse
• Long queues and waiting time	• Better control of movement of customers

Increase in customer-to-staff space ratio

Changes to the space within the branch have included the reallocation of space in favour of customers. Traditional branches had up to 90 per cent of their space devoted to staff and operations (Greenland, 1994). Now that many of the routine operations have been centralised, the space which they occupied in the branch can be used for other purposes. Thus, the change in space allocation has enabled customers to be drawn into the branches. The allocation of a greater amount of space to customers within the branch is likely to have a positive effect on customer-to-customer relationships. It has been identified that customers influence the enjoyment and experience of other customers in the service setting. Increasing the amount of space to customers increases the comfort factor as banking halls are less likely to become as crowded as they previously did.

Redesign of customer space

As well as increasing the amount of space allocated to customers, the customer area within the branch has also been redesigned. While the appearance of the banking hall would seem to be open-plan and free-form, it does in fact carefully control the flow and movement of customers in a similar way that a retail store would, encouraging customers to move past product displays (see figure 5.4). The banking hall has been separated into a reception area and personal banking areas. Speed is controlled by zoning which involves designating floor space to certain areas of business such as high-speed areas for cash withdrawals, off-the-shelf products such as loans and current accounts, and more complex products such as mortgages and pensions which require a slower approach offering privacy. Areas can be categorised as either 'hard' or 'soft' zones.

Hard zones are the high-speed areas which deal with transactions such as cash withdrawals, cash deposits, balance enquiries and statements. These transactions require speed in order to provide satisfaction to customers. The facilities are often placed just inside the door of the branch to allow customers to get in and out quickly and movement through these areas is often controlled by directional traffic flow methods using harsh strip lighting and guiding arrows. The fully automated self-service points situated at the entrance to the banking hall have enabled the speed and efficiency of such transactions to be improved.

In contrast, the soft zones of the branch use soft lighting and plush furnishings to slow down the pace of customers and encourage them to browse. Off-the-shelf products such as credit cards, current accounts and loan applications are provided in a separate area of the branch incorporating face-to-face contact. In this area there is a greater use of merchandising in the form of product displays and specialists are on hand to deal with specific enquiries. The more complex products such as mortgages and pensions are provided in a private part of the branch and offer a more personal approach.

Security and bandit screens

In addition, there has been the selective removal of bandit screens. These have been removed to improve service to the customer. It is difficult to carry out a discussion, particularly of a confidential nature, through a glazed security screen, and almost impossible to develop the discussion into a sales interview. While the modern open-plan layouts enable much more efficient use of sales techniques, security was a major concern during the refurbishments. Security is necessary for the protection of staff and customers but needs to be as unobtrusive as possible in order to allow staff to carry out their jobs. Thus, the issue of branch security raises a number of conflicts. As illustrated by the use of bandit screens, heavy security gets in the way of good customer service and prevents the creation of a relaxing and welcoming environment. It has been suggested (Hughes, 1994) that high levels of physical security can even stimulate more violent attacks on the branch, its staff and customers.

Security measures can be either passive or active. Passive devices include static bandit screens, time-delay safes, reinforced doors, windows and counters, and continuous videoing. Active devices include alarms, sirens, rising screens and auto-locking tills. In addition, measures can also be taken to prevent an attack from occurring by removing cash from the tills.

In order to overcome some of the conflicts, contemporary branches separate cash-withdrawal tills according to the amounts being withdrawn. Amounts that are typically less than £350 can be withdrawn from open tills without bandit screens, whereas larger amounts can be withdrawn from a screen-protected area. Video cameras monitor the cash tills and the higher amount cash tills tend to be located well within the branch, making a quick get-away more difficult for aspiring bank-robbers.

Centralised design control

The design of branches has moved towards more central control, having previously been regionally or locally controlled. Decentralised branch design had its disadvantages, since redesigns were often carried out on an *ad hoc* basis, often with little attention to the total corporate image and with local or bank manager preferences in mind. The central development and co-ordination of design strategies has obvious advantages for the development of a coherent corporate image. Due to the sheer size of networks, traditionally refurbishments were often embarked on by a piecemeal approach. Refurbishments are now planned with priority cases being identified initially, with the remaining branches organised on a roll-out basis. In addition, there is greater use of skilled marketing research in the selection of branch designs and the assessment of their impact on customers.

Despite the changes which have been made to branches, the question remains as to whether these reconfigurations can really be conducive to both the process of selling complex financial products, which tend to be expensive and purchased rather infrequently, and making low-value, regular transactions. The question, which a number of financial institutions seem to have failed to ask, is: do customers visit their branch to buy products or to conduct transactions? Indeed, do they want to do both at the same time, or do they view them as distinct experiences to be dealt with separately? In addition, how do purchases made during a short lunch break compare with weekend shopping for major purchases? The supermarkets seem to think that they are ahead of the traditional banks and building societies in terms of creating a more conducive 'shopping' environment (see, above, Financial Services Marketing in Practice: 'When is a bank branch not a bank branch?')

Branch personnel

Alongside the physical changes to the branch, branch personnel have also been forced to adapt. Bankers have metamorphosed into retail salespeople and have been required to adopt all the skills of selling. For many years now mainstream retailers have recognised the importance of selling skills and customer service in adding value to their existing offering. Financial institutions have come round to this way of thinking, although early attempts to adopt retail sales concepts left much to be desired. For example, Wilson (1994) notes that in the late 1980s many of the banks and building societies trained all branch staff to sell and a sales approach was adopted with nearly all customers who came into the branch. This resulted in the same customers being approached again and again, leading to frustration for both customers and staff.

Since this time, banks and building societies have attempted to alter their selling cultures to take account of a stronger emphasis on customer care and quality of service and almost all the main banks and building societies have undertaken some form of customer service training programme for branch staff. There is now the recognition that all employees in the bank have some influence on the sale of products and must, therefore, become more market-oriented. This is particularly true of employees who have direct contact with customers: they provide the link between the company and the marketplace and they sell and/or perform the service. To the customer they represent the financial institution and are seen as part of the product itself. Indeed, the quality of the service provided is inseparable from the quality of the service provider. Furthermore, they are ideally situated to take advantage of cross-selling opportunities.

Developing a sales culture has meant that financial institutions embrace the concept of customer loyalty, and that they are committed to building and maintaining customer relationships. The selling relationship should be defined as the attraction, maintenance and enhancement of customer relationships (Stephenson and Kiely, 1991). This is in stark contrast with earlier indiscriminate selling efforts which only focused on the attraction of customers. Tellers are now trained to identify sales leads and to transfer the lead across to a financial adviser. Thus, rather than taking a hard sales approach, the teller's role is to develop a relationship with customers in order to apply some soft selling techniques. The personal financial adviser is concerned with the more complex and time-consuming sales process. Hence, activities are categorised into transaction handling, lead generation, order taking (around simpler products) and specialist selling. All activities, except specialist selling, are performed by tellers. In contrast to the separation of cashiers and salespeople, which often meant that there was little co-operation between the groups as their roles were perceived as being totally separate, there is now much more of an emphasis on team effort.

While such sales training can increase cross-selling by 20 to 25 per cent, having a dramatic effect on new accounts and deposits (Parker *et al.*, 1993), it is really only effective where there is a quality contact situation with the customer, for example, when the customer approaches the counter or seeks advice from branch managers and specialists. Basic over-the-counter transactions, in which the customer requires a quick and efficient service, do not lend themselves to cross-selling opportunities.

Despite the benefits of sales training for branch personnel, there was initially some opposition. Some of these points were:

- bankers are professionals and true professionals do not sell;
- selling is a very visible activity with measurable results;
- many feared the concrete measurement that the results of selling activities might entail;
- selling is a dirty word and has a bad reputation.

Recognising the difficulty of achieving a good level of sales training, Wells Fargo, in the US, hires professional salespeople with several years' sales experience and then trains them up in the banking industry, suggesting that sales experience is harder to acquire than knowledge of the industry. These types of salespeople have been shown to outperform their traditional bank counterparts in terms of sales and earnings. The end result of sales training is more knowledgeable people who are more highly motivated, with a greater sense of team membership, contributing to an increase in customer satisfaction.

Network hierarchy

In addition to the changes which have taken place at the micro (branch) level, changes have also occurred at the macro (network) level. In the past, traditional institutions tended to offer more of a standard level of service across all the branches in the network. However, a standardised level of service is not always cost-effective or even necessary; customers in some areas do not demand the full range of services. Centralisation of routine processing has enabled certain branches to be downgraded, especially in urban or suburban areas where there are a number of other branches in the vicinity. In contrast to the past, institutions now differentiate the levels of service offered at different branches. If a customer requests a service which is not offered at that particular branch, they are simply referred to the nearest branch which does offer it.

As a result of this, branch networks now display more of a hierarchical arrangement than they previously did. Figure 5.5 illustrates the network hierarchy. Each level of the hierarchy offers a different level of service. At the same time 'hub and spoke' arrangements have evolved which deal with the spatial arrangement of branches in the network hierarchy. In any given area there will be a 'hub' branch providing the full level of services and support functions and a number of smaller surrounding 'spoke' or satellite branches offering a limited range of services, mostly the mainstream and regular services such as money transmission, current accounts, savings and personal loans.

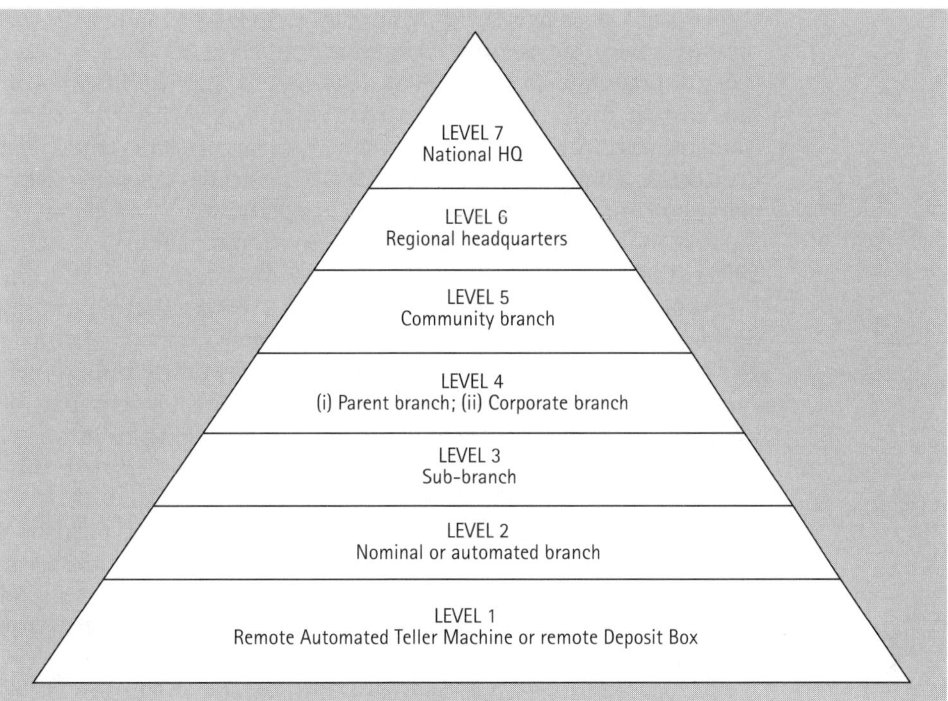

Fig. 5.5 Network hierarchy
(*Source*: Adapted from Greenland, 1994, 1995)

At the bottom of the hierarchy are the remote ATMs or deposit boxes. These serve the basic needs of cash accessibility and cash deposition. These services are often detached from the branch but are serviced by a local parent or community branch. The next level is the nominal or automated branch. This is predominantly a 'remote' or self-service outlet providing the basic services of cash accessibility as well as telephone links with community branches. Nominal or automated branches may be either manned or unmanned. If they are manned, there will only be one or two sales staff available, mostly to deal with enquiries and to refer customers to full-service outlets if necessary.

Remote deposit boxes and nominal or automated branches form only a small part of branch networks at present but are likely to form a larger part in the future. Greenland (1995) notes that the Co-operative Bank has developed the 'bank-point' kiosk concept. It is a portable hexagonal unit constructed of steel and glass weighing six tonnes and occupying a floor area of 120 sq ft. It is a totally remote facility, unstaffed and fully automated, offering ATMs, change machines, telephone interviewing links and interactive video-screen interviewing. Since it is portable, it can easily be installed in new locations or, indeed, moved from site to site to meet changing customer demand. This is likely to enable the Co-operative Bank to adapt its network quickly and at relatively low cost.

The third level is the sub-branch which is typically a small outlet offering ATM, manned cash counter, perhaps an interview facility, but a limited service-offering possibly operating within restricted opening hours. There is frequently no managerial presence in these branches, although they are visited by a sales adviser on a regular basis, thus necessitating appointments to be made with customers to receive product advice and information. Some concerns have been raised regarding these types of branches (Devlin, 1995). It is argued that the range of services may be so limited that there is the danger that customers will not visit them either in sufficient numbers or at regular enough intervals in order that relationships can be developed. Some banks have reportedly encountered some resistance to junior staff being left in charge of smaller branches as they do not inspire confidence in customers. In fact, some banks are having to put managers back into them which defeats the purpose of the rationalisation.

Level four consists of the parent branch, a retail outlet typically situated in a town or suburban location, offering a more complete range of personal banking services. The corporate branch is similar but caters to corporate, and not personal, customers; thus it differs in that there are no tills or retail area. By comparison, these branches frequently comprise management suites and parking facilities for customers, particularly those branches which operate from out-of-town business-park developments which occupy more space and have lower rents.

The next level is the community branch which is typical of a financial supermarket offering a banking hall divided into the specific product areas, a full service range including personal and business services, teleservice support for the lower-level branches and frequently processing and administrative assistance too. These branches tend to be situated in expensive city centre locations.

Level six comprises the regional headquarters which provide the administration and control centres for the regional networks and may also have a branch attached to them, depending on the location. At the top of the network hierarchy are the national headquarters which are the administrative and management centres responsible for determining and implementing the national network policy via the regional headquarters.

The extent to which this hierarchy is used differs from institution to institution. Each has its own policy for offering levels of service.

Direct sales force

During the 1980s there was a growth in the number of direct sales forces. This was partly as a result of increased competition and the increase in the number and complexity of products on the market. It was also affected by the polarisation brought about by the Financial Services Act which initially caused financial institutions to opt for tied status, thus reducing the number of independent intermediaries as the costs of compliance increased.

In the insurance industry, there is now a trend away from face-to-face selling by companies' own advisers. In the future, large-scale direct sales forces are expected to decline in numbers, particularly in the life and pensions business, where they will struggle to compete effectively against the bancassurers. Datamonitor predicted that up to 7,000 people in the life and pensions industry could lose their jobs by the turn of the century as direct sales forces are cut (*Financial Times*, 13 November 1997). Companies are paying the price for the pensions mis-selling scandal and for rising technology and compliance costs. Eagle Star Life, the life and pensions company, disbanded its direct sales force a couple of years ago to concentrate on telephone selling and sales through independent financial advisers (IFAs). It had one of the smallest direct sales forces in the industry and came to the conclusion that there was no strategic future for such small sales teams. It claims it can give customers who know what they want better value for money over the phone, while customers with more complicated needs seem to prefer IFAs.

Role and function of a direct sales force

The direct sales force (DSF) occupies a boundary-spanning position between the customer and the financial institution. This unique position at the interface between the organisation and its market requires the DSF to be capable of fulfilling a number of different roles. This position may lead to role ambiguity and conflict: conflict may arise because the DSF is expected to act in the best interests of the customers and the employer. This may even be further exacerbated if the DSF is remunerated on a commission basis, since its own interests will also come into play. This role conflict may be heightened in financial services where the provider of financial products also has a fiduciary responsibility towards the customer, and the customer places a great deal of trust in the salesperson and credibility on the advice given.

The Financial Services Act attempted to control the quality of advice through the guidelines of 'best practice' and 'best advice'. Despite this, sales forces or company representatives (in the case of tied status) are not obliged to point out that a rival company has a superior product. Thus, the customer is only offered the 'best' product from a limited range. The definition of 'best' is rather subjective. For example, Prudential, the UK's biggest insurance and pensions group, was ordered to re-test its entire direct sales force, some 5,500 people, after criticism over training and compliance procedures. The Securities and Investment Board accused Prudential of

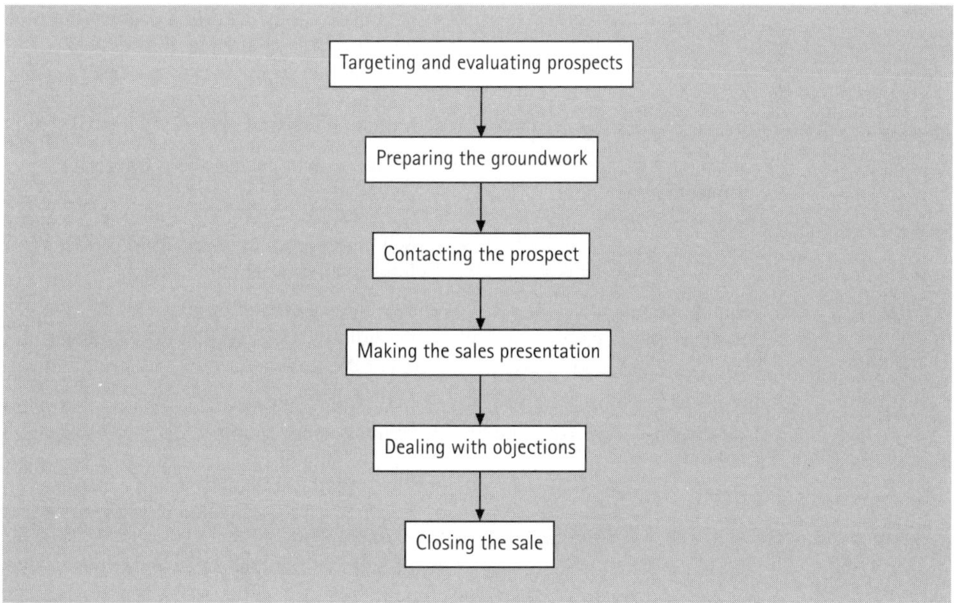

Fig. 5.6 The sales process

wrongly advising some of its non-taxpaying clients to buy one of its products when others would have been more suitable. The product in question apparently suffers from underlying taxation on the company's life fund.

The DSF roles include selling the product, becoming a problem-solver in many situations, building and servicing the continuing relationship and cross-selling other products. In order to do this, Howcroft and Kiely (1995) maintain that the sales force must possess certain characteristics and be able to:

- elicit information, listen and express technical information in layman's terms;
- control situations, take charge and instil confidence;
- display a good understanding of the full product range on offer;
- have an awareness of administrative procedures and policies and be able to manage their own time effectively.

In addition, the sales force needs to be aware of the stages involved in the sales process (see figure 5.6) in order that the prospective customer can be turned into an actual client.

Table 5.3 Sales force remuneration methods

Remuneration method	Characteristics
Commission only	• Pay is determined by what is sold • All sales are rewarded equally • Unlimited income to successful salespeople • Salespeople have little financial security • Less predictable selling costs • Allows sale of certain items to be encouraged • Many are self-employed, which can make commitment difficult to achieve • Money is not always a sufficient motivator
Quota-based systems	• Salespeople must aim for an agreed target • Flexible, offering a range of incentives • Emphasis on products can be altered by commission and rewards system • Motivating reward system, leading to high performance
Small basic salary with high commission potential	• Provides small degree of basic security • Limits company's fixed costs • Successful salespeople can increase income dramatically • Selling expenses are difficult to predict • May be difficult to administer
High basic salary with low commission or bonus	• Provides security of income • Requires careful selection of salespeople • If commission is too low, it may not motivate salespeople sufficiently
Salary only	• Provides security of income to salespeople • Easy to administer • Yields more predictable selling expenses • Requires careful selection of salespeople and monitoring of performance • As sales decline, selling expenses remain the same

(*Source*: Adapted from Howcroft and Kiely, 1995)

Sales force remuneration

The method used to compensate the sales force needs to be able to attract, motivate and retain salespeople. Methods include straight commission, straight salary or some combination of the two. Table 5.3 outlines the various methods used in the financial services sector, and their characteristics.

A straight salary is particularly useful when compensating new salespeople, or when the firm moves into a new sales territory. In both cases developmental work is often required and the straight salary reduces the initial pressure on the salesperson. A straight salary is also appropriate when salespeople need to perform a number of non-selling activities, such as extensive form-filling and computer work, which essentially reduce the 'selling' time available.

By contrast, a straight commission is useful when aggressive selling is required and when non-selling tasks are minimised. Although the commission-only method offers a highly cost-effective means of rewarding salespeople, it can result in a high staff turnover. This can happen because companies employing the commission-only method tend to be less selective with regards to whom they employ, and working on a commission-only basis puts salespeople under considerable strain. In this case, the financial reward can actually serve as a demotivator. Financial compensation is important but employers should also be aware that motivation of the sales force also requires satisfying non-financial needs. This may involve attention to the organisational environment (such as working conditions and job security), training and career progression (such as power and authority).

During the 1980s, commission-based selling was prominent in the financial services sector; it was blamed for the use of hard sales tactics and the reports of mis-selling. According to Shelton (1995), commission-based selling resulted in the following set of behaviours:

- product-driven advice
- pressure on the salesperson to sell
- pressure on the customer to buy
- the sale of inappropriate products
- over-concentration on new business and less interest in customer servicing and repeat business
- a dreadful reputation for many companies, life and pensions salesmen and the industry overall

Shelton (1995) also notes that customers in such situations feel:

- pressurised
- suspicious
- disadvantaged
- inadequate
- not in control
- uncertain
- confused

Recently, there seems to have been a shift away from commission-only remuneration of the sales force. The hard sales-driven approach is no longer appropriate for the sales culture of the new millennium which emphasises customer care and loyalty. Chapter 8 provides more details on the sales force in relation to communicative benefits of personal selling.

Independent financial advisers (IFAs)

In contrast to tied agents or direct sales forces, which have a duty to recommend to customers the most suitable product from their company's range, IFAs provide advice and information on a range of financial products from a variety of financial service providers. While company representatives are not required to point out that a rival company has a superior product, IFAs should point out the differences in various companies' products and should recommend the product which best suits the requirements of the customer.

There are currently around 25,000 IFAs in the UK regulated by the Personal Investment Authority (PIA) (*Financial Times*, 5 August 1997), most of whom work on a commission basis; commissions are paid by the firms whose products the IFAs sell. Only a minority of IFAs work on a fee basis, charging the customer an hourly rate. Since January 1996, the costs associated with the distribution of financial products via intermediaries have become more transparent to customers since they have had to disclose how much commission they receive for the sale of various products.

Anticipating that the disclosure of commissions and charges would cause customers to become more price-sensitive, a number of insurance and investment companies sought to adopt direct distribution methods, enabling them to bypass intermediaries and commission expenses. The Britannia Building Society stopped taking new business via IFAs at the end of 1997 to concentrate entirely on selling its life and pensions products through its own branch network. The decision was taken as a result of intense price competition; prices are falling faster than costs, making it difficult for small companies to compete against larger ones which can use their size and deep pockets to stay afloat. The Society hopes to generate better returns by focusing on its branch networks as the main distribution channel.

Despite this initial worry, IFAs have grown in popularity as a distribution channel. While direct sales forces still dominate in the distribution of life and pensions products, the amount of business channelled through IFAs has increased: their share of retail sales of life assurance, pensions and investment has grown to around half of the total from a third five years ago (see Financial Services Marketing in Practice: 'Pandas give financial services industry a black eye'). A number of factors have contributed to the strength and appeal of IFAs:

- customers are shopping around more;
- customers want to know exactly what is being provided and at what cost;
- customers desire to buy only parts of products (unbundling);
- customers need to feel that the product and its price give value for money compared with competitor products.

In theory, IFAs provide greater choice, convenience and value for money by allowing the customer to select from a complete range of financial services. Furthermore, IFAs offer the promise of impartial and independent advice. A key role of IFAs is that they are expected to operate within the bounds of 'best practice', as stipulated by the FSAct, and to offer 'best advice'. In terms of best practice, the IFA should examine the customer's specific financial circumstances and requirements before making a recommendation. Offering best advice means checking out what is available across the marketplace in order to find those products which best suit a particular customer's needs. At the same time advisers should also make sure that customers understand the nature of the investment and the associated risks.

FINANCIAL SERVICES MARKETING IN PRACTICE **FT**

'Pandas' give financial services industry a black eye: Instead of heading for extinction, independent financial advisers are emerging as the main players in the market

Independent financial advisers are the pandas that bit back. An industry pundit once forecast that IFAs, who are often self-employed, would become as rare as those endangered creatures. Instead they have emerged as the main people through whom financial services companies distribute many of their products to the public.

IFAs' core business is advising clients on life assurance and pension investment. Insurers pay them commission in return for selling their products, but this is not supposed to compromise the intermediaries' objectivity.

Tightening regulation and competition from sales teams employed by financial services companies were expected to drive the majority of IFAs out of business.

Instead they have increased their market share. Recent figures from the Association of British Insurers show that they sold 42 per cent of life and pensions policies designed to take yearly premium payments in the first half of 1997, 5 percentage points more than in 1996.

Insurance company salespeople still dominant this £1.2bn-a-year market worth around 66 per cent of sales. Many IFAs have won a clear lead in the much more important market for policies bought with one-off payments, worth £17bn a year. They now sell 60 per cent of the policies by value, against 50 per cent in 1993. Sales by company agents have fallen from 48 per cent to 39 per cent over the same period.

Meanwhile gross sales of unit trusts by IFAs hit a peak of £7.1bn in the year to July 1997, according to the Association of Unit Trusts and Investment Funds. This was 40 per cent more than unit trust managers' agents.

The influence of IFAs has become so strong in the unit trust business that AUTIF is changing its categorisation of funds so that it more closely matches that for the life and pensions investments familiar to the intermediaries.

Meanwhile, financial services businesses with a strong commitment to selling directly are hedging their bets by trying to boost distribution through IFAs. Barclays earlier this week announced the establishment of a new business group to promote a simplified range of unit trusts to them.

IFAs have prospered by cultivating wealthier customers who have been attracted by the IFAs' freedom to shop around on their behalf. Because these customers spend large amounts on investments, IFAs need to make only a few sales to generate healthy commissions.

Salesmen employed directly by financial services companies have typically been stuck with lower-income clients. Their smaller investments generate correspondingly less in commission and charges.

Successful IFAs' relatively high commission income allows them to take less of it in percentage terms on each sale than some salespeople. It also finances the high fixed costs of running their own businesses.

The survival of IFAs is a rare example of small entrepreneurs triumphing over big business. Some IFAs have hundreds of staff and are simply subsidiaries of large financial concerns – the Woolwich for example plans to double staff at its IFA wing to 200 by the end of the next year.

But the majority of the 25,000 practitioners licensed by the Personal Investment Authority, the retail investment watchdog, work in partnership with two or three colleagues, or as one-man bands. They rely on personal recommendations to build up client bases of around 200 customers each. Only 35 per cent have retail premises, the rest operate from anonymous offices over shops or from home.

Garry Heath, chairman of the IFA Association, estimates an IFA with a client base of wealthy Londoners can earn up to £500,000 in commission annually, after expenses. But £25,000 to £35,000 a year is more common, he says.

Many IFAs were formerly sales staff for big insurance companies. They leave, taking their experience, training, and often clients, with them because according to Mr Heath 'they want to run their own businesses, which will develop their own saleable value in time'.

FINANCIAL SERVICES MARKETING IN PRACTICE FT

Source: Jonathon Guthrie, *Financial Times*, 1997.

Questions:

1 Why have IFAs become popular?

2 How 'independent' is the advice received from Independent Financial Advisers?

3 What advantages/disadvantages do IFAs have over the direct sales force?

Since most IFAs' incomes depend on their ability to sell, it has been argued that they are not strictly independent. According to Tony Holland, the ombudsman who fields complaints against members of the PIA, 'independent' means free from the influence or control of others ... not relying on the support, especially financial support, of others' (*Financial Times*, 27 September 1997). The fact that most IFAs work on commission undermines their claims to independence. Since IFAs need to sell in order to survive, they should perhaps be called salespeople and not advisers. The term 'adviser' should perhaps be reserved for those who charge customers a fee for the advice they provide. It is also noted that companies or products which do not pay commission, such as National Savings, are seldom recommended.

The issue here is that few people who buy financial products are experts. Indeed, many people are looking for someone to advise them how best to invest their inheritance or save for their retirement. Most customers would, not surprisingly, assume that advice obtained from an independent financial adviser is guaranteed to be unbiased. Under the present PIA rules, however, the term 'adviser' has a rather limited meaning. It is used purely to distinguish salespeople who sell products from a number of companies from those selling only the products of a single company, such as tied agents or direct sales forces. The word 'independent' is a legacy from an earlier set of rules but has been adopted by the advisers. Admittedly, the term 'commission-based financial salesperson' would not be so appealing to customers as independent financial adviser.

In response to criticisms surrounding the conduct of financial advisers, all advisers must now possess a 'benchmark' or basic qualification of competence. Virtually no adviser is exempt from the requirement: all 100,000-plus people authorised to give advice on investments, including IFAs, direct sales forces, professionals such as bankers, solicitors and accountants, must pass a test if they want to sell investments. The most common test is the Financial Planning Certificate (FPC) examined by the Chartered Insurance Institute (CII). The Securities Institute also runs a benchmark exam for IFAs (the Investment Advice Certificate), and accountants and bankers also have their own (for example, the Chartered Institute of Bankers' qualification is the Certificate for Financial Advisers (CeFA)). Anyone who does not pass the FPC, or an equivalent, is not permitted to give advice unsupervised. This has been the case since 1 July 1997 for all firms regulated by the PIA, and 1 October 1997 for firms (including the Prudential) regulated by the Securities and Investment Board (SIB), the City's chief watchdog (now the FSA).

The question is whether the tests will be able to raise standards of advice and help prevent future scandals like the £2.5bn pensions mis-selling debacle. While there is general support for a competence test, some advisers believe that the standard set by the FPC is too low, and the qualification is very broad-based. If customers want an adviser with a higher level of competence they can look for someone who has passed the Advanced Financial Planning Certificate (AFPC). The AFPC is the next

Table 5.4 How to find a competent financial adviser

DOs	DON'Ts
✓ Check for experience and records of funds managed by the adviser	✗ Assume that someone is competent just because they are qualified
✓ Ask which exams the adviser has passed to check for professional qualifications	✗ Assume that the adviser is competent because s/he belongs to a number of professional bodies.
✓ Check for area of specialism	✗ Assume that all advisers are 'jacks-of-all-trades'. While 91 per cent of IFAs regulated by the PIA are authorised to sell, for example, unit trusts some firms have a greater expertise in this area.

(*Source*: Adapted from *Financial Times*, 19 April 1997)

stage up from the FPC and includes a personal investment planning syllabus. The main drawback of this is that seeking only advisers who have passed the AFPC limits the choice: so far less than 3,000 advisers have passed the AFPC. Customers should also beware of advisers with many letters after their names – letters may just denote membership of an institute or association, and different bodies vary enormously in terms of their criteria for membership from examinations to the payment of annual subscriptions. Jean Eaglesham (*Financial Times*, 19 April 1997) outlines three simple guidelines for customers seeking a competent financial adviser (see table 5.4).

In the future, it is likely that the structure of the IFA sector will change. There will probably be a concentration of business in the hands of the large IFA networks as intense price competition forces the smaller IFAs out of the market.

SUMMARY

This chapter has outlined some of the key channels of distribution employed in the marketing of retail financial services. It began by categorising the differences between direct and indirect methods and noted that differences exist between types of financial institution, such as banks, building societies, insurance and investment companies, in terms of the type or mix of channels employed. The chapter then focused on three of the most used channels: branch networks, the direct sales force and independent financial advisers. The development of branch networks has been largely evolutionary and unplanned, resulting in vast, expensive branch networks. Competitive and cost pressures have resulted in several trends, culminating in a number of branch closures, relocations to better sites and a change in the roles and functions of branches. Banks and building societies have become more like mainstream retailers, focusing on the redesign of branch environments, the adoption of retail sales and merchandising concepts and training of branch staff into retail salespeople.

As bancassurance and the popularity of IFAs increases, a number of smaller life and pensions offices have reduced, or even disbanded, their direct sales forces. Managing a sales force involves attention to recruitment, training and remuneration methods. The commission-only method of remuneration, traditionally used, has been criticised for encouraging hard sales tactics, and some companies are beginning to realise the value of salary-based compensation. Contrary to early opinions, IFAs have grown in popularity and number. The appeal to customers is the independent and impartial advice offered, although the extent to which advice is truly independent has been questioned. 'Benchmark' qualifications hope to improve the standard of advice in the future.

While the distribution function has already changed quite dramatically over the last couple of decades, it is likely to continue to do so as financial institutions look towards distribution channels as a means of cutting costs and optimising efficiency.

DISCUSSION QUESTIONS

1. Compare and contrast direct versus indirect distribution of financial services. Can you think of specific cases where each method is more, or less, appropriate?
2. Critically evaluate the development of retail branch networks in the UK. What have been the key arbiters of change in this context?
3. To what extent has the refurbishment of traditional bank branches been conducive to the creation of financial services 'shopping' behaviour?
4. What advantages, if any, do you think supermarkets have over the traditional banks and building societies in terms of retail environments?
5. You have been asked to advise a large national retail bank on its branch location strategy. How might you use the concepts of the network hierarchy and 'hub and spoke' banking to make recommendations on the spatial arrangement of branches?
6. How would you ensure that a salesperson successfully guides a potential customer through all the stages of the sales process? Make specific recommendations for each stage of the process.
7. How might the remuneration of salespeople affect their behaviour towards the customer?
8. Account for the apparent popularity of IFAs in the particular distribution of pensions and life products.
9. Critically discuss the extent to which the advice provided by independent financial advisers really is independent and impartial.
10. To what extent do you think the 'benchmark' qualifications for IFAs will bring about an increase in standards of advice and prevent future mis-selling scandals?

6 Technology-driven delivery channels

INTRODUCTION

The previous chapter outlined and discussed traditional distribution or marketing channels used by financial institutions. While the bank and building society sectors traditionally have been distinguishable from the insurance and investment-management sectors by their channels of distribution, the advent of technology-driven delivery methods is bringing about a convergence of various forms of distribution of financial products and communication with customers.

Many of the traditional boundaries are being eroded as new technologies offering innovative forms of delivery enable new players to enter the market. Thus, financial institutions are being forced to spend heavily on technology in the new millennium, not just to reduce the costs associated with traditional distribution channels, but also to maintain a competitive edge in an increasingly competitive market. Indeed, a survey published by Price Waterhouse Management Consulting (*Financial Times*, 1 July 1997) revealed that almost two-thirds of UK financial institutions were planning to increase their IT spending, and that the overall level of IT spending in the sector had risen to nearly 17 per cent of average total costs, and almost 25 per cent among investment banks.

New direct operators, employing telephone technology and sophisticated call centres, are appearing almost daily. The impact of computer technology has rendered old geographic and other frontiers meaningless, as financial institutions move out of the high streets and into cyberspace. Brokerage firms offer on-line securities trading and access to real-time market data and sophisticated investment management tools. Currency and other commodity traders operate around-the-clock, passing the book from one office to the next in a continuous race around the globe.

This chapter reviews some of the main technological developments in terms of the delivery of financial services, incorporating: self-service technology such as automatic teller machines and telebanking; prepayment cards, including Smart cards; and, on-line banking in the form of home banking and internet banking.

OBJECTIVES

After reading this chapter you should be able to:

- assess the impact of technology on the delivery of financial services;
- examine various forms of self-service technology and their application to financial services;
- discuss the developments of smart-card-based prepayment cards;
- outline the developments in on-line banking;

OBJECTIVES

- comment on some of the issues surrounding the security of technology-based delivery systems;
- discuss the role of IT in creating enhanced customer service.

The impact of technology on the delivery of financial services

Advancements in technology have had a profound effect on the delivery of financial services over the last few decades, and the pace of change and level of impact is continually increasing. Technology was first used in the branches of banks and building societies as a means of reducing the cost of many routine processes, through centralisation and automation. Now it provides a cost-effective and competitive solution to the delivery of products and communication with customers. Figure 6.1 outlines some of the major applications of technology in the delivery of financial services, and the methods by which they are accessed.

Automatic teller machines (ATMs) have had an important role to play in terms of automating routine services, increasing customer convenience and accessibility to financial institutions and providing an innovative method of communicating new products and services. While investment in ATMs has been quite substantial in the past, evidence suggests that they will receive less attention in the future compared with other forms of delivery such as telephone and on-line banking (see figure 6.2). An explanation could be that ATMs do not allow a dialogue to be established with the customer and may therefore be less effective at building relationships with customers compared with other forms of delivery where person-to-person contact may be possible.

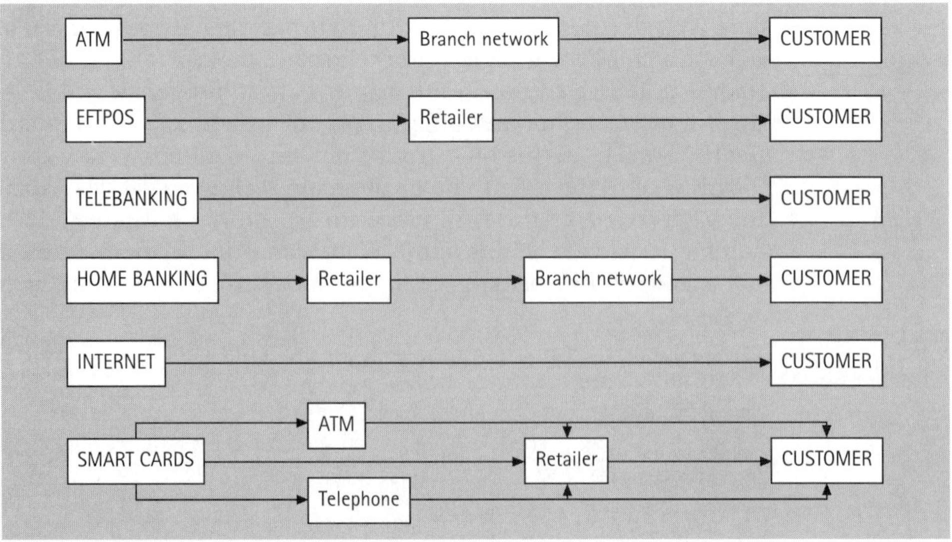

Fig. 6.1 Technology-driven delivery methods

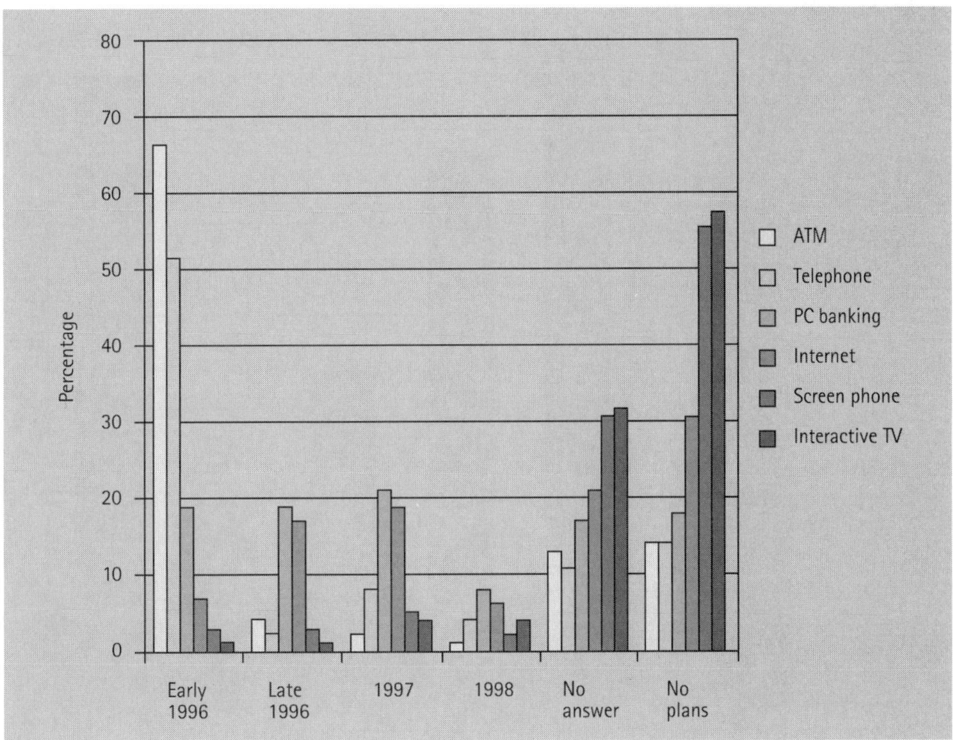

Fig. 6.2 Financial institutions' plans for investment in delivery systems
NB: Based on a sample of 659 respondents
(*Source*: Adapted from *Byte*, December 1996)

ATMs may be viewed as either a delivery channel or a product in their own right. They do exhibit qualities of both, and current pricing structures tend to reflect both these considerations. For example, access to account information is not normally charged, which reflects the delivery function of the terminals, yet some transactions performed via an ATM are chargeable, reflecting the product function of the ATM. ATMs provide cash accessibility from branch locations, retail or travel-centre locations or, increasingly, from remote sites.

Electronic funds transfer at point of sale (EFTPOS) is essentially a payment system, although it may be described as a delivery channel. It is worthy of mention because of the impact it has had on money transmission. Since the introduction of EFTPOS, retailers have been placed in a stronger position in terms of money transmission and, through the provision of 'cash-back' facilities have reduced the need for customers to visit either a branch or an ATM to withdraw cash from their accounts. It is perhaps this which has provided the logical step towards the provision of further financial services by retailers. EFTPOS is also worthy of mention because of the supporting role it will play in the wider use of smart cards.

Telebanking, conducting one's financial accounts over the telephone, has increased dramatically in popularity since the introduction of First Direct in 1989, reportedly winning 125,000 new customers in the UK every month. Datamonitor, a market research and management consultancy, forecast that telebanking could be serving 30 per cent of the population by the year 2000 (*Financial Times*, 29 March 1997). Consumers seem to be willing to conduct almost all transactions over the

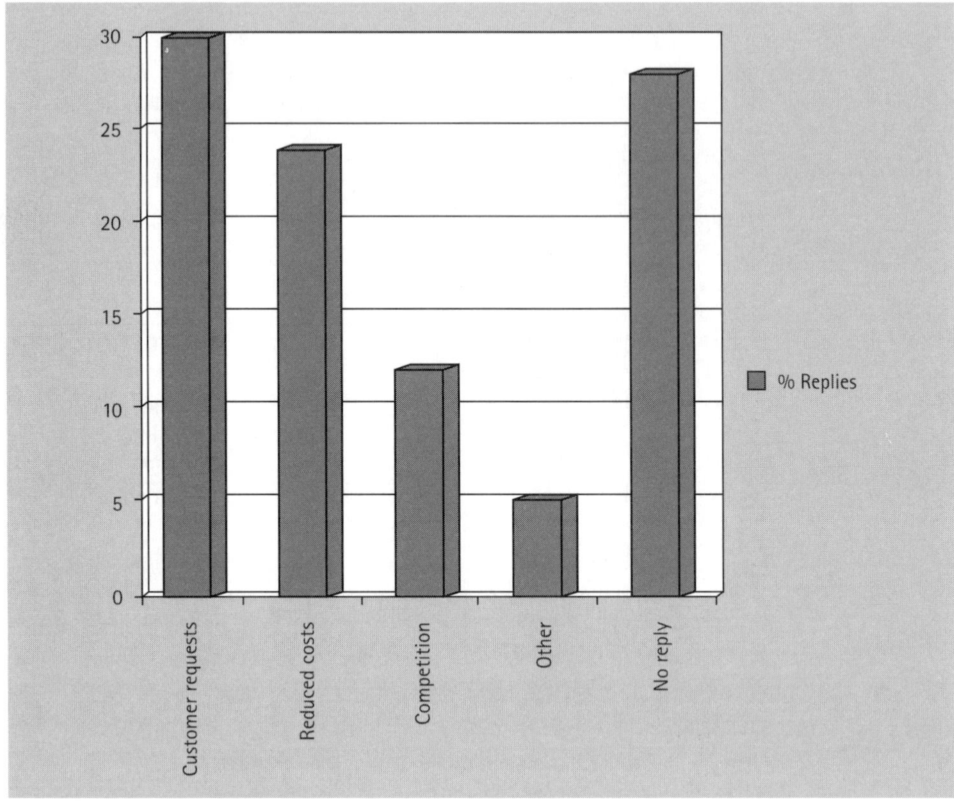

Fig. 6.3 Motivations for moving on-line
NB: Based on a sample of 659 respondents
(*Source*: Adapted from *Byte*, December 1996)

telephone. In fact, many are prepared to have conversations about almost anything on the phone. Thus, the level of interaction with the customer tends to be even higher than that achievable for branch banking, at considerably lower cost. The problem for the traditional banks and building societies is that telephone banking is creating the need for them to invest in new technology in order to compete with new rivals such as retailers and supermarkets, while at the same time leaving them with expensive branches. Some of the early telephone systems were directed via the branch network, but most telebanking operations are now conducted independently of the branch network from remote call centres.

On-line banking, consisting of home banking and internet banking, is also increasing in popularity. The speed of change has been quite dramatic over the last couple of years, and most of the financial institutions are developing home banking or internet banking services, or both. On the internet, a 'web-year' is now being defined as 35 days, reflecting the frenzy of on-line innovation. The motivations for moving on-line are primarily in response to customer requests (see figure 6.3), although the ability to be able to lower the cost of delivery is equally important.

Following substantial trials in the last few years, smart cards have recently made their way onto the UK market. These microchip-based cards have the potential to revolutionise payment methods and pave the way to a cashless society. Smart cards can be used between individuals to exchange electronic cash or can interface with ATMs, telephones and retailers to credit and debit value. It is likely that the future will see further integration of EFTPOS, smart card, telephone and on-line systems. The following sections of the chapter discuss each of these in more detail.

Automatic teller machines

Automatic teller machines (ATMs) were first introduced in the UK more than 25 years ago. Early machines were largely cash-dispensing terminals which were originally put in place to reduce queues in branches at peak times, cut down the amount of paperwork and cash handling and free up staff time in branches. Their introduction coincided with the onset of branch rationalisation programmes. Thus, they were viewed as a cheaper alternative to serving customers compared with expensive human tellers in branches.

ATMs were initially situated on an outside wall of the branch, providing increased convenience to customers out of restricted branch-opening times. Soon customers were taking advantage of the 24-hour access to cash provided by the terminals. Since this time, the nature and scope of functions performed by ATMs has expanded. From single-function cash-dispensing terminals have evolved a number of various multi-function terminals offering customers the choice of balance enquiries, mini-statements, cheque book ordering services as well as the possibility of accessing information on a range of other financial products. Indeed, as competition intensifies, the marketing potential of ATMs is also being exploited through the advertising messages which are screened and the announcements of new product offers. One of the problems associated with multi-function terminals is that they are more likely to malfunction and contribute to longer queues as a result of the number of services offered to customers. Because of this, financial institutions have introduced both simple single-function machines aimed at quick cash withdrawals and multi-function machines to serve a wider variety of needs.

Having initially forced their customers out onto the street in order to conduct their transactions, financial institutions soon began to realise that once the basic function of cash withdrawal was significantly reduced within branches, there was little incentive for the vast majority of customers to enter a branch any more. This had serious implications for the ability of branch staff to interact with customers face-to-face and to identify sales leads. Thus, branches have, for some time now, installed ATMs inside the branch in order to get customers back in and expose them to the variety of products and services available. Indeed, the modern semi-automated branches described in the previous chapter rely on a number of services being performed by ATMs within the branch environment.

Of the various types of ATMs, cash-dispensing terminals have attracted the most investment. A number of banks and building societies are focusing on these as the cornerstone of their self-service strategies. In contrast, deposit terminals have not made anywhere near as much impact on the market. There are perhaps two main reasons why this is so. First, people may feel less happy about depositing cash into a machine without immediate confirmation of what has been deposited. Second, while there may be less of a risk of cheques going astray, they are only really used on a wide scale in two main European countries: the UK and France. Similarly, while individuals seem to be happy to use self-service terminals for a number of routine transactions, such as cash withdrawals and balance enquiries, they appear to be more reluctant to make use of them for other more complicated services such as share purchases or obtaining financial advice.

One may argue that the number of ATMs in the UK has reached saturation. Despite this, studies show that investments are still being made. The reason for this is that different types of ATMs are being installed in different locations offering different services to cater to different requirements. While it may be argued that the banking community as a whole is more than adequately supplied with ATMs, individual banks are continuing to install them as part of a strategy of improving customer service, reducing costs and attracting new customers at the same time. Smaller financial institutions view ATMs as a means of compensating for their lack of a national branch network, and strategically invest in ATMs as a means of widening their delivery channels.

Because these terminals do not have to be located at or in branches, they can be, and are being, located in a number of remote locations, at supermarkets, train stations or unstaffed kiosks. They allow the financial institution to get closer to the customer by locating in an area where the institution does not have a presence. This overcomes the passivity of the traditional branch networks where the financial institution had to wait for the customer to make a visit. Now the institution can come to the customer. Shop-based ATMs, located at or in retail outlets or shopping centres, offer many interesting co-marketing opportunities for both the financial institution and the retailer. For example, they can be used for store-specific advertising, special promotions and coupon dispensing. Coupled with smart cards they can be matched to fit the purchasing patterns of individual consumers.

EFTPOS

There were several forces driving the introduction of electronic funds transfer at point of sale (EFTPOS). Consumers were demanding easier methods of payment, retailers wanted to reduce the amount of cash in the payment system, financial institutions wanted to reduce the amount of cheque-based payments and technology suppliers obviously wanted an outlet for their product.

When EFTPOS was first developed in the UK it was slow to take off. Now around two-thirds of the population use plastic payment cards. Around 80 million cards are in circulation, issued by over 20 different financial institutions and accepted in approximately 450,000 outlets.

In order for the cards to be used in retail outlets for payment of goods, retailers must be equipped with the correct terminals in order to read the cards. It took some time before a significant number of retailers were able to accept EFTPOS payment cards. It is estimated that under half the total retail outlets in the UK have EFTPOS equipment, those that do not are mostly smaller and independent retail outlets. Attempts were made initially to establish a national EFTPOS system involving all the major clearing banks and some of the larger building societies. Delays in the development of a national system gave way to the development of two main systems under the branding of Switch and Visa Delta.

The way in which EFTPOS developed, with the banks taking the lead, meant that they were obliged to take on the responsibility for a number of services required to run the system, including terminal supply and management, transaction processing, clearing and settlement. However, such activities as terminal supply, installation, training and maintenance are not core banking functions. While transaction processing and clearing are banking activities, they do not necessarily need to be performed by a bank. This led the way for independent sales organisations (ISOs) to offer some or all of the acquiring services on behalf of the banks which have established retailer relationships.

The recent growth in the use of debit cards has been fuelled by some retailers which pass the costs of credit cards on to the customer in the form of higher prices for credit card purchases. Debit cards are used free of charge and represent an instant cash transfer to the retailer's account. Reliance on EFTPOS is likely to increase in the future as smart cards become more commonplace.

Telebanking

People who enjoy conducting business over the telephone and prefer the telephone as a method of buying goods have been dubbed 'telephiles'. According to the Henley Centre for Forecasting, this includes half the population (*Financial Times*, 23 April 1998).

Girobank was the first to introduce banking services over the telephone almost two decades ago and Nottingham Building Society offered Britain's first subscription telephone banking service, Homelink, in 1983. Since this time, the majority of major banks, building societies and insurance companies have added the telephone to their delivery channels. Initially telephone services merely allowed the customer to ring the branch to make balance enquiries, order cheque books and ask for advice or information on products and services. Increasingly, however, telephone operations are being conducted from call centres which route calls away from busy branch staff. Some of the telephone services operate quite independently from the traditional branch network.

Midland Bank (HSBC) made the biggest and boldest step in 1989 with the launch of First Direct, the first ever stand-alone, telephone-only, 24-hour, 365-days-a-year bank with no branches. Admittedly, Midland did have an established branch network, which First Direct customers can make use of, but the operation was designed so that customers would be able to conduct all their financial transactions without having to visit the branch at all (see Financial Services Marketing in Practice: 'First Direct: the world's first direct bank').

The cost advantages of telephone banking are very attractive when compared with the costs associated with a branch network. The cost of servicing retail bank customers by telephone can be as little as 10 per cent of the cost of similar transactions via a branch teller (Baldock, 1997). Furthermore, for telephone services operated from call centres, there are the additional cost savings in terms of premises to be considered. Many centres are located in out-of-town or edge-of-town warehouse-style office accommodation which is plentiful and considerably cheaper than high street locations.

Telebanking systems can be operated via one of three main methods which differ in terms of the amount of technology involved:

FINANCIAL SERVICES MARKETING IN PRACTICE

First Direct: The world's first direct bank

First Direct, the world's first all telephone bank, offering 24-hour person-to-person service 365 days a year, commenced business on 1 October 1989. Since then over 750,000 customers have joined First Direct, over a third of whom have been through word-of-mouth.

The predictions from industry commentators were rather gloomy. There was a general belief that the conservative British consumer would not be willing to accept the innovative telephone-based channel. Yet, First Direct has proved all predictions wrong. Using the UK's 47 million telephones as a low-cost delivery channel, it now covers a customer base equivalent to some 200 branches, but with almost half the number of staff.

It was, and still is, successful because Midland did their homework before setting up the operation, and provided customers with what they wanted. The research showed that 51 per cent of customers would rather visit their branch as little as possible, and expressed a wish to conduct more transactions over the telephone. The service was also carefully targeted at ABC_1 individuals, whose time is limited and who are more accustomed to doing business over the telephone.

Through the use of IT, First Direct has been able to avoid the expense of maintaining an expensive branch network.

At the heart of First Direct is the call centre. Premises, with an operational floor the size of Wembley football pitch, were selected in Leeds to take advantage of attractive rates and labour costs compared with the south of England. Another plus was the local accent which was thought to be warm and friendly as well as easy to understand. Customers can call First Direct any time of day or night using a special lo-call number which charges the caller at the local rate no matter where they are in the country.

The cheque account has been designed to take all the hassle out of banking, with most customers being able to do all their banking in one three-minute call a month. Calls are answered by human operators, Banking Representatives, who are trained to deal with over three-quarters of customer enquiries. More specialist requirements are passed on to advisors who are available to deal with requests relating to their own specific area.

Each BR has a terminal which provides the complete history of the customer. Screen and telephone functions have been integrated to allow calls to be passed between BRs without the customer having to repeat the conversation, thus maintaining continuity and personalising the call.

The call centre is supported by a sophisticated customer information system embracing transactional information and behavioural data which enables the bank to predict which product the customer is likely to buy next. BRs use this information to create selling opportunities when the customer calls to make a routine request.

Sticking to person-to-person contact has allowed First Direct to maintain service quality. The bank leads the field in this respect with 87 per cent of customers reporting that they are very satisfied with the service provided by First Direct. The careful selection and training of staff has contributed much to this.

Personalities were crucial in the hiring of suitable people to become BRs. Many of the skills required were often found among the social professions – teachers, nurses, social workers – rather than traditional bankers. Consequently, banking skills took second place. Training is particularly intensive, requiring new recruits to successfully complete seven weeks of training before coming into contact with a customer. Only a small part of the customer interaction is scripted, at the beginning and end, allowing the BR to develop a more natural conversation with the customer.

First Direct has also been successful in adopting a more innovative style of management not traditionally associated with the banking profession. There is an open and approachable culture, with no executive offices, closed doors, hierarchies or pecking orders: everyone is on a first name basis and eats in the same cafeteria. In addition, BRs do not have their own desks, but employ a concept known as 'hot-desking' whereby stationery and personal belongings are transferred on mobile units to an available desk during the shift.

First Direct was set up as a division of Midland

FINANCIAL SERVICES MARKETING IN PRACTICE

(now HSBC). Anticipating that other institutions would be quick to develop their own telephone services, the bank did not want to delay the launch by waiting to obtain a separate banking charter. The surge in telephone operations in the last few years proves that Midland was right to act when it did.

Sources: Adapted from *Financial Times*, 4 October 1997, 8 November 1997 and 23 April 1998.

Questions:

1 What factors have contributed to the success of First Direct?

2 What value does the customer information system offer?

3 How different is First Direct from traditional banks, and what impact does this have on customer relationships?

Person-to-person

Person-to-person telephone operations were the first to be established. The customer has direct contact to the personnel at the financial institution to process transactions and deal with enquiries. In technological terms it is the least sophisticated of telephone delivery channels since it is merely a development of the *ad hoc* service which any customer enjoys from their financial institution. Yet, it does have several advantages. Perhaps the most useful feature of person-to-person contact is that it allows the call operator to pitch their communication to the level of the individual customer. The less financially adept can receive more time and more detailed explanations. However, for this to work, the representatives of the financial institution must be carefully selected and trained to be able to adapt their verbal skills to the requirements of different customers. In addition, since the range of requests from customers can be potentially limitless, the staff must be knowledgeable enough to be able to answer a wide variety of queries and requests. As a result of this, person-to-person operations are relatively expensive when compared with fully automated versions.

Early person-to-person systems operated within restricted hours, but did expand the banking hours offered through traditional branches. Most systems now operate 24 hours a day. This has been partly enabled by technology, although there has been no shortage of telephone operators willing to work through the night. Many routine calls, such as balance enquires, which do not need person-to-person contact, have been replaced by automated systems operated via push-button telephones. A smaller number of staff are available through the night to answer any other queries, although studies have shown that many people either telephone during the day from work or during the early part of the evening from home.

While the telephone initially offered the promise of reduced costs to the provider and increased convenience to the customer, it is now providing a means by which improved customer service can be delivered. One of the initial concerns surrounding telephone banking was that each time the customer telephoned they would not necessarily speak to the same telephone operator. In the traditional branch network, customers had the opportunity to visit the same teller each time they entered the bank, and establish a relationship. The teller would get to know the customer and the types of transactions routinely performed. With the telephone, the customer remains somewhat anonymous. However, many of the call centres employ sophisticated software which allows all call operators access to all customers' information. Some of the systems allow notes to be added about customers, so that the next time the customer rings, whoever they speak to will know exactly what the last communication was about. This allows a relationship to be developed with the customer (see Financial Services Marketing in Practice: 'Call centres: a vital role in customer service').

Tone/speech-based

Tone or speech-based telephone services are based on communication via tone generation and can be operated by one of two main telephone-based methods. The first of these operates via a push-button telephone or a tonepad and pulse/click phone. Essentially the customer dials the financial institution and is asked to respond by dialling the number on the telephone which corresponds with the service required. When the customer has completed their transaction, they will usually be asked if they require any other service. If the customer wishes to execute another transaction, the appropriate button is pressed, or the receiver is replaced if the customer has finished.

The second method is automated voice response. In this method communication occurs via speech or voice recognition followed by automated voice response. Rather than pushing a button on the telephone to select a service, the customer merely voices their request by speaking clearly and slowly into the telephone. The reply is given by a computer-generated voice response.

While both these services can be used easily for routine transactions, they do not lend themselves particularly to the open-ended discussion required for most complex advice-giving situations.

Screen-based

In screen-based systems communication occurs between the customer's computer, television or videotext system and the financial institution's computer system. The telephone merely provides the link between the financial institution's and the customer's technology. If the customer interacts via computer, they execute transactions via the keyboard. The computer must be linked to a modem in order for the connection to be made over the telephone line to the computer system at the financial institution. Alternatively, if communication occurs through a videotext system via the television, the customer may use a specially adapted remote-control panel to execute transactions. Although these systems rely to a certain extent on telephone technology, they are more commonly known as 'PC' or 'home-banking' devices. Due to the different skills and expertise required by the customer to interact with the financial institution in this way, these services tend to appeal to a specific target of the market compared with more mass-consumer use of mainstream telephone banking services. Further information on screen-based services is provided below, in the section on home banking.

The extent to which each of these telephone delivery methods is used by financial institutions varies. National Westminster bank offers all three of the above telebanking systems, each primarily treating different segments of the market:

FINANCIAL SERVICES MARKETING IN PRACTICE FT

Call centres : a vital role in customer service

In their bitter battle for market share, retail financial institutions have placed call centres firmly at the forefront of their strategies to improve customer service while reducing costs. The internet may one day become a mainstream banking channel, but until that day arrives, banks and insurance companies see the humble telephone as the most cost-effective way of expanding delivery channels, improving service and winning new customers. 'There is much interest in internet banking, but you should not forget that many more people have a phone than an internet connection', says Thierry Scellef, a Madrid-based consultant with Anglo-French IT, services company Sema. The firm has helped set up call centre services for the French direct banking service Banque Directe, part of the Paribas group, and several large Spanish banks including Banco Central Hispano and Caja de Madrid.

Spain's smaller banks are just as keen as their bigger sisters to set up phone banking operations. Sema has also developed services for Ceca, a confederation of 50 small savings banks and Cajas Rurales, which groups 79 rural banks. The aim is to allow these smaller participants to pool their call centre operations and so share the costs and overheads.

The price tag of a call centre can run to several million dollars but the savings in operational costs it produces can pay for the investment in just four months, according to a report by the UK-based consultancy firm, Ovum. In the worse case, the payback time is 19 months. 'However, the decision to build a call centre should never be a purely financial issue', says Mr David Bradshaw, senior consultant at Ovum, who sees customer service improvement as the most important reason for considering a call centre.

Indeed, many financial institutions, after initially turning to call centres to unload low-margin activities from their branch networks, such as balance consultations and funds transfers, are discovering that the telephone can be used to open up many new opportunities.

Halifax, the UK bank, set up a call centre in 1995 to service the current account customers of Halifax Direct, its new telephone banking division, as well as to generate new business for the company. The volume of business created by Halifax Direct in its first year far exceeded forecasts and calls rocketed from 42,000 in the first month to over half a million a year later.

To help its 400 agents answer the calls, the bank turned to a software product called CBR2 supplied by US firm Inference. CBR2 uses a technique called case-based reasoning to allow agents to follow a sophisticated 'script' when a customer calls. It is based on an expert systems engine which accumulates knowledge by analysing examples of questions and answers and stores that knowledge in the form of a 'case base'. CBR2 allows its 400 agents to answer calls in an average of 2.5 minutes, which the bank claims is up to 30 per cent faster than other systems.

This is important as direct banking operations usually have a freephone number and so the bank has to pay for the calls. Also, quicker handling allows the agents to handle more calls, so increasing productivity. CBR2 has become a principal component of the Halifax Direct call centre and has been used for nine different products or services, including an insurance emergency line and a tax advice service ... says Mr Phil Padfield, European vice president at Inference ... 'Most banks see call centres as simply a means of conducting a transaction, but customers can also have a relationship with a call centre.'

The latest generation of call centre products aim to achieve this 'relationship building' by, for example, allowing banks to automatically identify their most prized customers when they call and give them preferential treatment – routing them to a specific human operator, rather than the next available one or a computer voice. Less-prized customers will first be filtered through an interactive voice response unit that asks them questions which they answer using a touch tone telephone or by voice. Low-value operations, such as balance enquiries, can thus be routed to a computer. 'Banks want to be able to differentiate between different customers and do not want to use a human operator on low-value customers', says Mr Bob Summerfield, marketing manager for call centres with Tandem Computers.

FINANCIAL SERVICES MARKETING IN PRACTICE FT

Source: Geoff Nairn, *Financial Times*, 2 July 1997

Questions:

1 Why do people like banking on the phone?

2 How can a customer have a relationship with a call centre?

3 How does the call centre contribute to the delivery of customer service?

'Actionline' is a tone or speech-based system which caters for the majority of personal customers, 'Bankline' is a computer link system targeted at business customers, and 'Primeline' is a person-to-person system which is targeted at the professional market. From the point of view of some customers, particularly the professional segment aged 25–45 years, these systems are unlikely to be mutually exclusive. Many of these customers are likely to require elements of all systems. Thus, there may be a need for greater integration of the technology to allow for customers to choose the method by which they prefer to communicate with their financial institution depending on the transaction.

Accompanying the growth in direct telephone operations are increasing numbers of call centres which support the behind-the-scenes functions. While the only technology visible to and used by the customer is the telephone, call centres are increasingly high-tech operations. Staff, typically wearing headphones, sit at desks with a computer terminal in front of them. Automated call distribution (ACD) switching enables incoming calls to be sent out in orderly queues to waiting operators. If necessary, calls can be transferred to less busy centres in other cities or even continents. Computer telephony integration (CTI) allows customers' records to be called up on screen as their calls are answered.

Most estimates put current numbers of call-centre employees in the UK somewhere between 150,000 and 320,000. Datamonitor expected 2 per cent of the UK working population (some 480,000 people) to be employed in call centres by the year 2000. Across Europe the total could be more than 1.2m. These figures represent an annual growth in the UK of nearly 20 per cent, and even higher in continental Europe (*Financial Times*, 23 April 1998). Yet, it is the financial services sector which is making the most use of call centres in the UK, controlling 27 per cent of all workstations, followed by manufacturing, distribution and consumer products with 22 per cent. Other main areas account for 10 per cent or less of total workstations, and remote shopping controls just 6 per cent.

Having initially been established around the Midlands, the favourite location for call centres is currently Scotland, and Glasgow in particular. Labour costs and local-government support have, no doubt, contributed to this. The main reasons generally cited for choosing locations for call centres include:

- evidence of existing call centre success
- availability and quality of local labour force
- local business network
- financial incentives
- availability of premises
- local amenities (particularly for workforce)

- telecommunications expertise
- support from local/national development agency

(*Financial Times*, 23 April 1998).

Smart cards

Smart cards are a relatively recent innovation which offer a variety of possible applications including prepayment functions, advanced identification of cardholders, road-pricing schemes and retailer loyalty cards, as well as electronic cash. The card uses a microchip, instead of the magnetic stripe which is currently used in debit and credit cards and many other plastic cards on the market. There are several advantages which the microchip offers over the magnetic stripe:

- It enables increased amounts of data to be stored on the card – simple smart cards can hold 100 times the data held on normal magnetic-stripe cards.
- The microchip allows the data to be accessed and processed remotely as well as on-line – payment systems, such as debit and credit cards, currently in operation, require the cards to be verified from a central location via a network. Sometimes this can noticeably add to the waiting time in retail outlets at the check-out.
- The microchip is more secure than the magnetic stripe as the technology required to read data on a chip is beyond the reach of all but the most determined counterfeiters. Thus, the smart card has the potential to reduce fraud in payment systems.

However, the readers required to process the smart card transaction in retail outlets are estimated to be five times more expensive than magnetic-stripe readers (*Financial Times*, 3 September, 1997). It is this and other problems associated with the necessary infrastructure to support the cards which has held back the widespread infiltration of smart cards.

France has been at the forefront of developments in smart cards. For more than a decade, smart cards have been used as the basis for telephone cards in France, and smart cards have been used for EFTPOS since 1993. More than 23 million smart cards have been issued by French banks and total investment in the associated infrastructure is estimated at £250 million (Harvey, 1997). Elsewhere in Europe a more cautious approach has restricted widespread adoption of smart cards. The initial use of smart cards in the UK has been limited to applications mostly outside the financial services domain, in such areas as satellite television receivers, telephone cards and loyalty cards. Its use as an electronic purse has been limited.

While the technology required to produce smart cards has been available for a number of years, widespread adoption has been slow as a result of the lack of a suitable infrastructure. In order to operate fully, the smart card requires the involvement of several parties which include: technology suppliers, financial institutions, retailers and consumers. In order to function as a payment system, the smart card requires a supporting network of card readers at each point-of-sale terminal. This enables the card to be read and verified and value debited or credited. In addition, the supporting infrastructure requires the various parties involved to arrive at an agreement regarding who should pay. Some degree of collaboration is required since retailers may be unwilling to bear the cost of new smart-card terminals, having footed the bill for EFTPOS terminals to support debit cards in the mid-1980s.

Smart cards functioning as electronic purses can be designed in one of two completely different ways:

- They can be designed to be cleared through the banking system, thus preventing them from being passed between people in the same way as physical cash is.
- They can be designed to be more cash-like, essentially bypassing the clearing system. With this option banks face the risk of disintermediation and being rendered obsolete. Yet notes and coins have worked fairly well on this basis for over 7,000 years.

Two rival systems have been developed, each functioning by one of these methods. Mondex, developed by Midland (HSBC), NatWest and British Telecom, functions by the second method, by-passing the clearing system. Extensive trials were carried out for two years from 1995, and the roll-out commenced in 1997 (see Financial Services Marketing in Practice: 'Smart cards get smarter'). Visa Cash, a fully accounted system, commenced trials in September 1997, some way behind Mondex. One concern is that as the range of different systems grows, there is a need to ensure compatibility between different cards so that retailers can accept various payment methods using just one reader at point-of-sale. The principal card-issuers are working towards this with the Eurocard–MasterCard–Visa (EMV) standard for smart-card-based payments. Unlike Mondex, which is a unilaterally developed system, Visa Cash is based on the EMV specifications. A number of UK financial institutions are reportedly considering the adoption of Visa Cash as a rival to Mondex for electronic purses.

Electronic purses, such as Mondex and Visa Cash, are being positioned as replacements for cash in low-value transactions, competing with debit and credit cards. They could save £4.5 million a year in processing costs (*Financial Times*, 1 October 1997) and are estimated to replace between 40 and 50 per cent of cash transactions in merchant outlets within 5 years of the infrastructure being established (George, 1996). Yet, a survey conducted on behalf of Girobank, the banking subsidiary of Alliance & Leicester, noted that 80 per cent of the 2,000 adults questioned reported a preference to use notes and coins to buy items costing about £10. This figure represents a slight downward trend on the 82 per cent the previous year. While debit cards, such as Switch, have quickly overtaken cheques for personal payments, they have only recently made inroads into lower-value payments where cash rules (*Financial Times*, 9 June 1997).

On-line banking

On-line banking systems have wider reaching implications because they do not rely on ATMs or EFTPOS and they are not dependent on co-operative schemes with other banks. They do, however, require the intermediation of communications companies to provide the interactive communication networks.

On-line or PC banking, from a personal computer at home or place of work, pro-

FINANCIAL SERVICES MARKETING IN PRACTICE

Smart cards get smarter

The smart card branded Mondex is owned by a consortium including Midland (HSBC) and National Westminster banks and British Telecom. It offers a unique and simple way of providing electronic cash, offering all the attributes of money, allowing one individual to transfer value to another individual or retail outlet without having to go via a third party. At the same time, unlike physical cash, it can be sent down the phone line.

Individuals charge their Mondex card with encrypted cash from an automatic teller machine, from a BT public telephone, from their own smart card-enabled phone or (as a result of a link-up with Cellnet since September 1997) from their own mobile phone. The card is then used in the same way as a debit or credit card at retailer outlets which are capable of accepting the card.

The difference between Mondex and other payment cards is that it is 'unaccounted'. This means that there is no need to link each transaction back to a specific bank account where checks are made to discover whether funds are available and to authorise payment. Each time the card is used the chip on it generates a unique 'digital signature' which can be recognised by the other Mondex card involved in the transaction. This digital signature is the guarantee that the cards involved are genuine. This recognition process also identifies the card to which the cash is to be transferred, ensuring that funds are not intercepted by a third party.

Thus, Mondex requires no authorisation calls, no signatures to be checked, no PIN numbers to be typed, no clearing process and no delay in funds being transferred. The necessary requirement is that sufficient value has been loaded onto the card to cover the transaction. Providing sufficient value is available, the card can deal with any transaction up to a value of £500 which is transferred directly to an electronic purse in the retailer's terminal in the same way that cash moves from one's wallet to the retailer's till.

To enable transactions between individuals, Mondex comes with an electronic wallet, a pocket-sized device about the size of a slim calculator and similar in appearance to the electronic databanks, incorporating a small keyboard, display screen and a card reader into which the cardholder can slot their card. An integral part of the wallet is an electronic purse, similar to the one on the card itself.

To transfer money from one person to another the individual must first transfer funds from their card onto the purse chip in the wallet. The card onto which funds are to be transferred is then placed in the wallet and funds are moved from the purse chip in the wallet to the chip on the card.

The wallet also comes with a small balance reader which lets you know how much is on the card at any one time. It also enables details of the last 10 transactions to be accessed.

In addition, a number of safety features are provided. The wallet allows the cardholder to lock the card and unlock it using a four-digit code. Money can still be loaded on, but it cannot be taken off while the card is locked. So, unlike cash, if the card is lost, it can be frozen, offering protection from theft.

Furthermore, Mondex is capable of handling over 100 different currencies, and five are able to be used at the same time. This feature has made the card particularly attractive as a possible payment device for Europe's toll motorways.

In the Summer of 1996 Mondex International (51 per cent owned by MasterCard) was formed in a bid to franchise the technology beyond the UK. It has been successful in expanding the concept of electronic cash to 27 countries in 5 continents. Wells Fargo are involved in the venture in the US. Mondex claims more than 30,000 cardholders in Hong Kong – the full roll-out commenced towards the end of 1997.

The introduction of Mondex to the market began with trials in Swindon in 1995 which lasted for two years. 700 retail outlets were adapted to accept the card, 250 Mondex-compatible BT payphones provided cash-loading sites, and about 10,000 consumers had adopted the card by mid-1996. This figure was fewer than anticipated. Following that, trials moved to the University of Exeter where 11,000 students adopted the card, and the University of York where a further 1,500 cardholders were enlisted. The Universities of Edinburgh, Nottingham and Sheffield have also become involved.

Source: Adapted from Harvey (1997), *Financial Times*, 5 February 1997, 28 February 1997, 1 October 1997

FINANCIAL SERVICES MARKETING IN PRACTICE

Questions:

1 What impact will 'unaccounted' cards have on the role of traditional banks?

2 What are the applications/limitations of Mondex?

3 What can be done to increase the adoption and use of smart cards?

vides the customer with the facility to perform common banking transactions that would normally require a visit to the branch or perhaps a telephone call to process. Thus, it creates convenience allowing the sometimes onerous task of financial management to be fitted around individuals' busy lifestyles.

There are two main approaches to on-line banking which can be distinguished. The first of these is home (or office) PC banking. Home banking services require the user to dial directly into the financial service provider's system. The other method is internet banking, where access to the financial institution is made across the internet using a web browser. Both systems offer similar facilities to the customer, although the internet offers a more portable service, allowing customers to access their account details from any computer with an internet connection. Home banking services are tied to a particular computer terminal, at home or work. In addition, some financial institutions are providing hybrid solutions to on-line banking where the customer uses an existing internet browser to dial directly to their financial institution. One of such hybrid solutions is the service provided by Alliance & Leicester as described in Financial Services Marketing in Practice: 'E Bank: Alliance & Leicester's home banking service'. This combination of internet browser and direct-dial provides some degree of added security over the purely internet-based approach, although improvements to internet security are being made all the time.

Home banking

Basic facilities offered by most home banking services include: the ability to check account balances, view transactions records and account history, pay bills, apply for other services, communicate with the financial institution, and transfer money instantly between accounts. Some services also enable customers to download information onto their own PC, which means that customers can manage their own finances without needing to stay on-line. Customers only need to go on-line in order to process transactions. Some systems even provide compatibility with Microsoft's Money software, providing customers with a range of money management facilities from their own PC.

The technology needed to provide home banking has been available for some years. In fact, the Bank of Scotland developed their HOBS (Home and Office Banking System) more than 20 years ago. Yet, the acceptance of home banking has been slow. One of the main reasons for this was that personal computers in the home were only owned by a very small segment of the market, thus restricting home banking's widespread adoption. Since that time, however, consumers have

FINANCIAL SERVICES MARKETING IN PRACTICE

E Bank: Alliance & Leicester's home banking service

Alliance & Leicester recently moved into home banking following a six-month trial with 2,000 of its customers. The vehicle for the service is a system developed by Olivetti and refined in Denmark. The product, named E Bank, is produced under a new identity of Olsy, the wholly owned services arm of Olivetti. E Bank is being pushed as a cost-effective tool for banks across Europe.

While the internet provides the communications backbone for E Bank, the delivery mechanism is a closed loop between the Alliance & Leicester and its customers. In other words it is a virtual private network, or an intranet. BT provides the E Bank network for the customer, but by acting as an internet service provider the bank ensures both security and speed of response, thus side-stepping common complaints about slow internet response times.

Security is also cited as a main consumer objection to conducting financial transactions over the internet. However, both Alliance & Leicester and Olsy claim that the service offers an impenetrable level of encryption for signals.

Customers wishing to use the £500,000 service need a Windows personal computer and a modem. The service is designed to offer a broad level of access to customers. While some home banking systems are limited to people using Windows 95, Alliance & Leicester's service can also be accessed from Windows 3.1. E Bank is primarily PC-based with the bank's own servers linked into customer databases resident on Tandem and IBM hardware.

Alliance & Leicester already has some considerable expertise in direct banking, and inherited a vast electronic banking infrastructure when it acquired Girobank in 1990. Girobank is now Alliance & Leicester's commercial banking arm. Alliance & Leicester's telephone banking service for personal customers was adapted from the Girobank service, which also handles the state social-security payments on a commercial basis. For Alliance & Leicester, home banking would seem to be a logical extension of what it already does.

Source: Adapted from *Financial Times*, 2 July 1997

Questions:

1 What advantages does E Bank offer over purely internet-based banking?

2 Who is E Bank likely to appeal to?

become more familiar with computers, initially through workplaces, and a significant proportion of the population now own a PC at home, as indicated in Chapter 1. In addition the cost of PCs and modems, also required to run home banking, have come down in price considerably since home banking was first developed.

Furthermore, the costs associated with running a home banking system were initially quite high, but these are also coming down and many financial institutions now offer free internet access. The costs associated include the software (although in the case of proprietary systems which require the financial institution's own software, this is often provided free of charge), equipment costs (modem and PC if not owned already); there is usually an initial service fee and sometimes an annual fee. The customer also foots the bill for the telephone costs incurred in making the link between the two computer systems. When compared with the fees charged for running some accounts, home banking fees are not particularly expensive.

Security is a common consumer worry and an issue that has also restricted widespread adoption of home banking. Financial institutions are aware of this and are working towards tighter security controls in an effort to raise consumer confidence of on-line banking systems. Many financial institutions use the latest encryption technology to prevent unauthorised access to personal account records. Customers

Table 6.1. Examples of on-line banking services

Financial Institution	Technical specifications	Proprietary system	Browser-based	Fully internet based	Cost
Alliance & Leicester	Based on a viewdata service	✓	✗	✗	Monthly fee
Bank of Scotland	HOBS (Home and Office Banking System) based on a viewdata service	✓	✗	✗	Monthly fee
Barclays	Direct-dial-in based service. Also works off-line and supports MS Money	✓	✗	✗	Initial set-up cost plus a monthly fee
The Co-operative Bank	Internet-based, using Java. No downloads available to MS Money	✗	✗	✓	Free
First Direct	Browser-based with direct dial-in. Restricted to Windows 95 with Internet Explorer. Allows account details to be down loaded and used with MS Money	✗	✓	✗	Free
Royal Bank of Scotland	Internet-based service restricted to Windows 95/NT with Internet Explorer. Allows account details to be downloaded and used with MS Money	✗	✗	✓	Free
TSB	Direct-dial only available via Compuserve	✓	✗	✗	Free

NB: Proprietary systems require the customer to dial directly, via a modem, to the service provider.
Browser-based systems use an internet-based browser to dial directly into the provider's network.
Fully internet based systems operate on the open internet.

FINANCIAL SERVICES MARKETING IN PRACTICE FT

Guide to personal finance on the internet

When the internet was first conceived, as a communications system immune to nuclear attack, no-one thought that within a few years it would have led to predictions of the end of financial services as we know them.

Every study comes to the same conclusion: the global computer network will lead to a 'step change' in personal finance, increasing competition and the flow of information, empowering consumers and challenging the role of traditional service companies and banks.

But how far down the road to this consumers' paradise are we? In the US it is already possible to apply for a mortgage on-line, take out a personal loan and transfer money between accounts held with a virtual bank. Here in the UK, however, interactive services are lagging behind.

Financial services companies are in what a recent report labelled the 'learn, not earn' stage. Sites on the world wide web, the graphical part of the internet, are mainly promotional tools, established to allow companies to put a toe in the virtual water and show a presence on the net. Indeed, several admit in private that the only reason they are on-line at all is to keep up with competitors; any revenue is seen as a bonus.

The financial services sites that are breaking new ground in the UK are, in the main, not those of the biggest companies in the market: Guardian Royal Exchange has an insurance policy available exclusively on-line; Bath Building Society offers a 'one-stop shop' for house-buyers in conjunction with an estate agent. And the first UK internet banking service came not from a bank but a building society – albeit Nationwide, now the country's largest. Consumers of off-the-shelf financial services such as mortgages and insurance policies have not yet gained financially, but many small investors are already looking back to the time before the web and wondering how they coped.

Detailed information on share prices, company fundamentals and market conditions are available for free after a short delay, and live share-price tracking, previously the preserve of City professionals, has dropped in price dramatically and is now within the reach of investors of moderate means. 'The internet has the potential to strengthen the position of investors significantly', Sir Andrew Large, Chairman of the Securities and Investment Board, the Chief UK Financial Regulator, said recently. He added that the net could 'deliver a more educated investor and thus redress the "knowledge balance" between those offering financial services and the customer'.

The internet is already driving down the fees charged by execution-only stockbrokers; again, the US is more advanced, with more than a million on-line trading accounts, and fees dropping all the time. At the beginning of the year, one Florida stockbroker even offered fee-free trading over the net. In the UK there is only a handful of on-line brokers, but Electronic Share Information, the Cambridge-based information provider and gateway to three brokers, says it is recruiting 500 new users a day, with more than 100,000 signed up to the service.

The promise of the internet, however, also holds threats: scams operating out of unregulated countries could fleece investors before the swindlers disappear into cyberspace. Even the US President, Mr Bill Clinton, a proponent of electronic commerce, has described the internet as the 'Wild West' of the global market.

Virtual pyramid schemes have sprung up across Europe and America, and millions of dollars – scams usually originate in the US – have disappeared into the accounts of fraudsters. The risk of hackers intercepting credit card details or withdrawing money from someone else's virtual account also worries consumer watchdogs and finance groups thinking of starting web services, and although there have been no reports of large-scale losses, hackers break new codes almost every week.

So how does the average investor stand to gain? At present, the main advantage is access to information: comparisons of saving and mortgage rates, up-to-date share prices and historical performance data for unit and investment trusts are all available with a few clicks of the mouse.

But information is also holding back the development of the internet: a hunt for 'mortgages' on Altavista, a popular search engine, or guide to the net, found 87,723 relevant sites. Navigating through this morass can be time-consuming and frustrating. Ease of use, however, is continually improving, with the development of 'intelligent

FINANCIAL SERVICES MARKETING IN PRACTICE FT

agents', which use human-like reasoning to carry out searches, and there are now several UK sites that act as financial guides.

Perhaps the highest-profile electronic service at the moment is PC banking, whereby customers run an account from the home or office computer. Both Barclays and Citibank, the US group, are bombarding the public with advertisements for their electronic banking services. However, both have opted for direct-dial systems, where the user's computer calls the bank's computer, rather than internet-based services.

Nationwide 'opened' the first net bank in May [1997], and the heavily trailed Royal Bank of Scotland internet service was launched at the beginning of the summer [1997]. All the big banks are testing systems either for the internet or direct-dial.

Internet banking could be the death of traditional bank branches, continuing the process begun by telephone banking, as customers find they can set up standing orders and direct debits, pay bills and transfer cash between accounts without leaving their desks. Even more radical could be the rise of cyber-cash – consumers could use electronic payments to order goods from home or pay with a cash card in shops or on buses.

When will this happen? Predictions from within the industry vary wildly – but everyone agrees that change will be speedy. Mr David Lascelles, a director of the Centre for the Study of Financial Innovation (CSFI), a London think tank, says: 'Within the next five years it is likely that most people will be banking on the internet', and a CSFI study says that 'in the next two or three years' the net will have enough impact to trigger 'deep structural changes' among finance businesses already struggling to cope with the advent of direct telephone services.

Internet companies measure research in dog years – what other industries do in seven years the net does in one. With the number of on-line potential customers in Britain already more than 5m and almost doubling every year, according to NOP Research, financial services companies believe they must be wired to survive – and that means the smarter investors will find the best deals on the net.

Source: James Mackintosh, *Financial Times*, 16 August 1997

Questions:

1 How does the internet empower the consumer?

2 Why do so many financial institutions in the UK lack a clear internet strategy?

3 How strong do you think the impact of the internet will be on distribution of financial services?

are issued with a personal identification code and password. However, for added security it is also advised that the computer used for home banking is not connected to a network.

Internet banking

The internet offers an alternative and more portable means of operating on-line banking. The internet is a world-wide collection of linked computer networks connecting a diverse group of users. It has the potential of becoming a colossal transborder marketplace covering tens of millions of customers. Many companies are going on-line in an effort to increase business, and a number of 'virtual' organisations are being established. Virtualisation is the removal of the constraints of time, place and form and is made possible by the convergence of computing and telecommunications technology and visual media as manifested through the internet. It puts the consumer in greater control by increasing consumer choice through access to greater amounts of information at the touch of a button. Yet, the sheer amount of information accessible can be bewildering, as outlined in Financial Services Marketing in Practice: 'Guide to personal finance on the internet'.

According to the Centre for the Study of Financial Innovation (CSFI) (*Financial Times*, 1 July 1997) the internet has the potential to bring about revolutionary change by transforming the way business is conducted. It suggests the internet can do this by:

- stimulating more intense competition in the financial services market by admitting new entrants, making pricing more transparent and raising service expectation levels;
- switching the balance of power towards the service suppliers with technology and marketing know-how and diverting it away from those with traditional skills and cost structures;
- empowering the customers by giving them direct access to market information and greater control over the execution of their own deals;
- removing geography as a constraint on the business of financial services, particularly for traditional institutions which have been constrained by branches and national preferences, thus creating an industry that exists almost entirely in cyberspace.

From the point of view of the provider of financial services, new marketing possibilities could be opened up. However, the beneficiaries may not necessarily be the traditional financial services providers – new opportunities will open up for non-traditional players whose competitive capacity previously would have been limited without the existence of an extensive branch network or direct sales force. Yet, given the increasing amounts of information available to customers, the internet is likely to further undermine the ties of loyalty (or indeed inertia) built up through the branch networks.

When considering the cost savings available, the case for virtualisation of delivery through the internet is compelling. Several studies have concluded that the internet is far more cost-effective as a delivery method than the traditional methods used to deliver financial services. For example, a study by Booz, Allen and Hamilton (*Financial Times*, 1 July 1997) revealed that the cost of a typical bank transaction in a full-service branch was $1.07 compared with 54 cents for telephone banking, 27 cents for an ATM and perhaps as low as 1 cent for a transaction conducted over the internet.

Because the internet has the potential to reduce costs, improve convenience and increase information to the customer, the main beneficiary should be the consumer. Consumers will be able to roam the electronic marketplace, checking out deals, conducting their own transactions and even running their own bank account.

Interactive TV

Interactive TV offers the integration of television cable, satellite and internet services. The concept has been around for more than 20 years, yet its adoption could herald a whole new world in retailing and banking. British Interactive Broadcasting

(BIB), a collaborative venture involving British Sky Broadcasting (BSkyB), British Telecom (BT), Midland Bank (HSBC) and Matsushita Electric, was established to bring interactive television services to viewers of BSkyB's 200-channel digital satellite service from Spring 1998. Interactive services include shopping, banking, holiday booking, education, computer games, and internet access.

HSBC wants to pioneer TV banking in the same way its subsidiary, First Direct, did with telephone banking, and also to position itself for developments in the payment market. The bank expects to handle all the payments traffic for BIB using the Mondex card as a personal payment mechanism over the set-top box. Money could be downloaded from a bank account onto a card for use in purchasing small-value items across the BIB platform. Apparently the interactivity is limited with satellite – there are other possibilities with cable; and Telewest, the UK's second largest cable company, is planning a digital service including multi-channel television, a virtual video store, and interactive services similar to those planned by BIB. The UK has recently experienced the launch of digital terrestrial television (DTT) from the BBC, ITV and satellite and cable groupings. Estimates are that in ten years' time digital satellite TV could be in five to seven million homes, with digital cable and terrestrial services in a further three to five million each (*Financial Times*, 2 July 1997).

Security and fraud

As advancements in technology increase and we become more dependent on technology as a means of interacting with financial services providers, concern heightens over the security of such systems and the ability to protect them, and their users, from fraudsters. Technologies which have evoked the most concern have been, not surprising, the most recent developments in the delivery of financial services, such as smart cards and the internet, services which have not yet achieved mass acceptance. While, as the saying goes, familiarity breeds contempt, unfamiliarity can breed a great deal of scepticism. This scepticism surrounding the use of new forms of technology-based delivery channels has not been helped by the lack of legal protection available.

The closest one gets to legal protection is through the voluntary arrangements set out in the Code of Banking Practice. The Code was updated, with effect from 1 July 1997, to incorporate smart cards, and is supported by all the large banks, building societies and card issuers. It is the first time that the Code has applied to electronic purses. It stipulates that smart-cardholders will be liable for the loss of money on their card if it is stolen, in the same way that they would be liable for stolen cash. But if the stolen card is loaded up with more money from the legitimate cardholder's account, the cardholder's maximum liability is £50 before notifying the card issuer and nothing thereafter. This mirrors the existing provisions for credit and debit cards.

Another contentious issue surrounding smart cards is data protection. The potential for data gathering via smart cards is vast and a number of parties would be interested in claiming ownership of it. The question is, will the data become the preserve of the card issuers, the financial institutions or the retailers? One view is that it should be owned by the consumer, not least to avoid the watchful eye of 'Big Brother'.

The Code of Banking Practice does not, however, extend to internet banking where the speed of change has made it difficult for the law to keep pace. Here the fears relate to sophisticated computer hackers intercepting credit card details or diverting funds from one person's virtual account to another's. While the fears are very real, reports of large-scale losses are still to come. The potential for credit card fraud through internet payments is no greater than the threat imposed from divulging credit card details over the telephone. The difference is that individuals generally feel more comfortable with the telephone and more confident that the details are being transferred to their intended destination.

IT and customer service

While financial institutions may have turned to the use of technology initially to cut the cost of expensive forms of distribution, the potential for generating and improving customer service was soon realised and has become a key issue. Indeed, as the vast majority of financial institutions now offer a variety of technology-driven means of delivering products and services to their customers, the need to create a differential and sustainable competitive advantage through customer service is paramount.

Just by offering more convenient forms of access, such as the telephone and computer, which allow customers to fit their banking activities into their busy lifestyles, financial institutions have been able to increase the level of service offered to their customers. First Direct has shown this with the high service ratings it receives from customers. Yet increased access is not the only benefit – financial institutions are making greater use of information technology (IT) to allow them to understand consumers' financial requirements and be in a position to offer customers what they want when they want it.

One of the worries traditional financial institutions harboured when remote delivery channels were first established, was that they would no longer see the customer. When branch banking was in its heyday, customers frequently visited their branches and provided branch staff with the opportunity to get to know them and cross-sell products to them which suited their current requirements. As clearly demonstrated in Financial Services Marketing in Practice: 'Call centres: a vital role in customer service' (pp. 161–2), Halifax uses a case-based system which allows information to be built up about each individual customer each time they contact the call centre. This information is available to all call operators, so that next time the customer rings, whomever they speak to will know who they are and what their recent interactions with the call centre have been about. First Direct utilises a similar system which incorporates both screen and telephone functions, allowing calls (and customer details) to be passed between telephone operators. The sophisticated software also analyses customers' transaction data gathered from account usage and behavioural data, incorporating information gleaned through interactions with call operators, to predict the products the customer is most likely to want next. The cynical may argue that IT has provided financial institutions with the power to create better selling opportunities, yet the customer no doubt welcomes more targeted and relevant service than that of a more indiscriminate approach.

SUMMARY

This chapter has focused on the developments in technology which have had an impact on the way in which financial services are being delivered. With the introduction of ATMs, banks and building societies were able to streamline many routine banking transactions and free-up staff time. Yet, the widespread adoption of ATM terminals has created an extended delivery channel for many financial institutions and, in some cases, multi-function terminals at remote sites have offered a cost-effective alternative to small-scale branches. While ATMs have not been very effective at cross-selling products, the telephone has proved to be a valuable means of contact with the customer in this respect. Consumers seem to be willing to conduct a wide variety of financial transactions over the telephone and the surge of call centres provides evidence of this. Telebanking has also lowered the barriers to entry for many non-traditional financial services providers.

Yet consumers seem to be more reticent about the use of smart cards and on-line banking. These systems are also hampered by the need to have a suitable infrastructure in place. Smart cards particularly require the co-operation of several parties, including financial institutions, retailers, equipment suppliers and customers. On-line banking is dependent on the customer having access to a personal computer and, for many of the new services being offered, access to the internet. The other issue affecting the adoption of these technologies concerns the security of the systems. There is a need for the development of legal protection to cover all parties concerned.

One of the main advantages of technology-driven delivery channels is that customers have been provided with greater convenience, increased access and generally better service. There is also greater choice available: individuals can choose the way in which they want to interact with their financial services provider, putting the consumer in greater control.

DISCUSSION QUESTIONS

1 Examine the changing role of automatic teller machines since their introduction. What role do you think they will have in the future?

2 Evaluate the reasons for the increase in self-service technology from the point of view of the customer and the financial services provider.

3 What type of information might smart cards provide about their users?

4 How should the data gathered by smart cards be harnessed and used? Who should have control over it?

5 How close are we to a cashless society?

6 To what extent do you think home banking will render the branch network obsolete?

7 To what extent do you think internet banking will be as popular as telebanking? What might be some of the factors inhibiting its popularity?

8 What is your understanding of the notion of a 'virtual bank'?

9 As new players have entered the financial services market through the use of technology-driven delivery channels, what impact might this have on the traditional financial services providers in the provision of financial services?

10 How has customer service been improved through the use of IT in the delivery of financial services?

7 Pricing for financial services

INTRODUCTION

For commodity goods, price operates as the major determinant in purchase decisions. While price may be an important factor influencing consumers' financial decisions, it is not always easy to identify what the price of a financial product or service is. 'Price' may be represented in a number of different ways, depending on the product in question. Thus, in identifying price it is useful to consider the cost of the product or service to the consumer, which may be expressed as a financial cost or a non-financial cost, or indeed both.

The reason why this may occur is that financial institutions use both covert (implicit) and overt (explicit) pricing methods. Covert pricing methods have arisen as the result of the pricing of financial intermediation and the payment of so-called free banking services. The customer is, thus, implicitly charged for the service through higher loan rates or lower savings rates. Overt pricing methods are more straightforward and there is a general trend towards the charging of explicit fees for financial services.

Prices are influenced by a number of different factors both internal and external to the financial institution, as is the case for pricing decisions in other contexts. Yet, certain factors exert particular influence over the pricing of financial services. For example, changes to regulation have made prices more transparent. Consequently, consumers are shopping more carefully. As a result, prices have been experiencing considerable downward pressure in recent years as price competition has increased.

OBJECTIVES

After reading this chapter you should be able to:

- understand the concept of price for financial services;
- outline the differences between price and non-price competition;
- discuss the factors affecting pricing decisions for financial products and services;
- specifically examine mortgage pricing determinants;
- appreciate the role of financial intermediation on the pricing of financial services;
- compare and contrast covert and overt pricing methods;
- offer pricing examples for savings and investments and for credit and loans.

Definition of price

The question of what constitutes the price of a product may seem rather straightforward to answer: for many products it is simply the amount which appears on the price tag. Yet, the *price* of a financial product or service can appear in many guises: some prices are obvious, some are not, some are based on a monetary value, others are not. For example, the price of financial services may be the *interest rate* on a loan, the *notice* required to withdraw money from an account, the *penalty* incurred on the early withdrawal of money from a notice account, a *fee* charged for advice given, *commission* paid to an intermediary such as a broker or IFA, a *premium* paid on car insurance, the *tax* paid on the interest earned on savings, and the *insurance tax* added to insurance premiums.

Thus, price can mean many different things. In a general sense the price of a product or service has a number of important implications for both the seller and the buyer, as outlined in table 7.1. Yet, financial services are different from other products and services and the characteristics shown in the table do not always hold true.

Importance of price to the seller

From the seller's point of view it is generally recognised that prices are set to cover the costs incurred in the production, distribution and marketing of the product or service. While in the short term it may be possible to price a product below its cost, this is not seen as a viable long-term strategy. For many physical goods it may be possible to clearly identify what the costs of production are. For financial services, the costs attributed to individual product lines or customers are far less easy to identify due to shared facilities (such as computer systems, branch networks and call centres) and joint costs (such as staff, administration and marketing). In many cases, financial institutions are merely concerned with recovering the total costs of production and distribution. Hence, the prices charged to customers may or may not represent the costs directly associated with the products or services being bought or used.

Table 7.1 The importance of price to the seller and the buyer

To the seller	To the buyer
• *Price* represents the costs involved in producing the product or service	• *Price* represents the cost to the customer
• *Price* signifies the revenue that can be generated from the sale of the product or service	• *Price* signifies the value of the product or service
• *Price* indicates the profits and long-term survival of the organisation	• *Price* indicates the quality of the product/service and/or provider
• *Price* represents the ability to respond quickly to market conditions	• *Price* is affected by buying power

In addition, price is generally considered to be the only element of the marketing mix to produce revenue and profit: all the other marketing-mix variables represent an expense or create a cost to the organisation. While revenue (and profit) may be generated, they may not be generated as a result of the price charged for the product. For example, current accounts are usually provided free of charge to the customer, in the sense that the customer generally is not charged a fee for having a cheque book and using the ATMs. If the customer is not charged anything for using the facility, how can the financial institution generate revenue? Revenue is generated from the collective funds deposited in current accounts which the institution uses to furnish loan applications.

Finally, in relation to the seller, price is generally considered to be the most flexible element of the marketing mix, providing the organisation with the ability to respond quickly to market conditions by raising or lowering prices. By contrast, new product development, changes to distribution channels and promotion are considered to be more complex and time-consuming to take effect. For financial institutions the price, in terms of the interest rate for example, may not be as flexible as the prices charged by other organisations. Interest rates are controlled, to a certain extent, by the Bank of England, which determines the base rate. Any changes to the interest rate are made in response to changes to the base rate made by the Bank of England. Thus, pricing may be less flexible than for other types of products. In addition, it has already been discussed in Chapter 4 that the development of new financial products can take place very quickly in comparison to the development of physical goods, and may offer even more flexibility in terms of competition than price changes.

Importance of price to the buyer

From the buyer's perspective, the price of a product or service represents the cost to the consumer. As already mentioned, there may be hidden costs as well as obvious costs, and costs can be non-financial as well as financial. In addition, the price also usually represents the value the consumer places on the product or service. As already discussed in Chapter 2, there are a number of factors which affect the decision process in relation to the purchase of financial services and which make it difficult for the consumer to ascertain the value of what is being purchased. For example, the intangibility of the product creates a lack of pre-purchase information and necessitates the use of alternative sources of information, and the often long-term nature of the product means that it can be difficult to assess the value of the product even after purchase since consumption has still not taken place. Furthermore, the value of a financial product is, to a large extent, dependent on both the performance of the financial institution after the point of purchase and other factors outside the control of the financial institution which impact on the fund's performance.

Another aspect, from the buyer's point of view, is that for many products there is an implicit price–quality relationship which assumes that a higher-quality product commands a higher price (and vice versa). Similarly to the assessment of value, the quality of the purchase and the provider are equally as difficult to evaluate. Many financial products are bought infrequently (or perhaps just once in a lifetime). This means that the consumer often has no previous experience or benchmark to provide comparisons of quality. In addition, many financial services of a long-term nature are bought before they are actually consumed. Hence, consumers are forced to evaluate the quality of the product on the basis of its attributes. The problem with this is that there are often few physical attributes which can be used to evaluate financial services' quality levels. Thus, consumers tend to use peripheral cues to make assumptions about the level of quality received, such as the physical facilities, the technology, the reputation of the organisation, the professionalism of the staff and the service provided. In addition, due to many financial services being high in credence qualities, it may even be impossible for some consumers to judge the quality of the outcome even after consumption. This is why consumers often tend to base assessments of quality on 'functional' cues (such as those mentioned above) rather than 'technical' cues (such as the fund's performance).

Finally, price is affected by the consumer's buying power. What this normally means is that prices can be set according to the buyer's propensity and willingness to pay. Thus, those who can afford to pay more will be targeted with higher-priced products. This is not always the case. For conspicuous purchases, such as charge cards, certain segments of the market may be willing (as well as able) to pay higher fees for the kudos and prestige associated with having such a card. For car loans, the reverse is often seen due to the inverse relationship between purchasing power and risk: the higher the purchasing power, the lower the risk; the lower the purchasing power, the higher the risk. Price is set according to the risk attributed to consumer groups. Finance companies, such as GE Capital, which provide the finance for car loans through major car dealerships, have recently introduced higher-priced loans for higher-risk customers. These customers are people who would normally be rejected from a standard credit check as a result of low incomes, poor credit history or high risk of defaulting (among other things). The higher rate of interest charged on the loan, as well as the security of the car itself, represent the price the customer pays.

While pricing of financial services is, in many respects, similar to other marketing contexts there are still differences, and these need to be taken into account throughout the rest of the chapter.

Price versus non-price competition

It is worthwhile taking a look at the differences between price and non-price competition and the extent to which each form of competition has been used in the financial services sector. As can be seen from table 7.2, price competition involves using low prices as a competitive tool to attract customers. In order to be able to offer lower prices than competitors, the financial institution needs to be able to take advantage of low costs of production. Price competition does have its disadvantages. It can result in a price war as competitors continually try to beat each other's prices. Also, while price competition provides an effective means of acquiring new customers, it generally does not support customer loyalty programmes: price-cutting encourages customers to become price-sensitive and to switch for better prices.

By comparison, non-price competition involves competition along some other dimension which does not involve price. This could involve emphasising unique or distinct features of the product which set the financial institution apart from its competitors. It might involve focusing on customer service or on technology in

Table 7.2 Comparison of price and non-price competition

	Price competition	Non-price competition
What is it?	• An emphasis on price as a competitive tool	• An emphasis not on price but on some other distinctive features of the product or service
When is it appropriate?	• If the firm is a low-cost producer • If firms offer standard or commodity-type products	• If the firm can distinguish its products or brands from competitors' and obtain a unique image which is of value to the customer • If the customer is less price-sensitive
How does it work?	• The firm attempts to match or beat competitors' prices	• The firm charges a price which represents the value customers place on the product.
What effect does it have on behaviour?	• It can encourage customers to become price-sensitive, leading to switching behaviour	• It enables the firm to build customer loyalty

terms of innovative forms of delivery. Whatever the feature is, it must be of some value to the customer so that a price can be set. It works well when customers are less price-sensitive. Different products will have different price elasticities, which determine the extent to which customers are price-sensitive. For example, the general insurance market is notoriously price-sensitive. The majority of advertising messages for car and home insurance focus on price as the key issue. Some companies have tried to reduce the emphasis on price by adding in features and benefits to car insurance, but to little avail. If companies can create unique advantages, they are more likely to build customer loyalty.

Traditionally price was not used as a key competitive weapon in the financial services sector. Price competition was weak due to cartelised oligopolies for both the banks and the building societies. Thus, non-price competition was pursued which largely involved expansion and growth of distribution networks and investment in premises. These issues were discussed more fully in Chapter 5. The lack of price competition created relatively stable profits, had the effect of raising costs and allowed less efficient institutions to survive. Similarly, for life and pensions companies price competition was not an issue until the hard disclosure ruling came into effect. Prior to this, there was a practice of soft disclosure which meant that the price of products sold was not fully known to either customers or competitors.

In 1971 the 'corset', or interest rate cartel among the banks, was dissolved, and in 1983 the building societies cartel was abolished. Institutions began to take a more serious attitude towards price as a competitive weapon. Other deregulation at around the same time increased the competition between banks and building societies; both types of institution were beginning to encroach on each other's traditional domains, creating the need to defend market share and growth. Since 1995 life assurance companies have been required to make their pricing more transparent. They are now required to state clearly at point of purchase the charges and commissions which are deducted from the premium payments and the early-surrender values of investments.

In addition, consumers have also become more price sensitive. Prior to the dissolution of interest rate cartels and the emphasis on price, consumers were more likely to exhibit some degree of loyalty towards their financial provider. As discussed in Chapter 2, loyalty is now thought to have been merely behavioural loyalty and not based on a strong attitude or affinity to the organisation. Since financial institutions have begun to emphasise price and use it as a competitive tool, consumers have become less loyal and have increased their switching behaviour in search of the best deal.

Faced with intense competition, not only from other traditional financial institutions but also from new entrants to the market, financial institutions have made some attempts to reduce the emphasis on price in the hope of increasing customer loyalty. However, as indicated in table 7.2, in order to successfully implement non-price competition the company needs to be able to identify unique features or benefits of the product and emphasise a brand image. The lack of branding and product differentiation in financial services makes non-price competition very difficult to employ. Products are very similar and are easily copied. Recently institutions have focused on customer service as a means of creating differentiation. Yet, for many customers, good service is not considered to be an extra worth paying for, but rather an expected feature of the product. Information technology is the tool most institutions are now using to create distinctiveness through targeting and relationship development.

Factors affecting price

There are a number of factors which exert varying degrees of influence over financial institutions' pricing decisions. These are depicted in figure 7.1. The influencing factors can broadly be divided into internal and external factors. Internal factors are those which are internal to the financial institution and are within its control. They include: company and pricing objectives, the other marketing-mix variables, costs and risk assessment and analysis. The external factors exert influence outside the financial institution. Hence, the company has little or no control over them, but must monitor them and be aware of the likely impact they may have on the company and its pricing decisions. Some of the external factors are closer to the company than others. Thus, the external factors may be further divided into (internal) industry factors (such as competitors, shareholders and intermediaries) and external market factors (such as customers and regulation).

Internal factors

Objectives

Pricing objectives should be set to achieve consistency with organisational objectives. For example, if the organisational objective is to 'be the largest financial services provider' the pricing objective should be set to achieve volume growth. This may involve beating competitors' prices in order to increase demand and sales volume. Figure 7.2 outlines some other common pricing objectives. As mentioned earlier, it may be necessary to set prices below costs in order to stimulate cash flow

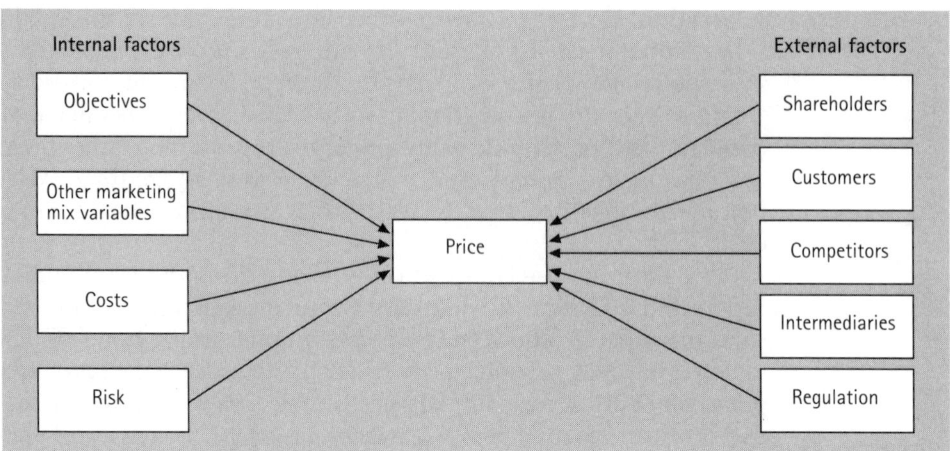

Fig. 7.1 Factors affecting financial services pricing decisions

in the short term. However, this is unlikely to be a viable long-term strategy. Rather than aiming for volume growth, a financial institution may attempt to achieve value growth. This objective aims to increase total income, not by increasing the number of sales, but by increasing the profit margin on each sale. This may or may not be linked to superior product quality or differentiation enabling a premium price to be charged.

Profit growth is also important as a means of generating capital through retained profits, thus enabling the institution to maintain its capital-to-assets ratio. This can be determined either by regulators or voluntarily on the basis of its own judgement of capital adequacy. Capital adequacy acts as a cushion against losses, whether it is in the form of mortgage arrears or a fall in the value of assets, allowing the institution to continue to conduct business.

Other marketing-mix variables

The marketing-mix variables of product, price, promotion, distribution, people, physical evidence and process of service assembly are all closely interrelated: changes to any one of them can have a wide-reaching impact. Thus, it is important

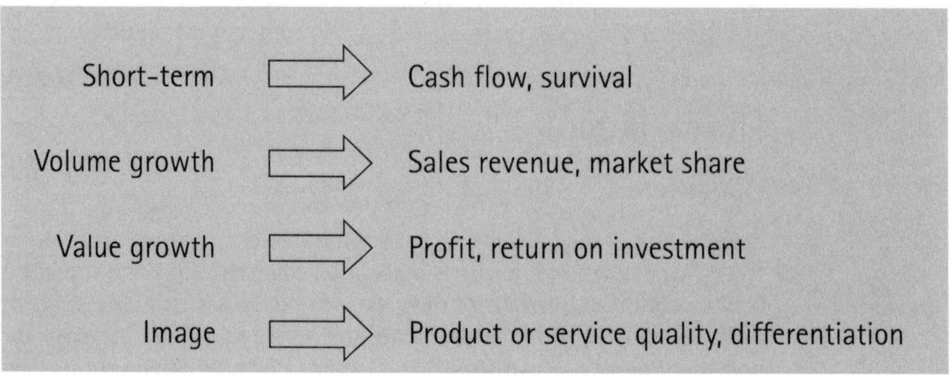

Fig. 7.2 Some pricing objectives

that the relationship between price and the other marketing-mix variables be understood.

As previously discussed in Chapter 4, the nature of the financial services product is quite unique: financial services are often multi-dimensional, being comprised of a bundle of services. This can create difficulties in terms of pricing the product, and make pricing complex in that the 'product' may actually be a package of products each with a different pricing consideration. Take, for example, an endowment mortgage. This is made up of essentially two products: a home loan and an endowment policy. To further complicate matters, the endowment policy contains both a saving element and a life assurance element, creating three different pricing considerations. However, the customer may not actually be aware of this.

Many financial products involve continuing relationships with the financial institution providing the opportunity to price on the basis of cross-subsidies. Payment services are a classic example of this. Pricing is based on the assumption that customers will make use of other services provided by the institution and will pay for the use of payment services in this way. In addition, many products, such as mortgages, rely on the long-term relationship to generate income. Thus, in order to protect the longevity of the relationship, substantial penalties may be imposed on the early termination of contracts, increasing the switching costs to customers.

Chapters 5 and 6 discussed how changes to the distribution of financial services have enabled delivery costs to be reduced. Indeed, financial institutions are beginning to price according to distribution channels in an attempt to encourage customers to make greater use of less costly methods such as the telephone and the internet. In some cases, intermediaries and their charges and commissions have been bypassed in favour of more direct contact with the customer. Greater use is being made of direct response advertising and 'execution-only' telephone operators in the promotion and sale of 'straightforward' products such as loans and general insurance, whereas the more costly form of personal selling, through either the direct sales force or IFAs, is reserved for the sale of more complex and expensive products such as pensions and investments which require some degree of advice to be given.

Costs

As already mentioned, it is not always easy to identify the precise costs attributed to a particular product line, due to shared facilities and joint costs. Indeed, prior to the dissolution of interest rate cartels, banks and building societies were largely unaware of their costs as they did not form part of the price-setting decision. In general pricing decisions, customer demand usually sets the ceiling on prices which can be charged and company costs set the floor below which prices often do not fall, unless the objective is to generate short-term cash flow.

A financial institution needs to cover a number of different costs. These can be broadly categorised as costs of capital, fixed costs and variable costs (see table 7.3). The costs are slightly easier to identify for a traditional building society than for a clearing bank, since the latter has the added complication of a payments system which is often provided free of charge to customers, but which incurs a cost, thus further complicating the pricing system.

For an institution which operates in the mortgage business, for example, the costs associated with the business might seem fairly straightforward to identify. A building society, will acquire its money from the wholesale market at a cost (i.e. it bor-

Table 7.3 A financial institution's costs

Type of cost	Example
Cost of capital	• The costs associated with interest paid on deposits, the cost of money acquired from the wholesale market (interest rate), and the cost of risk capital supplied by shareholders
Fixed costs	• General business costs: staff and management, administration, insurance and advertising, etc.
	• General overheads: buildings, land, branch networks, call centres, equipment, data processing, fixed costs associated with setting up accounts
Variable costs	• All costs which are dependent on the use of the service, such as part-time staff, correspondence, etc.

rows the money and must pay an interest rate). The money is then packaged into mortgages and made available to the retail market at a higher rate of interest than that charged to the building society. The margins are calculable. However, the building society still has to consider the branch network, its advertising of the mortgage, the staff and data processing etc. While it might be easy to calculate the costs associated with borrowing and lending money, it is less easy to calculate how the other costs should be apportioned to the product. Generally, the fixed and variable costs must be covered. They may not, however, be covered by the products or customers which incur the costs, but elsewhere through the system.

In a market where competition ensures that prices are very similar, the control of costs is viewed as a means to obtaining better profit margins. Since the costs of capital are fairly similar between financial institutions of similar sizes, the area where most financial institutions can attempt to reduce their costs is through the control of fixed costs. The widespread rationalisation programmes discussed in Chapter 5 in relation to distribution networks and the automation of many services, is a key area where financial institutions have attempted to reduce their costs and increase profitability.

Risk

In a sense risk is another cost to the financial institution, and should be taken into account in pricing decisions. Risk is created if the price of a liability (such as a loan) is set irrespective of the performance of the financial institution. For example, people are generally confident that deposits made with a bank can be quickly converted to cash. Indeed, should a customer demand that their deposits be paid in full, the bank is obliged to do so regardless of whether borrowers repay their loans. Not everyone will want to have all their deposited money at once, but in order to honour the repayment of deposits, the bank will have equity capital which serves as an internal insurance fund. The suppliers of equity capital (shareholders), are essentially providing risk capital to the bank and need to be compensated for it (usually in the form of dividends). This cost needs to be incorporated into the pricing of the product – if it is not the company's equity capital may eventually become depleted.

Insurance risk is based on an actuarial assessment of the likelihood and severity of a claim being made on the policy. Despite this, an insurance company must still honour its claims regardless of its performance (see Financial Services Marketing in Practice: 'Motor insurance profits hit by prolonged price war').

FINANCIAL SERVICES MARKETING IN PRACTICE FT

Motor insurance profits hit by prolonged price war

The price of personal motor insurance has hit a long-term low after several years of fierce rate-cutting. Industry experts said yesterday that competition was so intense in this traditionally cyclical market that profitability may never return to previous levels.

Rapid development of technology and alternative distribution channels have fuelled a deep and prolonged downturn. Bob Scott, chief executive of General Accident, said the volatile swings in profitability that have tended to drive prices would cease. There was too much capital in the market, he said. Furthermore, statistical data had become so sophisticated that insurers were able to act quickly enough to avoid problems.

'It's increasingly difficult to put rates up', said Mr Scott, who is to head the new group formed by the merger planned between GA and Commercial Union. 'Pricing has become more targeted and across-the-board rate changes are a thing of the past. Premium rates will move, but they won't bail out poor underwriting.'

According to a report by Moody's, the credit ratings agency, the tough conditions will lead to a frenzy of mergers and acquisitions. It said legislative changes to the legal aid system that benefited consumers, and an increase in the number of bodily injury claims, threatened long-term profitability.

Motor insurance premiums, which act as an indicator for other areas of the personal market, have fallen sharply since 1994. While rates began to rise again last year, gains have only matched an increase in the costs of claims, said analysts.

Telephone-based insurers that operate more cheaply by cutting out brokers were continuing to grab market share from intermediaries, according to Merrill Lynch. By the end of the decade, they would control about 40 per cent of all premiums.

Industry indices that showed sharp increases in premium rates were misleading, because they were based on projected assumptions that differed from what was achieved, said Merrill Lynch. 'With little sign that capacity is going to decline significantly, the outlook for the rest of the decade remains pretty grim.'

Companies which had bought or set up telephone-based operations, hoping to mimic the success of Direct Line, could be forced to exit the market. Others, seeking to build up critical mass in a sector where cutting costs and owning big books of business may be the only strategy for survival, could pay high prices for loss-making businesses.

Source: Christopher Adams, Insurance Correspondent, *Financial Times*, 10 March 1998

Questions

1 What factors have contributed to the intense price competition in the personal motor insurance industry?

2 What, if anything, can the insurance companies do to shift the emphasis on price?

3 How can targeted pricing strategies help?

With credit cards, companies know that a certain proportion of their credit card holders will default on their payments. However, it is not always possible to identify which segments these are. Thus, the risk associated with defaulting is added to all credit card holders' prices and everyone pays.

External factors

Shareholders

Shareholders need to be remunerated for providing equity capital. This can be done in a number of ways: through the payment of dividends, through capital appreciation or through undistributed profits which increase the equity holder's claim on the company. The impact which shareholders exert on prices is evidenced by the recent demutualisation of building societies. Demutualisation changes both the ownership and the aims of the organisation. A mutual organisation is one which is owned by its customers (members) and the aim is to maximise payment and service to policyholders. In contrast, a joint stock company (demutualised organisation) is one which is owned by its shareholders and its aim is to maximise shareholder wealth. Since a proprietary office is accountable to its shareholders and expected to pay dividends, it must attempt to generate revenue in order to do so. Thus, the policies and products offered by a proprietary office become a means to an ends rather than an end itself, as in the case of a mutual organisation.

Customers

Customers, their perceptions of the product and service, and their level of demand all have an effect on the ultimate price of the product. As already mentioned, consumers of financial services may find it difficult to assess the value and quality of what is being purchased, due to a lack of information, the sometimes hidden and obscure elements of both cost and value, and the fact that the value of most financial services is not discernible until some future date, if at all. As a result of this, it might be assumed that financial services are less price-elastic than many physical goods for which the price–quality relationship and costs are clear. Yet, there is evidence of different price elasticities for both different products and different buyers.

When demand for a product is inelastic, it is relatively unresponsive to a change in price. Thus, a product with an inelastic demand provides the opportunity for revenue to be increased: demand will not be adversely affected even though the

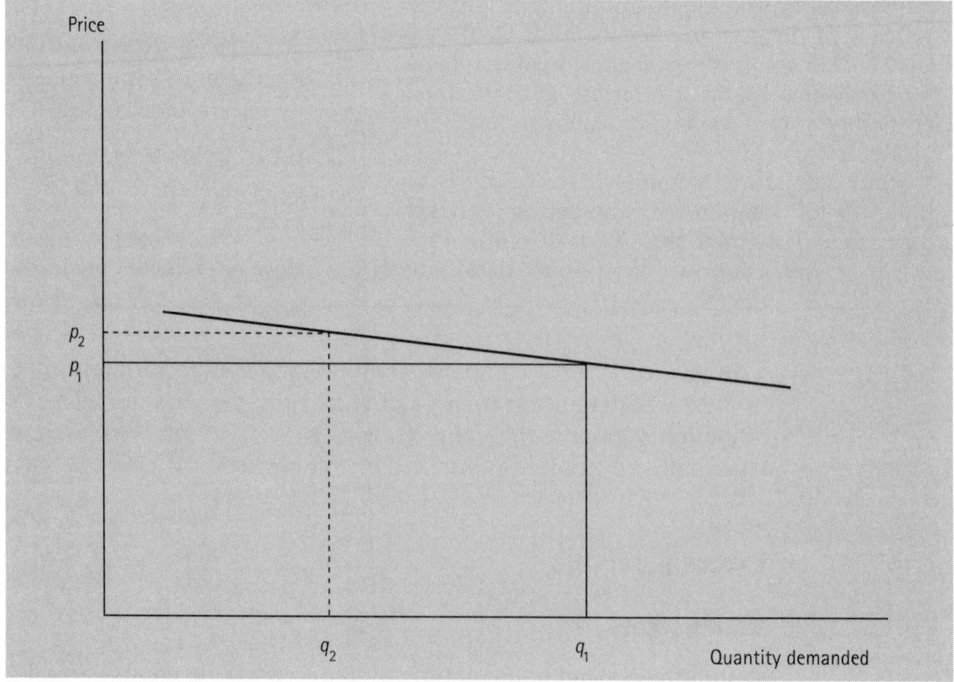

Fig. 7.3 Inelastic demand

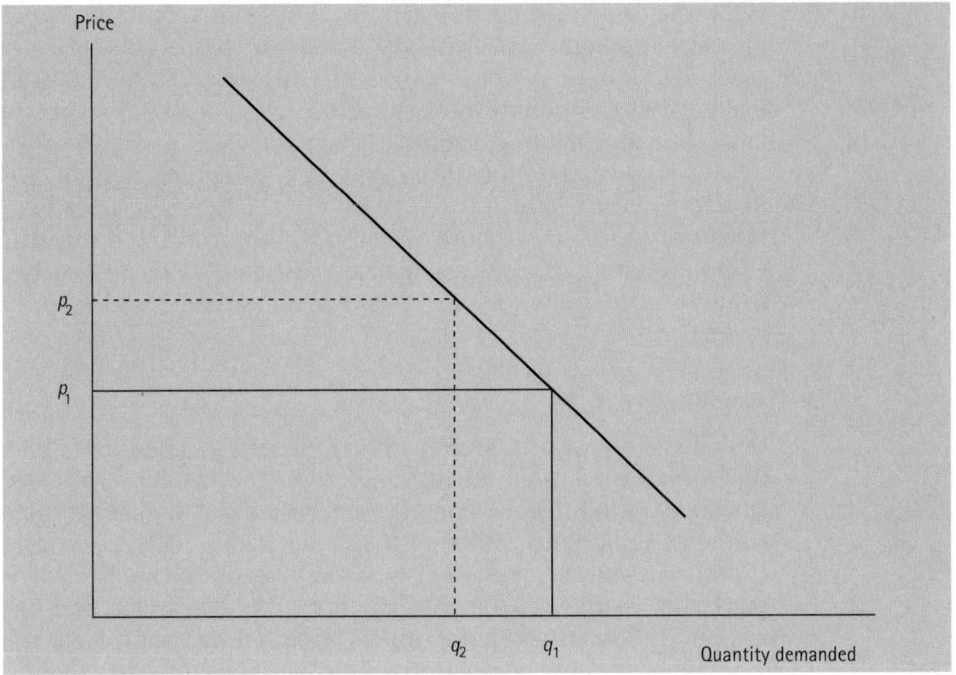

Fig. 7.4 Elastic demand

number of units sold may have gone down. This is illustrated in figure 7.3. An increase in the price from p_1 to p_2 has only a slight effect on the demand, reducing it from q_1 to q_2. On the contrary, figure 7.4 illustrates that even a slight price increase for a product with an elastic demand can result in a reduction of total revenue because the effect on demand is significant.

The insurance market is very price-sensitive, probably because there is often a legal obligation to buy certain types of insurance (such as car and house insurance) and the prices (premiums) are far more transparent and easier to compare than for other financial products. Financial institutions need to identify which products are more elastic than others, as this will determine the extent to which prices can be changed and price competition be used.

Different types of buyers can have higher price elasticities than others. Take, for example, the mortgage market. Even though first-time buyers represent a higher risk than 'seasoned' borrowers (due to their having no track record and typically less equity to put into the property), they tend to be offered more favourable terms such as discounted mortgages, low-start mortgages, cash-back incentives, etc. The reason for this is that first-time buyers are more price-sensitive. In addition, they represent a lower cost to the institution because they do not incur the transaction costs associated with switching between lenders. Furthermore, the mortgage represents the beginning of a long-term relationship with the customer, providing cross-selling opportunities.

Competitors

In highly competitive markets, such as financial services, it is important to know what competitors' prices are so that the institution can adjust its prices accordingly.

While the company may not want to always match or beat competitors' prices, it is important to know what effect a change in competitors' prices will have on the company. Prices have become more transparent in the financial services sector, making it easier not only for customers to ascertain exactly what the price of a product is, but also enabling competitors to see.

To a certain extent prices are kept very close as a result of the base rate set by the Bank of England. When a change in the base rate is announced, financial institutions will watch to see how quickly their competitors respond to the change by either increasing or lowering their deposit and lending rates. The larger financial institutions typically take the lead, with the smaller institutions waiting and following.

Intermediaries

Intermediaries perform several useful functions in a marketing channel. As a result, they have expectations about the level of compensation in terms of pay, training and support. Intermediaries add to the overall cost of making the product available to the customer, thus inflating the price. Traditionally, contact between financial institutions and their customers was face-to-face. The addition of middlemen to the marketing channel enabled distribution to be expanded and service levels to be improved. Prior to 1995 consumers were not aware of the costs associated with including the intermediary in the distribution channel.

Since the hard disclosure ruling, intermediaries have been required by law to state how much of the premium constitutes commission payments and fees. Consequently, the cost of intermediaries in the distribution channel has become more apparent to customers and also competitors. A number of financial institutions which previously used intermediaries have since set up direct distribution channels. These moves have been facilitated by technological developments which have enabled direct contact to be made with customers which is cheaper than face-to-face contact but, for the most part, offers person-to-person contact by telephone. This has enabled middlemen to be cut out of the distribution channel, thereby reducing the costs of distribution.

Regulation

Regulation exerts a number of influences on the financial services sector, as discussed in Chapter 1. There are some specific examples that can be given that indicate the impact on regulation specifically on the pricing function.

One of the most important regulations related to building societies is the wholesale funding limit proportion in relation to societies' total assets. For larger building societies the access to corporate funding (in addition to retail deposits) as a potential source of funding for mortgage demands is of some significance, meaning cheaper funds for larger ones and significantly affecting the costs.

The bank base rate is also significant. The bank base rate is the minimum bank lending rate which is fixed by the Bank of England. For mortgage lending, the building societies have the mortgage base rate that fluctuates with changes in the bank base rate. Unlike the bank base rate, the mortgage base rate is determined by individual societies, rather than governing bodies.

Factors affecting mortgage pricing

The above sections discussed the general factors which have an impact on pricing decisions for financial services. The extent to which each factor exerts influence over the pricing decision is likely to differ between different types of financial institution and possibly different types of financial products. This section examines the extent to which the factors discussed above specifically relate to the pricing of mortgages by building societies.

Mortgage pricing is the determination of standard mortgage rates offered to mortgage borrowers. In a survey by Meidan and Chin (1995) of 45 building societies (half the total number of building societies in existence at the time of the survey), mortgage pricing policies were found to vary according to whether the society was a national, regional or local society. Distinctions between national, regional and local building societies were made according to the societies' total assets and number of branches. Thus, national societies comprised those with assets of £5,000m or over and in excess of 150 branches; societies with assets between £500m and £5,000m and between 30 and 150 branches accounted for regional societies; and local societies were classed as having assets less than £500m and under 30 branches.

Figure 7.5 shows the factors which were considered and their rank order of importance for each category of society. Cost was found to be the most important

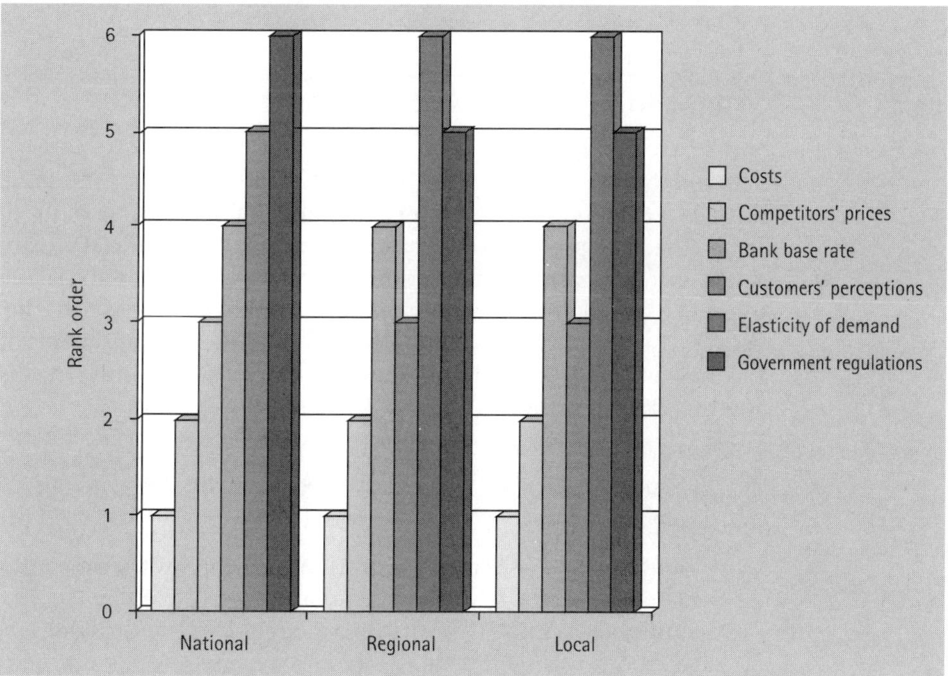

Fig. 7.5 Rank-ordered importance of mortgage price determinants for national, regional and local building societies
National: assets £5,000m+, over 150 branches
Regional: assets £500m–£5,000m, 30–150 branches
Local: Assets less than £500m, under 30 branches
(*Source*: Adapted from Meidan and Chin, 1995)

factor for all three types of society. This might seem surprising given that many financial institutions still find it difficult to identify costs specific to products. Yet, the result no doubt reflects the intensity of competition in the marketplace and societies are keen to reduce the total costs of the business, particularly focusing on the fixed costs such as the branch networks.

Competitors' prices were found to be the second most important factor for all types of society, indicating that societies closely watch one another in terms of price movements. Again, this reflects the intense price competition in the sector.

The bank base rate was ranked third in importance by national building societies, but the regional and local building societies deemed it to be less important than customer perceptions. Customer perceptions may be of less importance to large national building societies because they cater to a larger (and more diverse) customer base; demand may be less affected by changes in customer perceptions. Smaller building societies are more likely to operate niche strategies, which possibly have a closer bearing on customer relationships. This would also fit with the ranking of elasticity of demand in final place of importance, suggesting that smaller societies are less focused on price, which may explain why the base rate and elasticity of demand are perceived to be less important to these societies.

Generally, the results indicated that mortgage pricing as a whole is more influenced by internal industry factors, such as costs and competitors, rather than by market-related external factors such as customer perceptions and elasticity of demand.

Pricing of financial intermediation

The role of intermediaries, such as brokers and IFAs, as channel members was discussed in Chapter 5 in relation to the movement and flow of products and services from financial providers to customers. However, financial institutions are themselves intermediaries, and perform the very useful function of financial intermediation. Financial intermediation is an essential feature of the borrowing–lending process. Any financial institution which takes deposits and lends out funds is in the business of financial intermediation. There are two main functions which financial intermediaries perform:

- *Bridging the gap between borrowers (deficit units) and lenders (surplus units):* Financial intermediaries act as brokers, facilitating the flow of funds from savers to borrowers at costs lower than would be incurred privately.
- *Transmutation of funds:* Financial intermediaries transform the funds, matching maturity (different time horizons), volume (e.g. the repackaging of a number of small deposits into a larger loan) and risk (e.g. the probability that borrowers will default), thereby reconciling the often incompatible needs and objectives of borrowers and lenders. For example, the lender (or supplier of funds) wants to achieve safety of funds and liquidity (the ease of converting to cash with no loss of value). However, the borrower may find it difficult to promise either of these. Through the process of financial intermediation financial institutions can reconcile these needs by using collective deposited funds for loans and investments with varying degrees of

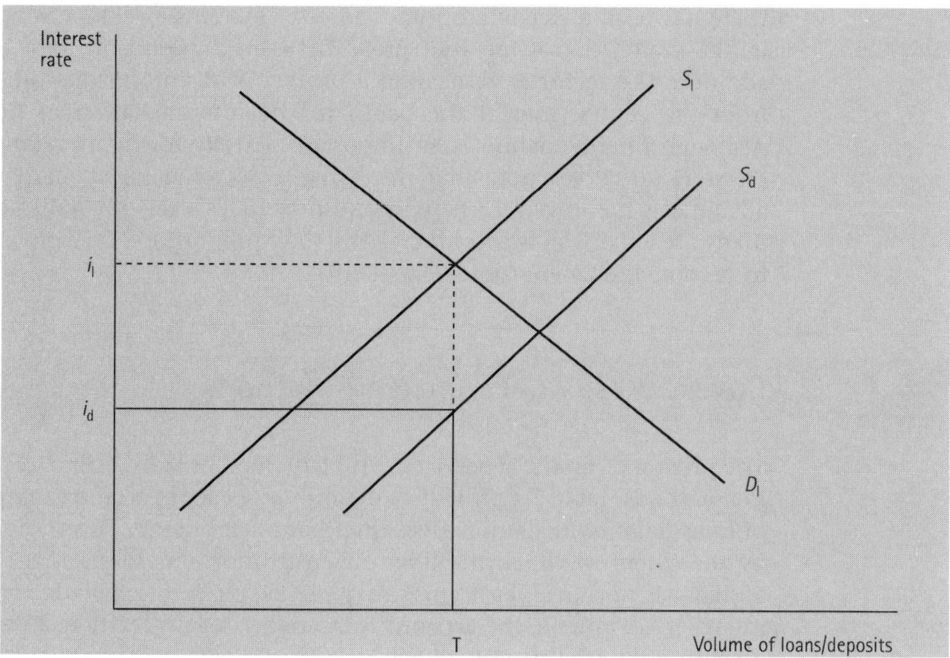

Fig. 7.6 Pricing of financial intermediation

risk and liquidity. Under financial intermediation, the lender's asset or financial claim is more liquid and there is less risk than would be the case in the absence of a financial intermediary. In addition, the borrower's funds are more certain.

To illustrate the pricing of financial intermediation, consider the simple model illustrated in figure 7.6. The vertical axis represents the interest rate (determined outside the control of individual banks) and the horizontal axis represents the volume of deposits and loans. As the interest rate rises, the financial institution experiences an increase in deposits (saving becomes more attractive for customers). This produces an upward sloping supply curve (S_d). An increase in the interest rate also creates the opportunity for the financial institution to generate more profit through the provision of loans. Hence, the financial institution will want to offer more loans to customers as the interest rate rises. This also produces an upward sloping supply curve (S_l) but at an interest rate higher than for deposits. Unlike the deposits supply curve, the increasing supply of loans is unlikely to be infinite; it will be discontinuous at some point since higher rates attract riskier borrowers (adverse selection) and encourage borrowers to undertake riskier activities (adverse incentives). The demand for loans is represented by D_l which shows that the demand increases as the interest rate decreases.

In equilibrium the financial institution pays a deposit rate of i_d to savers and charges a loan rate of i_l to borrowers. The volume of deposits received and loans demanded is OT and OT loans are supplied. The interest margin is equal to i_l minus i_d and represents the price paid by customers for the service of financial intermediation. A major part of a financial institution's revenue is based on the interest rate margin, the other major source of income being derived from fees. In recent times, there has been a steady erosion of interest margins as competition has intensified in the sector, narrowing the spread between deposit and loan interest rates. In addition, the sector is witnessing a process of disintermediation: the move away from the central role of the banks in the intermediation of financial services. Although intermediation is an important activity for many financial institutions, Piesse *et al.* (1995) note that the banking sector has lost many of the inherent advantages it enjoyed in the past and now plays a less pivotal role. Consequently, many are looking at ways of increasing their proportion of fee income in an attempt to become less interest-rate-dependent.

Covert versus overt pricing methods

The pricing of financial services can be divided broadly into covert and overt pricing methods. Table 7.4 provides a definition of each type and examples. The process of financial intermediation gives rise to implicit pricing. This is further complicated by the extent to which the financial institution provides a 'free' banking service. Banking is not 'free': customers may not be charged explicitly for the use of payment services (while the account is in credit), however, there are costs incurred in operating the facility which have to be recovered.

Payment services, or free banking facilities, have served traditionally as loss-leaders for financial institutions, providing the initial contact with the customer and creating a basis for the cross-selling of additional (income-earning) products. Assuming loyalty and long-term customer relationships, customers would pay for the use of the 'free' payment service through the purchase of other products, such as mortgages and loans. However, customers have become less loyal and more footloose in their banking behaviour, and many have contracts with several financial institutions. Consequently, those who incur the costs in the use of some services do not end up paying for them, leaving them to be covered elsewhere within the financial institution. In some cases, this creates a complex series of cross-subsidies involving other products and/or customers in the process. For example, the service may be paid for by any combination of the following means:

- charging another customer a higher price;
- charging higher prices on other products;
- paying lower dividends to shareholders as a result of lower profits from non-pricing;
- widening the interest margin on financial intermediation (creating either lower deposit rates or higher lending rates).

One of the problems associated with covert pricing through cross-subsidies is that it necessitates there being subsidising and subsidised parts of the business. For example, the interest rates charged for credit cards or loans may be priced higher than the market level in order to subsidise the cost of operating a payments system. As competition has intensified, and customers have become more price-sensitive and willing to switch to take advantage of better prices, the higher prices of subsidising parts have been forced down.

Another problem with covert pricing is that it is interest-rate-sensitive. Thus, the price charged to the customer and the revenue generated by the financial institution both change with changes in the rate of interest. Consider the effect of interest rate changes on the cost and revenue generation of operating a current account which is provided free of charge to customers while in credit but is such that the customer receives no interest payment on credit balances. When interest rates are high net revenue increases for the financial institution since the customer is in effect providing an interest-free loan to the financial institution. The financial institution earns interest on using these interest-free deposits to acquire interest-earning assets. Thus, the greater the volume of interest-free deposits, the more net interest income rises as the general interest rate rises. This is known as the 'endowment effect'.

When the interest rate rises, the cost to the customer also increases (when the account is in credit), since loss of income through receiving no interest occurs. However, when the interest rate falls, the cost to the customer decreases, but the interest revenue to the financial institution also decreases. Furthermore, the costs associated with operating the service are not dependent on changes in the rate of interest. At very low interest-rate levels the costs of supplying the service may not even be covered. Moreover, since customers are not aware of the costs associated with using the service (they are not charged per transaction), there is no incentive to limit the use of the service which may add to the total costs.

The endowment effect has been eroded in recent years due to building societies entering the payments services market and paying interest on credit balances. Interest margins have also been squeezed as a result of greater price competition. As a result of this, there is a general trend towards the more explicit or overt charging for the use of financial services and products in an attempt to reduce the emphasis on interest income and increase the proportion of fee income. This trend has also been fuelled by changes to regulation which have created greater transparency of prices.

Overt pricing methods attempt to overcome some of the problems identified above. In particular, explicit charges aim to recover (at least partially) the costs incurred by the customers who use the service. Thus, prices are set in order to make a contribution to fixed costs and may also include an estimate of the variable cost element. Flat fees are an example of this. Customers may be charged a set fee, paid annually, quarterly or monthly, irrespective of account use. Some current accounts are priced on this basis, allowing customers to make unlimited use of the facilities provided (i.e. writing cheques and making cash withdrawals from ATMs) and perhaps also offering an agreed overdraft limit.

From the customer's point of view, this pricing method is attractive: customers know how much the service will cost and it will not vary with use. However, from the point of view of the financial institution, it does present some disadvantages. One problem is the difficulty of estimating the amount of use customers will make of the service. Some will make greater use of the service than others, incurring greater costs than others. Across the whole customer base, it might be expected that these variances in over- and underuse might even out. Despite this, it does raise the issue of fairness to the customer: some customers will be paying for services that they are not using, while others are getting something for nothing. Furthermore, some customers may be encouraged to overuse the service if there are no additional charges to curtail behaviour.

A variation on the flat fee method would be to specify the amount of use or number of transactions covered by the fee, and to charge additional fees for use of the service above the specified amount. For example, the flat fee might include the writing of *x* number of cheques per accounting period, or it may mean increasing the minimum withdrawal amount from the ATMs in order to reduce the number of frequent and small withdrawals, thus changing the behaviour of customers in order to control costs.

As noted in Chapter 6, telephone banking has enabled costs of delivery to be controlled, with resultant price reductions for customers. Yet, a proportion of the cost of delivery is passed on to the customer in the form of telephone charges (usually charged at the local call rate). This in itself can influence the extent to which customers make use of the service (i.e. call the financial institution); as use of the service increases, so too does the cost to the customer. The same also applies to internet connections, since the customer again pays the connection fee.

The opposite of a flat fee is to charge customers according to the volume and frequency of account use. Thus, charges are levied on each transaction. This form of pricing is more effective at covering the variable costs than a flat fee. In addition, transactional charges do have some effect on behaviour and can limit the extent to which the customer makes use of the service. One of the problems, however, is that (depending on customer behaviour) the revenue generated may not cover all the fixed costs associated with running the service.

In the late 1980s many credit card companies found that customers were holding multiple credit cards from different card issuers, were taking advantage of the deferred payment period and were paying balances in full. Hence, they were not having to pay anything to the company. Yet, there are fixed costs associated with these customers, such as setting up the account, calculating account balances and issuing monthly statements. Thus, in 1990 credit card issuers began to introduce annual fees to contribute to the fixed costs associated with running the accounts. For customers who do not pay their balances in full (revolvers), this results in a two-part tariff including the annual fixed charge and the interest which varies according to the outstanding balance and the interest rate. Some credit card issuers waive the flat fee if the card has been used, thereby generating interest income.

Table 7.4 A comparison of covert and overt pricing methods

Pricing method	Definition	Examples
Covert	The hidden pricing of products, or 'free' banking. The cost to the customer may not be purely monetary	No or low interest on deposits (as in the case of current accounts), the requirement to give notice for the withdrawal of savings, the requirement to maintain a minimum balance in the account
Overt	The explicit charging of services and products. The cost to the customer is obvious and mostly financial	Flat fees (such as an annual or quarterly charge for the use of an account, irrespective of use), transactional charges (customers are charged according to the amount used – charge per ATM visit or withdrawal from savings), or some combination of the two

Pricing of specific financial products

Savings and investments

For simple savings and deposit accounts, there would appear to be no price involved: customers deposit money with the financial institution and receive interest for doing so. However, the financial institution incurs a cost in the running of such accounts – they use staff time, computer systems, branch networks, marketing, etc. – and these costs need to be recovered. Thus, price, in the context of simple savings and deposit accounts, is represented by the difference between the interest received by the customer for savings made and the interest which could have been received if no costs had been apportioned to the running of the account.

Having said this, it is clear to see, from looking around the high street at the savings accounts available, that the interest rates offered vary between different types of simple savings accounts. Table 7.5 shows a comparison of interest rates for instant access and notice accounts and bonds. Instant access, as the name suggests, provides customers with access to their savings instantly, allowing them to make withdrawals as and when required. By comparison, notice accounts and bonds require customers to give a specified period of notice before making withdrawals. As indicated in the examples in table 7.5, these can be 30, 40, 50 or 60 days.

The different accounts appeal to different savings motives. As outlined in Chapter 3, these might be to 'save for a rainy day', to 'save to spend', to 'save for a particular purpose or purchase'. Understanding the various motives for saving helps to explain some of the differences in interest rates on savings accounts. Customers who are saving in order to spend or saving for emergencies may wish to have instant access to their funds. Thus, they forgo higher interest rates in order to be able to make withdrawals when they wish. Instant access becomes a price of the account. By comparison, customers who are willing to forgo instant access to their savings can achieve higher interest rates. Hence, lack of access becomes a price. This becomes apparent when customers wish to make withdrawals sooner than the specified period of notice. A fee and/or loss of interest is usually incurred.

Table 7.5 Comparison of savings rates

Instant access	Interest rate	Notice accounts and bonds	Interest rate
Standard Life Bank *Direct Access*	7.35%	Scarborough Building Society 7.60% *Scarborough 30*	
Cheltenham & Gloucester *Instant Transfer*	7.50%	Chelsea Building Society *Post-tel 40*	7.80%
Safeway *Direct Savings*	7.55%	Standard Life Bank *50 Day Notice*	7.55%
Saga (for over 50s) *Postal Savings*	7.90%	Legal & General Bank *60 Direct 5*	8.00%

(*Source*: Adapted from *The Express*, Wednesday 26 August 1998)

A longer-term saving motive of 'saving for retirement' or 'saving for children and their education' may involve customers in a number of longer-term investments. These are likely to be investments (either directly or indirectly) in equities. Due to the long-term nature of these investments, there are often explicit charges in the form of management fees which cover the cost of managing the fund over its life. In addition, a percentage of the premiums or investments made by customers may be absorbed by the company. The Prudential Assurance Company offers the Prudence Savings Account which is based on a flexible endowment policy offering customers the ability to increase regular premiums and make lump-sum investments while having no fixed maturity date. The charges associated with the account are £10 per year for the management of the fund, plus £6 for every £100 of regular and lump sum investments made (Prudential, 'Prudence Savings Account').

There are also a number of explicit charges associated with the buying and selling of shares and unit trusts. Any dealing through a broker will incur a commission, while other charges may include VAT, transfer duty and stamp duty on investments accrued. In addition, the slightly more covert price represented by the spread between the buying price and the selling price (the latter being less than the former) can make this form of investment costly for small and frequent transactions.

Credit and loans

The price associated with credit and loan products might seem more obvious than for savings and investments, since it relates more directly to the interest charged for borrowed funds. However, the rate of interest varies according to the type of loan or credit, whether it is short- or long-term, the degree of risk and whether any security is available. Thus, overdrafts, credit cards and store cards generally carry higher interest rates than personal loans, mortgages and home improvement loans. The

Table 7.6 Comparison of credit card rates

Credit card	Annual fee	APR*	Credit card	Annual fee	APR*
RBS MasterCard	Nil	7.9%	Royal Bank of Scotland Gold Visa	Nil in first year and then £35 for expenditures totalling less than £4000	13.3%
Barclaycard MasterCard and Visa	£10	22.9%	Barclays Standard Visa	£10	22.0%
Lloyds Classic Reserve MasterCard	£12	22.9%	Lloyds Standard Access	£12	21.8%
Midland MasterCard and Visa	£12	21.6%	Midland Standard MasterCard	£12	20.6%
MBNA MasterCard and Visa	Nil	19.9%	Co-operative Bank Gold Visa	Nil	21.7%

* On purchases and not cash advances.
Source: Royal Bank of Scotland product literature. Figures valid as at 20 October 1998

former are generally used for borrowing in the shorter term, offer no security and therefore carry a higher risk. For example, in the case of credit cards, one of the reasons the rate is higher is due to credit card fraud and the high probability of credit card holders defaulting. Credit card companies know that *x* per cent of their card holders will default on their payments, but they do not know which ones. Hence, all card holders pay through higher rates.

As already mentioned, many credit card issuers introduced annual fees in 1990. This added a further pricing element to the product in addition to the interest rate. Table 7.6 shows a comparison of pricing schemes for selected credit cards. The two-part tariff of annual fee and interest rate (shown here as the annual percentage rate) can make it difficult to compare products. The combination of no annual fee/low interest and annual fee/high interest reflect the different positioning strategies of the credit card companies in targeting revolvers and full-payers respectively. Indeed, most of the main financial institutions now offer a lower rate of interest for a fixed period to new customers who switch balances from other financial institutions.

A mortgage is a long-term secured loan, typically for 25 years, which uses the property as security. Thus, if the customer defaults on the payments the financial institution has the legal right to repossess the property and resell it in order to repay the loan. A mortgage can be repaid in one of two ways, which has an impact on the pricing. Either the loan is repaid in monthly (or weekly) instalments over the agreed term of the loan, or it is paid as a lump sum on termination of the contract with funds accrued from another source.

Under the first option the customer takes a standard repayment mortgage which involves making regular payments to cover both the interest and the capital. A variety of these exist which differ in terms of variable or fixed interest rates, low start or flexible payments. The other main route involves the customer making investments in either an endowment policy, a pension or personal equity plan (to name a few) which is designed to accumulate sufficient funds to repay the capital sum borrowed on termination of the contract. This type of investment can only be used for the repayment of the capital borrowed; the interest must still be paid on a monthly (or weekly) basis throughout the life of the contract. Endowment mortgages came under attack during the early 1990s as a number of policies maturing at this time were not sufficient to cover the outstanding loan on the property. As indicated in Chapter 1, endowment mortgages have decreased in popularity in recent years against an increase in popularity of standard repayment mortgages.

The interest rate is not the only price associated with mortgages. It is often the most visible element, but there are a number of other hidden costs which are not immediately apparent, and are difficult to compare between mortgage providers. It is quite common for financial institutions to charge a mortgage arrangement fee. This may be a fixed amount, irrespective of the amount borrowed, and can vary from under £200 to over £400. Alternatively, the mortgage arrangement fee may be calculated as a percentage of the amount borrowed, say 1 per cent. Until recently, most financial institutions also charged a mortgage indemnity fee. These varied enormously. However, the Halifax (the UK's largest mortgage lender) abolished its indemnity fee in 1998, setting a precedent for other mortgage lenders.

Another price associated with a mortgage is stamp duty payable on properties/mortgages over £60,000. This is essentially a tax levied on the borrower. The other costs associated with house buying, such as solicitors' fees and surveyors' costs may also be considered part of the price. In addition, the financial institution may attempt to tie the customer into the purchase of buildings insurance as part of the contract of the mortgage, adding the insurance premiums to the price. Another factor for consideration is the proportion of the value of the property the financial institution will lend. First-time buyers may be looking to borrow up to 100 per cent of the value, yet the amount can vary from institution to institution from as little as 75 per cent upwards. This increases the price to the customer in that as much as 25 per cent of the value of the property may need to be offered as a down-payment.

These examples show that the price of a product can appear in many different ways, some being obvious and others not. The sometimes hidden nature of price and the many elements associated with it often make it difficult for customers to compare products according to price.

Trends in pricing

Since the abolition of the interest rate cartels, financial institutions have become more focused on price as a competitive tool. This has resulted in more intense competition with regard to interest rates. Furthermore, this has been made worse by the new entrants to the marketplace which have further increased the competition. Thus, the effect has been that interest rates have been squeezed. Financial institutions have made use of implicit pricing or covert pricing which has been successful in hiding the cost of the product to the customer. However, this relied on good interest margins in order to absorb the costs of running the services. Under intense competition the interest margins have been squeezed as rates have been competed down. Also, legislation has made pricing more transparent to customers and made it less possible for institutions to hide costs from the customer. Hence, institutions are attempting to reduce their reliance on interest margins, and look for alternative sources of income.

The US situation where fees are charged for entering banking halls might seem a little extreme for the UK. Nonetheless, we are experiencing some forms of fee introduction and the pricing according to distribution, encouraging customers to use less costly forms, e.g. telephone banking. Thus it does not seem unrealistic to expect that charges and fees will continue to be introduced and used as a means of pricing the services and products.

SUMMARY

This chapter has attempted to give an overview of pricing considerations for financial services. It has shown that pricing for financial services is far from straightforward. For example, it is not always easy to identify what the price of a product is, due to the nature of covert and overt pricing methods. Covert pricing methods have evolved as a direct consequence of the pricing of financial intermediation and the provision of so-called free banking services. Such services are not free, they incur a cost to the institution, and the cost must be recovered somewhere through the financial institution, either by charging customers higher loan rates or by offering lower savings rates. Overt pricing methods use explicit charges and fees and these are being used more as financial institutions attempt to reduce their dependence on the interest margin for income.

Pricing is also complicated in that prices are influenced by a number of factors both internal and external to the financial institution. Regulation imposes certain limits and restrictions on financial institutions and these have a direct impact on the pricing of financial services. The hard disclosure ruling has made prices more transparent and may have contributed to increased price competition in certain areas of business, notably insurance. Interest rates also closely follow movements in the base rate set by the Bank of England. Internally, financial institutions' capital adequacy requirements impact on prices, as too do shareholders' expectations. All of this is made even more complicated by the fact that for many financial products it is not possible to identify the specific costs attributed to the product. Pricing issues are also becoming increasingly interrelated with distribution considerations as new distribution channels are being used to reduce costs and operate targeted pricing strategies.

DISCUSSION QUESTIONS

1. Choose a range of financial products and identify how the price of each product is represented.
2. Explain why price is important to the consumer of financial services.
3. To what extent has price and/or non-price competition been used in the financial services sector? Give examples.
4. In your opinion, what are the most important factors influencing pricing decisions and what influence do they exert?
5. How important are costs in the determination of price, and how easily are financial services costs identified?
6. Explain the pricing of financial intermediation and the impact this has on the pricing of financial services.
7. Compare and contrast covert and overt pricing methods. What are the advantages and disadvantages of each from the point of view of both the financial institution and the consumer?
8. Outline some of the ways in which financial institutions price savings and investments products.
9. Discuss the current pricing strategies employed by credit card companies.
10. Comment on the current and future trends in financial services pricing.

8 Communication and promotion

INTRODUCTION

No matter how closely the product matches the customer's needs, how innovative the delivery mechanism is, or how competitively priced the product is, if customers do not know this they cannot begin to consider the product as a suitable purchase alternative. Thus, one of the key functions of the promotion element of the marketing mix is simply to communicate the company and its products and services to the customer.

There are several ways in which a financial institution can communicate with its customers and other target audiences. The specific combination of promotional methods is known as the 'promotional mix'. The mix includes: advertising, sales promotion, personal selling, publicity and public relations, direct mail, direct response advertising and sponsorship. The extent to which each method is used depends, among other things, on the marketing communication objectives, the target audience and the products or services being promoted.

While the advertising and promotion of financial services bears some resemblance to the promotion of other goods and services, there are noticeable differences particularly in terms of how the various tools of communication are used. A number of factors necessitate this, including: the intangibility, heterogeneity and high risk of financial services, the legal requirements and limitations surrounding advertising and promotion, and the general consumer apathy and lack of interest in the product category.

This chapter addresses these issues in more detail, and also focuses on the specific use of the promotional mix elements.

OBJECTIVES

After reading this chapter you should be able to:

- outline the role of promotion in the marketing mix;
- illustrate the communication process and its importance in the promotion of financial services;
- outline the factors affecting the promotion of financial services and discuss their implications;
- categorise communication objectives and highlight communication tools appropriate for the achievement of specific objectives;
- compare and discuss the elements of the promotional mix and critically evaluate their relative importance in the promotion of financial services.

The role of promotion

As mentioned above, the most basic role of promotion is communication. While the customers of a financial institution are a key target for promotion, there are also a number of other target audiences or constituencies which the organisation will want to communicate with or promote itself to. These include, among others, employees, intermediaries, shareholders, the general public. As a result of this, the role of promotion is wide-reaching, from facilitating exchanges with customers to informing and educating audiences.

In a highly competitive marketplace, such as financial services, consumers are bombarded with various forms of promotion. Hence, another key function of promotion is persuasion; promotional efforts must be stimulating and motivating enough to generate interest in and promote a positive attitude towards the company and its products so that they will be considered favourably in comparison with competitors.

Promotion achieves this by working in harmony with the other elements of the marketing mix, thus, according to Kirk (1994), enabling the following to be achieved:

- *Customer acquisition* – Acquiring new customers is a key business activity. A business cannot hope to survive indefinitely with the same customers. There will come a time when the customer outlives the usefulness of the product or the product outlives the customer. Either way, the recruitment of new customers is essential even to maintain existing levels of business in the long term. New customers can be gained from one of two main sources. Some new customers may just be entering the life stage appropriate for the product, thus, representing new business. Other new customers may not be new to the market but merely new to the company, gained from competitors. Promotion has a key role to play in building awareness of the company and its products to new customers and, in the case of switching customers, outlining the key benefits offered in comparison to competitors.
- *Customer retention* – While customer acquisition is important and necessary, it is essential that the value of existing customers is not overlooked. The marketing and promotion costs associated with acquiring new customers far outweigh those required to retain existing customers and generate further business from them. Promotion has an important role to play in building and maintaining customer loyalty and cross-selling additional products to customers as the need arises or as they enter the appropriate life stage.
- *Staff morale* – Financial institutions should not focus all their attention on customers, forgetting their staff. In service organisations, in particular, the role of employees has a crucial impact on customer satisfaction and retention. Customer-facing staff in financial institutions occupy a boundary-spanning role and are often seen as part-and-parcel of the product or service being provided. Thus, internal marketing and communication are just as important as communication with the external customer. Promotion and communication can provide support for staff and serve to boost the image of the company and its products and services.
- *Corporate stability* – An important role of promotion, particularly for financial

institutions, is that of the creation and projection of corporate stability to customers, employees and wider audiences such as shareholders, intermediaries and other investors. Financial institutions have a fiduciary responsibility towards their customers and investors. It is a relationship based on and dependent on trust. Customers need to feel that the institution is trustworthy and reliable. Promotion serves as a statement of confidence and stability to the wider audience. It sends out the message that if the company can afford to advertise it is credible and immutable.

- *Public image and awareness* – In addition to communication with the targets and constituencies in direct (or near direct) contact with the financial institution, the wider public audiences with which the institution has either no or indirect contact should also not be forgotten. It is important to create awareness of the institution and maintain a positive public image and generally create good public relations. Promotion can inform the public of socially responsible activities (such as charitable work) and dispel any negative misconceptions of the institution.

The communication process

In order to understand the role which promotion plays in the marketing mix, it is important to appreciate the process through which communication works. Essentially, the process is understood in terms of who says what to whom through what channels, in what way and to what effect. A simple model of the communication process is depicted in figure 8.1.

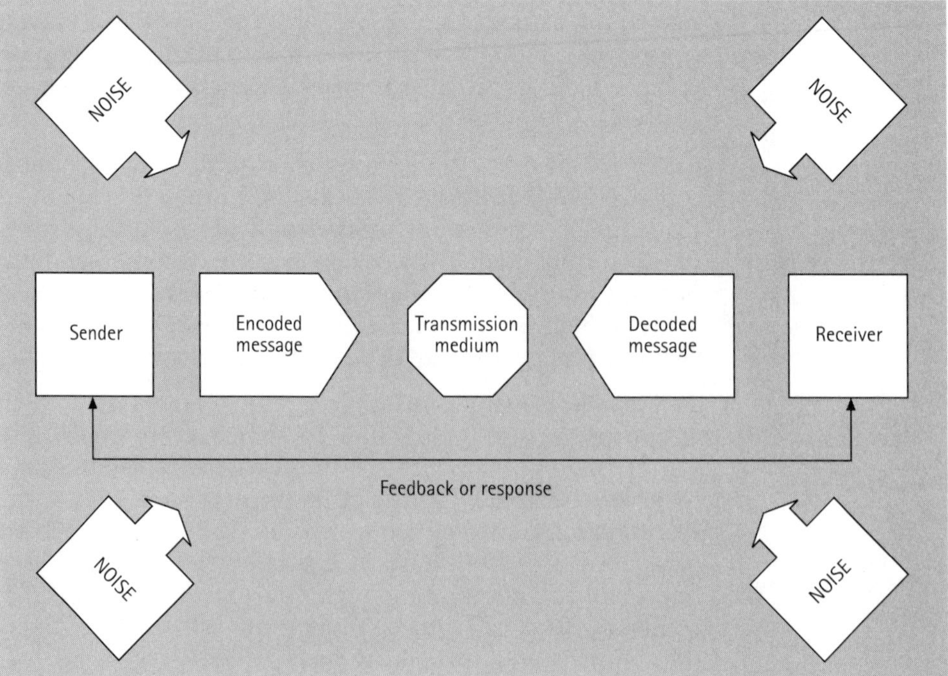

Fig. 8.1 The communication process

FINANCIAL SERVICES MARKETING IN PRACTICE

Researching the effectiveness of 'the little red phone': the case of Direct Line

The production costs and air-time of TV advertising can be immense, running to half a million to produce an ad and several millions to show it. It is, therefore, important to ensure maximum effectiveness. The way to achieve this is to run a pre-test.

Direct Line, the direct insurer, began selling motor insurance in 1985. The company operates by responding to calls from enquirers, providing quotations over the telephone as the operator keys in the caller's details.

In addition to storing customer information, the database also holds information on how and where the caller heard of the company, enabling Direct Line to build up a picture of how well different media are performing.

For example, the company has been able to test the effectiveness of different newspapers and different executions and to identify which produce the best outcome in terms of customer response and cost efficiency.

When Direct Line began advertising motor insurance, bottom-of-the-page strip in national newspapers fared the best. Yet, the success of Direct Line prompted a number of competitors to follow in their footsteps. Soon the direct insurance market was becoming crowded, with the result that Direct Line were finding it difficult to maintain share dominance.

A new strategy was needed to re-emphasise the benefits of Direct Line: the optimum impact, reach and communication potential could be achieved using TV. So, on January 3 1990, a new motor insurance campaign broke.

The ad was thoroughly researched and tested in animatic form, providing the opportunity to make changes before too much had been invested in the finished film. It was just as well. The findings of the pre-test showed that the ad: was not very enjoyable, provided low brand prominence, stimulated interest in the little red phone but general interest was low, and did not effectively communicate Direct Line's price competitiveness.

It was recommended that the red phone should adopt a more prominent role in the ad with a stronger personality, it needed to be positioned as 'the motorist's friend', but should not detract from the message about competitive prices.

Had the ad been left in its original form, it would have achieved an estimated awareness index (AI) of between one and two (i.e. for each additional 100 TVRs put behind the ad, there would have been an increase in only one or two percentage points of claimed ad recall). The majority of ads achieve AIs in the range of three to five. The ad was modified in accordance with the recommendations and achieved an AI of four.

Yet, the real benefit was found in the sales effect: following the TV ad, the slight downward trend, previously experienced, showed a rapid increase. Telephone enquiries for quotations rose by 70 per cent.

By late 1988 Direct Line had also entered the home insurance market. However, press advertising did not prove as successful for home insurance as it had for motor insurance. There were several explanations for this: strong consumer inertia, strong control from mortgage lenders – particularly building societies, and no habit of shopping around as with motor insurance.

Thus, it was decided that advertising for home insurance had to do more than merely announce Direct Line – it needed to shake up people's beliefs and opinions about home insurance so that they would begin to consider other providers in addition to their mortgage lender. Direct Line had something to shake up the market: a 20 per cent saving on current insurance premiums.

Following the success of the motor insurance TV ads, it was questioned whether a pre-test was necessary. The ad would have the same format as the motor insurance ads, the Direct Line proposition was clear and simple to grasp – a 20 per cent saving, and the personality of the red phone was understood from the earlier ad. Furthermore, the cost of a pre-test had to be considered – in the region of £20,000–£30,000 plus the time lag it would have on the launch of the campaign.

The arguments against a pre-test were compelling, yet the decision was taken to test the campaign, and it was just as well.

The pre-test threw up a number of problems: the ad did not rate well in terms of enjoyability or brand prominence. It seemed to fare well in terms of 'ease of understanding'; however, on further investigation it was found that around two thirds

FINANCIAL SERVICES MARKETING IN PRACTICE

of those tested clearly misunderstood the message and had got it completely the wrong way round.

Rather than perceiving the red phone as the agent offering the 20 per cent reduction, the saving was attributed to the building society manager. Consequently, the identity and role of the red phone emerged as something of a mystery and a source of irritation.

The misconceptions arose as a result of the sudden appearance of the red phone in the building society office. The phone needed to be seen as coming to the rescue from outside the building society to the aid of the couple discussing insurance premiums with the building society manager.

In the finished film the misconceptions were eradicated and the ad achieved a high AI of eight. Furthermore, 80 per cent found that the ad told them 'something of interest' – the offer of a 20 per cent saving on current premiums.

Source: Adapted from Ashman and Clarke (1994)

Questions:

1 What would have happened if the original animatics had not been tested and had not been amended in the finished films?

2 Was it right to assume that the home insurance ad would work because the motor insurance ad was successful?

3 Why is 'the little red phone' successful?

The process involves a sender, who sends a message via a transmission medium to the recipient or audience. In this case, the sender is the financial institution. The receiver typically represents the target customer audience but may also consist of employees, shareholders, intermediaries, the general public or any other of the company's targets or constituencies. The financial institution typically has an intended meaning which it wants to send to an audience. In order to transform the meaning into a message it needs to be converted into a series of signs and symbols which represent ideas and concepts. Thus, the meaning is encoded. For the message to be understood by those receiving it, the form of encoding used must be familiar to them. Thus, it is important that the financial institution fully understands who the target audience is and what appeals to them.

For the encoded message to be received and accessed by the target audience, it must be transmitted via a medium. The transmission medium merely represents the communication tool used to carry the message. This could be television or print advertising or personal selling via a salesperson. The choice of transmission medium needs to be specific to the target audience so that they can be reached.

Once the receiver or audience is exposed to the message it will be decoded in order that the full meaning can be understood. The audience may not always decode the message in a way which imparts the specific intended meaning. Direct Line discovered through pre-tests that their initial television advertisement formats for motor and home insurance did not get the intended message across. In fact, the home insurance ad message was interpreted to be the exact opposite of what Direct Line had intended (see Financial Services Marketing in Practice: 'Researching the effectiveness of "the little red phone": the case of Direct Line'). This is why it is important to fully understand the audience and how they will respond to the message. If Direct Line had not invested in a pre-test, their success in the direct insurance market might have been seriously jeopardised by a misunderstood message.

The communication process results in feedback or response. This may or may not be immediate, depending on the medium used. For example, advertising may result in a slower response than personal selling which is imperative and creates immediate feedback. Some non-personal forms of communication may evoke no feedback at all. Indeed, one of the key problems associated with mass communication, especially advertising, is that it is difficult to ascertain the effectiveness of the advertisement on sales due to a number of other potential intervening factors. Direct response advertising is measurable and this is one reason why it is favoured for financial services.

Communication objectives

Having established that the process of communication results in a response from a target audience, it is important that the financial institution decides what the desired response should be. The ultimate response is purchase behaviour. But, as discussed in Chapter 2, the act of purchase occurs at the end of a sometimes long process of consumer decision-making which involves the consumer progressing through a cognitive stage, an affective stage and finally a behavioural stage. In the cognitive stage, marketers need to put the company and its products and services in the mind of the consumer, in the affective stage an attitudinal change (in favour of the company and its products) needs to be effected, and in the behavioural stage marketers need to get the consumer to act.

Thus, the act of purchase is only one of the objectives of communication. A single communication, whether it is in the form of a television advertisement or personal selling, will rarely cause an individual to buy a previously unfamiliar product.

Table 8.1 Communication objectives

Communication objective	Communication tool	Example
Awareness	Mass communication sources. *Broadcast media (TV and radio) national or regional magazines and newspapers*	AA Insurance – *'That's the job of the AA'*
Interest	Mass communication sources. *Same media as above but not necessarily the same message*	Direct Line – 20 per cent reduction
Preference	Advertising, publicity and PR, and personal sources. *News story reports, comparative advertising and word-of-mouth from friends and relatives*	First Direct – TV and direct mail – *'Tell us one good thing about your bank'*
Trial	Sales promotion and personal sources. *Special offers, salespeople, relatives, friends*	Churchill insurance – *'Give the dog a phone'*
Adoption	Personal sources and, for reassurance, mass communication. *Salespeople, friends and relatives, broadcast and print advertising*	Bank of Scotland – *'Friend for Life'*

Marketing communication objectives need to be closely aligned with the stages of the consumer decision-making process and need to move the consumer closer to the stage of buyer readiness.

Table 8.1 outlines common communication objectives used to move the consumer closer to purchase and adoption of the product or service. The stages are adapted from a number of response hierarchy models which have been put forward to explain the affective, cognitive and behavioural stages consumers move through. Contrast this with the AIDA model (Awareness, Interest, Desire and Action) mentioned in Chapter 2.

- *Awareness* – For each communication objective (or stage of the decision process) different communication tools will have greater effectiveness. If the target audience is unaware of the product or service, as with a new product, the objective is to build awareness and name recognition. Mass communication sources are very effective at building awareness: they can reach a large audience quickly and at a relatively low cost per head. When Barclays Bank launched b_2 in 1998, its first television advertisement was aimed at building awareness of the name. The advertisement was deliberately vague: no spoken or written message was transmitted, and no people or objects were portrayed, just the projection of the mysterious name 'b_2' against a 'Barclays' blue background. The lack of information in the ad created an air of mystery and stimulated interest.

- *Interest* – Having made consumers aware of the existence of the product or service, communication needs to appeal to consumers' affective judgement. The air of mystery surrounding the b_2 ads may have stimulated some interest. However, to be truly interested in the product, the consumer needs to be informed of its features and characteristics. Mass communication sources may continue to be used to stimulate interest in the product, although the message may change from 'here we are' (the announcement of a product) to 'this is what we are' (the identification of specific features).

- *Preference* – Stimulating interest in the product may make consumers like the product but it may not make them want it over and above other competing products. Thus, the next objective is to gain consumer preference for the product. First Direct attempted to build a preference for its telephone banking service by asking its competitors' customers: 'Tell us one good thing about your bank'. This prompted individuals to evaluate their existing financial services provider against First Direct. The advertising resulted in some switching behaviour. Also Direct Line attempted to change individuals' beliefs about appropriate providers of home insurance and shook up the market with its first television advertisement for home insurance which portrayed the little red phone as the 'low-cost' hero coming to the rescue of house buyers paying high insurance premiums to building societies.

- *Trial* – Once a favourable attitude has been developed, communication must attempt to move the consumer towards buying action. The behavioural stage often comes in two parts: trial and adoption. For most physical goods, trial and adoption occur as distinct stages, often separated by time and place. However, as discussed in Chapter 4, the vast majority of financial services do not present the opportunity for trial. Hence, trial often forms part of the adoption stage in that consumers continue to evaluate the financial product once they have committed themselves to it. For the purpose of discussing communication objectives, trial can be perceived as the encouragement of consumers to interact with the financial services provider, perhaps to respond to an invitation to call for an insurance quote. Consumers may even engage in a 'pseudo-trial' of the product based on friends' and relatives' experiences of the product.

- *Adoption* – The ultimate communication objective is the adoption of the product or service. Yet, adoption does not mark the end of communication with consumers. Having adopted a financial product a consumer can terminate the contract and switch to another financial provider at any time. Thus, the role of communication is still important. Consumers need to be reassured and reminded of the benefits offered by the financial institution.

Communication message

The communication message is the key to the achievement of communication objectives. Considerations in the design of an appropriate message include: what to say, how to say it, and who should say it. This section will focus only on the message content (i.e. what to say). Knowing what to say is important, since a single message may not have the same level of effectiveness or even produce the same desired response from different segments of the market. Indeed, Britannia estimates that the effectiveness of their marketing communication was doubled by carefully targeting different customer segments with different communication messages via direct mail. As a result, the institution increased its direct marketing spend (see Financial Services Marketing in Practice: 'Targeted direct mailshot makes mortgage mailing meaningful').

In order to be effective, the message needs to have a theme, appeal or unique selling proposition. Appeals can be rational, emotional or moral.

Rational appeals

Rational themes appeal to logical reasoning. In the context of advertising financial services, rational appeals might focus on the actual product or service, its features, quality, value, performance, etc. As already mentioned, due to a number of factors associated with the advertising of financial services and consumers' difficulties in effectively evaluating them, it is not always possible to focus on product features and technical aspects of the offering. This is perhaps an explanation why few financial services ads use rational appeals, and those that do focus almost entirely on price or delivery as part of the appeal.

Emotional appeals

Emotional appeals attempt to rouse negative or positive feelings in an attempt to motivate individuals. Positive appeals may focus on the use of humour, love or pride. The Dunfermline Building Society attempted to elicit positive emotions in its television advertisements which focused on Scottish pride and nationalism.

FINANCIAL SERVICES MARKETING IN PRACTICE

Targeted direct mailshot makes mortgage mailing meaningful

UK financial institutions have found it difficult to build up accurate and detailed customer profiles. Indeed, the sector generally has been criticised for being poor at developing relationships with customers.

Britannia Building Society seems to have found the answer. The solution lies in the bonus scheme developed to illustrate to members of the society the value of mutual ownership against giving free shares through converting to a public limited company. In 1997 the bonus scheme paid out £35m.

Savers and borrowers are required to register in order to qualify for loyalty bonuses. Roughly, three-quarters of the society's members have registered for the scheme. The value to the society is that 60 per cent of those registered volunteered extra information about their tax band, occupation and financial relationships with other organisations. The information has enabled the society to segment its customers into nine categories and customise the direct mailings they receive.

This means that different groups of customers can be communicated to in different ways, with different messages that have specific meaning for them. Some groups are already knowledgeable and do not want to be patronised, others want to have their hands held and require a little more guidance. The different tones and messages are being used not only in direct mailshots but also in the branches.

The benefits of the database were realised when Britannia launched a direct mailshot to savers offering them the chance to switch their mortgage from their existing lender to Britannia. Based on the information gathered, the mailshot was able to take into account not only whether customers were likely to prefer lower monthly repayments to a cash lump sum, but how they would be most tempted to spend the cash.

Britannia believes that the effectiveness of the re-mortgaging mailshot has been doubled, even though the product remains the same. On the strength of this, the society increased its direct marketing spend from £1.5m in 1996 to £5m in 1997.

Source: Adapted from *Financial Times*, 21 April 1997

Questions:

1 How can the information gathered by Britannia improve customer relationships?

2 What other uses might direct mail be put to?

3 What are the advantages of direct mail for Britannia?

McKechnie *et al.* (1997) and McKechnie and Leather (1998) investigated factors influencing consumers' likeability of financial services television advertisements and the subsequent impact on their behaviour. Viewers' responses to financial services commercials seemed to be built on the following factors: the commercial should be stimulating; the context should be appealing and relevant; the message should be targeted and fresh; the people in the commercial should appear authentic. In addition, the organisation should be perceived as having a personal touch and be able to communicate in a 'down-to-earth' manner. In contrast to FMCG commercials, where likeability was determined by how meaningful and relevant the commercial appeared to the viewers, these studies suggested that for financial services commercials it depends very much on how original and amusing the message is and how appealing the music is.

Barclaycard successfully used humour to communicate its benefits in a way a more rational approach would not have been able to. Between 1991 and 1995 there were 14 advertisements made, communicating eight different benefits of the credit card. They featured Rowan Atkinson as Richard Latham, the bungling secret agent. In each one, his assistant, Bough, demonstrated the benefits of the card, providing the mouthpiece for information. Latham remained dismissive about the card's usefulness and repeatedly ran into trouble when things went wrong. The ads were successful because they made credit cards appear friendlier, dispelling many of the fears, and created a powerful visual demonstration of what can go wrong, providing many rational reasons to choose the card.

Negative appeals focus on fear, guilt and shame in order to motivate. According to Sternthal and Craig (1974), besides humour, fear is the most commonly used basis for persuasion. Yet, the use of humour is not so controversial. Fear is a powerful motivator and can influence buying behaviour. Marketing communications generally attempt to inform consumers of the benefits of purchasing and/or using a product or service. Communications using fear appeals do the opposite by informing consumers of the negative aspects associated with a product or the risks of using or not using a product. Thus, fear appeals are deliberately designed to arouse anxiety in an audience with the expectation that the audience will attempt to reduce that anxiety by adopting, continuing or discontinuing, or avoiding a specified course of thought or action (Spence and Moinpour, 1972). Positive appeals may also arouse anxiety but they do not set out to do so – it is incidental to the main thrust of the message.

Fear appeals generally have been used to modify social and health-related behaviour, for example the Health Education Board for Scotland makes extensive use of fear in its campaigns to encourage people to give up smoking, stop taking drugs and take care in the sun, by illustrating the consequences of not altering one's behaviour. In addition to this, financial institutions have also found a use for fear appeals in the advertising of a number of financial products, particularly pensions and life

Table 8.2 Examples of fear appeals

Financial product	Fear appeal	Example
Mortgage protection	Fear of repossession of property and home	'*You no doubt work hard to put a roof over your family's head . . . if the main mortgage payer is unable to work through sickness or unemployment, then plans have to be made to make sure the payments don't dry up*' (Clydesdale bank)
Pension	Fear of impoverished old age	'*Only 2% of the population with existing pension arrangements will retire on the maximum pension, 46% of pensioners rely solely on the State pension, 1 in 3 pensioners currently have to survive on less than £100 per month*' (Barclays Bank '1997 misery gap survey')
Home insurance	Fear of theft and loss of possessions and invasion of private space	'*You've probably spent a lot of time, effort and money on your home and though you may not want to think about it, accidents do happen and can be expensive without the right insurance cover*' (Bank of Scotland)
Life assurance	Fear of leaving dependants and loved-ones to fend for themselves in an uncertain future	'*The family is the most important thing in most peoples lives, and high priority is placed on making sure that they will be looked after if the worst should happen to you*' (Clydesdale bank)

products and general insurance (see table 8.2). A number of reasons can be offered to explain, first, why fear is used and, secondly, why it works.

Why fear is used in promoting financial services:

- Financial services are intangible entities and are difficult to display in advertising.
- Benefits are difficult to understand and difficult to communicate.
- Outcomes of products are often not known and therefore cannot be communicated.
- Financial products are high in credence qualities and many consumers do not have the know-how to assimilate advertised information.
- Lack of interest in many financial products has a negative impact on advertising.
- Regulatory limitations of advertising reduce its effectiveness.

Why fear works in the promotion of financial services

- The future is uncertain and many consumers may have a natural fear of their futures in a financial context.
- Many products have a legal obligation to buy, creating a fear of stepping outside the law.
- Families with dependants will have a natural worry for those they are responsible for.
- Fear can be induced – psychologists have shown that anxiety can be learned by observing another person produce such a response (Bandura and Walters, 1963) making advertising effective at inducing fear.

There are a number of important considerations in the use of fear appeals noted by Quinn *et al.* (1992).

- *Level of fear* – It is important to gauge the level of fear carefully, since it is possible that the message can be either too threatening or not carry enough threat. Increased levels of fear can actually be counter-productive because too much of a threat may cause people to either avoid the message altogether or simply ignore the recommendations within the message. On the contrary, a weak threat may not be seen as sufficiently motivating. In many situations it is thought that a moderate level of fear or threat may be best, yet this is a rather subjective measure and would need to be based on careful research specific to the target audience and product category.

- *Source credibility* – The fear appeal has the greatest impact when used in conjunction with a highly credible source. Some financial services advertisements promoting insurance products have portrayed the emergency services (police, fire and ambulance) in advertisements to add credibility and reality to the scenes depicted.

- *Type of fear* – There are potentially numerous types of fear. Perhaps the most relevant to financial services are the fear of physical or social harm and financial loss. Fear of physical harm may relate directly to the person and harm to themselves. Many insurance policies include a personal injury element to cover this. However, other forms of physical harm might relate to loss or damage of property from theft, fire or some other occurrence. Social harm may relate to the social consequences of loss of employment through redundancy, loss of status, position and responsibility, loss of standard of living, loss of home (due to repossession). A number of insurance policies are also designed to cater to these types of fear, offering redundancy protection plans, mortgage payment protection, etc. Other financial consequences may relate to the fear of an impoverished old age, often capitalised on in the marketing of pensions.

- *Interest value of the communication* – In order for the fear appeal to be successful the message must interest the audience and motivate them. Even if fear is high and credibility of the message is high, it will not guarantee success unless it stimulates interest.
- *Relevance* – The fear appeal is likely to have the greatest effect when the communication incorporates people to whom the threat is a relevant experience. This is why some financial institutions run a series of advertisements depicting different lifestyles and life stages in order to appeal to different segments of the market. For example, Pearl Assurance runs a series of television commercials around the theme of preparing for the future, which takes into account young, middle-aged and retirement age individuals in family and divorced situations. Ray and Wilkie (1970) suggest that fear motivation is most effective when consumers do not perceive themselves as part of the recommended market for the product. This approach has met some success in the portrayal of younger individuals in advertisements for pensions.
- *Ethics* – If fear appeals persuade individuals to buy products by preying on their heightened anxiety, the ethical issues should be considered. The use of fear appeals in advertising is open to question because of the possible negative effects of fear-induced behaviour. Indeed, it begs the question, should the use of fear appeals be regulated? Blatant ethical misconduct may be perceived in situations where the proposed solution to the feared condition is a product which does not meet the customer's expectations (or reduce their fear). The FSA is still trying to resolve the pensions mis-selling scandal, amidst a furore of advertising from both government and financial institutions.

Moral appeals

Moral appeals work on an audience's sense of what is right and wrong. Consumers are increasingly bringing their personal values and morals to purchasing situations as evidenced by the increasing demand for 'green' products and socially responsible businesses. In other product areas marketers have capitalised on this by appealing to consumers' morals. In the financial services sector success has been achieved in the area of ethical investments, yet the Co-operative Bank is the only bank to have positioned itself as an 'ethical' financial institution (see Financial Services Marketing in Practice: 'The Co-operative Bank: "Why bank with one that isn't?" – the development of an "ethical" advertising campaign').

FINANCIAL SERVICES MARKETING IN PRACTICE

The Co-operative Bank: 'Why bank with one that isn't?' – the development of an 'ethical' advertising campaign

In the late 1980s the Co-operative Bank was experiencing a number of problems: market share was falling although the market as a whole was growing, personal current account losses were outweighing the gains, the customer base was becoming increasingly downmarket, and the bank had a lack of special identity.

Thus, the bank decided it needed to raise awareness and develop a specific image while at the same time increasing the proportion of upmarket customers and customer loyalty. So, in the early 1990s the company began to develop an advertising campaign.

The Co-operative Bank is relatively small in comparison to the other main banks. Its advertising budget was limited, which meant that the effectiveness of the campaign was crucial. For these reasons is was felt that it would not be wise to attempt to position the bank alongside the other big banks. Hence, it was decided that a niche positioning strategy would be more appropriate.

The bank sought a unique competitive differentiator which could be emphasised and used in its positioning. It focused on how the bank was different from other banks, what type of people it attracted and how it was perceived.

How was the bank different from other banks?

A main difference was found in the ownership structure. Owned by the Co-operative Wholesale Society, the bank had strong ties with the co-operative movement and had developed areas of expertise in the provision of banking services for local authorities and community action groups.

Furthermore, the bank had an unwritten ethical code which meant that it never lent money to any of the larger environmentally or politically unsound organisations.

Whom had it attracted?

A high proportion of the customers of the bank were found to have a community focus with many customers from the social and caring professions, such as nurses, health workers, teachers, etc.

How was it perceived?

The image of the bank differed between the general public and its customers. The general public tended to perceive the bank as rather old fashioned and left-wing whereas the customers valued its heritage and had chosen the bank as a result of its ethical values.

It was acknowledged that the bank was never going to appeal to a mass market; a profitable niche market needed to be identified. An opportunity existed in the growing public awareness of the wider social and environmental implications of commercial behaviour.

Increasingly, consumers were bringing their personal values and morals to purchasing situations. The surge in 'green' goods provided evidence of this, but these values were also having an impact on financial services as the demand for ethical investments and affinity cards showed.

It was decided that the bank should attempt to capitalise on these ethical values and should position itself as the 'ethical bank'.

The creative challenge

The creative challenge was to impart the message of 'responsible sourcing and distribution of funds' in a way that consumers would understand but at the same time would find stimulating and motivating. It was important that the creative work was in keeping with the bank's values of honesty and integrity and did not fall into the trap of appearing 'holier than thou'. Indeed, the whole notion of advertising was somewhat at odds with the bank's values, and necessitated a simple approach.

The solution was based on an adaptation of the children's tale: 'This is the house that Jack built . . .'. It simply told the story of the actions and consequences in the sourcing and distribution of funds.

Four story lines were produced, each focusing on separate issues: the environment, human rights, animal testing and armaments. Each story told of a normal everyday family undertaking but with an ironic twist to it, revealing that the bank which the family used had loaned money to an organisation for purposes which were at odds with the family's values.

FINANCIAL SERVICES MARKETING IN PRACTICE

Black-and-white drawings and photographs were used to reinforce the simplicity of the message and to contrast with the glossy and colourful advertising used by the other banks.

The environment advertisement read: 'These are the trees that the Wilsons planted, with interest accrued from their savings, which their bank had lent to a chemical giant, that ceaselessly spews toxic waste'. The slogan running through all the ads made a very clever, yet simple, play on the name of the bank: 'The Co-operative Bank: Why bank with one that isn't?'

In terms of media selection, a focused execution was used. Sixty per cent of the budget was spent on ads in the quality press and the remaining 40 per cent was spent on TV. TV air time was bought to follow specific programmes, such as *Dispatches* and *World in Action*, which were thought to be in keeping with the values of the target audience.

The campaign was successful in attracting a greater proportion of ABC_1 individuals, resulting in a 9 per cent increase in the bank's personal current account deposits. Deposits increased by 49 per cent and the potential from cross-sales also increased. The campaign also boosted staff morale and improved public perceptions of the bank.

Source: Adapted from C. Baker (1995), 'The Co-operative Bank – "Profit with Principles"', *Advertising Works*, pp. 329–352, NTC Publications Limited, Henley-on-Thames

Questions:

1 How did the bank identify its unique competitive position?

2 What was the rationale for spending 60 per cent of the budget on press ads?

3 The campaign was deemed a success, but how reliable are the measures of success?

Factors affecting the promotion of financial services

There are a number of factors which impact on the promotion of financial services and make the task of promotion and its effectiveness more difficult. Some of these are related to the specific nature of the product, its characteristics and features, some are related to the nature of the customer, and others are related to the nature of legislation and external factors which control the environment in which financial services are promoted.

In Chapter 2 the impact of the specific characteristics of financial services on information processing and the purchase decision process was discussed. These influences on consumer buyer behaviour are the direct result of some of the problems associated with the advertising and promotion of essentially intangible and variable service offerings and warrant further attention in this chapter. Hill and Gandhi (1992) specifically noted the effects of intangibility, inseparability, heterogeneity and contextuality on the promotion and advertising of financial services (see table 8.3).

One of the key issues associated with advertising and promoting intangible products is that there is no tangible dimension. Consequently, it is not possible to display the product since it does not exist in physical form. Financial institutions have solved this problem by 'tangibilising' the product or service. This has been achieved by the use of physical evidence and symbols which portray the essence of what is being offered. For example, Direct Line use the red telephone to signify the delivery mechanism and Norwich Union uses the Great Wall of China to portray strength and protection.

Table 8.3 Effects of intangibility, inseparability, heterogeneity and contextuality on the promotion of financial services

Characteristic	Implications	Marketing actions	Examples
Intangibility	The greater the intangibility, the greater the need to create concreteness	Use physical evidence and artefacts such as branches and other delivery points. Use concrete, specific language and symbols	Lloyds Bank – Black Horse. Norwich Union – Great Wall of China. Direct Line Insurance – little red phone
Inseparability	The greater the inseparability, the greater the need to show participation of customers	Include both the service deliverer and the customer in the advertisement	Royal Bank of Scotland – '*We know where you're coming from, you know where we are*'
Heterogeneity	The greater the heterogeneity, the greater the need to stress quality	Show the process and scope of the service, performance records, etc. to gain credibility of performance	AA Insurance – insurance champions
Contextuality	The greater the specificity of context, the greater the need to characterise the service through the illustration of a sequence of events	Highlight the sequence of events which comprise the service experience	Barclaycard – loss of property and money Direct Line – insurance claims

(*Source*: Adapted from Hill and Gandhi, 1992)

The issue of inseparability hinges on the vital interaction between service provider and consumer in the production of a service product. Financial institutions have approached this by portraying both the service provider and the customer in the advertisement. The Royal Bank of Scotland emphasises the interaction between the bank and its customers in its TV commercials, assuring customers of a good deal by stressing that bank employees are also consumers.

The heterogeneity or variability of the service offering calls for financial institutions to stress quality in their promotion. This can be achieved by outlining the process and scope of the service and performance records. This serves to gain credibility of the quality of the service and reassures the consumer. Promotion can also be improved by highlighting the specific context of the service. For example, Barclaycard offers reassurance to its customers by stressing the sequence of events which comprise the service experience in the event of lost goods or lost money obtained via the card.

In addition to the above factors, Kirk (1994) argues that the promotion and advertising of financial services also has to contend with the following:

- *Consumer apathy* – One of the problems associated with financial services is that while many people may believe that they are important or necessary, few, unfortunately, are interested in them. This results in many people perceiving financial services and financial providers as a 'necessary evil'.

Indeed, segmentation research (Harrison, 1997a) mentioned in Chapter 3 identified only a small segment of the market really interested in financial services; the rest of the market was largely uninterested or disinterested. The consequence of this apathy is that many consumers are not sufficiently motivated to search for products and providers. Many products are 'unsought', which places greater stress on promotion in having to make the products and buying situations more motivating and appealing.

- *High Risk* – Another problem is the high perceived risk associated with many financial products. Many products involve a high degree of commitment from the consumer but present no opportunity for trial prior to purchase. Furthermore, the benefits derived from the products are largely intangible and are impossible to measure at the time of purchase, in many cases, due to the longevity of the contract. Also, the high credence qualities associated with financial services also renders the products impossible for many consumers to evaluate even after maturity.
- *Credibility of information sources* – Due to several of the factors mentioned above, it is difficult or even impossible to accurately advertise and display financial services. Consumers can, and in many cases are forced to, obtain information from sources other than those controlled by the organisation. These may include word of mouth from relatives and friends and independent sources. The problem is that these other sources of information may carry greater credibility from the customer's point of view than marketer-controlled sources. This is not necessarily a problem unless the sources are in conflict with advertised sources.

  One of the problems is that financial institutions do not always live up to their advertising. Does the 'listening bank' always lend an ear? Does 'the bank that likes to say yes' always honour loan applications? In fact, many customers agree that financial institutions are far from friendly and co-operative. Customer opinions are far more likely to be built up as a result of their experience with a particular financial institution than formed through advertising or promotion. This is perhaps typical of an experiential product.
- *Minority of consumers in the market* – Another factor influencing the effectiveness of promotion is that there will only be a small proportion of individuals in the marketplace who are in the 'ready-to-buy' stage at any one time. As previously discussed in Chapter 3, for some products it can be almost impossible to predict the 'ready-to-buy' windows. This presents a dilemma in terms of effectively targeting the right people and not wasting advertising. While it may be desirable to specifically target those individuals who are ready to buy, it has also been suggested that corporate advertising is nonetheless useful in order to keep the image of the company alive in the minds of other individuals until such time that they are also ready to buy.

  Despite there being a minority of consumers in the market, many financial institutions do themselves a disservice by snubbing around a quarter of the population. Research indicates that one in two women believe financial services advertising is not aimed at them. The feeling of exclusion was found to be strongest among women over the age of 65 (64 per cent) and between the ages of 15 and 24 (50 per cent) (*Financial Times*, 29 April 1997). These findings are likely to concern financial institutions, many of which are aware that women are responsible for the financial decisions in an increasing number of households.

- *Commodity purchase* – An increasing problem is the number of suppliers of financial products in the marketplace and the similarity between the products available. As previously discussed in Chapter 4, new products are easily copied, making any first-mover advantages extremely short-lived, and branding is very difficult to achieve, making differentiation almost impossible. The challenge this poses for promotion and advertising is that there are often few distinctive features which can be used in the communication message. Consequently, the method of delivery and the message appeal take on more important roles in attempting to stimulate interest and motivation among consumers.
- *Regulation* – The Financial Services Act (FSAct) ruling on advertising covers all media, including direct mail. Guidelines are being established under the new Financial Services and Markets Bill to cover advertising on the internet. The FSAct identifies three specific types of advertisement: image advertisements which specifically promote awareness of the company and its products; short form advertisements which include lists of fund prices; and specific product advertisements. The regulations regarding the advertising of investments, for example, stipulate that the advertisements must include: the basis of forecast performance, the level of future benefits, the risks associated with the investment and the penalties for early surrender.

  In addition to the FSAct, the advertising of financial services also comes under the scrutiny of the Advertising Standards Authority (ASA), the advertising watchdog. In early 1998 the marketing of personal savings accounts was thrown into confusion by a ruling from the ASA about the term 'instant access'. The ASA queried whether the time taken for a transfer of funds through the bank clearing procedures over three working days precludes an account from giving truly 'instant' access. The complaint was raised specifically in relation to telephone banking where the withdrawal of money can only occur by telephoning the bank to transfer the money to another bank or building society account. However, it has implications across the sector as a whole. While the ASA did not forbid the use of the term 'instant access' in the naming of accounts, it stressed that advertisements had to make clear that access to funds was not instant. Representatives of the financial services sector fear the ruling has the potential to cause more confusion than it resolves, arguing that the term instant access is well understood by customers.

The promotional mix

There are several ways in which a financial institution can communicate with its target audiences and promote its products and services. Not all of the promotional methods will be used to the same extent and degree by all companies. The specific combination of promotional methods used by an organisation to promote its products and services is referred to as the 'promotional mix'. A promotional mix can constitute any or all of the following: advertising, personal selling, sales promotion,

Table 8.4 Comparison of promotional tools

Promotional tool	Characteristics	Examples	Uses	Advantages	Disadvantages
Advertising	A paid form of non-personal communication through a mass medium	Television, radio, cinema, newspapers, magazines, outdoor, public transport, direct mail	• Promoting products and organisations • Stimulating demand • Off-setting competitors' advertising • Making sales personnel more effective • Increasing use of product • Reminding and reinforcing customers • Reducing sales fluctuation	• Cost-effective – reaches a large audience at low cost per head • Allows repetition of message • Can add value to the product • Enhances company's image	• Overall cost can be high • Rapid feedback is not usual • Measuring effect on sales can be difficult • Can be less persuasive than personal selling, say
Personal selling	Informing and persuading customers to purchase products through personal communication	Sales reps' visits, in-store/branch sales assistants, visits and consultations with IFAs and financial advisers	• Generating sales • Cross-selling • Enabling product strengths and weaknesses to be assessed • Reassuring customers in high-risk purchase situations • Enabling a dialogue with the customer	• Specific communication aimed at select target • Greater impact on customers • Immediate feedback • Flexible and allows message to be adjusted accordingly • Useful in complex buying situations and when buyers are close to purchasing	• Greater cost per head • Cannot reach large audiences effectively
Publicity and public relations	Non-personal communication in news-story form about an organisation and/or its products and services, transmitted at no charge	Magazine, newspaper, radio, television news story	• Creating awareness of the company's products, brands and activities • Helping to maintain positive public visibility • Enhancing company's image • Helping negative images to be overcome	• Free, but needs to be managed carefully to make sure the right message gets out • Informative as opposed to persuasive • Credible and impartial	• Lack of control over what is communicated • Can be good or bad publicity • Impact on sales is not immediate • Generally not subject to repetition
Sales promotion	Offering of an inducement or incentive to customers, channel members or salespeople in order to encourage purchase	Gifts, tokens, bonuses, contests, loyalty cards, free samples, money refunds, contests, sweepstakes. Monetary and non-monetary incentives	• Stimulating product trial • Encouraging switching • Shifting end-of-product lines • Reminding customers • Controlling sales fluctuations	• Stimulates short-term demand • Can shift end-of-product lines • Can remind customers of old product • Encourage trial of new customers	• Can devalue the brand if not supported by other forms of promotion • Increases price sensitivity and reduces loyalty of customers • Encourages customers to bargain-hunt
Direct marketing	Direct mail, telemarketing and direct response advertising	Direct leafleting, letters and contacts through mail, telephone and internet	• Creating brand awareness • Stimulating product adoption • Pre-sell technique • Generating product orders • Qualifying prospects for a sales call • Following up a sale • Announcing special sales	• Provides database of information • Offers variety of styles and formats • Can be personalised and customised • Can lead to accurate targeting • Effectiveness can be measured • Can be tied with sales promotion	• Perception as junk mail if not used properly • Can be expensive
Sponsorship	Financial or material support of an event, activity, person, organisation or product	Events or competitions, equipment, buildings, ideas, research, learning, animals or people, commercial or charitable causes, television programmes or services etc.	• Promoting company image • Identifying with a specific target • Creating positive relationships with the community	• Benefits of enhanced company • Philanthropic benefits • Identifies with specific targets • Improved morale and employee relations	• Can lack specificity • Effectiveness difficult to measure • Can miss out significant groups

publicity and public relations, direct mail, direct response advertising and sponsorship. Table 8.4 provides a summary of the characteristics, uses, advantages, disadvantages and examples of each of the promotional mix elements.

Advertising

Advertising is a form of non-personal communication through a mass medium such as television, radio, print, cinema, outdoor, public transport, etc. It has many uses, as outlined in table 8.4, although a great many financial institutions tend to use it for very general purposes. Most financial services television advertisements are mainly aimed at creating awareness of the company and its products, reminding customers and reassuring them of the stability and integrity of the organisation. For example, the Halifax ran a series of innovative and distinctive television commercials in which people were used to form objects (such as houses and bridges), illustrating the central theme of a building society. The black cloaked Scottish Widows woman reminds people of the existence and purpose of the organisation, but does not divulge any product details, and many insurance companies' advertisements simply announce the company and invite potential customers to ring for a quote.

Fidelity Investments, the world's largest fund manager, launched its most ambitious advertising campaign in a Broadway theatre in September 1998. Lily Tomlin, the well-known US comedienne, stars alongside Peter Lynch from Fidelity. In one of the commercials Mr Lynch is taking a physical check-up on a treadmill while the nurse, Lily Tomlin, conducts the medical. During the examination the treadmill bucks up and down sharply, to which Mr Lynch retorts: 'This reminds me of the stock market' (*Financial Times*, 4 September 1998). The advertisement may be funny and acknowledge the volatility of the stock market, but it does not tell anything about the company or its products.

There are several reasons for this focus on general or corporate themes rather than product-specific themes, some of which have already been mentioned. One reason relates to the specific nature of the product: it is difficult to display an intangible product via a visual medium. Nevertheless, it is possible to describe many intangible products using a visual medium through the careful sequencing of actions and events which provide a feel for what benefits the product provides. Indeed, insurance companies, such as the AA and Direct Line, have adopted this format to illustrate claims procedures.

Another reason for the use of general themes in advertising is that for many financial services the customer is required to enter into a contract with the financial institution. Before the contract can be agreed, several checks may need to be performed on the customer (in the case of mortgages and loans) to establish the financial status of the individual. Furthermore, the terms and conditions of the contract and, indeed, the price of the product may vary according to individuals' characteristics and financial status making it difficult to advertise the specific features of the product.

Perhaps one of the most important factors affecting the advertising of financial services is the Financial Services Act (1986) which set certain legal conditions on the advertising of financial services. For some products this means the inclusion of certain information in the advertisement. The information is designed to protect the customer and warn of the consequences of misuse of the product. Television com-

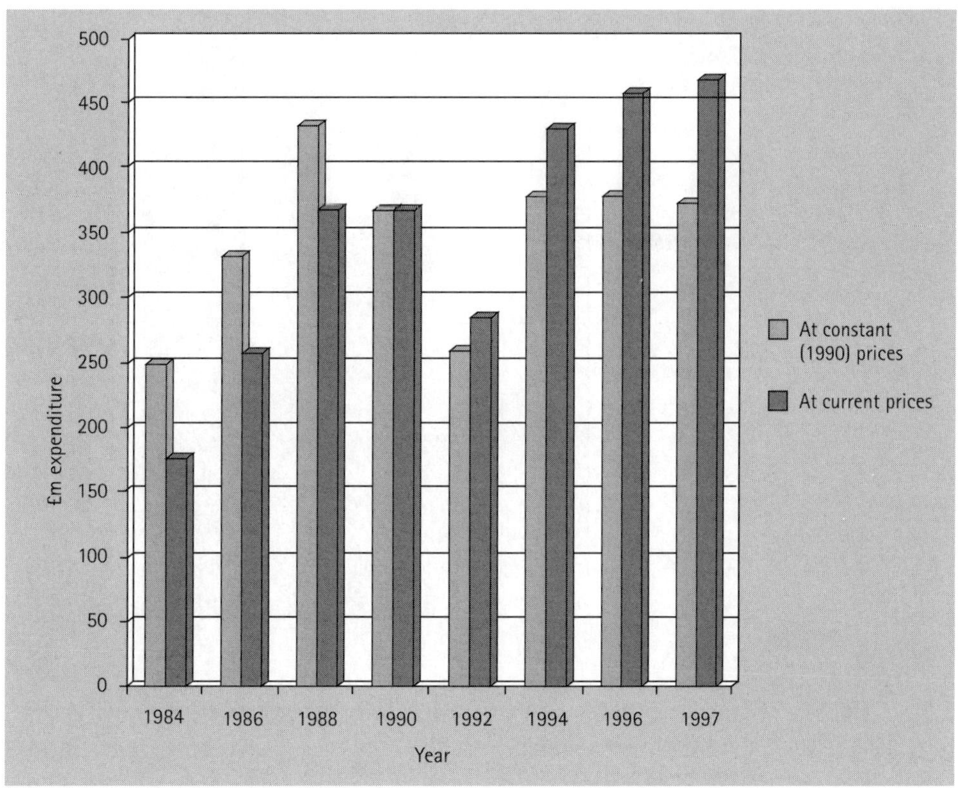

Fig. 8.2 Annual advertising expenditure
Based on adjusted Register-MEAL data. Excludes production costs and agency commission
(*Source*: Adapted from the *Advertising Statistics Yearbook*, 1998)

mercials are typically 30 second spots and do not offer much time in which to outline specific technical details of contracts, thus explaining why many of the broadcast advertisements tend to be rather general, thereby avoiding the issue of compliance with the FSAct.

Print media, on the other hand, provide the opportunity of presenting more detailed information. Yet, if too much detailed information is provided, the advertisement can appear too dense, too factual and not stimulating enough to gain and hold the interest of potential customers. For this reason, many print advertisements contain very little information, but simply invite interested parties to contact the company for further details. This type of direct response advertising is discussed in more detail below.

Given the limited ability of advertising for financial services, one may ask why financial institutions continue to spend so much of their promotional budgets on it. In 1997 total ad spend amounted to £5,280.7 million, 9 per cent (or £468.1 million) of which was spent by the financial services sector. Indeed, television advertising accounts for over one-third of total financial services advertising expenditure (McKechnie and Leather, 1998). Figure 8.2 shows that financial services ad spend fell during the recession in the early 1990s, but has remained at a stable level in the last few years. Financial products receiving the most ad spend in 1997 were personal equity plans, credit and charge cards, motor insurance and mortgages (see figure 8.3).

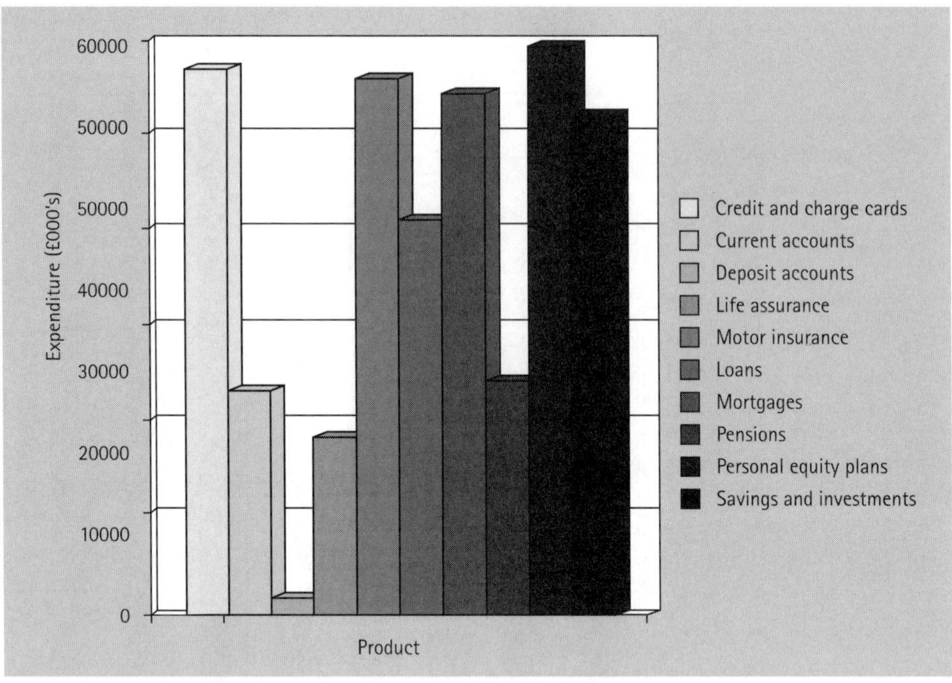

Fig. 8.3 Advertising expenditure (at rate-card) by selected financial services
Based on unadjusted ACNielsen-MEAL data.
(*Source*: Adapted from the *Advertising Statistics Yearbook*, 1998)

Advertising does, in fact, offer a number of advantages and may explain the high expenditure. Although the initial outlay is high, this is off set by the large numbers which can be reached at any one time. It also offers a high degree of repetition, which is useful in terms of reminding and reinforcing a message. This is particularly important for keeping the image of the company alive in the mind of potential customers. It was acknowledged earlier that few individuals will be in the market for a particular product at any one time, so it is important that the image of the company be kept alive in the minds of individuals until such time that they are ready to buy.

Personal selling

Personal selling uses personal communication to inform customers of products and services and to persuade customers to make purchases. Any employee who is in contact with the customer is potentially in a personal selling role. This could involve tellers, advisers, brokers, IFAs, the direct sales force. Many of these have an important role to play in the distribution of the products and services to customers (as previously discussed in Chapter 5), but also have an equally important role to play in terms of communication. They occupy a boundary-spanning role and as such present the communication link between the organisation and the marketplace. Personal sellers provide the medium through which messages are sent from the financial institution to the customer and through which messages are received from the customer. Consequently, personal selling is not only useful in a selling context but also in a market research context, enabling market information to be gathered and feedback to be elicited on the relative strengths and weaknesses of the institution's products.

One of the key advantages of personal selling for financial institutions, is that it is interactive: company representatives engage in a dialogue with the customer. This provides the institution with a great deal of flexibility in terms of tailoring specific messages to satisfy customers' specific information requirements. As a result of this it can be more persuasive than advertising, simply because the customer is provided with more detailed information which is specific to their needs and circumstances. It also provides every opportunity for compliance with the FSAct as specific details of the products can be explained fully to customers. Customers can also be furnished with the details in print.

The main disadvantage of personal selling is the cost. It is the most expensive form of communication per head, owing to the salaries of the sales representatives and their expenses. Furthermore, the costs of personal selling for financial services are increasing faster than advertising costs due to the increasing costs of compliance with the FSAct and such things as the IFA tests alluded to in Chapter 5. This is one of the reasons why the Prudential reduced its reliance on personal selling and stopped selling small premium cash-collection life insurance and savings products in 1995 (*Financial Times*, 12 February 1997). The high costs of collecting small amounts in person every four weeks ate into the returns that investors received. Yet, the company acknowledges the advantages from the personal touch and thus attempted to recreate and update 'The man from the Pru' so popular in the 1950s, 1960s and 1970s through television, poster and newspapers advertisements in which Sir Peter Davis, the company's chief executive, appears as the new man from the Pru.

Sales promotion

As competition has intensified in the financial services sector, prices have become more transparent and price competition more explicit, the use of sales promotion has increased. The combination of these factors has created an increased emphasis on short-term goals with a focus on customer acquisition. Thus, much of the sales promotion employed by financial institutions is predominantly used to encourage trial and generate switching. The problem is that without support from other media, it is unlikely to generate or build loyalty. It now becomes clear why financial institutions advertise so heavily. Advertising and personal selling work in the long term as well as the short term and serve to build up loyalty, whereas sales promotion has a tendency to break loyalty down.

Peattie and Peattie (1994) attribute the growth in sales promotion in the financial services sector to the following:

- *Rising prices and advertising 'clutter'*: as consumers become increasingly desensitised to advertising, the cost effectiveness of mass-media advertising is becoming eroded.
- *Growing respectability of sales promotion*: as market leaders increase their use of sales promotions it is becoming a more respectable element of the promotional mix.

- *Shortening planning time horizons*: time pressure on sales can make the short-term gains promised by sales promotion seem attractive.
- *Micro-marketing approaches*: fragmentation of the market (discussed in Chapter 3) calls for greater targeting and precision of communication.
- *A 'snowball' effect*: many financial institutions are jumping on the bandwagon for fear of losing market share.

Sales promotion techniques can be classified into one of two main types. So-called 'two for the price of one' offers and '25% extra free' offers are known as 'value-increasing' sales promotions. Such offers work by promoting an increased quantity to customers at the normal price. They do not work well for financial services since many financial services are not tangible products. How would a 25 per cent extra free loan work? The only way such offers can work for financial services is through dangerous margin- and image-eroding price reductions. The result can be intense competition based on price, or even a price war. The credit card market has become focused on this kind of price promotion.

The other main type of sales promotion is known as 'value adding' or 'packaged up' sales promotion. This form of promotion leaves the price and core product/service offering untouched and offers the customer something extra in the form of a free gift or a competition. Student and young persons' accounts typically offer free gifts as incentives to open accounts. The advantages of competitions for financial services promotions are outlined in table 8.5.

Direct mail

Alongside telemarketing, direct mail forms part of the direct selling category. Direct mail offers a number of uses, many of which are similar to other forms of promotion mentioned above. The advantages of direct marketing in general were outlined in Chapter 3. Yet, the real advantage of direct mail over other mass forms of communication is its ability, through a wide variety of styles and formats, to personalise and customise communication (see Financial Services Marketing in Practice: 'Targeted direct mailshots make mortgage mailing meaningful', see p. 208).

There has been a noticeable increase in the use of direct mail by financial institutions. This can be explained partly by the restrictions imposed on the advertising of financial products, discussed above, and partly by the advantages which direct mail offers over other forms of promotion for this type of product. Direct mail allows the financial institution to communicate the relevant product information to individuals and gives the customer time to consider the information and react to it. As a result, it is more likely to increase the customer's confidence in dealing with a financial services buying situation, since the customer is more knowledgeable when entering the buying process.

Another advantage of direct mail is that the financial institution can control when the message reaches the individual. Thus, messages can be extremely effective providing the financial institution can predict individuals' 'ready-to-buy' windows. Furthermore, since the company knows who has been communicated to and when, they are able to measure the effectiveness of communicated messages.

However, as mentioned in Chapter 3, not all financial institutions have had the same level of success with direct mail: a significant proportion still merely amounts to direct mass mailing where all customers receive the same indiscriminate mess-

Table 8.5 Advantages of sales promotions competitions for financial services

Advantage	Implication
Differentiation opportunities	It was acknowledged in Chapter 4 that differentiation is difficult to achieve in financial services: products are easily copied, making any innovation advantages short-lived. Competitions can create a point of differentiation. While copy-cat competitions can be established, they risk failure if early competitions have exhausted the supply of potential contenders
Link-up opportunities	Sales promotion activities can be linked to other forms of promotion, such as advertising and personal selling
Adding a tangible dimension to products	While many financial services are intangible and cannot readily be displayed using visual media, competition posters and leaflets provide a tangible and visible point-of-sale dimension to the business
Quality cue appeal	Consumers look for cues of service quality when choosing a financial services provider. While the physical premises and history of the organisation may serve as traditional cues of quality, the prizes offered in competitions provide an alternative dimension of assessing service quality
Demand-soothing	Controlling demand fluctuations can be a problem in managing financial services. Competitions can be timed to stimulate demand at slack periods
Consumer interaction	In contrast with other promotional tools, such as advertising, competitions can create valuable interaction with the customer
Cost certainty	Competitions generally involve predictable costs and are more effective at maintaining perceived quality levels than 'give-away' promotions
Price/quality stability	The competition adds value to the product or service without the need to alter the price or nature of the core product. This avoids any danger of a price war and devaluing of the product
Versatility	Competitions are versatile and can contribute towards a range of communication and marketing objectives both short- and long-term involving both new and existing products and customers

(*Source*: Adapted from Peattie and Peattie, 1992)

ages. This type of activity is responsible for the perception of direct mail as junk mail. Thwaites and Lee (1994) note this as a general criticism of the use of direct mail by financial institutions and argue that it could be integrated better with other marketing and communication activities. Specifically, there is a need for development in database quality and timing of direct mailshots.

Direct-response advertising

Direct-response advertising is a variation on direct mail. Whereas direct mail targets specific individuals with the objective of achieving a response, direct-response advertising works by providing individuals with initial product information with the minimal effort from the organisation and invites interested individuals to request either further information or products. Information is commonly provided in press or leaflet form and is delivered in a two-stage process. The individual responds to an initial advertisement in the press or leaflets and is mailed further details of the product prior to making an actual purchase.

It is thought that the financial services sector is probably the biggest user of direct-response advertising through the press. There are a number of reasons why this may be so. First, direct-response advertising overcomes many of the restrictions imposed on the advertising of financial services. Individuals can be sent information specific to their needs and requirements. In the case of insurance quotes, these can also be made specific to the individual. Second, direct-response advertising can be more cost-effective than indiscriminate direct mail: specific product details are only mailed to individuals who respond to the initial advertisement and specifically request additional information. Third, because it relies on customers' responding to an initial advertisement, the financial institution can establish a database of potential customers for particular products. Even if the individual does not buy the product at that particular time, the institution knows that they are interested and can continue to send them product details.

A variety of financial products are advertised in this way, although it is thought that products requiring a low amount of advice have the greatest success through this channel. However, the increase in execution-only telephone operators may eventually replace some of this business as the sector witnesses a greater convergence of distribution and communication activities.

Publicity and public relations

Publicity is often part of the function of public relations in an organisation.The two are very closely linked. In fact, publicity may be described as the activities undertaken by the organisation to build and maintain good relations with its public. Traditionally, it has been viewed as simply issuing press releases and seeking good publicity, but it has become more sophisticated and uses a variety of tools, such as annual reports, seminars and speeches, cause-related marketing, in-house magazines and press releases, to create a positive image about the company.

Financial institutions should carefully manage their public relations. Efforts should be deliberate and planned in order to be maximally effective and publicity should not be left to chance.

Publicity and public relations are different from the promotional tools already discussed. Whereas the promotional tools already mentioned attempt to persuade customers to purchase products, publicity and public relations are primarily informative. For example, they attempt to make people aware of the company's products and services and its activities, they attempt to maintain a certain level of positive visibility of the company, enhance its image and overcome any negative images. However, publicity may be persuasive through its credibility, impartiality and objectivity. In addition, whereas other forms of promotion already mentioned are designed to have a fairly immediate impact on sales, publicity and public relations tend to be more subdued. They are not subject to repetition and the impact may not be as intense as an advertised message, although this depends on the nature of the publicity.

Perhaps the biggest difference between publicity and public relations and other forms of promotion is that the focus on communication is not just the customer. Public relations concerns relationships with a wide number of internal and external parties which may have an impact on the organisation. These include: shareholders, suppliers, customers, local communities, employees, government. For this reason it is argued that public relations should not be the responsibility of the marketing function, but should be controlled at the corporate level in order to maintain consistency with the overall corporate image.

Perhaps one of the biggest hurdles for financial institutions in creating good public relations is attempting to create an image which is at odds with the general perception of the industry. Financial scandals, of which there have been a few recently, give the industry a bad press, and there is the problem that all financial institutions become tarred with the same brush.

Sponsorship

Sponsorship has a public relations dimension to it, and traditionally would have been considered part of the public relations function. However, it has increased in popularity and spend, is wider-reaching than public relations and is generally considered to be an important element of the promotional mix in its own right.

An organisation can sponsor almost anything from events or competitions to equipment and buildings, ideas or research, education, animals or people, commercial or charitable causes, television programmes or products or services. Acting as a sponsor, an organisation seeks to exploit the commercial potential associated with the sponsored event or activity in return for an investment in cash or kind. For sponsorship to be effective to the donor the sponsored event or activity must be recognised by the target audience.

Sports sponsorship attracts the greatest expenditure, probably because it offers large viewing figures and the opportunity of targeting a wide audience. Broadcast sponsorship is also increasing in popularity for financial institutions. For example, Midland sponsors films and Legal & General sponsors regional weather broadcasts. A wide range of audiences can be targeted including: customers and potential customers, suppliers, employees, the media, shareholders, the general public and politicians.

Some of the benefits of sponsorship are that it can increase general public awareness of the company, it may alter public perceptions (particularly if the sponsored event is a charitable event), it may build goodwill among opinion leaders, it can have positive effects on employees and improve employee relations, it can reassure customers and shareholders and it can create a general perception of community involvement.

SUMMARY

The promotion element of the marketing mix is essential for communicating the company, its products and services and their benefits to relevant target audiences. Promotion performs a number of functions and roles, including informing, persuading and educating individuals and groups, and works in harmony with the other elements of the marketing mix enabling the acquisition of new customers to take place, retention of existing customers, improvements in staff morale, and projections of a company image. In order for promotion to be effective, financial institutions must appreciate the process of communication and the factors likely to have an impact on the promotion of financial services.

Due to the specific characteristics of financial services and the limitations imposed by the FSAct on their advertising, emotional and moral appeals tend to be used more than rational appeals in communication messages. The fear appeal tends to be used, capitalising on life's uncertainty. With regard to the range of promotional tools, financial institutions make use of advertising, direct-response advertising, sales promotion, sponsorship, publicity and personal selling. Television advertising, direct-response advertising and sponsorship seem to attract the greatest expenditure, while many financial institutions have reduced their direct sales forces and the personal selling element.

DISCUSSION QUESTIONS

1. What role does promotion have for financial institutions?
2. How can a financial institution ensure the effectiveness of the communication process?
3. Select two or three financial services advertisements of your choice and comment on the communications objectives they attempt to achieve. To what extent do you think they are successful?
4. What can a financial institution do to stimulate interest in its advertised products?
5. Evaluate the effectiveness of fear appeals in the advertising of pensions and life assurance.
6. How might financial institutions make more use of positive appeals in communication? What should the positive appeals be?
7. In your opinion, which factors have the greatest influence on the promotion of financial services?
8. Suggest an appropriate promotional mix for a financial institution of your choice. Justify your recommendations.
9. How can sales promotion be used to encourage, rather than break down, loyalty, either on its own or used in conjunction with other promotional tools?
10. What role does sponsorship play for financial institutions in the promotional mix?

9 Building customer relationships

INTRODUCTION

In recent years there has been a growing interest among financial institutions in the cultivation of customer relationships. The reason for this is the recognition that building long-term customer relationships offers a way of reducing defection rates, reducing costs and increasing revenues. Consequently, it has resulted in such activities as the appointment of 'relationship managers' and customised mailings to initiate a 'dialogue' with individual customers.

While companies want to build relationships with their customers, few customers perceive themselves as having a relationship with the companies they deal with. Surprisingly, though, financial institutions seem to be among the few types of companies that customers do feel they have a relationship with. Despite this, many financial institutions have developed relationship strategies with little reference to what constitutes a good relationship from the customer's point of view.

Relationship marketing encompasses the activities of attracting, maintaining and enhancing customer relationships with an organisation. Building relationships with customers is more than just a marketing function: it is an organisational philosophy that impacts on operations and processes, employees, customer service and quality. Thus, financial institutions that wish to build and maintain long-term relationships need to take a holistic approach to dealing with their customers.

This chapter attempts to illustrate some of the complexities of relationship development and the interrelationships between various functional areas of the business which are required for customer relationships to be successful.

OBJECTIVES

After reading this chapter you should be able to:

- recognise the concept of relationship marketing;
- discuss the rationale for developing customer relationships;
- consider with whom relationships should be built;
- outline the stages involved in the relationship development process;
- discuss the key components of a relationship, paying particular attention to the role of trust, employees, service quality and the management of customer complaints.

The concept of relationship marketing

Relationship marketing has been defined variously, but is generally considered to encompass the activities of attracting, maintaining and enhancing customer relationships with an organisation. Thus, it takes into account both offensive and defensive marketing strategies while at the same time incorporating a customer service element. Offensive marketing concerns the acquisition of new customers and all that is involved in marketing to prospective customers or encouraging competitors' customers to switch. By comparison, defensive marketing is concerned with defending market share and protecting the customer base. Hence, defensive strategies attempt to retain existing customers and generate further business from them. Table 9.1 outlines the key differences between offensive and defensive marketing and suitable conditions for their use.

As the financial services sector has become more competitive and the threat to profitability from new entrants increases, financial institutions need to consider ways of developing relationships with their existing customers in order to defend their market share. The high street banks have been criticised for being too complacent with respect to new competition, and it is estimated that as much as 25 per cent of their profits could be lost in the next four years if they do not change their ways (*Financial Times*, 1 November 1998).

In order to develop relationships with customers, financial institutions must understand what relationship marketing entails. One way of doing this is to look at how relationship marketing has developed. The formal study of marketing has followed the evolution of specific market sectors. Thus, in the 1950s the focus was primarily consumer goods, in the 1960s it was industrial marketing, in the 1970s non-profit marketing, in the 1980s services marketing, and since the 1990s relationship marketing has become prominent.

The development of industrial and services marketing called for new perspectives based on closer links with customers, and other constituencies, over longer time

Table 9.1 Comparison of offensive and defensive marketing

	Offensive marketing	Defensive marketing
What is it?	Customer acquisition	Customer retention
Who is it aimed at?	New customers/markets	Existing customers
When is it appropriate?	New markets or market growth	Mature or saturated markets
Which competitive situations cause it?	Lack of significant competition	Highly competitive
What is its goal?	Market share growth	Profit growth
How is it operationalised?	Advertising and promotion, one-off incentives	Service, rewards and discounts to encourage loyalty
To what extent is it discernible?	Overt	Covert

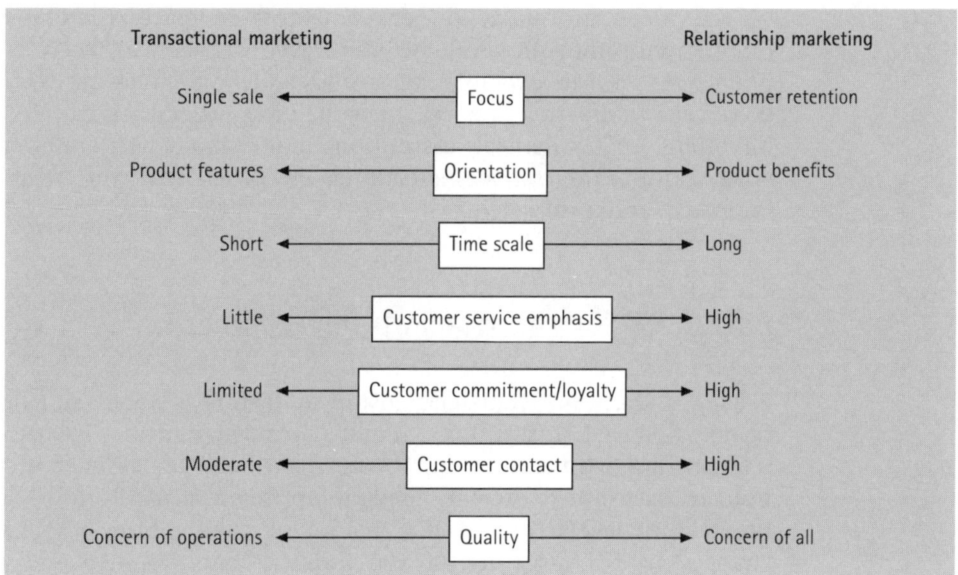

Fig. 9.1 Contrasts between transactional and relationship marketing
(*Source*: Adapted from Christopher *et al.*, 1991)

periods involving greater degrees of interaction and participation from both sides with the need to manage customer satisfaction through quality and service before, during and after the sale. As a result of this, the emphasis has switched from transaction-based marketing, focused on the single sale, to an ongoing relationship over the longerterm, based on high levels of customer service, customer contact and quality. Figure 9.1 contrasts transactional and relationship marketing.

What constitutes a relationship?

When a customer embarks on a new type of investment with a financial institution, he or she may have several meetings with a financial advisor to first ascertain which product best meets his or her needs. The meeting may have been set up by first making a telephone call, and there may be other telephone conversations which take place before and after signing the contract for the investment. Throughout this period the customer is engaged in a transaction, and each time the customer interacts with the financial adviser, a contact episode takes place. If the transaction period is managed well, the customer may return to the adviser for more products. Hence, the relationship continues as further transaction periods occur.

What this illustrates is that a relationship between an individual and a financial institution can actually be broken down into a series of perceived transaction periods. The transaction periods can be further broken down into distinct contact episodes. A critical element of the contact episode is 'the moment of truth' or 'service encounter'. It is at these points that direct interaction between the customer and the financial institution occurs. The interaction may take several different forms. For example, the customer can interact with personnel face-to-face, by telephone or by letter, or the customer can interact with an ATM or some other technology.

Every time an interaction or contact takes place, there is an opportunity for the customer to evaluate the level of service received and form an impression of the overall relationship with the financial services provider. A perceived transaction period may include several service encounters. It is important that financial institutions understand what the customer experiences during the service encounter, in order that the relationship can be improved and prolonged.

Rationale for relationship development

Having understood what relationship marketing is about and how it came into being, financial institutions might consider why it is necessary to build relationships with customers. It was mentioned above that increased competition in the sector is exerting pressure on financial institutions' abilities to retain profitability levels. Indeed, the nature of competition has changed alongside changes to the structure of the industry and its increased maturity. These changes are closely interlinked with other broader changes to the environment in which financial institutions operate and to the customers that they deal with (see figure 9.2).

Changes to the broader environment include those discussed in Chapter 1, and can be summarised as regulatory change, economic pressures and technological developments. Customer trends were discussed in Chapter 2 and include a more mobile, knowledgeable and cynical customer base much more likely to switch than previously, and with higher service expectations. The combined effects of these changes have resulted in decreased barriers to entry to the market and an increased need to retain existing customers and improve service quality levels.

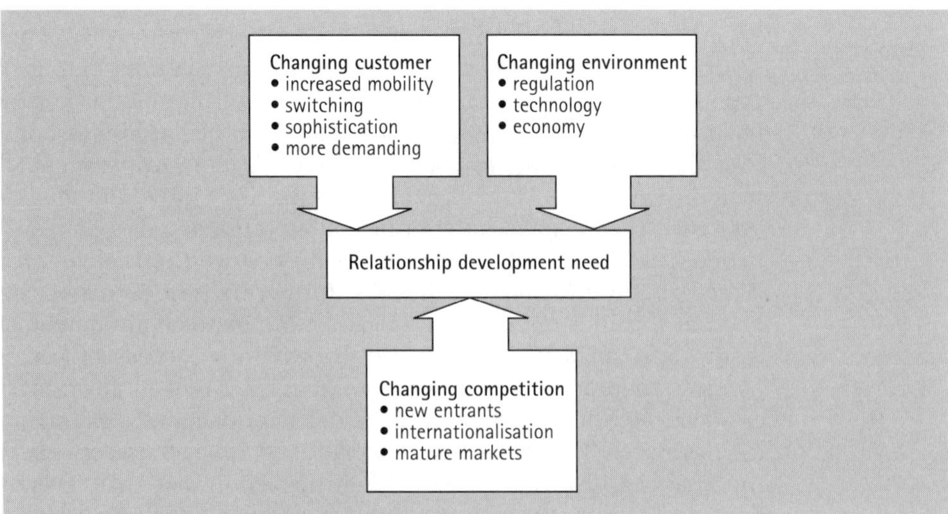

Fig. 9.2 Factors influencing the need for relationship development

Benefits of relationship development

In addition to the broader reasons driving financial institutions towards a relationship approach, there are a number of benefits associated with the retention of existing customers and the development of long-term satisfying relationships (see Financial Services Marketing in Practice: 'A blossoming relationship').

- *It takes time to make money from customers* – many customers are not immediately profitable. For example, students are generally unprofitable while at university and only start contributing to profit the year after graduation. After this, profit generation tends to increase, thereby increasing the need to hold on to them.
- *Sales, marketing and set-up costs are amortised over a longer customer lifetime* – linked to the above point is that associated with acquiring a new customer there are initial set-up costs which can be recouped over time. The ratio of acquisition costs to retention is high: it is costing up to five times more to create a customer than to keep one (Clutterback, 1989; Liswood, 1989). Reichheld and Kenny (1990) note that customers' economies generally improve over time, which is why it is important to take a lifetime-value perspective which considers the potential lifetime income from the customer relative to the costs attributed to the customer.
- *Repeat customers often cost less to service* – repeat customers can cost less to service, not only because of the above-mentioned factors, but also because they are more likely to be familiar with the company and its products and services and may make fewer requests or fewer demands on the time of employees.
- *It allows cross-selling opportunities, leading to increased customer expenditure over time* – for many financial institutions, the attraction of building customer relationships is the promise of cross-selling: selling additional products and services to the existing customer base. It is generally believed that longer-term customers will buy more and, if satisfied with the company and the company has what the customer wants, will buy from the same financial services provider.
- *It stops competitors knowing them* – retained and satisfied customers may be less susceptible to competitors' appeals or, as Stum and Thiry (1991) put it, may demonstrate an immunity to the pull of competition.
- *It allows for inter-generational relationships* – one of the key factors influencing the choice of financial institution for young people is parental influence. Hence, it is assumed that building a relationship with one family member will have an impact on other members of the same family.
- *Satisfied customers provide referrals and may be willing to pay a price premium* – satisfied customers may generate positive word-of-mouth and provide free and credible advertising for the institution. However, word-of-mouth is a double-edged sword and relationships need to be managed carefully to avoid any negative word-of-mouth. Sonnenberg (1990) notes that customers who leave a company because they are dissatisfied with the service are believed to tell nine to ten people of their experience.

FINANCIAL SERVICES MARKETING IN PRACTICE **FT**

A blossoming relationship

For most people, the idea of having a relationship with a large company seems patently absurd. But 'relationship marketing' – whereby companies know enough about their customers to differentiate between them – is having a profound effect on many industries.

The technique, which was first embraced by the airline industry in the early 1980s and later taken up by the telecommunications and financial services industries, is now making headway in the retailing sector. Over the past few years, a plethora of loyalty schemes have been launched in the US and UK in which retailers have tried to woo customers with promises of better treatment, discounts and perks.

For example, Tesco, which rolled out the first large retailing loyalty scheme in the UK, provides card holders with certain benefits, as well as discounts linked to their total spending. It analyses the shopping habits of its customers, so that it can add personalised discount vouchers to its mailings. It has also developed five versions of its clubcard magazines for different age groups and types of family.

By analysing the shopping habits of high-spending customers, Tesco is able to invite them to specific events such as cheese and wine tastings or hairdressing demonstrations.

Such schemes are manifestly successful in giving customers a warm feeling about the company and its products. But sceptics point out that pioneers of loyalty cards are invariably followed by others. Nearly a third of retailing customers have more than one loyalty card and remain intent on shopping around, according to one study. Ultimately, the critics argue, relationship marketing will turn out to be a zero sum game.

This unease about schemes' profitability may prove justified in some cases. But champions of relationship marketing argue that, correctly implemented, it can have a profound strategic impact on business.

'Using information has transformed the way companies do business and are organised and has led to very different relationships with their customers', according to the Boston Consulting Group, in a recently published study on 'Knowing your customer' for the Coca-Cola Retailing Research Group.

Mercer Management Consulting, another strategic consultancy, agrees. It argues that, properly implemented, customer relationship management can provide 'fundamentally new bases of competition' that can determine new winners and losers within an industry.

For example, it cites the experience of a credit card company that increased its overall profitability by 15 per cent by tailoring its offer to individual customers, instead of making a single offer to all its customers. Other examples include a car manufacturer that increased its customers' repurchase rate by 60 per cent and an on-line service provider that was able to reduce the number of customers leaving it in a particular period by one-third.

Behind all these examples was the ability to analyse customer information, so that different groups of customers could be targeted in different ways. For example, detailed analysis of customer data makes it possible to identify which types of customer are more profitable and so, in effect, cross-subsidise others. The company that goes out of its way to attract these profitable customers is likely to prosper at the expense of its competitors which are left with the less attractive customers.

One example of this was the US credit card market, where new players such as Capital One and MBNA were able to take the most profitable customers from the big banks, which saw a sharp fall in their profitability. As well as identifying customers who can be wooed with better offers, a careful analysis of customer data may identify customers who are less price sensitive than theirs. Mercer cites one insurance company that increased revenues by 7 per cent, at no extra cost, without losing market share, by focusing on particular types of customers.

Another benefit from skilful customer relationship management is its impact on customer retention. Analysts at Bain & Co, management consultants, found that a 5 per cent increase in customer retention could significantly lift profitability – ranging from 25 per cent in bank deposits to 85 per cent in car servicing.

But even if companies recognise the potential impact of using their customer information, few companies are yet making full use of their data. BCG identifies three stages in companies' use of customer information and points out that the

FINANCIAL SERVICES MARKETING IN PRACTICE **FT**

more sophisticated applications take many years to realise.

In the first phase, companies start to do mass marketing, usually with loyalty programmes and simple direct marketing initiatives such as newsletters.

In the second phase, loyalty programmes become more sophisticated, with differentiated pricing and communications for different customers.

In the third phase, the company reorganises itself around customer segments, tailoring products, services, pricing and communication to each segment.

The companies that are most advanced in relationship marketing are, by and large, those that find it easiest to implement and have the most to gain. BCG points out that airlines, telecom providers and banks have an in-built advantage because they know who their customers are. Retailers, by contrast, have to build a database at a cost that can be as much as 1 per cent of sales in information technology costs and incentives for customers to take part in the scheme.

Despite hurdles, BCG argues that the first results of retailers' attempts to use information are encouraging, citing a survey of 10 US-based retailers which showed margin gains of between 1 and 2 per cent.

But most commentators agree that some companies are paying insufficient attention to getting real value out of their customer data. Fiona Stewart, of the Henley Centre, the UK research group, is concerned that companies are using loyalty schemes as a 'cynical add-on', rather than a tool to improve service.

'I think there will be a huge amount of cash wasted', says Simon Hay, client services director of DunnHumby Associates, an agency that analyses relationship marketing data for Tesco and other companies.

Experts like Hay argue that the success of relationship marketing depends on the whole business adopting a customer-focused approach. The point is that successful relationship management is not just a matter of database analysis to be left to the manager in the marketing department. Only if it starts with a mandate from the top of the organisation can it change the way in which a company competes.

Source: Vanessa Houlder, *Financial Times*, 28 July 1997

Questions:

1 At which of the three stages would you place financial services?

2 Does relationship marketing offer a sustainable competitive advantage?

3 To what extent do loyalty schemes improve customer service and contribute to relationship development?

While these benefits are commonly associated with building customer relationships, Dowling and Uncles (1997) point out a few caveats:

- *The costs of serving existing customers may not always be less*. When specific start-up costs are involved, such as credit checks in an application for a loan or the entering of new customer details into the customer database, the costs do exceed those of serving repeat customers. However, specific start-up costs are not always present for all types of products. For example, the costs of issuing travellers cheques are the same for both first-time customers and repeat customers. Thus, the cost of serving the customer would seem to be determined as much by the type of product as by whether the customer is new or not.
- *Retained customers are not always less price-sensitive* – building up a relationship with customers does not always focus the customer's attention less on price. Why should it? Customers may just perceive a better quality and value for money, which is why they remain a customer of the

institution. Some retained customers may, in fact, expect a price discount or better service in exchange for their custom. It is not unreasonable that long-standing customers may expect some reward for their longevity and commitment to the company.

- *Retained customers do not always spend more with the company* – it should not be assumed that just because the financial institution has built a long-term relationship with the customer that they will automatically spend more. There could be any number of reasons why the customer does not purchase from the total available product lines or invest more than other customers. Indeed, retained customers who do spend more may just be heavy users of the product – it may have nothing to do with their relationship with the financial institution. If this is the case, customer spend is more important than customer longevity. By the same token, longevity does not automatically lead to profitability – the relationship needs to be managed in order to generate profit.
- *Long-standing customers do not always pass on positive word-of-mouth recommendations* – customers do not need to have a long-term relationship with the financial institution to generate positive word-of-mouth: any satisfied customer can do this, whether they are a one-off customer or a customer of thirty years standing.

Do customers want relationships?

While most companies want to have relationships with their customers, few customers think of themselves as having a relationship with the organisations they deal with. The Henley Centre (1994) conducted research into the extent of customers' relationships with companies. Customers who repeatedly bought a brand from the same company were asked whether they would describe their feelings about the brand as 'having a relationship with it'. There were only five product types where 10 per cent or more of those questioned felt they had a relationship. These are shown in figure 9.3

It is interesting to note that three of the five products in figure 9.3 are financial products. Thus, it would seem that the potential for developing relationships with customers bodes well for financial institutions. At one level it is not difficult to understand why customers use the term 'relationship' when talking about financial services providers: financial matters are of concern to most people. Yet, Mills and Geraghty (1997) suggest that relationships may have developed in financial services, more than in other contexts, as a result of traditionally limited methods of distribution used by financial institutions. Before technology revolutionised the way individuals could make contact with their financial services provider, distribution channels were largely restricted to the branch network and door-to-door. Both these methods relied on personal contact. Consequently, relationships developed by default.

By the same token, it is argued that as financial institutions become increasingly remote in their contacts with customers and encourage customers to make greater use of low-cost automated delivery channels, there are likely to be repercussions in terms of customer relationship development. As contact is no longer channelled

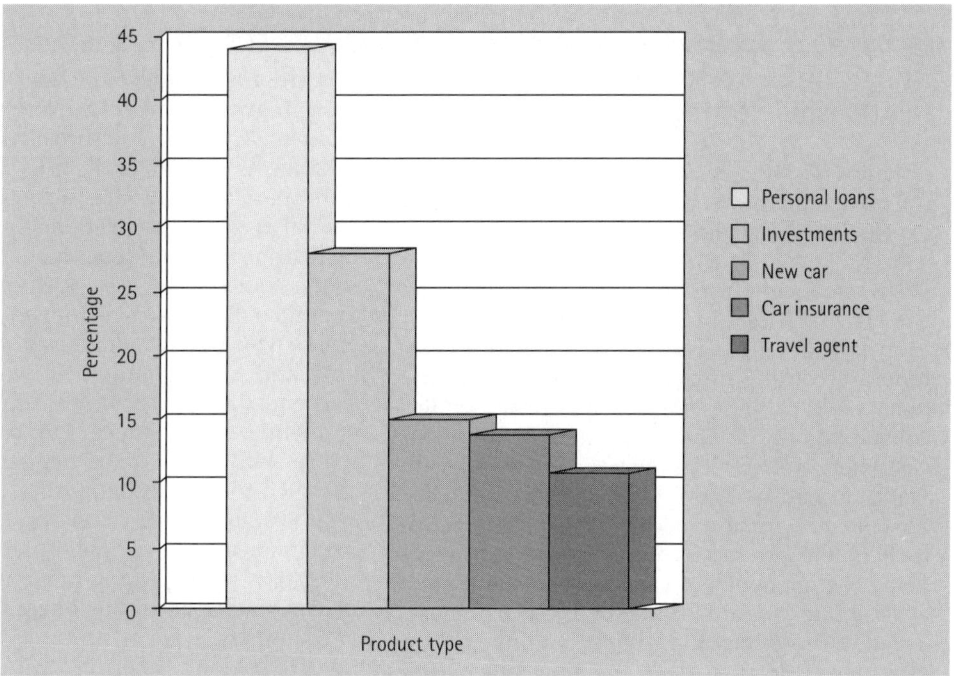

Fig. 9.3 Which products do customers have relationships with?
(*Source*: Adapted from The Henley Centre, Consumer Consultancy, 1994).

through person-to-person interaction, the emotional nature of the relationship changes. It was argued in Chapter 6, in relation to telephone banking, that remote forms of distribution put the customer in greater control of the customer–financial institution interaction: the customer essentially becomes empowered by the technology. While this is a good thing from the point of view of the customer, it could mean that customers will be more inclined to break their ties with financial institutions more frequently once the personal element is withdrawn. It may be argued that the relationship is no longer with the person (representative of the financial institution) but the technology.

With whom should relationships be built?

This question raises the issue of which customers the financial institution should be thinking about keeping and developing a relationship with. Implicit in this question is the assumption that not all customers are equal. Indeed, this is the hypothesis underpinning segmentation, and was discussed in Chapter 3. Some customers, for whatever reason, are worth more than others. Many financial institutions would agree that the most profitable customers are the most valuable and are the ones on whom the greatest amount of resources should be directed. Yet, this raises two separate issues:

- *How do you measure profitability?* The difficulties of calculating profitability at either the product or the customer level were discussed in Chapter 7 in

FINANCIAL SERVICES MARKETING IN PRACTICE

American Express: customer relationship strategy

American Express has been recognised as one of the few companies to have an explicit strategy for developing and maintaining customer relationships.

The products offered by American Express are the Green, Gold and Platinum cards. This division provides a basic means of segmenting customers according to customer requirements and financial capabilities. While American Express considers it has a close relationship with all its customers, the closest relationship exists with Platinum card holders.

Segmentation also occurs within and across each of the product groups: the primary bases being the frequency of card use and the type of expenditure the card is used for. Each customer is assigned a profitability score according to how often they use their card and how much they spend. Differential marketing and servicing policies are implemented according to individual profitability scores.

For example, if a customer with a high profitability score threatens to cancel their card, they might be offered a reduced fee in an attempt to win them back. If, on the other hand, a non-profitable customer threatens to cancel their card, American Express may just simply let them go.

Customer Recruitment

In contrast to most credit card companies, American Express does not have access to credit bureau data which would enable it to identify suitable targets. Consequently, the company engages in a large amount of mailings in order to solicit potential customers, review them and reject unsuitable ones.

Relationship Management

Once customers are on board, they are managed according to the stage in their relationship with American Express. New customers are allocated to a special department for the first sixteen months of their relationship where they are given special treatment. The reason for this is that the relationship is most sensitive in the early stages. Attrition rates are highest in the first one to one-and-a-half years.

To improve the likelihood of the customer remaining with American Express, they are subjected to a number of special offers and other activities to encourage them to make use of the card. Special attention is also paid to the pre-renewal stage in the relationships, especially for the first membership renewal.

After four or five years attrition rates are very low. Much of the early customer loss is due to customers who were acquired as a result of promotions and subsequently left when the special deals ended. Some customers simply try the card for a while and then give it up because they find that they do not have the frequent travel pattern for which the card is designed.

For customers that fit the card, they find that spend increases over time. There is also a close correlation with spend and retention – the more the customer spends, the longer they stay.

Because the use of the card is dependent on travel behaviour, American Express does what it can to increase travel behaviour. This includes Air Miles rewards and other affinity deals with hotels.

Service Quality

In order to improve the relationship with customers, American Express has focused on improving service quality through customisation and customer service. The relationship is customised in several ways, from the statements and direct mailings to the data provided to the customer service representatives when the customer calls.

Customer service is improved by soliciting feedback from customers on their experience of the level of service quality. There are several points in the relationship when feedback is sought. The first is the initial point of contact with the new customer. The information provided by the customer at this point helps determine what type of customer they are and what level of service they will require. Customer service questionnaires are administered to samples of card holders at specific intervals.

The quality of the relationship is measured in terms of the retention rate, the number of relationships (or products) the customer has with American Express and the usage rate and expenditure.

Interestingly, poor customer service is not the main reason for customers leaving. It stands to

FINANCIAL SERVICES MARKETING IN PRACTICE

reason that if customers do not receive a good service they will be offended, but they are very likely to tell American Express. In fact, American Express make it easy for customers to complain which gives them the opportunity to put it right and recover the customer.

Being able to put things right means enabling employees to deal with situations as they arise. At American Express, employees have been empowered to write off charges according to the customer's value, giving authorisation at the point of contact. This avoids the need for the customer to make a second call which can be very damaging to the relationship.

American Express places a great deal of importance on the management of customer relationships. It recognises that the benefits of relationships are: the retention of customers, increased use of the card and resultant profit, and positive word-of-mouth leading to the recruitment of new customers.

Customer relationships with American Express last, on average, four and half years. Roughly twenty per cent of customers deliver seventy per cent of the profits. The top seven to eight per cent of customers deliver forty per cent of profits. Some of the most profitable customers only give American Express half their spend.

Source: Adapted from Stone and Lowrie (1996)

Questions:

1 How can American Express use existing card holders to recruit new members?

2 Outline some of the ways in which card holders can be encouraged to make more use of their cards.

3 What can American Express do to increase the average length of the customer relationship?

relation to pricing. Thus, it may not be possible to know exactly how profitable customers are. American Express has devised a formula for calculating profitability scores for its customers. Marketing and service levels are pitched according to the customer's profitability (see Financial Services Marketing in Practice: 'American Express: customer relationship strategy').

- *Do customers need to generate a profit to be valuable?* The simple answer to this is yes, customers generally do need to be capable of generating profit for the financial institution. Relationship banking is practised very successfully at the top end of the market, but it should be remembered that private banks offer a service for a fee. This is radically different from the cross-purchase rationale which underpins mass retail markets. In the mass retail markets, Mills and Geraghty (1997) note that customer relationships that translate into the most profitable behaviour are prevalent among the 'middle-income' market, C_1C_2 groups. Consumers in this category are generally more attracted to the idea of concentrating their product holdings with a provider they trust. However, some customers, such as students, may not generate profit in the short term. Indeed, some customers may not be particularly profitable throughout the whole of their banking relationship. Does this mean, then, that these customers are not valuable? There may be some value to be gained from these customers, particularly if they generate profit indirectly, through valuable positive word-of-mouth which results in the referral of other customers. Thus, it is important to ascertain the value which each customer holds for the business, and the specific nature of the value.

The process of relationship development

People rarely move from being prospects one minute to loyal customers, committed to a long-term relationship, the next. Individuals progress through various stages before eventually becoming fully loyal. The stages are shown in figure 9.4. The prospect is a potential buyer for the company's products. Once the prospect has made a purchase, they become a customer. Some customers may only ever make one purchase from a company. Yet, the objective is to achieve regular repurchasing, thereby turning the customer into a client. Having established repurchase behaviour, the next stage is to move the individual towards the development of a favourable attitude towards the company and its products. In doing so, the individual may then become a supporter of the company and its products and may eventually become an active and vocal advocate for the company generating positive word-of-mouth and acting as a referral source.

In order to create advocates out of prospects, financial institutions need to understand the process involved in the development and management of customer relationships. The ladder of customer loyalty would seem to suggest that once the customer becomes an advocate for the company, they will remain an advocate. In reality, any of the stages along the way can be threatened at any time, causing the individual to terminate their association with the organisation. Thus, the process of relationship development involves acquiring new customers and attempting to move them up the ladder of loyalty while at the same time managing situations which may lead to the ultimate termination of the relationship with the company. Recognising which stage customers are at is important to the management of successful and long-term relationships.

The process of relationship development has been defined as consisting of eight distinct stages (Stone and Woodcock, 1997). Figure 9.5 illustrates the process.

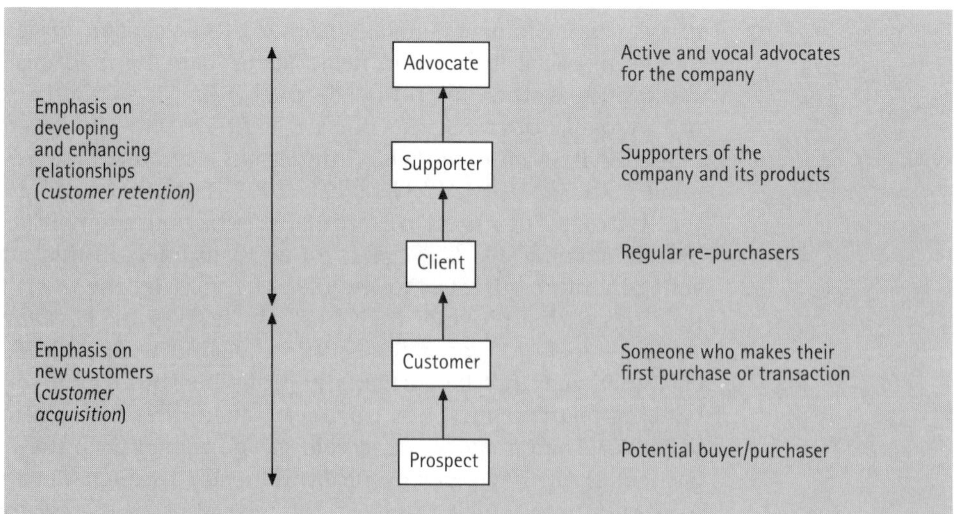

Fig. 9.4 Ladder of customer loyalty
(*Source*: Adapted from Christopher *et al.*, 1991)

- *Recruitment* – the first stage in the development of relationships is the recruitment of prospects. Potential customers can be targeted by a variety of means including direct mail targeted at individuals or mass forms of communication such as advertising. This is the first impression individuals will have of the organisation, so it is important that the necessary research is undertaken beforehand. Targeting should be specific enough to catch the people who have a need for the products offered, and ensure that time and effort is not wasted on those who are not interested. Communication messages also need to be meaningful and motivating. Every effort should be made to maximise the likelihood of the prospect becoming an actual customer.
- *Welcoming* – once the prospect makes a purchase and becomes a customer it is important that efforts are made to ensure that they are securely on board. Customers need to know who the key contacts are in the organisation. For example, new bank customers will be made aware of who the key personnel are with regard to enquiries or specific product information. Many telephone banking operations are assigning a personal banker to customers. This means that the customer has a key contact within the bank. This can provide security and assurance to the customer, knowing that there is a key individual responsible for their account.
- *Getting acquainted* – this stage is crucial to progressing the relationship any further and transforming the customer into a client. In order to encourage repeat purchase and cross-sell products both sides need to exchange information. The financial institution will want to find out what the individual's financial requirements are, now and in the future, and what their plans and aspirations are. The individual can assist the financial institution in providing the appropriate products at appropriate times by keeping them up-to-date on any changes to their personal circumstances. Getting acquainted with the customer is an important stage. Spending time here, and getting it right, can pay off later. The number of early cancellations on insurance policies may suggest that companies are still not spending enough time finding out what customers need. Financial institutions need to focus on what their customers want, not on what they can sell.
- *Account management* – at this stage the relationship is being managed securely and additional needs are being met as they arise. Individuals who develop a positive attitude towards the financial institution may become supporters or even advocates of its products and services, providing recommendations to other prospective customers. This is a desired state, and often viewed as the ultimate in relationship development. The problem which many financial institutions face is that few customers enter into this stage or stay in it very long. To prolong the length of time customers remain at this stage, it must be managed carefully.
- *Intensive care* – the relationship between a financial institution and its customers is unlikely to be totally problem-free. Problems can be experienced on both sides and are likely to threaten the continued existence of the relationship. While problems can develop during any of

the stages already mentioned in the development of the relationship, it is perhaps the account management stage where the greatest impact is likely to be felt. At this stage the customer is likely to have several products from the financial institution and may have also generated some positive word-of-mouth. When a problem does arise, it is likely to require intensive care to prevent the situation from getting out of control and the customer from leaving. A strategy of service recovery may be attempted to return the customer safely to the above stage. This involves a planned process of turning a dissatisfied customer into a satisfied one by putting things right. Service recovery is both emotional and physical and requires the empowerment of employees to allow them to act appropriately. The process involves apologising, putting the problem right and compensating. Successful recovery can have a significant impact on subsequent customer loyalty towards the organisation.

- *Potential divorce* – if intensive care has been unsuccessful, and the customer is still dissatisfied, divorce and exit may be imminent. Many companies fail to recognise that this is happening. Indeed, it can be difficult to spot, especially if the problem has not been brought to the attention of the financial institution by a customer complaint. However, even if the problem is known, some financial institutions just simply give up and resign themselves to the fact that the customer is already lost. But the customer is not yet lost!
- *Divorce* – if the financial institution does not attempt to rectify the situation the customer may terminate their contract, close accounts and leave. Even

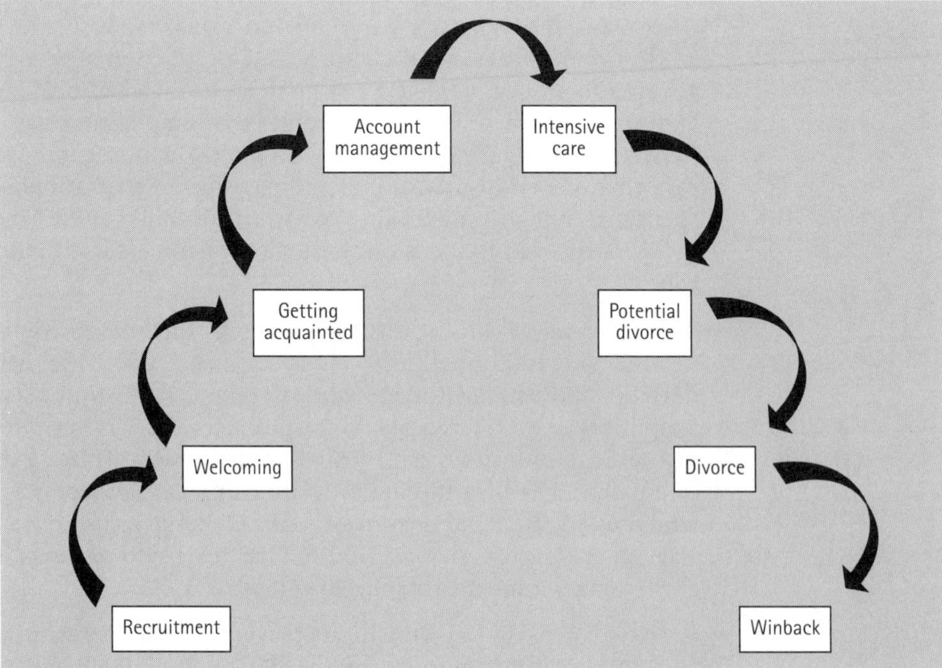

Fig. 9.5 Stages in the development of customer relationships
(*Source*: Adapted from Stone and Woodcock, 1997)

though the customer has gone, there may still be the possibility of winning them back after a sufficient cooling off period has elapsed.

- *Winback* – the success of winback depends very much on the customer's reasons for leaving. It the reasons were largely due to circumstances (such as changing a job or moving house), the likelihood of winning the customer back would be greater than if the customer had left because of dissatisfaction. If customers are won back, it can be possible to build even stronger bonds with them. In many cases, attempts to win customers back are not made because it is perceived to be too costly compared with focusing on acquiring more new customers.

The components of a relationship

The process of developing and maintaining relationships with customers rests on a number of key factors. If prospects are to become long-term customers they need to be able to trust that the financial institution will honour its promises and provide them with products and services which meet their needs over time. The continued satisfaction of the customer will depend, to a large extent, on the overall quality of service provided by the financial institution and the competence, efficiency and helpfulness of staff in processing transactions and gaining information. Furthermore, if customers should become dissatisfied with any aspect of their relationship with the financial institution and make a complaint, it is important that it is known how to deal with the situation in order to try to recover the customer and prevent them from leaving. Thus, several key factors which determine the ultimate success of a relationship are: understanding the nature and role of trust, service quality, the role of employees and managing customer complaints. The remainder of this section will consider the impact of each of these in turn.

The role of trust

The extent to which the relationship is successful will depend, in some part, on the amount of trust that exists between the customer and the financial services provider. Trust works both ways. For example, in the application for a loan, the customer needs to trust that the financial institution will deliver the loan on time, while the financial institution needs to trust that the customer will make the loan repayments as agreed. Trust is, therefore, a generalised expectancy that the word (and/or actions) of another can be relied upon.

It has been shown that the length of a relationship between a customer and a company is positively related to the customer's perceptions of the trustworthiness of the company (Cowles, 1997). Therefore, financial institutions should attempt to increase their trustworthiness in the eyes of their customers in order to improve relationships with them. The trust which an individual feels for a company is dependent on a number of key things. Increasing the overall trust for the company, therefore, requires some attention to these key determinants.

- *Perceived risk* – Situations involving trust, such as relationships between a financial institution and its customers, constitute a subclass of those involving risk. These are situations in which the risk one takes depends on the performance of another. In such cases there must be some degree of trust. This kind of trust, which is specific to financial institutions, was referred to in Chapter 2 as 'fiduciary responsibility'. Financial institutions are entrusted with the responsibility of their customers' money and, in many cases, their financial welfare. For many types of investments, customers depend on the behaviour and performance of fund managers. A way of increasing the trust would be to reduce the risk perceived by the customer. The provision of contractual safeguards can achieve this.

- *Contractual safeguards* – Contractual safeguards essentially preclude the need for trusting behaviour. For many customer purchases, safeguards have been devised. These take the form of guarantees, warranties and other implicit or explicit promises. In the context of financial services, it is difficult to find examples of safeguards which guarantee the product or the outcome of a financial relationship. For example, due to a number of factors outside the control of the financial institution it is not possible to guarantee the value of an investment plan in *x* years time. It is far more usual in financial services to find examples of safeguards or guarantees of the processes or procedures. First Direct provides compensation for any mistakes made in the running of accounts, as do many other financial institutions. With regard to the giving of financial advice, safeguards are contained in the guidelines outlined in the Financial Services Act (1986). These relate to the proper conduct of financial advisers with regard to working within 'best practice' and the giving of 'best advice'. Regulation generally can serve to infuse trading confidence into otherwise problematic trading relationships, but only really works if the regulation is understood by customers. The problem with financial regulation is that few customers understand it fully enough to feel confident in it.
- *Confidence* – An act of trust occurs when one person has some confidence in their expectations for the other's behaviour. Confidence that the financial institution will honour its promises can be built up from a number of sources. If the customer has had previous experience with the financial institution, and was satisfied with the experience, the customer has every reason to trust that a similarly satisfying experience will be had. A previous happy experience has the effect of reducing the risk to the customer. If customers have had no prior experience of the financial institution, recommendations (based on the experience of others) can serve to increase confidence and trust in dealing with the organisation. Recognising the importance of positive word-of-mouth, financial institutions should attempt to increase such positive exchanges between customers. Customer confidence can also be increased as a result of public relations or credible advertising sources.
- *Corporate culture* – all financial institutions operate within the same environment and compete against the same safeguards offered by regulation. However, some strategic advantage may be gained from organisation-specific safeguards, such as corporate culture. If the organisation is known for

investing in people or has won service quality awards, this can increase the customer's trust in it. Some of the banks are taking a novel approach to addressing problems – promise the customer money if something goes wrong. Sainsbury's Bank will automatically send out £10 worth of vouchers to spend in the supermarket if it falls short of the standards expected by customers. The initiative is designed to protect the integrity of the Sainsbury name. The Co-operative Bank has had a similar scheme in operation since 1995, making about 600 compensation payments a month. This, it claims, gives a 99.996 per cent efficiency rate (*Financial Times*, 15 November 1997).

Service quality

A major consideration in recent years has been the needs of customers in relation to service quality levels. High levels of customer service are seen as a means to achieving competitive advantage. As customers become increasingly aware of the alternatives on offer and standards of service rise, so too do customer expectations of service. Consequently, customers of financial institutions are generally becoming increasingly critical of the quality of service experienced. In order to maintain long-term, satisfying relationships with customers financial institutions need to understand how quality of service can be achieved.

Defining service quality is difficult. It is basically concerned with meeting customers' needs and requirements and how well the service level delivered meets customer expectations. Customer expectations basically relate to what the customer wants or desires out of the relationship with the financial services provider, and what he or she feels the service provider should offer. Thus, quality becomes a customer judgement. If a service level meets or exceeds a customer's expectations, it is generally considered to be of quality. If the service level falls short of expectations, it does not necessarily mean that the absolute level of quality is low; it is, however, unsatisfactory for the customer. Thus, the quality of a service is evaluated relative to what the customer expects it to be.

Financial institutions can raise expectations through advertising, but if promises are not delivered, customers can be disappointed. Poor service can also arise when demand is increased so dramatically for a company's product that the company is unable to meet customer requests on time. This happened to Tesco when it launched its instant-access account with a very attractive rate of interest compared with the main high-street banks. The supermarket fell victim to its own success when it became inundated with applications. Customers experienced delays in accounts being opened and there were a number of teething problems in the initial running of accounts.

Generally, customers' expectations are reasonable, but they do vary depending on the specific circumstances and experience of the customer. Each customer has a 'zone of tolerance' which determines the variation in expected service levels that the customer is willing to tolerate. Zones of tolerance tend to be smaller for outcome features (e.g. the value of an investment on maturity) than for process dimensions (e.g. the issuing of annual statements during the term of the investment plan). Outcome features tend to be more important to customers than process features. Furthermore, if options are limited, tolerance zones may be higher. However, in emergency situations expectations are usually higher than normal.

Various authors (Lehtinen and Lehtinen, 1991; Gronroos, 1984; Parasuraman *et al.*, 1985, 1988) have commented on what constitutes service quality. The common factors cited include process, outcome, physical, interactive and corporate quality.

- *Process quality* – process or functional quality refers to the quality of the processes and procedures in producing and delivering the service to the customer. Due to the often simultaneous nature of production and consumption of services, process quality is usually judged by customers while the service is being performed. In a financial services context, the processes may refer to any mechanical or technical aspects of process or service delivery or any interactions with employees and the manner in which they conduct themselves. Evaluations of these enable customers to make a judgement about service quality.
- *Output quality* – output or technical quality is judged after the service has been performed. The output is what the customer receives from the service organisation, or what the customer is left with after interactions have ended. It was mentioned above that customers' zones of tolerance are generally smaller for outcome features than for process features. What this means is that customers are generally less tolerant of deviations from expectations for service outcomes than for service processes. In the context of ongoing financial services relationships, customers may be tolerant of mistakes made on statements or ATMs occasionally not working (process quality) since there is the opportunity for the financial institution to put them right for the next time. However, customers are more likely to be far less tolerant if a matured private pension plan (output quality) has not performed as well as expected since this has a much bigger impact on the customer and it signifies the end of that product relationship with the financial institution with no opportunity for it to be rectified.
- *Physical quality* – physical quality refers to the products or support features of the products and service. Financial products have few physical dimensions so alternative physical cues are often used to evaluate the quality of service. Branches provide much physical evidence of the service quality. Customers use the décor, in-branch facilities, layout and comfort within the branch to make judgements of quality. This is one of the reasons why financial institutions have invested so much in branch refurbishments.
- *Interactive quality* – interactive quality refers to the interactions between the customer and service provider. Interactions may take place in many ways: in branches, face-to-face or by remote means, such as telephone or internet contact. Whichever form the interaction takes, financial institutions need to ensure that they communicate effectively with their customers. This means keeping customers informed in a language they understand and understanding the customer and knowing what they want. Any communication via printed media should be clear and free of ambiguity. And any communication from employees needs to be conducted in a courteous and helpful manner.
- *Corporate quality* – corporate quality refers to the general image and perceptions of the organisation. Corporate quality is an intangible

dimension. Hence, perceptions of the overall quality of the organisation are likely to be based on all of the above factors.

Service quality is very subjective. The extent to which each of the above factors influences a customer's perceptions of the overall quality is likely to vary. For some customers, the general quality of the relationship with a financial institution may be more affected by the quality of interaction with the branch personnel, whereas for other customers, the overall relationship may be more affected by the reliability of technology, such as the ATMs. Factors affecting service quality can be categorised into hygiene factors, enhancing factors and dual threshold factors.

- *Hygiene factors* are those things that are expected by the customer. For example, customers expect the ATM to issue them with the amount of money requested and to debit the amount from their account. Failure to do this will cause dissatisfaction. Hygiene factors, thus, represent the minimum level of service that the customer is willing to accept.
- *Enhancing factors* are those which lead to satisfaction, such as branch staff remembering the customer's name the next time they go into the branch. But failure to remember the customer's name will not normally cause dissatisfaction.
- *Dual-threshold factors* are things in which failure to deliver will cause dissatisfaction, but delivery above a certain level will enhance customer perceptions of service. For example, if staff are exceptionally friendly towards customers it can enhance their service experience. However, provided staff are not unfriendly, customers are unlikely to be dissatisfied.

Improving service quality can be very beneficial to a financial institution, having a direct impact on its relationships with customers. The following benefits can be expected from service quality enhancement:

- *Right-first-time* – reducing the mistakes and getting processes and procedures right the first time can lead to a dramatic reduction in the cost of corrective measures and compensation claims. In addition, it is likely to lead to a more satisfied customer and less complaints. Furthermore, reducing the number of mistakes can increase the customer's confidence and trust in the financial institution, with the possibility that the customer may wish to purchase additional products.
- *Increased productivity* – a reduction in mistakes and an improvement in processes and procedures can improve productivity and increase sales. If processes and staff are working effectively and efficiently, more time is spent on selling products than correcting them.
- *Increased staff morale* – improvements to service quality can also increase staff morale. Staff satisfaction can be increased as a result of dealing with satisfied customers and producing a quality service. Satisfied staff are also more likely to become loyal staff, staying with the financial institution for longer. If staff turnover is reduced, so too are the costs associated with staff recruitment and training of new staff. It is also likely that relationships between employees and their employer will be enhanced.

- *Enhanced corporate image* – better-quality products and service and satisfied customers and employees contribute to the enhanced image of the organisation. Enhanced corporate image can have an impact on brand value.

Employees

The role of employees is integral to the management of successful customer relationships. Employees have different roles within the financial institution, and the nature of the role can have a significant impact on the financial institution–customer relationship. According to Judd (1987), the influence which employees have on the customer relationship depends on two key factors: the extent to which employees are customer-facing, and in direct contact with customers, and the degree of employees' involvement in marketing activities. Figure 9.6 shows the four different types of employees in terms of their relationship with the customer.

- *Contactors* – the role which these employees occupy has perhaps the greatest impact on the customer's perception of the level of service delivered. Employees such as tellers, customer service staff and telephone sales staff are usually in frequent contact with customers. At the same time, they are also involved in marketing activities, generally in terms of implementing marketing strategies at the customer level. Thus, the interaction which the customer has with these employees often leaves an impression of the level of service the customer has received. From the customer's point of view, these employees are responsible for the service delivered. In order to enhance the relationship with customers, it is important that employees in these roles are given the correct training to enable them to communicate effectively with customers, respond effectively to their needs and be in possession of the required skills and knowledge to answer technical enquiries.

  Contact with customers is crucial to the development of customer relationships. Indeed, the relationship between customer contact and levels of customer satisfaction is well documented (Mills and Geraghty, 1997). However, much less attention has been paid to the nature of the contact. Contact between a customer and a financial institution can be face-to-face, by telephone, be letter, via the internet or via a number of other means. In studying relationships between financial institutions and their customers Mills and Geraghty (1997) came to the conclusion that customer relationships that develop into positive behaviour can best be achieved by having a human focus to the relationship. Basically, relationships are driven by personal contact.

  However, contact between customers and their financial services providers has become increasingly remote, to the extent that many people simply do not interact with their financial institution on a personal, face-to-face level. Contact occurs on a continuum from high-touch (personal interactions) to high-tech (remote interactions). The question to consider is whether it is possible to build relationships in high-tech situations. In such situations, financial institutions can enhance their relationship with their customers by ensuring that the customer's dialogue with them has a sense of consistency. In addition, it is important that customers feel that the organisation needs

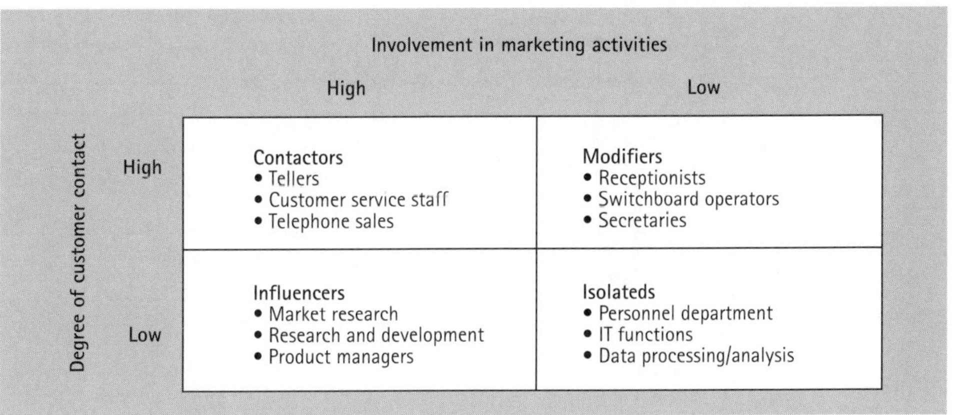

Fig. 9.6 Influence of financial services employees on customers
(*Source*: Adapted from Judd, 1987)

them as much as they need the product or service – customers need to feel valued. Even if face-to-face contact may not be available to reassure the customer of this, regular verbal recognition of the importance of the customer can still be achieved by simply phoning the customer up.

- *Modifiers* – another group of employees also in frequent contact with customers are the modifiers. This group includes receptionists, secretaries and switchboard operators. While these individuals are not directly involved in implementing marketing activities, they do have an important role to play. These employees must be trained to be courteous and friendly and responsive to customers' needs.
- *Influencers* – influencers are people involved in marketing activities, but not in direct contact with the customer. This would include those people working in marketing research and R&D departments. Although these employees do not come into daily contact with the customer, the extent to which these roles and/or departments are customer-focused and customer-responsive can greatly improve the general relationship with customers. One of the problems with most of the marketing departments of banks is that they are often quite remote from customers. Marketing, in banks, needs to be managed more as an integral part of the customer process. Many people working in marketing departments in banks are actually product managers responsible for a specific product or group of products. Hence, few product managers get to make up a picture of the whole customer. Some financial institutions have tried to overcome this problem, and have become more customer-focused by re-organising the company according to customer segments and not product categories, creating a more integrated customer relationship.
- *Isolateds* – these are employees who provide support functions such as personnel and data processing. They are often far removed from the customer and any marketing activity, mostly serving the needs of other employees within the organisation – the internal customer. The role that these employees play is important due to the indirect impact that they have

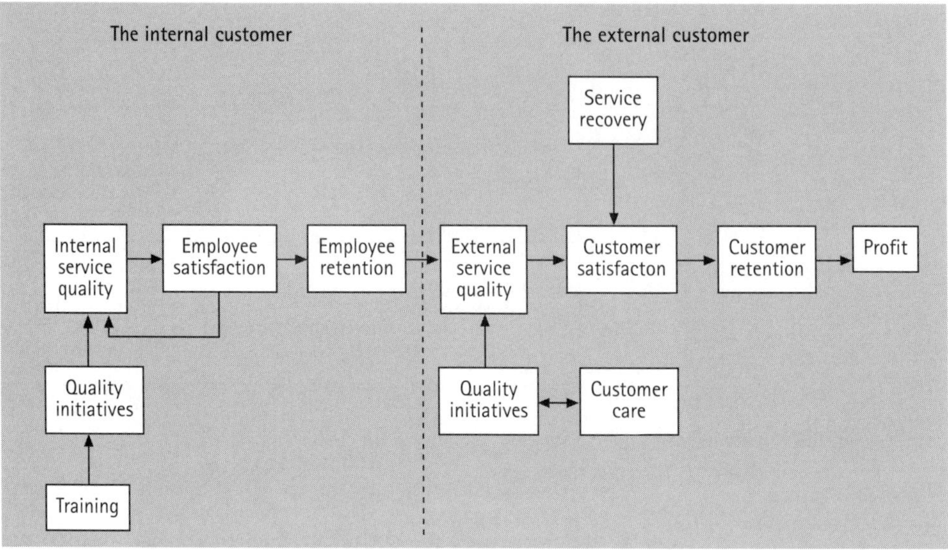

Fig. 9.7 The service–profit chain
(*Source*: Adapted from Schlesinger and Heskett, 1991)

on the overall (external) customer relationship. While it is important for customer-facing staff to appreciate the importance of marketing in managing successful customer relationships, the concept of internal marketing is relevant here. Internal marketing views employees as internal customers, and views their jobs as internal products. The financial institution needs to sell its jobs to its employees (internal customers) before employees can sell the financial institution's products and services to its external customers. The objectives of internal marketing are:

- to create an internal environment which supports customer consciousness;
- to foster customer-oriented and customer-caring staff;
- to sell service and marketing efforts to employees via training programmes.

Figure 9.7 shows that by satisfying the needs of internal customers, a financial institution can increase the likelihood of satisfying the needs of external customers and building long-term relationships with them.

Managing customer complaints

Financial services customers are becoming more discriminating in their purchasing behaviour. If service quality levels are not maintained, customers will become dissatisfied and may make complaints about poor service, poor quality or poor value for money. A proportion of dissatisfied customers will tell other customers, generating negative word-of-mouth. Thus, it is important that customer complaints be taken seriously, and their causes detected and rectified. Responding

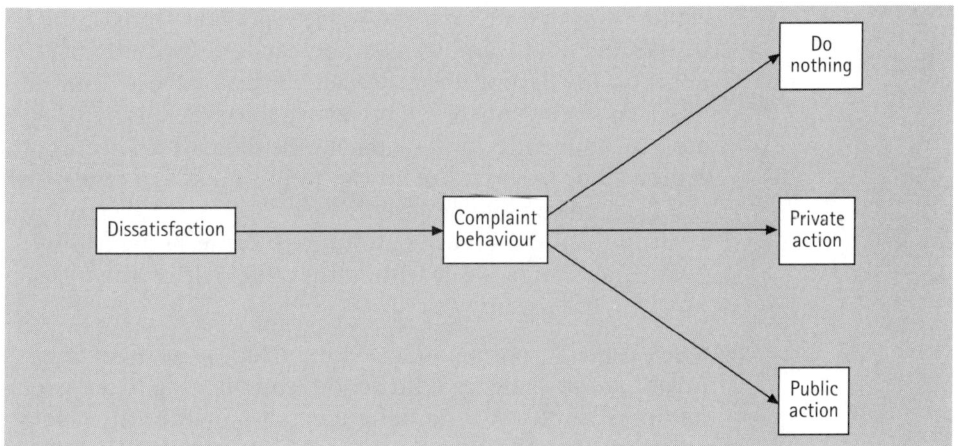

Fig. 9.8 Customer complaint behaviour
(*Source*: Adapted from Broadbridge and Marshall, 1995)

effectively to customer complaints is an area which financial institutions can address: it can provide a key point of differentiation and improve customer relationships.

As mentioned earlier, customers have different zones of tolerance. Thus, the point at which service quality levels are perceived to be below standard is rather subjective. A problem is a problem when the customer feels it is one.

Consumer complaint behaviour is considered a distinct process. It begins when the customer has evaluated a consumption experience (resulting in dissatisfaction) and ends when the customer has completed all the behavioural and non-behavioural responses to the experience. The length of consumption experiences depends on the nature of the product. Many financial products are extremely long-term in nature. Such products as personal pensions, which are consumed over a long period of time beyond the post-purchase stage, take longer to assess. However, during this time the additional experiences or interactions with the financial institution are assessed and may be treated as new episodes of consumer satisfaction/dissatisfaction.

Once a problem has been recognised, there are three options available under consumer complaining behaviour to resolve it. These are depicted in figure 9.8.

- *Do nothing* – when customers are dissatisfied yet make no effort to complain, a number of conditions are likely to prevail. For example, the purchased item may be of low cost or low value to the customer so that the loss to the customer is not great. Consequently, the dissatisfaction has no lasting impact. Alternatively, customers may choose to do nothing because they feel that it would not be worth the time and effort to complain. This situation typifies many which customers of financial institutions face. Stone and Woodcock (1997) note that, at any one time, there are typically between 5 and 15 per cent of customers who would like to change their bank. In reality far fewer actually do anything about it. Thus, many dissatisfied customers remain with the same financial institution out of inertia.
- *Private action* – an alternative response is for the customer to take private

action by switching financial services provider, boycotting the organisation or warning family and friends. Such actions generally may require little effort on the part of the customer, but may have a significant impact on the financial institution. Some private actions, such as negative word-of-mouth, are hard to identify, and it can also be difficult to measure the exact impact on the company. Yet, the impact can be great as a result of the influence it can have on the buying intentions of others. It is better for financial institutions to encourage customers to come to them with their complaints where they can be dealt with, rather than letting them leave and never knowing the reason why.

- *Public action* – taking public action includes seeking redress directly from the organisation, bringing legal action, complaining to an association or authority, such as the banking ombudsman or to the media. In many cases, customers will first take their complaints to the financial institution in question. If they are not dealt with satisfactorily customers are likely to then go on and seek further redress. When customers approach with a complaint, companies need to respond in order to prevent the process from continuing and the complaint being made public. It is generally high priced, complex items, with a relatively long life expectancy that generate a higher incidence of public complaints, as evidenced from the number of public complaints concerning pensions mis-selling.

SUMMARY

The level of interest in relationship marketing has increased in recent years. Financial institutions are keen to develop long-term relationships with their customers in an attempt to cushion themselves from competitive pressures, reduce operating costs and increase revenues. Before embarking on a relationship development strategy, financial institutions must consider with whom they wish to develop relationships. Some customer groups may offer greater profit potential, while other customer groups may not wish to have a relationship with their financial services provider. Developing relationships with customers can be a lengthy process. Individuals pass through several stages before becoming loyal, long-term customers. It is important that the process of relationship development is managed carefully. The longevity of the relationship can be threatened at any time and strategies need to be in place to win customers back if they decide to leave.

The process of developing and maintaining successful relationships with customers rests on a number of key factors. Customers need to be able to trust that the financial institution will honour its promises and provide them with products and services which meet their needs over time. The continued satisfaction of the customer will depend on the overall quality of service provided by the financial institution and the competence, efficiency and helpfulness of its staff. Furthermore, if customers become dissatisfied with any aspect of their relationship with the financial institution and make a complaint, it is important that complaints be managed effectively to recover the customer and prevent them from leaving.

DISCUSSION QUESTIONS

1 Outline the differences between offensive and defensive marketing strategies and show how they are being used by financial institutions.

2 What are the constituent parts of a relationship and how can they be managed?

3 Compare and contrast the benefits of relationship marketing with transactional marketing.

4 How does a financial institution decide which customers it should build relationships with?

5 What are the benefits of moving customers up the ladder of loyalty?

6 Suggest appropriate strategies for progressing customers from the recruitment to the account management stage in the process of relationship development.

7 Suggest appropriate strategies for recovering customers when the relationship breaks down.

8 How can financial institutions build more trust into their relationships with customers?

9 What recommendations would you make to improve service quality in a bank?

10 How can customer complaint data be put to better use in the management of customer relationships?

10 Customer retention and loyalty

INTRODUCTION

In order to build relationships with customers, financial institutions need to understand how to first retain existing customers and increase their loyalty to the institution. The previous chapter took a holistic approach to the development of customer relationships, emphasising the strategic importance of relationships and the inter-functional dependencies in relationship creation. This chapter focuses more on the tactical issues concerned with customer retention and loyalty.

Retention is an interesting issue, since customers may stay with, or indeed leave, an organisation for a number of reasons. These reasons may be attributed to the company and the level of service received, to the competition and the promise of a better offer, or external factors which essentially force customers to alter their behaviour. Interestingly, not all satisfied customers choose to stay; customers may be completely happy with the level of service received, yet still defect to the competition.

Institutions should not be lured entirely by retention statistics. Just because a customer stays it does not necessarily mean that they are satisfied. They may stay out of inertia or due to the lack of suitable alternatives. Loyalty is, thus, a complex phenomenon, comprised of a set of both behavioural and attitudinal factors. Any attempt to build customer loyalty should address both repeat purchase and emotional considerations.

OBJECTIVES

After reading this chapter you should be able to:

- provide definitions of customer retention and defection;
- discuss motives for customer retention and exit;
- outline a strategy for customer retention;
- define customer loyalty and discuss the components of loyalty;
- critically evaluate the extent to which customer loyalty programmes in the financial services sector actually build loyal customers.

Customer retention

Customer retention is an essential part of relationship development: in order to be able to build long-term relationships with customers, financial institutions must

FINANCIAL SERVICES MARKETING IN PRACTICE

The student market: a lesson in retention

Students represent a significant part of the youth market and have received considerable attention from the financial services sector over the last few decades. In the 1970s the major clearing banks began to develop student accounts aimed at school leavers going on to further education. The driving factor at that time was that a vast majority of students received local education authority grants paid by cheque for which a bank account was desirable.

Since the 1970s much has changed with respect to grants, and most students are now funded by student loans and/or parental contribution with an increasing number supplementing their financial means with part-time employment. Nevertheless, students still represent an attractive market segment for financial institutions for a number of reasons. Among these are that:

- students are easily identifiable in demographic terms;
- they are easily located and reached;
- they have specific, identifiable needs;
- they represent a captive market while at university;
- many will obtain employment in AB social class-type occupations – high paying jobs with extensive financial services needs;
- with little switching they present the opportunity to capitalise on the full lifetime value of the segment.

While at university, students are generally unprofitable; they only start contributing to the profits of financial institutions the year after graduation. Profitability has then been found to increase every year up to ten years. The costs of acquiring university students are high due to marketing expenditure from promotional offers used to entice them. Yet, once graduated, they are more likely to be in higher-paid jobs with salaries increasing at higher rates than their non-university counterparts.

For this reason, financial institutions are keen to retain their student customers beyond graduation. One problem with this is that recent graduates are highly mobile in the early years of their career, with serious consequences for their relationship with their financial services provider.

Defection rates among students have been found to vary up to 36 per cent in the UK and 18 per cent in Ireland. The average length of a student's relationship with a financial institution is around five and a half years. Research into the student market by Colgate *et al.* found that a reduction in the defection rate of less than 3 per cent can increase revenue by more than 100 per cent, and reducing the defection rate by a further 5 per cent can generate increased profits of over 500 per cent.

In order to reduce defection rates and increase retention rates, financial institutions need to understand why students switch. Studies have shown that students' initial motives for choosing a financial services provider are convenience of location and parental influence. High mobility on graduation may cause many students to switch their provider in order to achieve greater convenience. Indeed, the study by Colgate *et al.* highlighted convenience as the top reason for defection (33%), followed by dissatisfaction with the service provided (23%), refusal of an overdraft request (12%) and dissatisfaction with charges (11%).

Factors which were found likely to encourage students to stay with their financial services provider and not switch were ranked as: no charges, good customer service, interest paid on current accounts, competitive savings rates and competitive overdraft rates.

Thus, students would seem to be fairly price-sensitive, and it appears that financial institutions may be able to retain their student customers beyond graduation by offering more competitive prices, or perhaps rewarding their loyalty with discounts. At the same time, however, students also seem to place a great deal of emphasis on good customer service. Poor customer service can be a prime motive for switching.

Financial institutions need to be aware that young people today expect higher levels of service than their predecessors did. A study by Lewis *et al.* showed that while 72 per cent of the student sample surveyed were at least content with the level of service received, there was some room for improvement.

Students expect reliability from their financial

FINANCIAL SERVICES MARKETING IN PRACTICE

services provider in terms of accurate statements and being able to trust the employees' knowledge of the products offered. Tangibles, in the form of the branch décor and appearance, seem to have the least effect on perceptions of quality. While students are generally pleased with the 'people' aspects of the service, they do perceive some shortfalls in relation to aspects of service delivery such as product knowledge, speed and efficiency, slow queues and limited opening hours of branches.

If financial institutions are serious about retaining their student customers after graduation, they need to consider them as proper customers and not just as students.

Sources: Adapted from Colgate *et al.* (1995), Lewis *et al.* (1994), Lewis and Bingham (1991)

Questions:

1 Why do financial institutions want to retain students after graduation?

2 What can financial institutions do to improve service to student customers and retain them?

3 How can financial institutions overcome the inevitable mobility of students on graduation?

first be able to retain existing customers. The economic value of customer retention is widely recognised. Bain and Co. (Reichheld and Sasser, 1990) found that customer retention has a more positive effect on profits than market share, scale economies and other variables that are commonly associated with competitive advantage. The same research also showed that businesses generally lose between 15 and 20 per cent of their customers each year. A reduction in customer defections of only 5 per cent can boost profits anywhere from 25 to 85 per cent. The profit implications may be far greater for some customer segments. For example, research into the student market by Colgate *et al.* (1995) found that a reduction in the defection rate of less than 3 per cent can increase revenue by more than 100 per cent, and reducing the defection rate by a further 5 per cent can generate increased profits of over 500 per cent (see Financial Services Marketing in Practice: 'The student market: a lesson in retention').

In the financial services sector more widely, it has been reported (*Financial Times*, 16 November 1998) that, in fact, only as little as 3 per cent of bank customers move accounts to other providers every year. It is argued that this figure has fostered much complacency among financial institutions. Nevertheless, it is anticipated that the number of switchers will increase dramatically over the next few years as the costs of switching between providers are reduced by new technologies and new entrants. The question is to what extent banks will be prepared for increased customer switching behaviour. Many have been criticised for being too focused on short-term issues such as the millennium bug and the Euro, paying much less attention to the longer-term concerns of customer retention and relationships.

The problem is that once customers are lost, they are difficult to regain. Financial institutions need to strive to keep defection rates low and retention rates high. A high customer defection rate makes the market attractive to new market entrants since it makes it easier for new players to acquire customers. Low defection rates increase the barriers to entry and make the market less attractive for new entrants. A number of new players have recently entered the market, and traditional financial institutions may find it increasingly difficult to retain the big account balances and multiple product sales they have previously enjoyed if they do not pay due attention to customer retention programmes.

Definition of retention

Before financial institutions can retain customers, they need to understand what retention means. Furthermore, in understanding retention it is necessary to understand what defection means: retention and defection are two sides of the same coin. There are several facets to customer retention and defection. At the broadest level, it is necessary to make a distinction between *client* retention and/or defection and *contract* retention and/or defection.

- *Client retention/defection* – this refers to the retention (or defection) of a customer and all the contracts/business associated with them. It has important implications in terms of customer defection, since the true cost of losing a customer is not just the current business, which is lost, but the amount of business that person could have generated for the company over their entire lifetime. Client retention, on the other hand, provides the opportunity for the company to increase the number of separate contracts it has with the client. This concept has been called 'share of wallet' (SOW) (Dugmore and Reid, 1997). The objective is for the financial institution to obtain as large a share of the customer's expenditure on financial services (their wallet) as possible. In doing so, the likelihood of similar products being purchased from another financial services provider is reduced and the ties between the customer and the financial institution are strengthened. Hence, the chance of the customer defecting is reduced.
- *Contract retention/defection* – in contrast to client retention/defection, which deals with whole customers, this refers to the retention or termination of individual contracts by the customer. The distinctions between contract and client retention/defection can, however, become blurred. Some customers may only have a single contract relationship with the financial institution. In such cases, when the contract is terminated, the customer is also lost. Hence, the potential of cross-selling other products is also lost, reducing the possibility of contract retention developing into client retention. Just as contract retention can develop into client retention, the termination of a single contract (in the context of a multi-contract relationship) can signal the first step towards client defection. In such cases, financial institutions need to ascertain why the customer has terminated the contract and the future intentions of the customer with regard to remaining contracts. For some types of customers, it may be in the financial institution's interests to terminate a particular contract with a customer (or let the customer terminate the contract), but keep the customer for other contracts.

In addition to this, there are two further aspects to retention and defection: the visible and the insidious. In other words, retention and defection can be of either an active or a passive nature. The first is easy to see. For example, active retention would involve the customer in the purchase of additional products or, in the case of an investment product, making additional investments. Active defection would be the termination of contracts and the visible movement of accounts to another financial services provider. Thus, customers may be observed switching to competitors.

Passive retention and defection are a little more difficult to distinguish. A passively retained customer may be someone who does not add to further investments

Table 10.1 Active versus passive retention

Retention	Client	Contract
Active	Share of wallet, cross-selling, buying across the full product/ service range	Single contract/product relationship, but actively using the account/product to the full
Passive	When a customer is persuaded to buy a bundle of products when only one is sought – such as when insurance and current account products are bundled with mortgages	Dormant accounts, accounts which have been allowed to run down, no active use, or no new use of the account

Table 10.2 Active versus passive defection

Defection	Client	Contract
Active	Client closes all contracts and relationships with the company, breaks all ties and switches to another provider	Client closes one single account, terminates one single contract. If the client has multiple contracts, this could be a first step in client defection
Passive	Customer does not close accounts but no longer makes active use of them, and may even establish new accounts with another provider which receive more active use	Non-use of account, no new use, funds moving out but contract or account not closed down

and does not buy any additional products. Passive defection is harder to spot as it involves a steady evaporation of customers for less obvious reasons to less obvious competitors. An example of passive defection is a dormant account: where a customer runs down a savings account, for example, leaving only a nominal amount in the account, and no longer uses it, but does not actually close the account. This type of defection is costly to the financial institution, since the account still has to be administered. Hence, a number of financial institutions have made an effort to clean up their dormant accounts by writing to such customers asking them whether they wish to make any further use of the account, or whether the account can be closed. Tables 10.1 and 10.2 provide some specific examples of active and passive retention and defection.

Motives for retention/defection

Having understood what retention and defection are, it is important that financial institutions understand motives for retention and defection. In understanding why customers stay with the organisation, or why they leave, financial institutions can learn how to increase retention and decrease defection.

Motives for staying or leaving can be either positive or negative. For example, a positive reason for remaining a customer of a financial institution would be because

FINANCIAL SERVICES MARKETING IN PRACTICE

Loyalty schemes in the mortgage market

The mortgage provides the classic long-term relationship between the lender and the customer. Home loans are typically repaid over a twenty-five year period, during which there is much scope for the financial institution to reward customers for their longevity. Yet, do they?

It would seem that lenders are generally paying less attention to existing borrowers compared with the acquisition of new borrowers. The proportion of first-time borrowers still represents the significant proportion of new mortgage business, but it is shrinking.

Hence, lenders are focusing their attention on remortgagers for their new business. Much of the activity is, thus, the result of lenders chasing each other's customers, resulting in increased switching and a breakdown in the traditional long-term relationship.

Indeed, lenders have been criticised for not rewarding loyal borrowers, and using existing borrowers to fund the creation of new deals by charging them far higher rates than new borrowers. A survey commissioned by the Mortgage Guild suggests that more than 40 per cent of borrowers are paying the lender's standard variable rate (SVR), in effect more than they need to be paying.

Customers who switch from one mortgage lender to another are offered discounts, cash-back offers and low interest rates. It is argued that financial institutions have benefited from the ignorance and lack of sophistication of many of their customers, but as these better deals become more widely advertised, customers will not fail to notice that they are getting a raw deal.

In fact only 16 lenders in the UK offer discounts to long-standing borrowers, although the length of time the customer needs to be with the lender to qualify for a discount varies.

After seven years, customers of Northern Rock are rewarded with a reduction of 0.25 percentage point off the SVR, while customers of Hinckley and Rugby get a slightly better reduction of 0.5 percentage point after just five years of paying the mortgage.

Discounts may be awarded as a reduction in the monthly repayments or as an annual lump sum. Those that offer an annual lump sum tend to credit accounts at the end of the year. The benefit of this type of loyalty discount may be more tangible than a monthly reduction, and may provide a positive reason for staying with the financial institution, particularly if the cash arrives in time for Christmas shopping.

One may question why so many customers remain with their lender when they are paying higher interest rates. The answer is that they would probably incur a penalty if they tried to leave. Redemption penalties may improve retention rates, but do increased switching costs and barriers that lock customers in to deals really contribute to building loyal customer relationships? The likelihood of such customers' acting as vocal advocates for the financial institution is much lower. Indeed, if customers are locked in and just waiting for the opportunity to leave, they are perhaps more likely to generate negative word-of-mouth.

The Building Societies' Association was considering a ban on redemption penalties for mortgages. This could herald the end of widespread discounts, offers and cash-backs, since lenders would find it difficult to offer cheap deals unless they could then use early redemption penalties to lock customers in to paying the SVR for a minimum period of time. Financial institutions would then have to consider more positive reasons for encouraging customers to stay, when the barriers to exit have gone. This may mean taking more of a look at the whole of the customer relationship and linking in special deals and benefits for multiple-product holdings.

Britannia, the UK's third largest building society, has been criticised for operating one of the most complicated loyalty schemes. In 1998 it paid £39 million in loyalty bonuses to 1.1 million members. The loyalty bonus is part of the society's commitment to mutuality. The payout was £4 million more than in 1997, but the average payment per member was only £1 higher (£36 in 1998 against £35 in 1997) because more members became eligible for the bonus.

The bonus scheme is based on the extent of the customer's relationship with the society. Points are earned based on savings balances, size of mortgage, and purchases of other products from Britannia. In 1996 the points were worth 22p each. The maximum bonus would go to a 10-year member with a £500 a month mortgage, savings

FINANCIAL SERVICES MARKETING IN PRACTICE

of more than £20,000, and a range of additional products, such as PEPs and insurance, bought through Britannia.

In 1998, 795,000 members received bonuses of up to £50 (against 780,000 in 1997), some 230,000 received between £50 and £100 (against 217,000 in 1997), while 55,000 members received more than £100 (up from 43,000 in 1997). Some members received as much as £500.

The society says that its strategy is designed to retain customers and expand business from existing customers. However, it accepts that it is unlikely to win much new business on the back of the scheme.

Sources: Adapted from *Financial Times*, 4 July 1998, 6 June 1998, 14 February 1998, 13 February 1997

Questions:

1 Why do mortgage lenders pay so little attention to existing customers?

2 How can mortgage lenders reverse the trend towards switching, and build customer loyalty?

3 How far does Britannia's scheme go toward rewarding loyal customers?

of the rewards achieved. For example, tiered interest rates on savings accounts are designed to reward customers for saving more. Other rewards might include the giving of discounts on the purchase of additional products – some insurance companies give customers a discount on their insurance premiums if they purchase both their buildings and contents insurance from them.

Many financial institutions have moved to product bundles in an attempt to offer customers greater benefit and strengthen the ties. The bundling of additional financial services with products such as gold credit cards is well established: free travel insurance, free legal expenses insurance, free card-loss insurance, free banking, a year's warranty on household goods, etc. Yet, an increasing number of product bundles take the form of 'affinity' deals which bundle services and products offered by the financial institution with services and products offered by companies in other sectors. The rationale for this is the realisation that financial products themselves are not sufficiently motivating to individuals. Hence, financial institutions are teaming up with products and services believed to be more important or relevant to their customers. For example, Alliance & Leicester offers customers of London Electricity a mortgage that pays their gas and electricity bills. Discounts are offered to customers of Eastern Electricity paying by Barclaycard, and Tesco offers Norweb customers bonus points on its loyalty card.

One of the problems with bundling is that it makes it difficult to weigh up the relative costs involved in each product and the benefits. Some packaged products are genuinely attractive to customers and can serve as a positive reason for staying with the financial institutions. Yet, other bundles may simply lock the customer in and increase the barriers to exit, thereby creating a negative motive for retention. Financial institutions need to understand what kinds of product bundles customers would find appealing.

Negative reasons for staying with the same financial institution relate to the exit barriers put in place to prevent the customer from leaving, or to make it difficult for the customer to leave. These might include penalties for the early termination of contracts. In the mortgage market the costs of switching can be high. For example, it typically costs between £600 and £1,000 (e.g. £200 legal fees, £150 land registry and local authority search fees, £200 property valuation fees and £300 lender's fees). The exact fees obviously depend on the value of the property and how much the customer borrows, but the costs do act as an exit barrier locking many customers in (see Financial Services Marketing in Practice: 'Loyalty schemes in the mortgage market').

Positive motives for customer exit or defection relate to more attractive alternatives from competitors, whereas negative motives for defection are usually concerned with dissatisfaction with the financial institution and the level of service it provides. Financial institutions, thus, need to decide whether they want their customers to stay because of positive reasons or whether they simply want to lock them in. Customers can be encouraged to remain with the institution by offering better service quality. But if the objective is simply to prevent them from leaving, high switching costs such as penalties will do the trick. The problem is that once these customers do leave they are less likely to come back again and even more likely to generate negative word-of-mouth.

Figure 10.1 illustrates some of the reasons why people remain with a financial institution or why they switch. Retention and defection are behavioural responses to an emotional state. However, customers can be in one of many emotional states. For example, they do not need to be dissatisfied to leave, neither does satisfaction guarantee that they will stay. Conventional wisdom suggests that the link between customer satisfaction and retention, in markets where customers have choices, is a simple linear relationship: as satisfaction goes up, so too does retention. However, Jones and Sasser (1995) discovered in a survey of five different markets, that the relationship was neither linear or simple. They showed that completely satisfied customers, compared with merely satisfied customers, were far more likely to repurchase the company's products than anticipated. However, Reichheld (1993) discov-

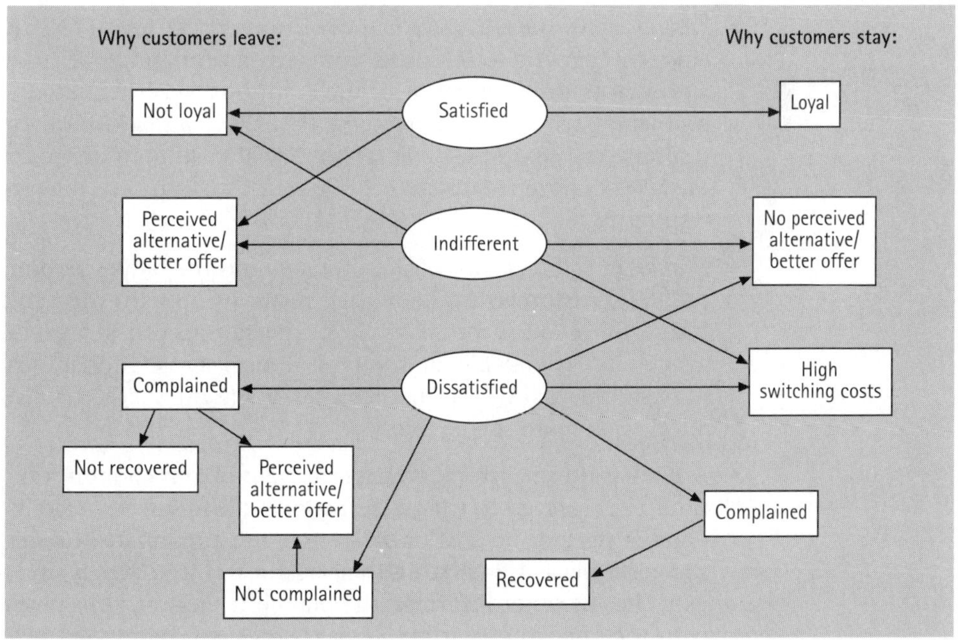

Fig. 10.1 Comparison of retention and defection motives

ered that between 65 and 85 per cent of customers who defect say that they were satisfied or very satisfied with their former supplier, suggesting that satisfaction alone is not enough to keep customers, although this may have something to do with the measurement devices used.

Process of customer defection

Stewart (1998) investigated the processes that consumers go through in ending a relationship with their financial services provider. Due to the difficulties of identifying passive defection, the research focused on active defection only, but specifically on situations where the customer was closing the last account held with the institution, hence severing all ties with the institution. A model of the customer exit process was developed, which defines the process according to the following stages:

- *The problem* – The process of customer exit or defection starts with the customer experiencing a problem. In approximately one-third of the cases investigated, the problem alone was enough to instigate the closing of the account. The problems experienced could be classified into one of four categories: charges and their implementation; facilities and availability thereof; provision of information and confidentiality; services and issues relating to how customers are treated.
- *Effort* – Having experienced the problem, the vast majority (85 per cent) of customers went to some effort to get the problem resolved. This included contacting the branch in person, by telephone or by letter. Often the response from the financial institution did little to alleviate the problem or resolve the situation.
- *Emotion* – As a result, over half of customers expressed emotional effects. The emotions experienced ranged from frustration and anger to embarrassment and disappointment. Some of the emotions were attributed to the initial problem, but to a much greater extent they were attributed to the bank's response to the problem. This shows that customers are relatively tolerant of mistakes but are less tolerant of financial institutions' inappropriate responses.
- *Evaluation* – As a result of the problem and the bank's response to the problem, customers evaluate their relationship with the bank. Evaluation takes into account the customer's expectations of the level of service and awareness of available alternatives. Hence, the relationship is not evaluated in isolation. If the customer feels he or she can get better elsewhere, this will affect subsequent behaviour.
- *Exit* – For those customers that felt the problem could not be resolved or had not been resolved to their satisfaction, exit followed. Account closure can be done in person, by post or by completing a mandate at a new bank to which the customer is transferring their business. Interestingly, in most cases of exit, the customer informed the branch in person, thus providing the bank with the opportunity to implement service recovery. Yet, few customers actually were asked why they were closing their account but were simply

allowed to leave the organisation. There is much that can be done here at branch level in terms of empowering employees to investigate such situations and offering compensation where necessary. Furthermore, many customers were surprised at just how easy it was to close an account.

- *Post-exit evaluation* – Having moved from one bank to another, the customer will evaluate the relationship with their new financial services provider. Not surprisingly, customers generally are happier after the switch. However, in the early part of the new relationship it is not easy to tell whether these feelings of satisfaction are the result of real contentment with the financial services provider or merely the consumer's way of avoiding cognitive dissonance.

A customer retention plan

In order that customers may be retained, financial institutions need to develop a retention strategy. Some customers may be retained by accident, but for the majority of customers retention needs to be carefully planned and managed. DeSouza (1992) outlines a simple four-stage plan to foil defectors and boost retention rates (see figure 10.2).

1 Measure customer retention

The first step to the retention of customers is to measure the current retention rate. DeSouza (1992) argues, if retention is not measured it cannot be managed. It is important to know what the current retention level is in order that improvements

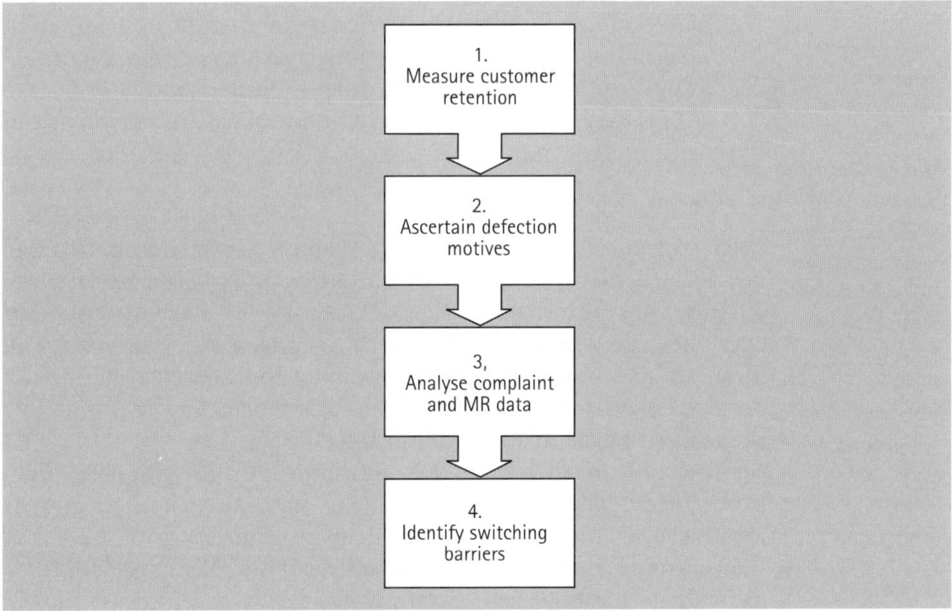

Fig. 10.2 Customer retention plan
(*Source*: Adapted from DeSouza, 1992)

can be gauged. Retention will mean different things for different products. For example, with respect to mortgage business, financial institutions may want to know the proportion of customers that remain with the institution until their mortgages are fully paid up compared with those that switch mortgage provider part-way through the contract. In terms of credit cards, the financial institution may be more concerned with measuring the proportion of customers that make regular use of the card compared with those that do not. And in terms of fixed-term investments, retention may be measured according to the proportion of customers that decide to re-invest their money on maturity of the investment.

Thus, it is clear that retention is sensitive to the means by which revenue and profit are generated by different products and customers. Therefore, in measuring retention rates it is important to understand the differences between the crude and weighted retention rates.

- *The crude retention rate* – this simply measures the proportion of customers that have remained with the institution over a time period compared with those that have left. For example, if the company has 1 million customers at the start of the year and has lost 100,000 by the end of the year, the retention rate is 95 per cent (or defection rate is 5 per cent). While this information may be useful at a broad level, its main problem is that it treats all customers equally. However, all customers are not equal: some spend more than others or buy higher margin products than others. Thus, some lost customers may be worth much more than others.
- *The weighted retention rate* – the problem can be solved by weighting customers according to their importance or value to the company (in terms of how much they buy). If the 100,000 lost customers above had double the buying potential of the average retained customer, the loss to the institution is greater. If these customers were likely to invest or borrow twice as much as other retained customers, the financial institution is, in effect, losing two customers each time one of these customers leaves. Hence, the retention rate is lowered to 90 per cent. In order to understand whether a retention rate of 90 per cent is good or bad, the financial institution must compare this figure with market trends.

2 Ascertain defection motives

Once customers have closed their accounts and/or terminated contracts with their financial services provider they are often simply written off and forgotten about. Financial institutions should not let customers leave without attempting to find out why they are leaving. Understanding consumers' motives for defection can tell financial institutions why others too may choose to leave and, indeed, what can be done to encourage them to stay. Customers defect for a number of reasons. Some of the reasons have already been outlined.

However, not all reasons for defection are preventable: some defections result from forces external to the business, such as customers moving to a different location and finding the financial institution is no longer convenient for them, hence, they switch to a competitor. Indeed, banks have found that changes in an individual's lifestyle, such as family upheavals, can increase the possibility of defection anywhere between 100 and 300 per cent (Reichheld, 1993). Other types of defection are preventable, or at least curable. For example, some customers may be

Table 10.3 Defector types

Type of defector	Characteristic	Example
Price defector	Customer switches to a competitively priced competitor. This was the third largest motive for defection identifed by Keaveney (1995). Reasons cited were: high prices, price increases, unfair pricing and deceptive pricing practices.	Examples can be found from the insurance and credit-card sectors, which are intensely price-competitive, and where a significant degree of discounting is currently taking place. (See 'Financial Services Marketing in Practice: Credit card loyalty schemes: how much is a customer's loyalty worth?' on p. 268)
Product defector	Customer switches to a competitor offering a superior product. Core service/product failures were identified by Keaveney (1995) as the largest cause of switching.	Examples here can be found from customers switching to new entrants which emphasise new product features and benefits.
Service defector	Customers switch because of poor service. Service-encounter failures can be attributed to some aspect of the service employees' behaviour or attitudes, including being: uncaring, impolite, unresponsive or lacking in knowledge. Keaveney (1995) found that these constituted the second largest motive for switching.	The same as above – customers are switching to new entrants which are more customer-focused and deliver better service quality.
Market defector	Customers are lost, not to competitors within the market, but to companies outside the market.	Switching to supermarkets, or purchasing antiques to accumulate capital in place of investments.
Technological defector	Customers switch as a result of better technology offers.	Switching to benefit from improved delivery systems such as switching to Direct Line or First Direct.
Organisational defector	Customers switch because they are unhappy with organisational 'politics'. Customers perceive illegal, immoral, unsafe, unhealthy, etc. behaviours that deviate widely from social norms.	Customers switched from Barclays and other banks in the 1970s to make a statement about Apartheid and the bank's involvement in South Africa. Also, more recently, the Bank of Scotland lost between 400 and 500 accounts as a result of its controversial involvement with Pat Robertson, the American TV evangelist.

(*Source*: Adapted from DeSouza, 1992 and Keaveney, 1995)

prevented from leaving if service levels are improved, whereas other customers may be won back by providing compensation or guarantees of better service in the future, hence curing possible defections. Table 10.3 summarises defector types identified by DeSouza (1992) and Keaveney (1995).

Price defectors can be won back with discounts and special offers. However, customers who switch as a result of price are perhaps some of the most difficult to retain since they will always be on the lookout for a better deal. Product defection can be more damaging to the organisation, often being irreversible. If customers perceive that a competitor offers a superior product, attempting to change those perceptions can be very difficult. Service defectors may be able to be recovered, particularly if they complain before deciding to leave. As mentioned in Chapter 9, if the customer brings the poor service to the attention of the financial institution through a complaint, it allows the company to respond either by improving the service or by offering some form of compensation. Dissatisfied customers who have complained and been recovered can make customers who are more likely to stay.

Whereas the financial institution can attempt to prevent price, product and service defectors, it can be far more difficult to prevent market defectors. The markets and companies which customers switch to may not be obvious, hence it can be almost impossible for the company to understand why such customers have defected. The increase in technology in the delivery and distribution of financial services has created much technological defection as customers switch to remote distribution. Organisational defectors may leave a financial institution, not because its loan rates are too high, its savings rates too low or its service poor, but because they disagree with the 'political' issues surrounding the organisation. What this means is that as well as providing competitively priced, good quality products and services, financial institutions must also be sensitive to the broader concerns of their customers. The Co-operative Bank recognises this and has attempted to build a loyal customer base of like-minded individuals founded on their common ethics, values and morals.

One particularly interesting factor highlighted by Keaveney's study is that there is considerable complexity and interdependency in factors leading up to switching. Over 55 per cent of critical switching incidents were classified as 'complex' in that they were composed of more than one category or motive.

3 Analyse complaint and marketing research (MR) data

With most things, prevention is better than cure. This also holds true for retention: it is better (and far easier) to prevent customers from leaving than attempting to recover them after they have already left. This is basically the difference between the financial institution acting proactively or simply reacting to a situation.

Conducting effective marketing research can enable the financial institution to highlight potentially problematic issues that may cause customers to become dissatisfied or leave. Thus, marketing information can enable the financial institution to be proactive in terms of retaining its customers. Financial institutions have increased the amount of marketing research which they undertake, yet simply conducting research is not enough: the findings also need to be acted upon. Furthermore, the issues explored in research need to be meaningful and insightful. Satisfaction surveys, for example, are not without their problems. Satisfaction is difficult to measure, and satisfaction scores are often quite meaningless. Most satisfaction surveys indicate that the majority of financial services customers are at least mildly satisfied with the service they receive, but the results do not help to explain why customers continue to leave.

Analysing customer complaints can also be very informative. However, when the customer makes a complaint it is an indication that something has gone wrong. Thus, the institution is no longer in a position to prevent dissatisfaction, but must attempt to cure the problem to the satisfaction of the customer in order to prevent them from leaving. While complaint data can be very useful, it is natural to regard customer complaints as a nuisance, but they can represent valuable information about the company and its products and services. For every customer who complains, there are probably ten others who did not voice their complaint but felt the same way. These customers may just go quietly from the organisation, leaving no obvious reason for defection. The problem with this is that customers leave due to bad service but since they make no complaint, the financial institution is not aware this is the reason for their leaving. Hence, service is not improved.

Financial institutions should make it easy for customers to complain; they should encourage customers to tell them what they think about the level of service received and should welcome suggestions for improvement. Freephone numbers can be provided for customers to ring in, posting boxes can be provided in branches for customers to post their written comments in, and customer service personnel can be appointed to deal with complaints and to harness the complaint data. Indeed, many financial institutions do have these in place.

4 Identify switching barriers

Using marketing research and complaint data and an analysis of reasons why customers leave, it should be possible for the financial institution to erect barriers to customer exit. The term 'switching barriers' tends to arouse negative connotations: keeping customers captive. Indeed, some examples of switching barriers do amount to 'locking the customer in'. However, switching barriers can generally be categorised as either positive or negative barriers to exit. Table 10.4 summarises some of the common ones.

In identifying switching barriers, financial institutions should attempt to look for

Table 10.4 Barriers to customer defection

Positive	✓ Better service ✓ Superior products ✓ Technological innovation ✓ Loyalty building ✓ Rewards ✓ Satisfaction ✓ Added value
Negative	✗ Exit costs ✗ Penalties ✗ Contractual agreements

FINANCIAL SERVICES MARKETING IN PRACTICE

How MBNA built customer loyalty

Following a number of letters from frustrated customers, MBNA's president, Charles Cawley, assembled the 300 employees of the Delaware credit card company and announced that the company was going to satisfy and keep every single customer.

It was a bold statement. The process began by gathering feedback from defecting customers. The reasons for customer defections were analysed,and the information was acted on by adjusting products and processes to meet customer needs more closely.

As a result, quality improved and fewer customers had reason to defect. In eight years the company had managed to achieve a defection rate of five per cent. This was one of the lowest defection rates in the industry. In fact, it was only half the average rate for the industry.

MBNA's efforts translated into huge earnings. Without making any acquisitions, the company's industry ranking went from number thirty-eight to four, and profit increased sixteen-fold!

The company succeeded because it reorganised its entire business system around customer loyalty and recognised that loyalty is earned by consistently delivering superior value and understanding the economic effects of retention on revenue and costs.

It is not until the second year of the relationship with a customer that the initial recruitment costs are covered through fee and interest income. After this, annual profits rise. A reduction in the defection rate from 20 per cent to 10 per cent means that the average lifespan of an MBNA customer doubles from 5 to 10 years, hence the lifetime value more than doubles. Similarly, a 5 per cent increase in retention can have a downstream effect of raising profits by 60 per cent in the fifth year of the relationship.

MBNA also put a lot of effort into understanding its customers' needs and tightened up its targeting. Credit cards were provided primarily to members of groups or individuals who had an affinity with a group – such as the Dental Association or university alumni. The rationale for this is that members of a group tend to share similar qualities, and have similar needs, making MBNA's marketing more effective.

Having mastered customer retention and loyalty, MBNA is now successfully expanding its customer base by acquiring new customers in foreign markets.

Sources: Adapted from O'Brien (1993); Buttle (1996)

Questions:

1 What prompted MBNA to begin a customer retention programme?

2 What steps did MBNA go through to earn the loyalty of its customers?

3 What factors contributed to the success of the programme?

best practice examples not only from within their own sector but also from other sectors. The benefit of this is that it surprises the competition and creates a further point of differentiation.

Creating positive barriers can lead to better service, superior products and technological innovation, thus eliminating several common reasons for defection. Negative barriers may increase the switching costs but the impact on customer satisfaction must be kept in mind.

While it may look like there are greater opportunities to create positive barriers to exit, there are still many examples from the financial services marketplace of negative barriers being used. The problem is that many of the positive barriers to retention are easily replicable by other financial institutions. As has been shown by the widespread adoption of customer care programmes, once all financial institutions implement the same service-improving initiatives, they eventually fail to differentiate, since all financial institutions begin to look the same again. Worse still, customers expect higher service levels as a minimum requirement, placing increased pressure on institutions. Thus, it becomes increasingly difficult to find a positive initiative that truly adds value and is not just copying what the competition is doing. In many ways, the negative barriers to exit are easier to implement and may even have greater effect in many cases; however, the emotional impact on the customer must not be forgotten if long-term relationships are the real objective.

American Express is one of the few companies in any sector which has an explicit strategy for recruiting, retaining and developing particular groups of customers. The most basic definition used by American Express is product group: green/gold/platinum cards, and the revolving credit card. But, segmentation is also carried out both within and across these product groups. Primary segmentation is by frequency and type of spend on the card. Customers are then assigned a profitability score. On this basis, the company makes use of different marketing and service policies. For example, if the customer threatens to defect and the profitability score is good, the fee may be reduced in an attempt to win the customer back.

American Express considers it has a close relationship with its customers at individual and group levels, particularly for the platinum card holders where the relationship aims to be very personal. Platinum card holders have a personal account manager and different communication streams. In addition, customers are managed differently according to the stage in their relationship with American Express. New customers are allocated to a special department for the first sixteen months. A number of activities take place during this time, including special offers. The main aim is to extend the relationship or, if the card is not used much, to increase its use. There is a higher risk of customers' leaving during this period, which is why more attention is devoted to it.

Financial Services Marketing in Practice: 'How MBNA built customer loyalty' illustrates the process that MBNA went through in improving customer retention and building customer relationships.

Loyalty

In many cases retention is taken as a proxy for customer loyalty, and defection or switching is seen as the reverse of loyalty. This is a somewhat naïve assumption to make since retention can be inflated by inertia or apathy. Loyalty is a complex phenomenon, comprising a set of behaviours and attitudes. Figure 10.3 illustrates the interrelationships between attitudes and behaviour. The behavioural dimension relates to the extent to which the individual exhibits either high or low repeat purchase. The attitudinal dimension relates to whether the individual feels either a high or low relative attachment to the financial institution.

Griffin (1995) notes that the attachment an individual has towards a company and/or its products/services is shaped by two dimensions: degree of preference (the extent of the customer's conviction about the product or service) and degree of perceived product differentiation (to what extent the individual distinguishes the company and its products/services from alternatives). Thus, attachment is highest when the customer exhibits a strong preference for the financial institution's products and clearly differentiates them from the products offered by other financial institutions. Combining behavioural and attitudinal differences results in segments that exhibit varying degrees of loyalty.

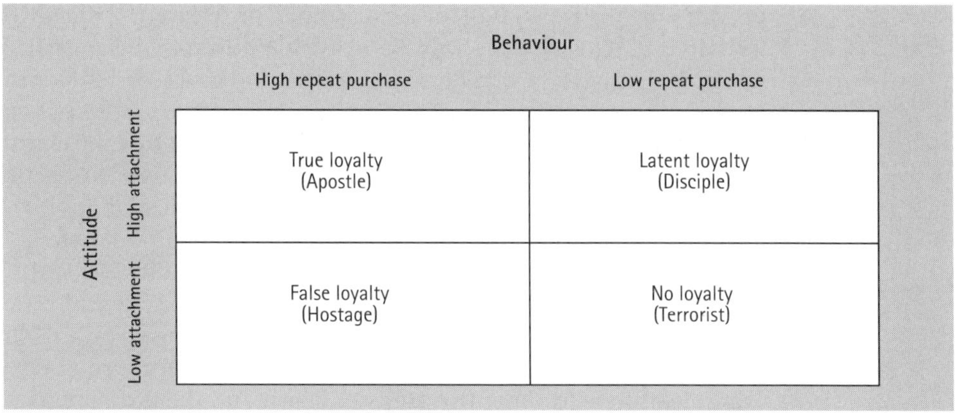

Attitude		Behaviour: High repeat purchase	Behaviour: Low repeat purchase
	High attachment	True loyalty (Apostle)	Latent loyalty (Disciple)
	Low attachment	False loyalty (Hostage)	No loyalty (Terrorist)

Fig. 10.3 Loyalty segments
(*Source*: Adapted from Dick and Basu, 1994 and Griffin, 1995)

FINANCIAL SERVICES MARKETING IN PRACTICE

Credit card loyalty schemes: how much is a customer's loyalty worth?

The battle of the credit card issuers is hotting up. Customers are being tempted by ever-better loyalty schemes – but are they?

Credit card issuers have been offering points-based loyalty schemes for a while. The psychology of such schemes is that customers spend more because they feel they are getting something back by earning points. The evidence from supermarket loyalty schemes would seem to suggest that people do spend more if points are offered.

Yet, in reality the discounts received from credit card issuers rarely cover any increase in spending, leaving few credit card loyalty schemes actually rewarding customers for their allegiance and increased spending.

With NatWest's Air Miles card, customers need to spend £9,000 in order to earn enough points for a flight to Paris. Customers of Barclaycard, the UK's credit card leader, need to spend £10,000 to earn a toaster and a child's ticket to the zoo!

Aside from the fact that many credit card loyalty schemes require their customers to spend a lot to acquire anything at all, is the complaint that many of the products and services offered by the schemes are limited in choice and uninteresting.

Some schemes also require the customer to put up hard cash, in addition to the points earned, to pay for goods and services. The cynics among us may argue that these gimmicks are being used as a sales channel to a captive customer base.

With more than twenty main credit card issuers fighting for their share of the UK market, providers need to re-evaluate their loyalty rewards or run the risk of watching their customers leave to better deals.

New entrants to the UK market, such as MBNA and Banc One Corporation from the US, are driving rates down and increasing the competition. While the high-street banks are trying to encourage their customers to spend more by offering loyalty programmes, many customers are being lured away by better offers from new entrants.

No-frills cards with rates as low as 6.9 per cent for as much as the first nine months of the relationship are attracting a lot of consumer interest. Credit card issuers hope that apathy will set in long enough to charge the standard rate; however, customers tempted to switch credit cards by a temporary low-rate offer are perhaps just as likely to switch again when the low-rate period expires.

Barclaycard has built a loyal following based on offering a number of additional services to customers. Clever advertising has positioned Barclaycard as a credit card offering a bundle of benefits, including travel insurance, card loss insurance, purchase warranties etc. Thus, Barclaycard has emphasised its differentiated offering rather than using price as a competitive tool.

FINANCIAL SERVICES MARKETING IN PRACTICE

Indeed, Barclaycard's customers would seem to be less price sensitive – since its rate is one of the highest charged by credit cards, almost twice as high as the discounted rates offered by new entrants – or, are they?

Over the last few years, Barclaycard has experienced a steady decline in its market share (from 32.1 per cent in 1989 to 25.4 per cent in 1997). During this time, the credit card market was expanding, and the number of cards issued by Barclaycard actually increased.

However, this is not the real issue, since around a third of credit card customers have two or more cards, and it is estimated that the number of multiple cardholders will continue to rise. Card issuers need to ascertain what customers are using their card for, and try to make sure theirs is the first choice.

On the face of it, it is hard to imagine why so many people stay with some of the card issuers which charge high rates and offer little reward. The companies claim that customers value their range of free services, but apathy must also have a role to play.

It is important to keep in mind what loyalty is: it's not just about repeat purchase, it's about the customer having a sense of belonging to the company. This is one reason why affinity deals have become popular as a means of building a loyal customer base. Many charities, clubs and associations operate affinity credit cards.

The success of MBNA has been built partly on targeting members of groups, or individuals who have an affinity with a group. The rationale for this is that members of a group tend to share similar beliefs and have similar needs, making target marketing more effective. Customers of affinity cards are proud to use their card, knowing that each time they use it they are supporting the organisation or assisting a good cause.

Capital One, the US credit card company, believes that to understand loyalty, financial institutions need to look at the family and personal relationships. This is the reason why its customers could soon be carrying pictures of their loved ones on their credit cards.

The Royal Bank of Scotland and Frizzell Bank already allow their cardholders to have photographs of themselves on the back of their cards in an attempt to reduce fraud. However, Capital One's latest venture has nothing to do with combating fraud, but rather attempts to strengthen its ties with customers by capitalising on the loyalty people feel to their family and friends rather than to an anonymous brand.

Sources: Adapted from *Financial Times* 14 October 1998, 16 May 1998, 25 October 1997, 27 August 1997, 15 March 1997

Questions:

1 Why do customers remain with the same card issuer when the rewards are so low?

2 What can be done to make loyalty schemes more motivating for customers?

3 To what extent are the low rewards and discounted offers contributing to an increase in customer switching?

- *True loyalty* – this is indicated by high repeat patronage and a high relative attitude towards the company. For many organisations, this type of customer loyalty is desired. At the highest level of attachment, these customers are proud to be associated with the financial institution and take pleasure in sharing their satisfaction with others, becoming vocal advocates for the institution's products and services. At the same time, these individuals are least likely to be persuaded by competitive offers and price discounts. For many companies, the goal is to upgrade as many customers as possible to this type of loyalty and devote the most attention to them.

While it may be desirable to achieve such loyal and vocal advocates of the company, Gofton (1995) notes that only around 17 per cent of the population may be called 'loyals' in the sense that they nearly always buy the same brand in more than half of the product/service sectors they use. The majority of people (46 per cent) exhibit divided or polygamous loyalty (i.e. they tend to be loyal in between a quarter and a half of the markets/product sectors used), while 36 per cent may be classified as 'promiscuous' (regularly buying the same brand in less than a quarter of sectors).

It is not surprising, then, that the proportion of buyers exhibiting 100 per cent loyalty is much less. Dowling and Uncles (1997) note that there is evidence to suggest that only about 10 per cent of buyers for many frequently purchased consumer goods are 100 per cent loyal to a particular brand over a one-year period. Even in service situations, loyalty seems to be confined to a small number of buyers. Moreover, they note that customers who are 100 per cent loyal tend to be 'light' buyers and are not necessarily the heaviest spenders.

Companies should perhaps focus more attention on those of their customers who exhibit divided loyalty. A first step would be to ascertain the reasons why customers exhibit divided loyalty. There are possibly several explanations for why many people exhibit loyalty to several companies at the same time. For example, people buy different products/brands for different reasons and may choose different suppliers accordingly. On the other hand, some people simply seek variety and may not want to patronise the same provider for all purchases. Another reason may be that different companies simply offer better deals, hence it would not be in the individual's interest to stay with the same provider.

With regard to the purchase of financial services, there may be more specific reasons why individuals decide to use a number of financial institutions to satisfy their financial needs. For some individuals, using a number of financial services providers may be part of a risk management strategy which allows them to optimise their financial dealings by selecting the best products from different providers. However, there may be an even simpler explanation. Even though the boundaries have come down between various types of financial institution, allowing them to offer the same products, there is still a tendency for many people to consider certain types of financial institutions for certain types of products. For example, banks are still commonly associated with current accounts and personal loans, building societies are commonly associated with mortgages and insurance companies with insurance. Hence, when the customer wishes to make a new purchase they may not automatically choose their main financial services provider, but what they consider to be the best supplier for that product.

- *No loyalty* – low repeat purchase combined with a low relative attitude towards the company signifies the absence of loyalty. Hence, no loyalty is the inverse of loyalty. The low relative attitude may occur due to the financial institution's inability to communicate the distinct advantage of its products and services or may perhaps be due to specific marketplace dynamics. The problem which most financial institutions face is that many consumers perceive no difference between the various financial providers and their products and services. Consequently, these individuals are more likely to be defectors. While there may be little to gain in the longer term from attempting to convert non-loyals to loyals, there may be some short-term gains to be had.

- *Latent loyalty* – low repeat patronage but a high relative attitude signifies latent loyalty. Thus, the customer is favourably disposed towards the financial institution and its products and services, but is not a heavy user of them. There could be several explanations for this: there may be situational factors inhibiting the purchasing behaviour or the individual may be patronising other suppliers. Attempting to create an even higher attitudinal attachment to the organisation would be expensive and is unlikely to alter this latent loyalty. Hence, managerial effort would be best spent addressing the situational constraints and attempting to remove them. If individuals are patronising other financial institutions, the company needs to understand why they are patronised.
- *False loyalty* – despite a relatively low attitude towards the financial institution the customer continues to patronise it. From a purely behavioural perspective, these customers appear to be extremely loyal. Several factors can generate false loyalty or make customers appear to be deeply loyal when they are not. These include government regulations that limit competition, a logistical infrastructure which essentially holds the customer hostage to the bank by increasing the barriers to switching, or proprietary technology that limits alternatives. All of these have contributed to a certain degree of false loyalty among financial services consumers. However, through successive deregulation, the lowering of switching barriers and the emergence of alternative technology (most notably in the form of telephone and internet banking), financial institutions have found that their hold on customers has diminished to a certain degree. When customers have choices and feel free to make a choice, there is a tendency for them to behave like customers in markets characterised by intense competition. In such situations, customers may only remain loyal if they are completely satisfied with the service and products received from their existing supplier.

  Yet, a number of customers remain with their financial services provider even though they are not completely satisfied with them. This can be explained by a high degree of inertia which essentially describes the unwillingness of the customer to switch. The customer stays because of habit or because it is believed that switching to a competitor will bring no additional benefit. While these individuals may not be highly satisfied with their financial services provider, there is no real dissatisfaction – just indifference. It can be possible to convert inertia loyalty into a higher form of loyalty by attempting to increase the degree of positive differentiation perceived by the customer.

Loyalty schemes

In their attempts to build customer loyalty, companies have turned to loyalty schemes. Loyalty schemes work by rewarding customers for their repeat business. In theory, the schemes add value to the relationship, thereby encouraging the customer to come back. Individuals who perceive benefits from the reward scheme may be motivated to increase their allegiance to the organisation and develop into a 'loyal' customer.

Some of the most popular loyalty schemes are based on loyalty cards. For millions of customers, loyalty cards have become part of the weekly shopping. They took off after Tesco launched its Clubcard in February 1995. Sainsbury initially sniffed at them, dubbing them 'electronic Green Shield stamps', but they were forced to follow suit when Safeway launched its ABC card. Between the three supermarkets, they have more than 25 million cardholders which represents well over two-thirds of their shoppers. ASDA initially decided to refrain from launching a loyalty card, believing that customers are more interested in 'good value today than the possibility of something in a few months' time' (*Financial Times*, 25 October 1997). However, by 1997 it had started to introduce its own loyalty scheme in selected supermarkets.

Retailers' initial motives for the introduction of loyalty cards were to identify the top 30 or so per cent of their customers and concentrate marketing effort on them. These prime customers would receive targeted communication by direct mail and personalised offers providing them with better deals at the expense of less profitable customers. Thus, the real objective of loyalty programmes is not to acquire more customers, but to keep the best ones by offering them better service. The expansion of supermarkets into financial services can further enhance the benefits to customers. For example, if customers of Tesco use Tesco's own credit card in its supermarkets, they can receive even bigger discounts than if they were to pay by cash or debit card. In the longer term, supermarkets could be using points accrued on loyalty cards to provide discounts on financial products.

Credit card issuers have also introduced similar schemes to both encourage and reward increased use of the card (see, above, Financial Services Marketing in Practice: 'Credit card loyalty schemes: how much is a customer's loyalty worth?'). Yet, few loyalty schemes operated by UK financial institutions are focused on the whole of the customer relationship. Many of them merely attempt to retain individual accounts. One of the reasons for the product, rather than customer, focus can be attributed to the systems responsible for holding customer and account information.

Halifax, the UK's largest mortgage lender, found that the process of conversion from a building society to a bank in 1997 forced the company to reorganise its information from account holding to customer holding. Now the bank has an all-round picture of its customers and can identify the full range of services that a single customer uses. Lloyds TSB, the UK's largest banking group, offers a loyalty scheme for customers using several of its products and services. Thus, customers holding a savings account, current account, mortgage and credit card may be offered preferential loan rates if they are looking for a loan. The idea is that the bank rewards its most loyal customers.

Just how far, however, do so-called loyalty schemes go towards building and rewarding loyalty? Are financial institutions really attempting to build customer loyalty, or are they merely paying lip service to it? One way to answer this question is to examine some of the failings of loyalty programmes. Financial institutions need to critically evaluate their programmes to ensure that they do not fall into the same trap:

- *Launch motives* – Dowling and Uncles (1997) note that companies' decisions to launch a loyalty programme are often influenced as much by their desire to achieve competitive parity as anything else. Simply jumping on the bandwagon may mean that financial institutions lose sight of the objective of building customer loyalty, resulting in the loyalty scheme contributing little to the customer's relationship. Another reason for the launch of a loyalty programme is because the institution pre-empts the entry of a new player to the market. A number of new players have entered the financial services market, and traditional institutions have become defensive about market positions.

- *Long-term discount* – A poll of marketeers by Equifax (*Financial Times*, 3 June 1998) at the Direct Marketing fair in 1998, revealed that while 49 per cent of those questioned possessed three or more loyalty cards, and 23 per cent possessed even more than that, some 41 per cent believed that the current spate of loyalty cards do not create loyalty. In fact, many loyalty schemes seem to offer little more than long-term discount. While discounts may encourage repeat purchase, they are unlikely to have a significant attitudinal impact on the customer. Thus, emotional ties are not likely to be strengthened.

- *Customer apathy* – As the number of loyalty schemes has proliferated, there are growing signs of customer apathy. The schemes are very similar, based on points and discounts, and offer little in the way of differentiating features for the companies offering them.

- *Incentives* – Many of the schemes offer few real incentives to customers. Customers have to spend more in order to get anything back, and often the gifts and prizes are uninteresting. A survey commissioned by the People's Bank of Connecticut, revealed that only a third of those eligible to claim reward points actually do so. Many people find they are too busy to claim the rewards, or simply forget to, suggesting that they hold limited value for the customer.

- *Ineffective at changing behaviour* – Many loyalty schemes require customers to change their established patterns of behaviour in order to benefit from the rewards. Surely loyalty schemes should be designed to reward the already loyal behaviour of customers rather than attempting to make them jump unrealistic hurdles to achieve one-time discounts. Prior to 1995 there were no loyalty schemes in the UK grocery market, with the exception of Co-op's stamp scheme, but once Tesco introduced its Clubcard the other supermarkets were quick to follow. Once everyone has a loyalty programme, most customers are able to accumulate points with whichever shop they patronise, leaving loyalty patterns unchanged. Similar loyalty scheme proliferation has taken place in the credit card sector, and the increase in multiple cardholding seems to suggest that a similar effect is being had on customer behaviour. Some may argue that rather than increasing exclusive loyalty to one company, loyalty schemes have encouraged polygamous or divided loyalty – loyalty (or repeat patronage) of a number of providers.

- *Difficult to differentiate from other marketing initiatives* – Do loyalty schemes really offer a better return to the company than alternatives, such as price cuts, increased distribution or increased advertising, in stimulating demand? Evidence from the credit card market would seem to suggest that customers do value discounted interest rates over points and prizes.

- *Data analysis* – One of the reasons why loyalty schemes are not working is

> that companies are failing to use the data captured to generate meaningful marketing information. Britannia Building Society has successfully used the data gathered from its loyalty scheme to segment its customers into nine categories and customise the direct mailings they receive. The different messages are not only being used in direct mailshots but also in branches. The benefits of the database were realised when Britannia launched a direct mailshot to savers offering them the chance to switch their mortgage from their existing lender to Britannia. Based on the information gathered, the mailshot was able to take account not only of whether customers were more likely to prefer lower monthly repayments to a cash lump sum, but how they would be most tempted to spend the cash. In addition, the costs of datamining are important considerations. For example, supermarket loyalty card schemes cost on average 2 per cent of group sales, equating to £40m at Tesco and Sainsbury and £20m at Safeway. Data storage groups believe that the large up-front costs of setting up the schemes dwarf the costs of storing and analysing the data. They also disregard the benefits accruing from information provided by the data, such as improvements to product lines and store administration and targeting of sales promotions.

If a loyalty scheme is to be successful at building customer loyalty it needs to offer incentives that are deemed attractive by the customer so that they are more likely to stay with the financial institution and are less likely to defect. Thus, financial institutions, need to identify the positive factors that can be used to encourage loyalty, rather than simply increasing the negative barriers to exit. Furthermore, the incentives must work by enhancing the core value propositions. If they are simply 'me-too' responses to competitive moves, they are unlikely to achieve the objective of building loyalty and will simply become an added cost burden to the institution.

Finally, it must be remembered that loyalty must be earned. The difference between repeat behaviour and loyalty is that the former is for sale while loyalty is earned through the excellence of the offer and the value to the customer. As already noted in this chapter, many of the loyalty schemes offered by financial institutions, while they may increase purchase activity, do so as a result of price discounts. If loyal customers are indeed less price-sensitive, it could be argued that the loyalty schemes based on discounting and incentives attract primarily deal-prone consumers who might be more likely to switch again. Indeed, it may even be argued that many of the schemes have, in fact, created much of the switching and price-focused shopping, forcing financial institutions into a vicious circle of price promotions and discounting.

SUMMARY

This chapter looked at customer retention and customer loyalty. It began by defining customer retention and defection, outlining the differences between client and contract retention/defection and between passive and active retention/defection. Motives for retention/defection were also discussed. It was noted that retention and defection are responses to emotional states, yet satisfied customers can still leave, while dissatisfied customers may still remain with the institution. Although satisfaction may be a necessary component of customer retention, it alone does not prevent defections.

Financial institutions should be wary of assuming that retained customers are loyal, simply because they continue to patronise the organisation. Loyalty is a complex phenomenon, consisting not only of the behavioural dimension of repeat purchase, but also an attitudinal or emotional dimension which suggests a certain attachment to the organisation. Different degrees of loyalty exist, and the extent to which true loyalty can be achieved depends on the organisation, the customer and the product type. In financial services, a great deal of apathy prevails, making a real attachment to either the product or the institution difficult. Financial institutions have attempted to increase loyalty by introducing loyalty schemes. Many of these have been based on points and rewards; however, they can be criticised on a number of counts. While many of the schemes may increase purchase activity, they often do not have any emotional impact. Many companies fail to realise that, while repeat purchase can be bought, loyalty must be earned.

DISCUSSION QUESTIONS

1. For a customer segment of your choice, suggest a suitable strategy for customer retention.
2. What can financial institutions do to convert passive retention to active retention?
3. What are the problems associated with passive defection? How can financial institutions detect customers who quietly exit?
4. Taking the financial services which you yourself use as an example, examine the extent to which your financial services provider uses either negative or positive retention motives.
5. Financial institutions are keen to build long-term and satisfying relationships with their customers. To what extent are the customer retention programmes employed by such institutions fit for this purpose?
6. It was noted earlier in this chapter that in fact only 3 per cent of bank customers change account each year. To what extent is this statistic a reflection of customer loyalty, and are financial institutions worrying themselves unnecessarily about building customer loyalty?
7. Customer loyalty in banking: rhetoric or reality?
8. Retailers of financial services are seeking to develop multi-product relationships with consumers. At the same time people are becoming more sophisticated and less loyal to one company. How should financial institutions respond to this challenge?
9. How might a financial institution attempt to convert 'latent loyalty' and 'false loyalty' into 'true loyalty'?
10. Loyalty is one of the current 'buzzwords' in the financial services sector. To what extent would you agree that financial organisations must earn the loyalty of their customers? How far are the current strategies in the marketplace aimed at promoting loyalty?

11 Corporate financial services

INTRODUCTION

The basic concept of marketing applies equally to the personal and corporate markets, and the material presented in the earlier chapters is largely relevant to the corporate sector. However, it must be recognised that the corporate market possesses some distinct characteristics which make it different from the personal market and which affect the way in which marketing is applied in this context. For example, corporate markets generally consist of fewer customers, often larger customers which are individually more significant to the financial institution than an individual personal customer, have more complex financial requirements, but at the same time have a more complete understanding of the alternatives available.

In order to market effectively to corporate customers, financial institutions need to understand how companies choose financial services providers and what they require from them. Corporate financial decisions are likely to be taken by a group of individuals, the members of which will have varying degrees of influence over the final outcome and different buying criteria. The buying group often serves to lengthen the decision process and increase the degree of negotiation both within the buying company and between the financial institution and the company.

Research suggests that the banking community is lacking somewhat in its understanding of corporate customers' requirements. Banks are failing to recognise the factors that corporate customers perceive as important in the corporate customer–bank relationship. Indeed, banks seem more preoccupied with what they can provide for the customer, rather than what the customer actually desires of them. Furthermore, it is important to recognise that the requirements of small businesses differ from those of large corporations. Small business have had a bad deal from banks in the past, although there is evidence to suggest that relationships are improving and the services offered to small businesses are getting better.

The purpose of this chapter is to highlight some of the distinct characteristics of corporate markets and their implications for marketing. It is a very large area, and the subject of corporate finance especially is a complex and specialised topic. It is, therefore, not possible to cover the subject in any great detail in one chapter, but merely to provide an overview of some of the key points of departure from the personal market.

OBJECTIVES

After reading this chapter you should be able to:

- highlight the key differences between the personal and corporate markets;
- provide an indication of the types of both providers of corporate financial services and corporate buyers;
- understand the nature of organisational buying behaviour and the role of the buying group in corporate decision-making;
- highlight some of the variables used to segment corporate markets;
- review some of the issues associated with corporate banking relationships;
- discuss the specific characteristics and requirements of small businesses and their relationships with financial services providers.

Differences between corporate and personal markets

Marketing is generally applicable to both personal and corporate markets, although there are some fundamental differences which exist and which exert influence over the nature of marketing. The key points of departure are summarised in table 11.1. Several characteristics warrant particular attention, and are discussed below.

- *Market structure* – As a general rule, corporate markets have fewer sellers and, in particular, fewer buyers in any market compared with consumer markets. While corporate customers vary widely in size and requirements, some of them often bigger than their suppliers, corporate marketers, in many cases, are not dealing with mass markets. On the contrary, corporate marketers tend to talk about their customers individually, and to a large extent deal with them individually. As a result of this, the opportunities for developing closer relationships with customers based on a deeper understanding of their requirements are far more likely.
- *Balance of power* – The fact that corporate markets tend to be largely oligopolistic has an impact on the balance of power between buying and

Table 11.1 Key characteristics of corporate markets and transactions

Characteristics of organisational markets	Characteristics of organisational transactions
• Fewer buyers • Larger buyers • Close supplier–buyer relationships • Geographically concentrated • Derived demand • Power of customer • Networks	• Larger order quantities • Infrequent orders • Importance of purchase • Customised offerings • Professional purchasing • Several buying influences • Direct purchasing • Lengthy negotiations • Interactive • Complex transactions • Risky and expensive • Purchase decisions involve committees

supplying firms. While the balance of power can vary greatly from one customer and supplier to another, and is also a matter of continuous negotiation, the likelihood of customers' having some degree of power or influence over their suppliers is greater than in a consumer market situation.

- *Knowledgeable buyers* – Corporate buyers buy products not for personal use but as component parts of products and services to be produced or to serve the operations of the firm in some way. As a result of this, corporate buyers tend to place greater concern on the technical aspects and specifications of the product, its performance, service and support. Corporate buyers are in a better position to evaluate such factors, being professionally trained and technically qualified.
- *Strategic role of purchasing* – The purchasing function in corporations makes a major contribution to cost reduction and profit enhancement. Purchasing also enables a company to achieve a competitive advantage by using the skills and resources of suppliers. Thus, purchasing performs an important strategic function for the organisation. Because of this, it is necessary that firms build relationships with suppliers to ensure both the quality and quantity of supply.
- *Derived demand* – Consumer demand is direct demand. Corporate demand is derived demand, since it is derived from the end-user or consumer market. Both the organisation, and the provider of financial services need to be aware of the direct demand situation, which means understanding not only the organisation's customers, but also its customers' customers.
- *Interactive relationships* – Many corporate transactions take place over an extended time period, involving varying degrees of interaction and meetings. Thus, each corporate purchase is not simply a single transaction, but merely an episode among many in an ongoing relationship between two companies. As a result of the specific conditions shaping the structure of corporate markets, the importance of purchasing and the nature of the transaction, it has been argued that corporate exchanges are more interactive, based on a greater degree of mutual dependence and founded on commitment and trust than personal consumer exchanges. The interaction approach sees buyer–seller relationships taking place between two active parties. Thus, corporate markets do not consist of active sellers and passive buyers. Often a buying company is extremely active and takes the lead role in specifying and defining requirements and negotiating terms and contracts. Indeed, suppliers may even adapt their products or processes to fit the buyer's requirements. The supplying company effectively becomes an extension of the buying company. Thus, the process is not one of action and reaction, as is often the case in consumer markets, but one of interaction. This is in contrast to the more traditional view which analyses the reactions of an aggregate market to a seller's offering. Either buyer or seller can take the initiative in seeking a partner.
- *Mutual interdependence* – The existence of fewer supply alternatives and the complexity and risk of the product and purchase mean that customers often become dependent on their suppliers. In many cases, the dependence is

mutual, since the customer may be a significant customer and the seller needs them as much as the buyer needs the seller's product. It has been noted that buyer–seller interdependence is a crucial characteristic of corporate marketing. This means that firms establish relationships that are often close, complex and frequently long term. The concept of mutuality rests on the importance of collective goals or common interests between more than one company. Many firms will share technology with suppliers. Mutuality can only really be demonstrated over time. It is the mirror of trust that exists between parties.

- *Network relationships* – Companies do not operate in isolation. The network approach takes the view that each company is enmeshed in an even more complex network of relationships. According to Ford *et al.* (1986), a company can be viewed as an ever-widening pattern of interactions, some of which occur independently of it. The web of interactions has been described as being so complex that it defies full description or analysis. The relationship one company has with another company will affect that company's relationship with other companies. For example, a powerful retailer may seek to affect the operations of its immediate suppliers and, thus, their suppliers, thereby influencing the chain of derived demand.

  Tyler's (1996) research into the marketing of equity securities to institutional investors shows that a network of relationships exists, of both a voluntary and an involuntary nature. Involuntary relationships exist between Government, Parliament, Treasury, the Department of Trade and Industry, the Bank of England, the Stock Exchange and the Financial Services Authority. Voluntary relationships exist between securities houses, salesmen, analysts, institutional investors and other companies. Securities houses initiate the communication and seek to establish relationships with institutional investors. Each securities house salesperson will initiate, develop and maintain a relationship with between one to eight fund managers. Although the relationship is initiated by the salesperson, it becomes reciprocal. Securities houses communicate with a number of institutions, but the institutions do not communicate with one another; however, they know of each other's existence. The interaction between the securities houses is known as 'network players knowledge', and it is shared. There are also multiple layers of interactions between fund managers, traders, analysts, salespeople and service executives. As a result of the level of interaction, corporate entertaining is important (see Financial services marketing in practice: 'Brokers search for new ways to woo female high-flyers').

Corporate financial services providers

The area of corporate finance is a complex and specialised one. It would be impossible to do justice to the topic in one small section of a chapter, and this is not the intention of this chapter. A great number of books have been devoted to the subject, and readers are directed to these for a deeper understanding of the subject. The purpose here is merely to identify some of the providers of financial services to cor-

FINANCIAL SERVICES MARKETING IN PRACTICE **FT**

Brokers search for new ways to woo female high-flyers

A meal and a game of rugby at Twickenham is still a favourite way for City stockbrokers to entertain investors, as are horseracing at Cheltenham and cricket at Lord's.

But what may seem like an ideal way to mix sport and maybe a little business on the side has failed to impress the new breed of female high-flyers. 'Gorging myself and getting drunk in a rugby tent isn't my idea of fun', says one female fund manager.

As more women break into the traditionally male domain of fund management, stockbrokers are finding the need to look for new means of corporate entertainment. 'Brokers have started to realise that rugby and cricket isn't going to work with women', says Veronica Berger Collins, assistant director at Foreign & Colonial, a fund management company.

Some women share the passion for rugby, cricket or golf, and tickets to the opera and ballet go down well with arts aficionados. However, many female fund managers point out that there are too few group events tailor-made for women. 'There are quite a lot of things which are boys oriented but they've only just started to catch on with imaginative ideas for women', says Amanda Forsyth, fund manager at Standard Life.

Courting female fund managers has become increasingly important as women make headway in the industry. Nicola Horlick, who moved to SocGen Asset Management from Morgan Grenfell amid a storm of publicity last year and Carol Galley, vice chairman of Mercury Asset Management, are the biggest stars.

According to the Institutional Fund Managers Association, women are finding it easier to make their mark in fund management rather than in other areas such as corporate finance because of a flat management structure and the results-oriented nature of the business.

Women fund managers tend to concentrate on their work rather than spending a day out or being wined and dined, while many have families and are reluctant to spend work-related time outside the office, making them less 'entertainable' than their male counterparts.

But they tend to respond well to events with glitz and glamour such as fashion shows and film premiers, while corporate hospitality with an element of cosseting, such as makeovers or sessions at a health farm, is also popular. 'A spot of pampering seems to go down better than rugby or football', says Suzie Kemp, fund manager at Credit Suisse Asset Management.

A gourmet dinner and a day by the pool with masseurs and beauticians in full attendance arranged by NatWest Markets' Edinburgh office won high approval ratings from female fund managers who participated in its ladies' weekend in St. Andrews.

Ladies' shopping nights out at high street retailers such as Harvey Nichols and Selfridges where stockbrokers rent out a store for a group of female fund managers in the evenings are also well received.

But one male fund manager suggests that organising 'ladies only' events may be sexist. "I'd rather go to a shopping night than rugby', he says.

Source: Emiko Terazono *Financial Times*, 6 April 1998

Questions:

1 What is the purpose of corporate entertaining?

2 What are the advantages/disadvantages of corporate entertaining compared with other forms of promotion and communication?

3 How can financial institutions select suitable events for entertaining corporate customers?

porations and to indicate the differences from the personal market. Commercial banks and investment or merchant banks are particularly relevant to the remainder of the chapter:

- *Commercial banks* – A commercial bank is any bank licensed under the

Banking Act 1987. The large clearing banks, such as Midland, Lloyds TSB, NatWest, Barclays, etc., are commercial banks. However, the term is often used to refer to banks involved in international trade and corporate banking. A more accurate description of these activities would be 'wholesale banking'. 'Wholesale banking' generally describes the business of commercial banks in their dealings with other banks, large national and international companies, government departments or agencies. Thus, wholesale banking is distinct from retail banking which deals with the personal market.

- *Investment/merchant banks* – An 'investment bank' is the US equivalent of a merchant bank in the UK. According to the Dictionary of Banking (Klein, 1995), the appropriate description of merchant banks is 'Acceptance Houses' since they are all members of the Accepting Houses Association and their main functions are dealing with the acceptance and discounting of bills of exchange and finance of international trade. They are also involved in dealing with mergers, take-overs, share and stock placings, new issues, investment management, etc. Historically, merchant bankers were merchants dealing in overseas trade with specialised knowledge in certain commodities or areas of the world. As banking services became more important to the traders than acting as merchants, they assumed the name 'merchant banks'. Many merchant banks are well known, for example Rothschilds, Lazards, Schroders.

  Chu (1990) identifies two basic functions of investment (merchant) banks: raising capital and giving advice on mergers and acquisitions, all other services being either supportive of or developed from these functions. With regard to the function of raising capital, Hayes *et al.* (1983) specify three activities: origination and management of new financial issues; underwriting of issued securities; and distribution, involving selling securities to ultimate holders. The function of merchant banking can, therefore, be defined as creating and mediating the flow of assets between issuers and investors. Issuers are companies and other entities that sell assets such as stocks, bonds and even part or all of the company itself. Investors are investment banks or merchant banks, companies, institutions and people who buy these assets.

Types of corporate customers

As with retail customers, corporate or organisational customers can vary in terms of type, size and financial services requirements. Generally, though, they can be categorised into one of the four following groups:

- *Producers* – Producers or manufacturers buy products or services for use in the production of other products or services or to be used in the daily operations of the firm. The types of products purchased may vary from raw materials or component parts to finished or semi-finished items. The products/services purchased by such companies have a direct impact on the output of the organisation, and its sales and profit generation. The demand for raw materials and component parts is derived from the demand for the final product, which may be a consumer good. Depending on the nature of the final product, producers may have to quickly increase production. Since demand may fluctuate, producer markets may find that they have a particular need for overdraft and credit facilities, at least in the short term, which financial institutions need to be sensitive to.

- *Resellers* – Resellers are companies that buy finished goods and sell them on. They essentially represent intermediaries in the chain of distribution. Their business is derived from buying goods in, marking them up and selling them on for profit. There are a wide variety of resellers, including brokers, industrial distributors, wholesalers and retailers. In all cases, firms may buy direct from the manufacturer or from another reseller, and then sell the product on to the ultimate consumer or to another reseller in the chain.
- *Government* – National and local governments form a distinct type of organisational customer, not least because of their size and significant power, but also because of the specific circumstances under which purchasing and transacting takes place. Many government agencies have clearly defined policies and practices for purchasing and operate within clearly defined budgets. There may also be restrictions placed on the types of organisations they can do business with. The Bank of Scotland's controversial joint venture with Pat Robertson caused a great deal of concern among a number of trade unions and local councils. In fact, West Lothian Council threatened to pull out of a £250m deal. Organisations such as local councils and trade unions cannot be seen to be in business with companies or individuals which have values and beliefs that are in conflict with those of the people they serve.
- *Institutions* – These are organisations with charitable, educational, community or other non-business goals. While such organisations may not have profit as their main goal, they do have financial requirements. However, the ethical and moral values of these organisations may lead them also to have policies regarding the types of organisations they can do business with. The Vermont National Bank in the US established a successful Socially Responsible Banking (SRB) fund, aimed at such organisations. Both small businesses and personal customers can deposit funds in the SRB fund which they know will only be used to furnish loans for local, community-based projects and socially responsible businesses.

Corporate financial services needs

Corporations can have many different financial requirements and expectations of their financial services providers. Their needs may differ according to the type of organisation, the type of business and the size of the business, among other things. The general financial services needs, outlined in Chapter 2, are also relevant to organisations. The core needs of cash accessibility, deferred payment, money transmission, etc. are just as relevant for companies as they are for consumers, yet companies may seek further benefits at the augmented-product level which make their financial services requirements different from consumers' requirements.

In a study of small businesses, Schlesinger *et al.* (1987) noted three particular financial services requirements: lending rates, accessibility of borrowing and the range of services on offer. The price of the service offered was also found to be an important requirement in work undertaken by Buerger and Ulrich (1986). It is perhaps not surprising that small businesses focus predominantly on price, since they are more dependent on banks as a source of funding than larger corporations and, hence, more sensitive to interest rate (price) fluctuations. Accessibility of borrowing is an important requirement, particularly to gain access to short-term credit or overdrafts, and the range of services on offer is likely to be of importance to small businesses looking to grow and expand the business and increase their demand for financial services. Despite this apparent preoccupation with price and short-term cash accessibility issues, other studies (Prince and Schultz, 1990; Freeman and Turner, 1990) have shown that small businesses also require confidentiality and professionalism.

In contrast to small businesses, Turnbull and Gibbs (1989) found that price was not such an important factor for large corporations. Presumably, the size of larger organisations places them in a better position with regard to bargaining on price. In addition to this, larger corporations also have access to other sources of funding, making them less dependent on banks and other financial institutions. The main considerations of larger corporations tend to rest with the quality of service provided and the knowledge of staff (Rosenblatt *et al.*, 1988; Chan and Ma, 1990).

Buying behaviour

Having looked very briefly at the types of financial institutions and organisations involved in corporate financial services exchanges, let us now turn our attention on the processes and decisions associated with corporate buying behaviour.

Purchasing operates at the interface between a company and its supply market environment. It involves a number of activities including determination of purchasing requirements, selection and handling of suppliers and buyer–seller negotiations. Purchasing tends to involve a number of people from both the purchasing and selling organisations. As a result of both social and economic interactions, corporate purchasing tends to be a complex process, not an instantaneous act.

From the marketer's point of view, there are a number of strategic implications for the corporate buying process. First, the financial institution must be able to anticipate customers' needs. Second, the seller needs to be able to help define and meet the buyer's information needs. Third, the supplier must examine the sequence of decisions taken by the buyer and understand how they translate to the final decision.

From the buyer's perspective, organisations may have a number of purchasing objectives:

- availability, when and where needed;
- product quality consistent with specifications;
- lowest price consistent with availability and product quality;
- service to maximise the value of the product in use;
- good long-term supplier relations.

This is not a complete list of organisational purchasing objectives; moreover, not all objectives will be equally important. Depending on the product or service being purchased, some objectives may take on greater importance.

The buying process

A popular model of industrial buying behaviour was developed by Robinson *et al.* (1967). The model identifies eight distinct stages that industrial organisations go through in the purchase decision process. Figure 11.1 presents an adaptation of those eight stages, focusing predominantly on the stages of significance to corporations in the selection and evaluation of financial services and financial institutions.

- *Problem recognition or anticipation* – The first stage in the process occurs when the company realises or anticipates a need for a financial product or advice from a financial institution. The recognition or anticipation of a need may arise from a number of different sources, but broadly speaking will come either from sources inside the organisation or from outside the organisation. For example, the same need to raise a loan to buy new capital equipment may arise from a significant machine breakdown or machine obsolescence

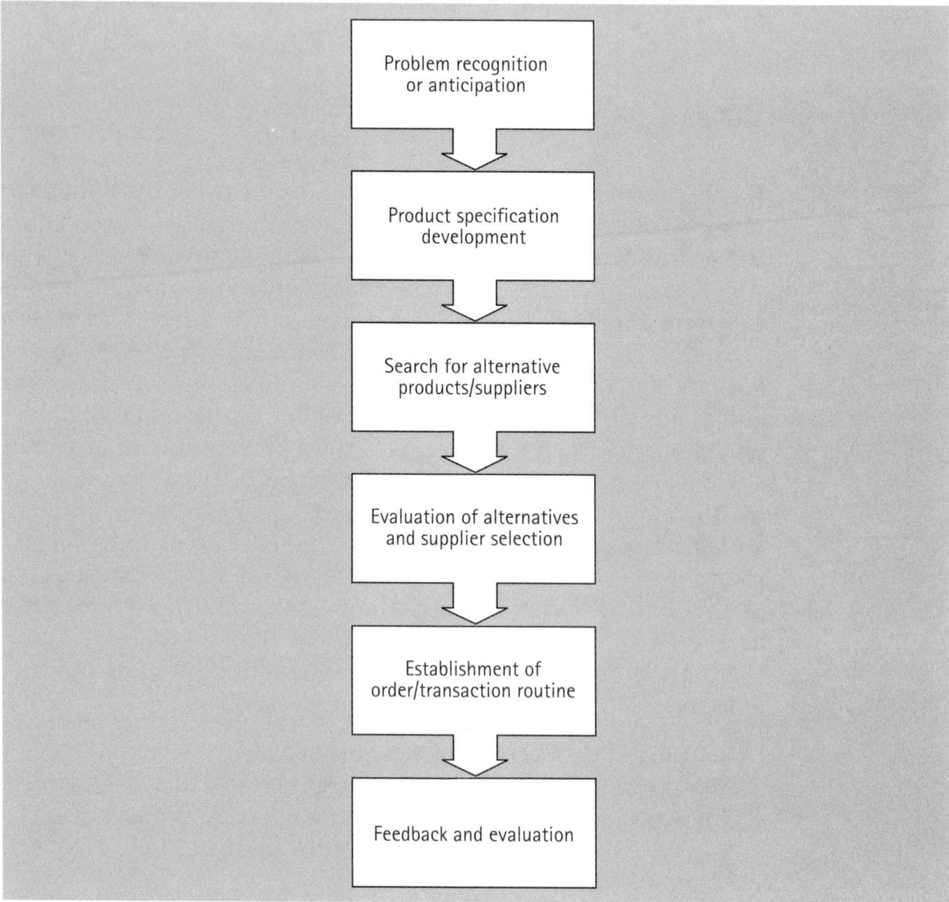

Fig. 11.1 Stages in the corporate buying process

(i.e. an internal source), or from an increase in consumer demand for the company's product, requiring new equipment to increase production capacity (i.e. an external source).

- *Product specification development* – Having realised the need for a product, the company must then decide on product specifications. If the company is seeking to borrow from a bank it will need to specify the amount required and the term of the loan and decide on fixed or variable rates of interest. Such factors will need to be discussed with the lender. For some forms of lending, firms may be required to put up collateral as security.
- *Search for alternative products/suppliers* – At this stage, the company must make a list of potential suppliers. Depending on the nature of the product, the company may be faced with many or just a few alternative sources. The company will also need to consider the merits and limitations of using either existing or known ('in') suppliers or new ('out') suppliers. The size of the organisation will also have an impact on the potential number of sources available. Research has shown that large companies are more likely to have relationships with several banks compared with small firms which are more likely to use just one bank (Zineldin, 1996). This limits the choice of potential products and suppliers for small firms and may place the small firm in a poorer position with regard to bargaining for better deals. The size of the firm also affects the level of dependence the company has on its bank. By operating with multiple financial institutions, larger corporations are able to reduce their dependence on commercial banks and may get better deals by shopping around.
- *Evaluation of alternatives and supplier selection* – The previous stage in the decision process should result in a list of potential sources. This stage involves evaluating the alternatives in order to make a final choice. Companies will evaluate both the products on offer and the financial institutions according to a number of criteria deemed important to them. From the point of view of the financial institution, it is important that they understand what their corporate customers are looking for and can provide it. A study conducted by Nielsen *et al.* (1998) of small, medium and large Australian firms, concluded that the following four factors are generally considered to be the most important in the selection of a bank: the ability to provide a long-term relationship, competitive prices, efficiency in daily operations, and willingness to accommodate the firm's credit needs. Each of these criteria was selected as one of the top three choices by at least one-third of the firms surveyed. Nielsen *et al.* (1998) then went on to compare the factors businesses noted as important with those the banks perceived were important to businesses in the selection of a bank. The findings raise some interesting questions about the extent to which the banking community understand the needs of its corporate customers.

Table 11.2 lists the 15 factors, first in rank order of importance to the businesses and, second, in rank order of the banks' perceptions. None of the factors were ranked the same by both groups, indeed six of the differences were found to be significant at the 10 per cent level, indicating that Australian bankers do not have a good understanding of the needs of their

Table 11.2 Comparison of businesses' and banks' need expectations

Business firms' perception		Banks' perception		Difference
1	Long-term relationship	1	Competitive prices	+1
2	Competitive prices	2	Long-term relationship	−1
3	Efficient operations	3	Personal relationship	+3
4	Accommodate credit needs	4	Service delivery	+4
5	Knowledge of business	5	Efficient operations	−2
6	Personal relationship	6	Accommodate credit needs	−2
7	Convenient location	7	Make decisions quickly	+2
8	Service delivery	8	Knowledge of business	−3
9	Make decisions quickly	9	Innovative	+2
10	Financially healthy	10	Friend's recommendation	+5
11	Innovative	11	Community reputation	+2
12	New technology	12	Convenient location	−5
13	Community reputation	13	Below market rates	no score
14	Below market rates	14	New technology	no score
15	Friend's recommendation	15.	Financially healthy	no score

(Source: Adapted from Nielsen *et al.*, 1998)

business customers. In contrast to banks' dealings with the personal market, we would expect knowledge of corporate customers to be far greater as a result of the importance of the customers individually and as a result of perhaps closer relationships which should allow a more detailed understanding to develop.

Looking collectively at the differences between business and banks, it would seem that business customers generally are more concerned with: the banks willingness to accommodate their credit needs, efficiency of the bank operations and the fact that the bank has knowledge of their specific business. The banks, on the other hand, felt that it was more important to offer competitive rates, offer a full range of products and services and provide a personal banking relationship. There is not only a discrepancy in the expectations of both, but the banks do not seem to be focused on the needs of customers at all, but on what they can best provide or supply the customer with. This suggests not a market orientation but a product orientation.

- *Establishment of order/transaction routine* – Having selected a suitable financial services provider, both parties need to establish a routine to conduct the transaction. Until this point, the corporate customer and the financial institution are likely to have been engaged in detailed and lengthy discussions, possibly over an extended time period. From this point onwards, the interaction between the two parties is likely to become more arm's length and routinised. For example, if the customer requires a loan, the transaction routine will simply involve the regular payment of instalments as agreed by the two parties. Provided the company has no further requirements during the loan term, and does not default on payments, repayments are likely to be made automatically with limited contact.

- *Feedback and evaluation* – As previously discussed, in relation to consumer buying behaviour of financial services, evaluation can occur at several points in the decision-making process. One of the key points is post-purchase, but the true evaluation is unlikely to be conducted until post-consumption, which may be some time, even years, after purchase. Evaluation of the continued service will also take place at discrete episodes during the relationship when the customer and financial institution come into contact. Evaluation is important in building up an opinion of the financial services provider and the level of services provided. These opinions are useful to future purchase decisions and may result in the same provider being chosen again or avoided. Indeed, evaluation during an extended relationship can cause the company to terminate the relationship early if it is dissatisfied with the service received (see Financial Services Marketing in Practice: 'RFR: portrait of a serial switcher').

FINANCIAL SERVICES MARKETING IN PRACTICE

RFR – portrait of a serial switcher

Rider, Fenn and Ridgway (RFR) made its first switch, from Bank A to Bank B, about six months before current finance director Alan Brunskill joined. Although the company had been with Bank A for some time, it had never discussed using an overdraft facility because it had never needed one. But when RFR began negotiating for work with the Department of Transport, it discovered a performance bond was part of the deal.

A performance bond is provided by a bank, and means that if a company defaults on the work, the bank will pay. This bond can be covered by the company either by an overdraft facility or by lodging money in a specific account.

'RFR had to submit the tender for the work very quickly, so the company approached Bank A for a bond, which it was very reluctant to provide', says Brunskill. 'The bank told us it needed forecasts and accounts but, due to time constraints, RFR could not provide them. Instead we offered to deposit £30,000 in a special account, an offer Bank A was unable to accept.'

The episode irritated the company's managing director so much that he went to Bank B, which provided the bond without even demanding a deposit in a special account. RFR decided to leave Bank A because it felt the bank understood neither the needs of the business nor the special level of service it demanded.

The company's relationship with Bank B began reasonably well. An overdraft of £75,000 was negotiated, which could be increased to £100,000 overnight. The business continued to grow. In 1992, turnover was £6.5m. By 1994, this had almost doubled to £12m but as the company grew, so did its need for funding.

'At first we dealt with the bank's local regional director, who was very sympathetic to our needs', says Brunskill. 'But, as we grew, we were handed over to the local business centre, which adopted a far more cautious approach. Money was flowing into our account every day, but there came a time when our account was going to go £100,108 overdrawn overnight.

'We would be brought back within our overdraft level the next day, when we were expecting payment of £70,000. The bank, however, refused to let us exceed our overdraft limit, and threatened to block out-going cheques. We ended up taking £109 out of petty cash and depositing it with the bank to cover the shortfall.

'As the company's turnover increased, the local business centre manager for Bank B remained cautious and did not appear to understand what RFR were trying to do. Disappointed, Brunskill arranged a meeting with the manager of Bank C. He proved extremely keen to help and offered RFR an overdraft facility of £250,000. The company switched banks again.

Everything went well for the next 18 months, until the directors decided they needed to re-equip the business to provide more production capability. They devised a three-stage plan to buy a new factory: first they would buy the bricks and

FINANCIAL SERVICES MARKETING IN PRACTICE

mortar; then get a lease from the local council; and finally refurbish the buildings. After that, RFR planned to take out a mortgage on the new factory to pay for the three stages.

'We asked Bank C to help us buy the bricks and mortar with a £500,000 bridging loan for six months while we negotiated the lease with the council', Brunskill says. 'Initially Bank C agreed but, two weeks before we were due to complete, it pulled out. We decided to go ahead and took the money out of the cash flow. But we had an uneasy feeling that decisions at the bank were now being taken by the men in grey suits in the back office.'

Unhappy with Bank C's failure to support the company's plans, RFR's directors met with the UK Industrial Fund (UKIF), a front manager for banks and institutions, in spring last year. The fund was willing to take over RFR's debt funding at lower rates and charges. It also offered short-term overdraft facilities and was able to advise RFR on restructuring. With the backing of a new bank, Bank D, RFR has switched the bulk of its borrowing to UKIF and is saving between £50,000 and £60,000 a year in charges.

'We moved from Bank B to Bank C because we preferred the latter's style of management', says Brunskill. 'But when the business grew, we found the UK Fund suited our needs best. The fund understands how to finance growing companies and promise strategic planning within a less bureaucratic framework.'

Source: *Chartered Banker*, February 1996, p.11. Reprinted with permission.

Questions:

1 Why did RFR switch banks – what were the underlying reasons?

2 Was there anything that could have been done by RFR or the banks to resolve the issues?

3 Is RFR the type of customer the banks would want to lose? Why?

The buying group

Corporate financial decisions usually involve a certain degree of risk and may require complex solutions. As a result of this, purchase decisions tend to be taken by a group of participants rather than by a single individual. The participants in the buying decision tend to adopt certain roles in the decision-making process and perform certain tasks. Unfortunately, the job titles and positions held within organisations often are not very informative as to the roles played. Bonoma (1982) identified several roles:

- *Initiator(s)* – these are people who essentially begin the purchase process by recognising that the organisation has a financing need. Initiators can be from within the organisation, or they may be from outside the organisation from a supplying organisation.
- *Influencer(s)* – one or more individuals in the buying organisation may influence the buying decision. These people do not necessarily have buying authority, but they have a say in the ultimate decision that is taken.
- *Decider(s)* – this is the person that ultimately decides 'yes' or 'no'. In many cases this person will hold a senior position within the corporation. Although the ultimate decision may rest with this person, the outcome is likely to be based on information and opinions supplied by other buying group participants, particularly influencers.
- *Purchaser* – this is the person who places the purchase order. In many cases,

the selling company may confuse the purchaser with the decider, mistakenly assuming that they have more authority and influence over the purchase decision than they actually do. However, the purchaser is mainly acting on instructions and performs a purely clerical task of order placing and does not usually have buying authority.

- *User(s)* – these are people who will be using the purchased product or service. They may be involved in the decision-making from an early stage and can influence the outcome. They may also be responsible for initiating the purchase process.
- *Gatekeeper(s)* – these are people who, either deliberately or unknowingly, control the flow of information. For example, a secretary may forget to pass on information from a potential supplier, thereby 'structuring' the final decision.

The structure of the buying group can vary according to the type of decision being taken. It can vary according to the level of influence of participants and their involvement. Johnston and Bonoma (1981) note that the structure of the buying group can vary according to the degree of:

- *Lateral involvement* – lateral involvement refers to the extent of horizontal involvement of members of different department or functions from within the organisation.
- *Vertical involvement* – vertical involvement refers to the levels of hierarchy involved in the decision-making process.
- *Extensivity* – extensivity refers to the number of people involved in the decision-making group.
- *Connectedness* – this refers to the extent to which members of the decision-making unit are linked via direct communication and can exchange information and opinions freely.
- *Centrality* – this refers to the centrality of the purchasing department or purchasing manager to the whole decision-making process and communication network.

As a general rule, more complex, unfamiliar and risky decisions tend to result in greater degrees of both lateral and vertical involvement, tend to be more extensive in terms of the number of people involved, and are likely to involve regular and direct forms of communication, possibly centred through the purchasing department.

The characteristics of the buying group also change depending on the novelty or newness of the purchase. New task situations tend to result in larger buying groups, which are slower to decide, may be more uncertain about their needs they may also be more concerned about finding a good solution to the problem than getting a low price and may be more willing to entertain proposals from 'out' suppliers (i.e. suppliers not currently used). The influence of the purchasing department is likely to be less. By contrast straight rebuy or slightly modified rebuys are more likely to result in smaller buying groups that are quicker to decide. They are likely to be confident in their appraisal of the problem and its solution. They may be more concerned about supply and price and may be satisfied with 'in' suppliers. Purchasing agents may take on more of an influence in such situations of routine re-ordering.

Research by Turnbull and Moustakatos (1996) found that decision-making for investment banking services is taken at a high level in all companies surveyed. The buying centre generally constitutes the CEO, the board of directors, the finance director and the group treasurer, but tends to vary according to the specific product being purchased. For example, for debt instruments decisions are taken within the treasury department, while for equity instruments or advice-related services the decisions are usually taken at the highest level with the involvement of not only the finance director but the CE or chairman and often the whole board of directors. The objective of the financial institution should be to ascertain who in the company has the greatest influence over the final decision.

Segmentation

Differences in the structure of corporate markets and the nature of buying behaviour necessitate different market segmentation criteria. While the rationale for segmenting customers and the general approaches to segmentation remain the same as for personal markets, corporate markets require the use of slightly different bases for segmentation which match their circumstances more closely.

At a very broad level, Chéron *et al.* (1989) suggest that a distinction should be made between large corporate customers and small businesses since they differ both in the nature and scale of their financial requirements and the level of expertise in financial management. Large corporations are likely to need customised marketing

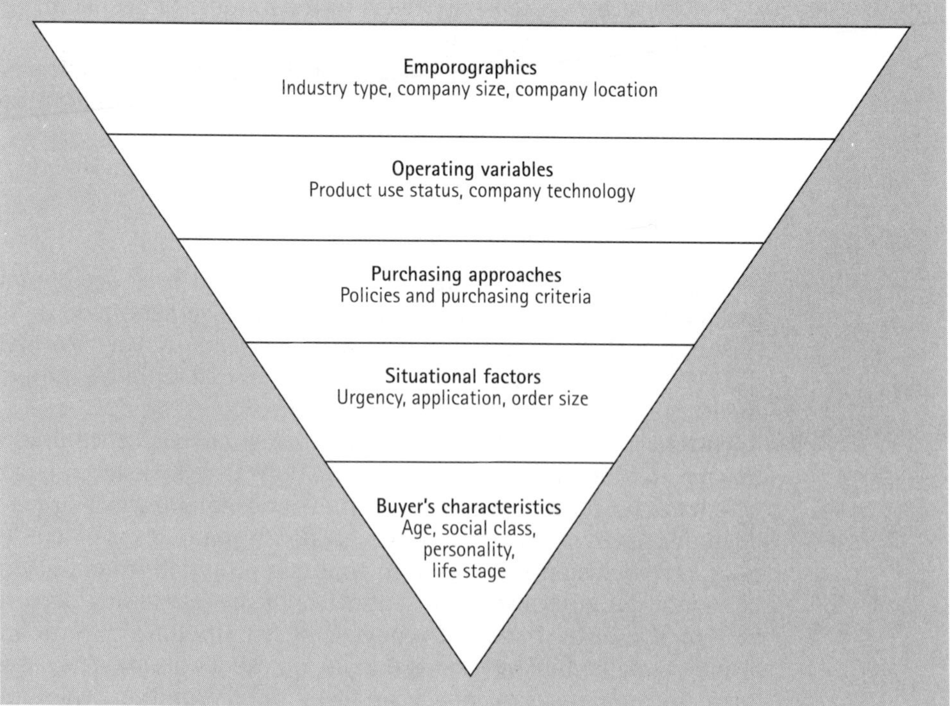

Fig. 11.2 Corporate segmentation variables
(*Source*: Adapted from Shapiro and Bonoma, 1984)

programmes and relationship management. Smaller businesses are likely to be still in the development stage of their life cycles and have less business experience.

Shapiro and Bonoma (1984) offer a useful categorisation of segmentation variables for corporate customers. The variables, depicted in figure 11.2, suggest that segmentation can occur at various levels, from the more general to the specific. The variables are closely related to the factors that influence purchasing behaviour, including external company factors, organisational factors, purchasing policies, situational factors and the individual characteristics of the buyer.

Research by Turnbull and Moustakatos (1996) into the investment banking industry indicates that investment banks do segment their clients and, in fact, use rather elaborate methods. The traditional bases, such as size, geographic location and industry type seem to have wide appeal through the sector, but other bases used to a much lesser extent include: the value and nature of the transaction, and the level of activity in buying investment banking services.

The size and value of the transaction is important because of the economies of scale which operate in the industry, and since profitability is usually linked to the size of the transaction or deal. The complexity and difficulty of the transaction is used in the belief that deals will become more complex in the future with higher added value and profitability. Finally, the level of activity in buying investment banking services is used in the belief that activity is linked to profitability. Thus, there is evidence to suggest that investment banks are attempting to segment their clients according to the profit they are likely to generate for them. It was also noted that a number of investment banks combine different segmentation criteria to increase their effectiveness in identifying segments.

Corporate banking relationships

As mentioned earlier, both buyers and sellers are interactive participants in the relationship. The relationship is frequently long term, close and involving a complex pattern of interactions both between companies and within each company. During the relationship the bank attempts to solve the problems of the company and satisfy its needs through a series of transactions. The corporation not only participates in the production of the product or service, but also evaluates its effectiveness.

The decision to purchase banking products or services involves interactions between at least two individuals, one from the client organisation and one from the financial institution, usually the finance director or corporate treasurer. It is important that the banker recognises that his or her personal interaction with the corporate financial officer is not the only interaction that takes place. The company representative will also be subject to a variety of influences from within their own organisation as well. The banker needs to understand what these influences are and to adapt the services to meet the requirements of the client.

Unfortunately, there is a general feeling that commercial bankers understand little about the environment, financial problems and decision-making process of their corporate clients. This is surprising given the importance and power of some customers, and the fact that there are fewer customers generally compared with consumers, allowing a more individual treatment of them. It is, therefore, import-

Table 11.3 The relationship life cycle and objectives for relationship management

Stage	Characteristic	Marketing objectives
Early stage	Uncertainty about what each party hopes to gain from the relationship and unaware of other's performance and abilities	• Create interest in the bank and its products • Identify target corporate clients • Understand customer requirements and extent to which they are currently being met • Identify the strategic fit between the bank's products and customer needs • Emphasise product of most appeal to customer
Development stage	Corporate customer and bank have agreed/ identified a product solution. Increased information is gathered and knowledge of other's norms and values	• Convince customer that product offers the desired benefits • Identify future customer needs more effectively • Identify level of customer satisfaction • Improve ability to communicate with existing and potential customers
Long-term stage	Strong, close and interactive relationship has developed, characterised by mutual trust and satisfaction; client loyalty is high	• Maintain service quality and performance • Offer product development • Adapt, innovate and make product attractive to changing needs • Use information to fine-tune client's needs • Offer professional/individualised service
Partnership relationship	Client is confident of the bank's ability to service current and future problems. Mutual interdependence, social bonds and complex psychological relationship. Clients feel valued and are willing to pay a premium for benefits offered	• Seek to solidify institutional bonds • Offer products valuable to clients but not readily available from competitors • Technological innovation to maintain relationships

(*Source*: Adapted from Zineldin, 1996)

ant that financial institutions understand the various stages in the client–bank relationship, are aware of the characteristics of each stage, and can identify clear marketing objectives to ensure the successful progression to the next stage. Table 11.3 highlights these issues.

Early writings on relationships seemed to suggest that business relationships were closer and more co-operative than is always the case. It may be fair to say that perhaps most of the business relationships are close, complex and long term. However, this does not define all relationships. In many cases, firms do not know everything about each other, neither do they always act in the other party's best interests. Some relationships merely focus on a single transaction, even though the decision to purchase and the period of negotiation may take a long time. Some business relationships are not balanced, one party may dominate. They may not be based on honesty or trust but deceit. Indeed, the risk of viewing relationships as if they must involve commitment and trust is to ignore the rich diversity of relationships which not only exist but are appropriate in different contexts. Furthermore, relationships may not always be harmonious but based on conflict. Some are short term and opportunistic, leaving one party taking advantage of the other. Thus, relationships can be close or arm's-length.

Moriarty *et al.* (1983) identify five factors which are believed to affect the perceived value of the banking relationship by the firm:

- *Competition* – If the client has access to multiple banks/financial institutions, there is essentially no need for a relationship to develop with one bank in particular. The fewer the supply alternatives, however, the more likely it is that corporations will seek to develop relationships with firms in order to secure access to funding.
- *Need for non-credit products/services* – If there is a need for other complex products, the relationship potential is likely to be greater because the ability of a wide range of institutions to offer complex products may be reduced, leaving the company facing fewer supply alternatives.
- *Need for flexibility* – Unconventional or complex businesses may force companies to place greater value on the banking relationship due to their need for customised skills and services.
- *Financial health* – If the company is less strongly capitalised, has poor earnings or may be involved in risky ventures, this will place greater emphasis on the banking relationship.
- *Attitude towards management of the financial function* – This relates to decisions over whether to make or buy. If services are bought in, the company will be likely to place greater emphasis on the relationship.

Small and medium-sized enterprises (SMEs) are more likely than large corporations to value a stable relationship with a principal bank. Significant information and transactions costs will cause a small firm to conduct its transactions with a single bank and maintain a long-term relationship. Because larger corporations are less affected by such costs, they are able to have multiple relationships, but they

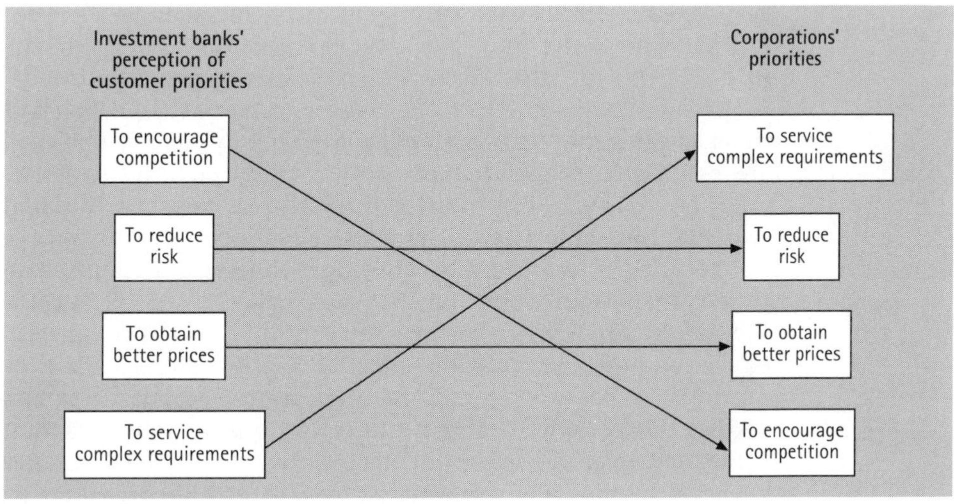

Fig. 11.3 Justifications for multiple bank relationships

may also need to have multiple relationships due to more complex requirements. A survey by Turnbull and Moustakatos (1996) notes that companies buying investment banking services are mostly multi-sourced with a range of 3–25 principal relationships. Corporations cited several reasons for using multiple investment banks (see figure 11.3), although there were some differences between corporations' priorities and investment banks' perceptions of their priorites.

Relationship breakdown and switching behaviour

Customer defections and switching behaviour are just as important, if not more so, in the bank–corporate customer relationships as they are in the bank–personal customer relationship. The previous chapter outlined the characteristics and motivations for switching behaviour and strategies for retaining customers. The material contained in that chapter is just as relevant for corporate customers as it is for personal customers.

Defection among established corporate customers is a growing trend. More worrying is that most businesses that switch are the kind of corporate customers that banks actively seek and presumably would wish to keep. As with the consumer market, there is a great deal of inertia. A study of corporate customers, carried out by PDA Consultants (*Chartered Banker*, February 1996), found that while 60 per cent were prepared to switch there was no evidence of mass defections. Indeed, in the year to June 1995, 2.56 per cent of businesses switched bank (an increase from 2.07 per cent the previous year).

What this means is that for those businesses that do switch, they must have very strong reasons for doing so. While inertia may cause businesses to remain with their bank longer than they would wish to, it does create a difficult task as far as loyalty building is concerned, and banks need to address this area more fully. This means recognising that companies want constructive relationships with banks that care enough to provide and support the appropriate transactions.

Until recently, banks believed that only the higher-risk customers switched, either to obtain increased borrowings or to make a fresh start elsewhere. Believing they were high risk, the banks were relatively happy to let them go. Yet, a survey by Risk & Opportunity Intelligence (ROI) (*Chartered Banker*, February 1996) suggests that 90 per cent of switchers are either medium- or low-credit-risk. In fact, the switching activity of high-risk businesses has more than halved in recent years. The trend towards lower-risk customers leaving may suggest that banks are providing greater support for their higher-risk customers in return for higher margins. On the other hand, it may just mean that higher-risk customers are finding it harder to switch as competitors show a preference for poaching lower-risk customers.

One thing is clear: healthy growing businesses now appreciate the advantages they can gain from a more fluid banking market. Switching is less of an issue among the larger corporate customers, since nearly three-quarters of them are multi-banked and use an average of 10 banks. Such switching is done less in terms of the relationship, but more to increase or reduce the emphasis of transactions with the various banks; switching the entire relationship is carried out more by small companies where a banking arrangement with a single bank is most appropriate.

Eighty-nine per cent of businesses bank with either one of the big four banks: i.e. Barclays, NatWest, Lloyds TSB, HSBC, or one of the two main Scottish banks; however, there is a net migration away from these traditional suppliers towards smaller players and foreign banks.

Small businesses

The attractiveness and importance of large corporate customers to a financial institution is not difficult to understand, yet small and medium-sized firms should not be forgotten, or labelled as less important customers even, since they represent the nation's future and provide valuable potential to grow and develop into significant longer-term customers. Businesses with less than fifty employees now account for roughly 40 per cent of economic activity and almost half of total employment in the UK (*Financial Times*, 17 May 1999).

Despite the apparent importance of small businesses, their treatment from banks and other financial institutions has left much to be desired, particularly in relation to lending (see *Financial Services Marketing in Practice*: 'It pays to be friends with your bank: self-employment'). Banks have been criticised for giving small businesses overdrafts rather than loans and demanding the entrepreneur's home as collateral. Demanding collateral means that the risks are shared, but can also mean that the businessperson with good ideas cannot get started. The problem with overdrafts is that the small business is sensitive to changes in short-term interest rates. When overdrafts have been the only form of funding on offer, this has forced small businesses to make inappropriate use of the funding to fund asset acquisitions etc.

Financial institutions have also been criticised for allowing small businesses to 'go under'. By the time the banks found out the company was in trouble, it was too late. This, in part, reflected the fact that small businesses are hard to monitor. Large corporations typically are quoted on the stock market and reported in the papers, making it easier for the financial institutions to keep track of the company. Banks are often far less informed of the state of small businesses.

However, since the start of the 1990s, there has been a steady shift in the way small companies raise finance, leaving them better equipped to cope with the ups and the downs of the economy. Small businesses now rely less on overdrafts and more on medium-term loans with fixed interest rates. In 1992, the balance between overdraft and term lending was evenly split. By 1998, term lending accounted for 70 per cent of total finance from banks to small businesses. Furthermore, two-thirds of banks' committed funds have maturities of more than five years (*Financial Times*, 17 May 1999). This means that small businesses are less vulnerable to the short-term swings of the economic cycle, and financial institutions are locked into the provision of finance during such times when they may have withdrawn credit in the past.

In addition, bank lending has fallen from 61 per cent of total small business finance to 27 per cent from 1992 to 1998. While the four main clearing banks (NatWest, Barclays, Lloyds TSB and Midland (HSBC)) have maintained a steady 85 per cent share of lending to small businesses throughout the 1990s, NatWest and Barclays have lost share to Lloyds TSB and HSBC, particularly in business start-up lending. Between 1992 and 1998 hire purchase and leasing increased from 16 to 27 per cent of total small business finance. In 1987–1990, only 39 per cent of small businesses sought external finance, by 1995–1997 this had risen to 65 per cent

(*Financial Times*, 17 May 1999). Not surprising, perhaps, is that small businesses also rely more on internally generated funds than in the past.

The experience of banks has also prompted them to try harder, a number of improved codes of small business practice and industry standards mean that the information problem is also being addressed. In short, financial institutions are doing more to keep a closer eye on small businesses and be ready to give advice.

Small business–bank relationships

Commercial banks provide a key source of finance for small businesses. In the past banks were the main source of funding, making small businesses very dependent on their bank. However, the relationship was not often perceived as mutually dependent, as banks were quick to call in loans and drop small businesses in times of trouble. Yet there have been a number of changes and improving relations, such that Ennew and Binks (1996) note that relationships between small businesses and their banks are improving. Small business banking is becoming competitive. NatWest and Barclays may still dominate the market, but they face increasing competition from Lloyds TSB and HSBC, and from other smaller banks. Banks have developed small business units, reflecting an acceptance of the need for improvement in the relationship and signalling the importance of the relationship.

Butler and Durkin (1995) suggest that poor small business–bank relationships may be explained by the differences in structure and organisational culture between large commercial banks and small firms. The bank is essentially a 'machine bureaucracy' which places rules and regulations above managerial discretion. By contrast, the typical entrepreneurial firm is organic and informal: the owner/manager makes the decisions, often quickly and intuitively. In short, they are polar extremes. The problems are further compounded by the differences between banks' and small firms' perceptions of themselves and each other (table 11.4). Butler and Durkin (1995) argue that many of the problems in the relationship are due to these gaps in perception and expectation. For example, the bank wants track records, forecasts and some form of collateral, and the small business wants support, empathy and advice.

Intermediaries in the small business–bank relationship

Small firms usually engage the services of an independent accountant who acts as an intermediary in the small firm–bank relationship. The accountant performs a

Table 11.4 Banks' and small businesses' perceptions of themselves and each other

Organisation	Self-perception	Other's perception
Bank	Procedural, systematic, prudent	Obstructive, procrastinating, fearful of natural commercial risk
Small business	Risk-taking, entrepreneurial, innovative	Foolhardy, immature, lacking in understanding of commercial consequences

(*Source*: Adapted from Butler and Durkin, 1995)

number of useful tasks for the small firm, including assisting in the production of a business plan and financial projections, which are prerequisites to securing funding from a bank. The accountant generally facilitates the effective transfer of information between the small business and the bank.

Although the small firm employs the accountant, one may question the extent to which he or she really acts in the small firm's best interests. In many cases, the accountant merely advises the client to meet the demands of the bank and does not attempt to negotiate with the bank on behalf of the client or encourage the bank to adapt procedures or policies to meet the needs of the small business (Butler and Durkin, 1998). Thus, the accountant does not add any bargaining power to the small business, and it could be argued that the presence of the accountant may even serve to further weaken the strength of the small business in some ways by reinforcing the power of the bank.

The role of the accountant changes at different stages of the small business–bank relationship. From the accountant's point of view, he or she needs to know what the small business requires at each stage. In the early stages of the relationship, the

Table 11.5 Role of the accountant in the small business–bank relationship

Relationship stages	Meaning	Role of accountant
Awareness	Awareness of the role of the bank as a source of funding	To ensure small firm is aware of services on offer
Exploration	Choice of bank, analysis of terms and conditions of business, agreement to lender requirements	Ensures client meets bank's requirements. Presence of accountant at meetings signals commitment, professionalism and team effort. Use of a well-known firm of accountants may add greater credibility. Accountant needs to present the potential of the business alongside past track records and cash-flow projections
Expansion	Occurs when the situation is felt to offer potential in the longer term. There is a degree of reappraisal and realignment for the parties. Further resourcing may be necessary	Develop established transactions and exchanges further. Reiterate success to date and press for funding on further potential
Commitment	Clear to parties that long-term relationship is beneficial. Small firm has moved up the learning curve of financial management and reliance on accountant may be diminished	The role of accountant changes from brokering the initial deal to deepening the existing relationship and to getting each party to perceive a level of trust and bridge the information gap
Review	Relationship and roles are reviewed based on past performance and future requirements	The accountant may exit the network. The services may no longer be required or may be perceived as integral to the relationship. The accountant will then play the role of expert, facilitating information flows and relationship maintenance is the primary task

(*Source*: Adapted from Butler and Durkin, 1998)

FINANCIAL SERVICES MARKETING IN PRACTICE FT

It pays to be friends with your bank: self employment

The brave decision to become your own boss often means establishing a new relationship with your bank. This is especially true if you need to borrow money to get your business going.

In the past, banks have put self-employed people into a high-risk category because their income is often erratic and more than 30 per cent of start-up businesses go under within two years. As a result, borrowing costs are usually higher and there is an ever-present threat of the lender pulling the plug on your overdraft or loan just when you need credit facilities most.

Indeed, if your venture is considered particularly high risk, be prepared to pay up to 6 percentage points above base rate on a term loan. The long, deep recession of the early 1990s did nothing to help the image of budding entrepreneurs. Bad debt rose to record levels as business after business went to the wall, and many lenders got their fingers burnt badly.

According to research by the Forum of Private Business (FPB), a small business lobby group, the big four banks in 1990 were demanding collateral of around five times the size of a loan from self-employed business people (although, with the economic recovery, this ratio has now dropped to around three times). Often, they would not offer credit at all.

Have things really improved? A recent survey of 16,000 members by the Federation of Small Businesses revealed that more than a third had applied for a refund of charges from their bank – and nearly all succeeded. Moreover, a third of those businesses that negotiated with their bank managers managed to change their fee arrangements. The message is clear. Everything is negotiable, and you should never assume that charges are always correct.

There are now 3.9m self-employed people, compared with 2.5m in 1985. Banks realise that this rapidly-expanding, if loosely-defined, sector offers lucrative opportunities. But their risk assessment methods have had to become more sophisticated, along with their understanding of the businesses to which they are lending.

Aidan Berry, Professor of Accounting and Finance at the University of Brighton, says: 'Banks are moving dramatically towards credit scoring for very small businesses and self-employed people. The concern here is that their scoring systems seem quite reliant on home ownership rather than the traditional income criteria. Does this mean there can be only middle-class entrepreneurs?'

In a bid for their business, National Westminster Bank has appointed more than 1,200 small business managers to advise and provide services for the self-employed, and 400 more are planned. The cynical observer might consider this unsurprising, since the FPB identified NatWest as having the highest margin over base rate for overdrafts in 1996.

But Peter Ibbetson, the bank's head of small business services, says: 'A self-employed person is not necessarily more risky than an employee in a large company. Depending on their respective repayment track records, an employee might have to pay a higher rate of interest on a loan than a self-employed person. The uncertainty of the modern workplace now puts people in the same boat.'

The recession has taught banks to move away from an over-reliance on overdrafts – short-term borrowing facilities often used, incorrectly, to buy long-term capital assets – and towards other forms of lending such as personal loans, hire purchase agreements and leasing services. The banks are finding that a more structured form of lending encourages greater repayment discipline from small businesses. And the FPB's research, which involved interviews with 10,000 self-employed bank customers, showed clearly that those who have a close and honest relationship with their bank benefit from lower borrowing costs and better service.

This involves discussing excess borrowing requirements before you need them, providing regular updates on how your business is faring, and showing a willingness to negotiate on rates and methods of repayment. Marry this with a bank that makes a genuine effort to understand your business and clear savings can be made across the whole range of services and products.

A small business with a poor banking relationship is four times more likely to have a loan application rejected than one that enjoys a relationship of mutual trust and co-operation. Similarly, there can be a difference of more than

FINANCIAL SERVICES MARKETING IN PRACTICE FT

1 per cent on borrowing rates for 'good' and 'bad' customers.

John Hutton-Attenborough at Berry Birch & Noble, an independent financial adviser, says newly self-employed people should make a big effort to prepare a proper business plan for the bank manager to consider. 'If you just walk in off the street and ask to borrow money without any evidence of planning or thought, you are likely to be shown the door', he adds. If you don't have an existing relationship with the manager, it can be a good idea to find an accountant who does.

The British Bankers' Association (BBA) says average bank charges for small businesses are £200 a year, although charges can mount for those who need specialist advice or non-standard lending facilities, such as a capital repayment holiday.

Most self-employed people who sign up as business customers are offered free banking in the first year. Mike Young, assistant director at the BBA, adds: 'Thereafter, there is more room for negotiation on charges than people often realise'. If you are about to become self-employed, it might be tempting simply not to tell your bank. But this is a potentially dangerous course to take – if your bank found out, it could put you on a punitive charging tariff or even withdraw the banking service altogether.

Source: Matthew Wall, *Financial Times*, 16 January 1999

Questions:

1 Why are small businesses generally considered to be high-risk?

2 What are the advantages and disadvantages of applying credit scoring principles to small businesses?

3 What can small businesses do to ensure they get the best out of their bank?

accountant provides an information-gathering service, acting as translator of the small business's information for the bank. As the relationship progresses, the role changes from one of broker to problem solver in which the accountant can assist in deepening the relationship between the bank and the small business. Table 11.5 outlines the various stages of the relationship, the characteristics and the role of the accountant.

SUMMARY

This chapter has attempted to offer an insight into the specific nature of corporate financial services marketing. It began by highlighting the specific characteristics of corporate customers and their implications for marketing. It showed that corporate customers tend to be larger than personal customers with more complex financial requirements, but generally they are more knowledgeable customers.

One of the main differences between personal and corporate financial services customers is the nature and complexity of the purchase decision process. Purchase decisions tend to be taken by groups of individuals; each individual takes on a specific role in the decision-making process. Some individuals exert more power and influence than others and have the ability to shape the final decision. Corporate financial services providers need to understand the roles adopted by the various individuals, their specific buying criteria and the level of influence they have.

Understanding the processes that corporate customers go through in making decisions is important, yet there is evidence to suggest that financial services providers are still lacking in their perception of corporate customer needs. While many businesses are concerned with the ability of the bank to develop a long-term relationship and its willingness to accommodate credit needs, many banks show a tendency to ignore these desires, focusing predominantly on what the bank can provide the business with. It is these gaps which need to be addressed further in the corporate banking relationship.

It is also important that financial services providers understand the differences in needs between larger corporate customers and small business customers. Small business customers are more dependent on banks as a source of finance, compared with large corporations which usually have multiple banking relationships and can use their bargaining power to obtain better deals. As a result of this, small businesses tend to be more focused on price than larger corporations which favour quality of service and relationship development.

DISCUSSION QUESTIONS

1 What makes corporate customers different from personal customers?

2 Identify some different types of corporate customers and summarise what you think their financial requirements would be.

3 For an organisation and financial product of your choice, outline the stages the company would go through in the purchase decision process.

4 What can financial institutions do at each of the stages of the buying process to assist the buyer with the decision?

5 How would you explain the differences in businesses' financial requirements and banks' perceptions of their requirements? What can be done to narrow the gaps?

6 Why is it important to understand the buying-group roles and participants? Who might be involved in the buying group in a small firm?

7 Why do large corporations use a number of financial institutions to meet their financial requirements, and how can a financial institution ensure that it is selected?

8 What can banks do to retain their corporate customers?

9 Why has the relationship between small businesses and their banks often been unsatisfactory?

10 Analyse the role of the accountant in the small business–bank relationship and comment on its effectiveness.

12 Projects

INTRODUCTION

This chapter contains 10 projects which take into account the different areas of marketing covered in the book, and different types of financial institution. Many of the projects are multi-themed, highlighting the interrelationships between the material presented in the chapters. All of the projects contained in this chapter represent actual problems or issues currently experienced by financial institutions, thus enabling students to experience and execute the same decisions made by marketing managers in many financial institutions.

The projects can be used in a number of ways: 1. as assessed assignments, conducted either as group or individual projects; 2. as the basis for class discussion; 3. for examinations, with either closed or open book. In addition, the projects are also adaptable. For example, in the case of individual assignments or class discussions, only some of the questions may be required. Alternatively, further questions can be added, or completely new questions can be used which fit the course material more closely.

Each project comprises: 1. *Background* – this sets the scene for the project and provides general background to the problem, or the issues leading up to the problem. Further material on the background to the problem can usually be found in the relevant chapters to which the project relates or, indeed, the mini-cases within the relevant chapters. The background material is also useful in guiding further reading on the problem and directing students to appropriate texts. 2. *Questions* – for each project there are a number of questions to be answered. These can be used as they are presented, or, where time is limited, they can be simplified or used in part. 3. *Research method* – this provides an indication of the means by which the problem can be researched. Depending on the nature of use, primary research may not always be possible. Hence, every attempt has been made to ensure that most projects are equally researchable by either desk research or a combination of desk and primary research. 4. *Reading* – each project is accompanied by a small suggested reading list. In most cases the reading material is optional, and serves only as a guide to the problem. Alternative readings may be used, or further readings may be added to those indicated.

OBJECTIVES

After reading this chapter you should be able to:

- highlight the issues of key concern to financial institutions;
- benefit from the practical experience of financial services marketing;
- appreciate the interrelationships between key issues covered throughout the book.

Table 12.1 Core chapters which relate to the projects

	Chapter 1	Chapter 2	Chapter 3	Chapter 4	Chapter 5	Chapter 6	Chapter 7	Chapter 8	Chapter 9	Chapter 10	Chapter 11
Project 1	✓	✓	✓					✓			
Project 2		✓	✓	✓				✓			
Project 3		✓	✓	✓					✓	✓	
Project 4	✓				✓	✓	✓				
Project 5			✓							✓	
Project 6					✓	✓					
Project 7				✓			✓	✓		✓	
Project 8			✓	✓				✓			
Project 9				✓				✓	✓	✓	
Project 10									✓	✓	✓

Table 12.1 indicates the relevant chapters of the book for each project.

PROJECT 1

Investor education

Background

One of the key objectives of the Financial Services Authority, through the Financial Services and Markets Bill, is to promote public understanding of financial services. This is a new objective and takes the financial system into new territory. One of the reasons why this has been introduced as a key objective, is due to the amount of mis-selling that has occurred in recent years; the Financial Services Act 1986 was not adequate to protect consumers in this respect.

However, the Financial Services Authority (FSA) would also suggest that there has been a certain amount of mis-buying, and the financial institutions and regulatory authorities cannot be held accountable for this. Consumers need appropriate information on which to base purchase decisions and the ability to understand the information. Overall, the objective of the FSA is to improve the quality of decision-making by consumers. The FSA plans to achieve this by putting measures in place to enhance general financial literacy and provide generic advice, which stops short of recommending a product, but which helps people to arrive at a more informed judgement.

Questions

- Why should financial institutions be concerned about educating their customers. Are there any ethical issues to be considered?
- Choose one of the organisations listed in the directory of financial education programmes for consumers, and critically evaluate their educational activities.
- Analyse the gaps in financial education identified in the report and comment on what can be done either at an institution level or at an industry-wide level to improve the situation.
- Choose *one* of the segments identified in the report and develop a campaign for investor education that takes into account the specific learning required and the preferred learning methods.

Research method

Most of the research is based on a critical evaluation of the material contained in the Financial Services Authority report (detailed below). However, some primary research will need to be undertaken to obtain the necessary material needed to address the second objective outlined above. If it is not possible to contact any of the organisations listed in the directory, similar leaflets or material may be gathered from local bank branches.

In addition, it is expected that a wider understanding of the issues and factors affecting consumer behaviour decisions will be brought to the discussion. It is also important that the evaluation of the financial literacy activities is made as critical as possible, merely describing the activities is not enough. To assist in this matter, it is a good idea to identify particular evaluative criteria by which to assess the effectiveness.

Reading

Vass, J. (1998), 'A Guide to the Provision of Financial Services Education for Consumers', *Financial Services Authority*, March 1998.

McKechnie, S. (1992), 'Consumer Buying Behaviour in Financial Services: an Overview', *International Journal of Bank Marketing*, Vol. 10, No. 5, pp. 4–12.

Harrison, T. (1994), 'Mapping Customer Segments for Personal Financial Services', *International Journal of Bank Marketing*, Vol. 12, No. 8, pp. 17–25.

PROJECT 2

The mortgage purchase process

Background

The 1980s were characterised by growth in terms of both the size and the number of suppliers of mortgages, and also in the choice of products available. This was both a function of and a contributor to the rise in the number of households. At the same time, government policy actively encouraged owner-occupation, and many individuals perceived property ownership as both an investment and a form of security. The 1990s, however, signalled a downturn in the housing market and the opportunities of the 1980s, in terms of mortgage sales, were reduced.

The combined effects of a depressed economy and demographic shifts towards an older population have meant that the potential customer base of first-time buyers has been reduced. While the first-time buyer market is still important, emphasis is now being placed to an increasing extent on the second-time buyer market and the remortgage market. The market has become increasingly competitive, with lenders offering cash-backs, fixed, capped and variable loans, making up a plethora of marginally different products derived from the basic mortgage loan. Therefore, the need to understand the buying process, in relation to mortgages, is of paramount importance. Equally important, is the need to understand where remortgaging is likely to occur, and how this fits in with the overall buying process.

Questions

- Consider the various stages within the mortgage buying process.
- Identify the stages within this process where customers are most receptive to product information and promotion.
- Provide recommendations of ways in which promotion, during these identified stages, should best be handled.

Research method

This project can be conducted in one of two ways. It is possible to base the research entirely on desk research by reviewing previous research undertaken in this area and extrapolating the findings to this particular project. Yet, there is also scope to conduct some primary research with mortgage customers to explore the decision processes they went through in the choice of mortgage product and provider. Whichever approach is adopted, a comprehensive review of research studies in the area of purchase behaviour should be undertaken in order to ascertain the factors affecting purchase decisions. Attempts should also be made to identify target segments for mortgage products and the type of promotion and marketing which is appropriate to the target groups.

Reading

Talaga, J. A. and Buch, J. (1998), 'Consumer Trade-offs among Mortgage Instrument Variables', *International Journal of Bank Marketing*, Vol. 16, No. 6, pp. 264–270.

Park, C. W. (1982), 'Joint Decisions in Home Purchasing: A Muddling-through Process', *Journal of Consumer Research*, No. 9, pp. 151–162.

McKechnie, S. (1992), 'Consumer Buying Behaviour in Financial Services: an Overview', *International Journal of Bank Marketing*, Vol. 10, No. 5, pp. 4–12.

Verhallen, T. M. M., Greve, H. and Frambach, R. T. (1997), 'Consultative Selling in Financial Services: An Observational Study of the Mortgage Mediation Process', *International Journal of Bank Marketing*, Vol. 15, No. 2, pp. 54–59.

PROJECT 3

Flexible mortgage segmentation

Background

Employment trends are causing various effects on consumer financial services consumption. These trends include: the increased importance of self-employment and part-time work, the increase in temporary employment and the fall in job stability. Coupled with other social trends such as divorce, remarriage and demands on care for the elderly, they have a marked effect on traditional life-cycle cash flows, bringing about greater fluctuations in income and expenditure and possible periods of unemployment. Indeed, increased job uncertainty and employment gaps do not bode well for the traditional mortgage which is inflexible, relies on a stable income and regular payments. Many families may find that they simply cannot keep regular payments going, but rather have periods of high earnings during which higher repayments can be made, and periods of lower earnings during which repayments may need to be reduced or even stopped completely. Thus, there is a greater need for flexibility in the mortgage product which takes account of families' changing social and economic circumstances.

A more flexible product may be seen as a means of attracting second-time buyers and retaining existing customers as it provides for changes within the customer's life cycle, or possibly encourages loyalty by future incentives. It is necessary to understand what the characteristics of customers are who are most interested in such features, when in their mortgage buying life the product would be most applicable, and to what extent this may encourage loyalty, so that financial institutions can target customers for a flexible product more efficiently and effectively.

Questions

- Briefly review the current options on the market in terms of flexible repayment mortgages.
- Identify those customers who are most likely to be receptive to the notion of flexible mortgage repayments.

- Provide a specific profile of the segment that can be used for targeting and communication.
- Provide recommendations of ways in which promotion of such a product might take place.

Research method

The research will be based mostly on desk research, although it is expected that a reasonable review of flexible mortgage products currently available on the market be conducted. This may require visits to local bank/building society branches. A review of research studies in the area of the mortgage market should also be conducted in order to glean any relevant information. The research can also draw on more general theories and research on life-cycle patterns, patterns of income and wealth, etc. A critical analysis of products already on the market may provide an indication of target groups perceived by other institutions.

Reading

Lawson, R. W. (1988), 'The Family Life Cycle: A Demographic Analysis', *Journal of Marketing Management*, Vol. 4, No. 1, pp. 13–33.

Gerdes, M. (1996), 'How Demographic Shifts and Undercurrents will Mould the Financial Services Market', *Journal of Financial Services Marketing*, Vol. 1, No. 3, pp. 239–248.

Murphy, P. E. and Staples, W. A. (1979), 'A Modernised Family Life-Cycle', *Journal of Consumer Research*, June, pp. 12–22.

PROJECT 4

Changing distribution channels in the life assurance market

Background

The onset of hard disclosure and own charge projections in the financial services sector has heightened the importance of distribution channels selection in this intensely competitive market. Many life assurance companies are restricted in their selection of distribution channels, with most business going through independent financial advisers. Over the last few years there has been an increasing desire to have more direct contact with customers for reasons of cost as well as access.

The direct route offers a number of advantages to life assurance companies wanting to create closer links with customers. Innovative direct telephone operators, such as Direct Line, have shown that it is possible to diversify from general insurance into mortgages with publicly quoted success. Others have also followed. Life assurance companies are interested in understanding the potential uses of the direct telephone channel across the complete product range and the attitudes and opinions of customers towards the use of direct methods.

Questions

- Provide a report on the changing distribution channels currently affecting the mortgage market, with specific reference to direct telephone marketing.

- Examine the advantages and disadvantages of setting up a direct telephone channel for a life assurance company.
- Suggest a strategy for entry to the direct mortgage market.

Research method

The research will be based primarily on desk research. You may choose to focus on a particular life assurance company that you are familiar with, or alternatively may identify a company from newspaper reports. You will need to conduct secondary data analyses of the success of other direct operators in the mortgage market, and also be expected to show a critical appreciation of various distribution channels in the marketing of mortgages.

Reading

Worthington, S. (1998), 'The Card Centric Distribution of Financial Services: A Comparison of Japan and the UK', *International Journal of Bank Marketing*, Vol. 16, No. 5, pp. 211–220.

Mols, N. P. (1998), 'The Behavioural Consequences of PC Banking', *International Journal of Bank Marketing*, Vol. 16, No. 5, pp. 195–201.

Dannenberg, M. and Kellner, D. (1998), 'The Bank of Tomorrow with Today's Technology', *International Journal of Bank Marketing*, Vol. 16, No. 2, pp. 90–97.

PROJECT 5

Holes in the bucket

Background

Due to the combination of low interest rates, increased competition and increasing customer promiscuity, financial institutions are currently finding it harder to maintain and increase their current deposit books. New players are entering the market with competitive rates and are attracting customers from traditional financial institutions. One of the key segments under attack is the over-49s. The over-49s are a valuable segment in the sense that they are empty-nesters in the main, have fully paid-up mortgages, are likely to still be in employment with a good source of income and have a higher-than-average propensity to save.

The key issues financial institutions are concerned about are: what factors are most likely to persuade customers to keep existing funds within the institution, and what factors are likely to attract funds from new customers.

Questions

- Establish why customers with deposits in excess of £5,000 are switching their savings.
- Ascertain to what degree switching is occurring.
- Suggest a possible range of factors that could trigger switching behaviour.
- Establish where and into what types of accounts funds are moving.
- Offer suggestions as to how a financial institution can retain such customers.

Research method

There are two possible ways of researching this topic: either by desk research or by a combination of desk and primary research. The research should focus specifically on the over-49s market, male and female, professional/working households. Savings may have been built up over a number of years, or could have been recently received in the form of inheritance. It is likely that this segment is cautious in their financial dealings and is unlikely to contemplate risk ventures into the stock market. Security is important to this market, in both a psychological and a physical sense.

Reading

Stanley, T. O., Ford, J. K. and Richards, S. K. (1985), 'Segmentation of Bank Customers by Age', *International Journal of Bank Marketing*, Vol. 3, No. 3, pp. 56–63.

Banks, R. (1990), 'Money Management for the Mature, their Needs and the Services Competing to Meet them', *Admap*, March, pp. 26–29.

Bartos, R. (1980), 'Over 49: The Invisible Consumer Market', *Harvard Business Review*, January–February, pp. 140–148.

Buck, S . (1990), 'Turning an Old Problem into a New Opportunity', *Admap*, March, pp. 20–22.

Kreitzman, L. (1994), 'Quantifying the "Third Age" ', *Admap*, July/August, pp. 19–22.

PROJECT 6

Self-service banking

Background

Economic pressures on the financial services sector have caused financial institutions to examine the profitability of their distribution systems. The large and expensive branch networks, which have traditionally been important in providing the primary point of contact between the financial institution and the customer, have become the focus of attention in terms of rationalisation and streamlining of branch activities. Hence, there has been a reduction in the number of branches over the last decade in the sector as a whole. At the same time, advances in technology have facilitated this rationalisation in that they have provided alternative distribution channels.

The introduction of ATMs has increased the possibilities in terms of cash accessibility outside normal banking hours. Other developments, such as telephone banking, now offer 24-hour service for a wider range of transactions. The implications of such services can be seen at both an operational and a marketing level. In operational terms the use of electronic technology has created a shift in the burden of the branch time, which in marketing terms, allows branch staff to concentrate on the services and products requiring personal contact with branch staff. Yet, developments are still occurring with on-line home banking and use of the internet and interactive TV. As these technologies increase further, their impact on the market and the way in which consumers use and purchase financial services is undoubtedly likely to change.

Questions

- Assess the current situation with regard to the adoption of self-service technologies in the financial services sector.
- Establish who are the primary users of self-service banking, and what are the primary uses.
- Provide an insight into the attitudes and behaviour of users of self-service technology with an indication of current barriers to use.
- Critically evaluate the future implications of advances in self-service technology in terms of financial institutions' operations and delivery of services, and the marketing of financial services through such channels.

Research method

Extensive desk research can provide much of the information required for this project, for example, in the form of previous studies and academic papers. However, the project also lends itself to observation research, which would provide a deeper insight into the users and uses of such technology and behaviour. If possible, qualitative research in the form of individual interviews or focus groups would provide a deeper insight into the attitudes and opinions of individuals.

Reading

Mols, N. P. (1998), 'The Behavioural Consequences of PC Banking', *International Journal of Bank Marketing*, Vol. 16, No. 5, pp. 195–201.

Prendergast, G. P., and Marr, N. E. (1994), 'The Future of Self-Service Technologies in Retail Banking', *The Service Industries Journal*, Vol. 14, No. 1, pp. 94–114.

Leblanc, G. (1990), 'Customer Motivations: Use and Non-Use of Automated Banking', *International Journal of Bank Marketing*, Vol. 8, No. 4, pp. 36–40.

PROJECT 7

Product bundling and loyalty building

Background

In recent years, banks have diverted from their traditional customer acquisition strategy in favour of customer retention and loyalty. The financial services market is somewhat saturated by large numbers of financial institutions offering what are essentially the same products. Scope for new customer acquisition is, therefore, limited. Resources are now diverted towards retaining existing customers and encouraging them to buy as many products from the same institution as possible.

The concept of product bundling represents one way in which banks can entice customers to direct more of their business to them. For example, if customers maintain a minimum balance of £2,500 in a deposit account for one year, they may be offered a discounted mortgage rate by 0.5 per cent for two years. Such an offer may divert a customer from approaching another financial institution for finance.

The concept of bundling has been used to a greater or lesser extent by a number of financial institutions in recent years, and is a particular feature of the banking industry in the US and other countries.

Questions

- Consider the concept of product bundling and how it can be applied to financial services.
- Approach the concept from the customer point of view and determine how a financial institution can encourage its customers to buy more of their financial products from them.
- Provide recommendations on how these proposals could be promoted to customers.

Research method

A certain amount of desk research will be required concerning existing practices both at home and abroad. In order to establish customer opinions, it will be necessary to carry out some qualitative research. This information should facilitate informed decisions which should be made with full cognisance of the economics of the proposals made, as well as consideration of budgetary constraints.

Reading

Hughes, T. J. (1992), 'The Customer Database: Cross-selling Retail Financial Services', *International Journal of Bank Marketing*, Vol. 10, No. 7, pp. 11–16.

Drake, C., Gwynne, A. and Waite, N. (1998), 'Barclays Life Customer Satisfaction and Loyalty Tracking Survey: A Demonstration of Customer Loyalty Research in Practice', *International Journal of Bank Marketing*, Vol. 16, No. 7, pp. 287–292.

Bloemer, J., De Ruyter, K. and Peeters, P. (1998), 'Investigating Drivers of Bank Loyalty: The Complex Relationship between Image, Service Quality and Satisfaction', *International Journal of Bank Marketing*, Vol. 16, No. 7, pp. 276–286.

PROJECT 8

The design and launch of a bank's student package

Background

Students represent a significant part of the youth market and have received considerable attention from the financial services sector over the last few decades. In the 1970s the major clearing banks began to develop student accounts aimed at school leavers going on to further education. The driving factor at that time was that a vast majority of students received local education authority grants paid by cheque for which a bank account was desirable. In addition to this, there are several other reasons why financial institutions wish to target students: they are easily identifiable; they can be easily reached and located; they have specific, identifiable needs; they represent a captive market while at university and they represent a potentially profitable market for the future.

In order to retain their share of the student market, banks and building societies review their student packages on an annual basis, taking into account aspects such as current market conditions, competitor activity and customer expectations. Depending on the marketing objectives of the individual financial institutions, student packages are launched between May and September every year, in an effort to capture a share of the new student market. Banks recruit new student customers with a view to long-term customer retention. Their aim, therefore, is to successfully retain these customers during their time at college or university, and, following graduation, trade them up through a range of products.

Questions

- Consider the needs, requirements and expectations of first-year students in terms of the products and services available from banks.
- Consider how your findings could be incorporated within a student package to appeal to new first-year students.
- Provide recommendations regarding how this package can be promoted.

Research method

A certain amount of research will be required concerning the content of existing student packages. This can be achieved by visiting banks and building societies and obtaining product literature on their student packages. Some form of critical evaluation of the packages will need to be carried out. In order to establish customer opinions of the packages, it will be necessary to carry out some primary research. This can be of either a qualitative or a quantitative nature. This information should facilitate informed decisions which should be made with full cognisance of the economics of the proposals made, as well as consideration of budgetary constraints.

Reading

Lewis, B. R. (1982), 'Student Accounts – A Profitable Segment?', *European Journal of Marketing,* Vol. 16, No. 3, pp. 63–72.

Lewis, B. R., Orledge, J. and Mitchell, V.-W. (1994), 'Service Quality: Students' Assessment of Banks and Building Societies', *International Journal of Bank Marketing,* Vol. 12, No. 4, pp. 3–12.

PROJECT 9

Long-term retention of graduating students

Background

Banks and building societies make considerable investments in terms of resources and expenditure in their efforts to attract and retain student customers during their time at college or university, and of course beyond. Student customers are not particularly profitable for financial institutions while they are at college or university; they only begin to become profitable in the year after graduation. After this, profit rises rapidly as the demand for financial products increases.

The initial outlays can only be recouped if the student customers can be retained on a long-term basis following graduation. It is important that banks actively encourage their final-year student customers to remain with them after graduation, therefore allowing them to be traded-up through the range of accounts available, and providing further opportunities for selling products such as savings, loans and mortgages.

Questions

- Consider the features of current student packages and identify those that may be of greater importance to student customers during their final year.
- Consider how these features could be incorporated within a graduate package, with a view to encouraging long-term customer retention.
- Provide recommendations regarding the promotion of such a package.

Research method

Desk research can be used to address the first objective outlined above. This will involve gathering product literature and evaluating the services offered to students in the final year of their degree. However, in order to assess fully the needs of students in their final year and how these needs may change beyond graduation it will be necessary to conduct some form of primary research.

Reading

Chan, R. Y.-K. (1993), 'Banking Services for Young Intellectuals', *International Journal of Bank Marketing*, Vol. 11, No. 5, pp. 33–40.

Colgate, M., Stewart, K. and Kinsella, R. (1995), 'Customer Defection: A Study of the Student Market in Ireland', *International Journal of Bank Marketing*, Vol. 14, No. 8, pp. 23–29.

Colgate, M. and Alexander, N. (1998), 'Banks, Retailers and their Customers: A Relationship Marketing Perspective', *International Journal of Bank Marketing*, Vol. 16, No. 4, pp. 144–152.

PROJECT 10

Small business–bank relationships

Background

Small businesses represent potentially big business for banks: companies with less than fifty employees now account for approximately 40 per cent of economic activity in the UK and almost half of total employment. Yet, small businesses seem to be at the end of the queue when it comes to receiving good service from banks. The way in which banks have treated small businesses suggests a lack of understanding of the specific needs of small businesses and a lack of appreciation for the importance of the role of the bank in small business finance.

Recent reports suggest that banks cannot afford to be complacent where small businesses are concerned. While the NatWest and Barclays still dominate the small business sector, there is evidence to suggest that small business banking is becoming increasingly competitive. The market leaders face competition from Lloyds TSB and HSBC and other smaller banks. In order to retain their share of the small business market, the traditional players need to re-evaluate their approach to small business banking and gain a better understanding of the requirements of small businesses.

Questions

- Critically evaluate the level of service small businesses have tended to receive from their banks.

- Identify the specific needs of small businesses, and how they may differ from the needs of larger corporations.
- Discuss what banks can do to improve their relationship with small business customers.
- Suggest a plan for the retention of a small business customer.

Research method

It is possible for this project to be based entirely on desk research using secondary data sources. A number of reports, papers and newspaper articles have brought the plight of small businesses to our attention. However, primary research would offer an interesting insight into the problem. Depending on the nature of access to small businesses, interviews or questionnaires might be used specifically to address small business needs, small businesses' perceptions of their banks and the level of service received, and to inform a successful retention strategy.

Reading

Butler, P. and Durkin, M. (1998), 'Relationship Intermediaries: Business Advisers in the Small Firm–Bank Relationship', *International Journal of Bank Marketing*, Vol. 16, No. 1, pp. 32–38.

Tyler, K. and Stanley, E. (1999), 'Marketing Financial Services to Businesses: A Critical Review and Research Agenda', *International Journal of Bank Marketing*, Vol. 17, No. 3, pp. 98–115.

Nielsen, J. F., Terry, C. and Trayler, R. M. (1998), 'Business Banking in Australia: A Comparison of Expectations', *International Journal of Bank Marketing*, Vol. 16, No. 6, pp. 253–263.

References

Abell, Derek F. (1980), *Defining the Business: The Starting Point of Strategic Planning*, Prentice-Hall, Englewood Cliffs, NJ.

Advertising Association, *Advertising Statistics Yearbook* (1998), 16th Annual Edition, June, NTC Publications, Henley-on-Thames.

Armitage, S. (1997), 'The Future of Mutual Life Offices', in H. Macmillan and M. Christophers (Eds) *Strategic Issues in the Life Assurance Industry*, Butterworth-Heinemann, Oxford, pp. 43–63.

Ashman, S. and Clarke, K. (1994), 'Optimising Ad Effectiveness: Quantifying the Major Cost Benefits of Painstaking Television Pre-tests', *Admap*, February, pp. 43–56.

Baker, C. (1995), 'The Co-operative Bank – "Profit with Principles" ', *Advertising Works*, pp. 329–352, NTC Publications, Henley-on-Thames.

Baker, M. J. (1992), *Marketing Strategy and Management*, Second Edition, Macmillan, London.

Baldock, R. (1997), 'The Virtual Bank: Four Marketing Scenarios for the Future', *Journal of Financial Services Marketing*, Vol. 1, No. 3, pp. 260–268.

Bandura, A. (1977a), *Social Learning Theory*, Prentice Hall, Englewood Cliffs, NJ.

Bandura, A. (1977b), 'Self-Efficacy: Toward a Unifying Theory of Behavioural Change', *Psychological Review*, Vol. 84, pp. 191–215.

Bandura, A. and Walters, R. H. (1963), *Social Learning Theory and Personality Development*, Holt, Rinehart and Winston, New York.

Banks, R. (1990), 'Money Management for the Mature, their Needs and the Services Competing to Meet them', *Admap*, March, pp. 26–29.

Bateson, J. E. G. (1977), 'Do We Need Service Marketing', in P. Eiglier, E. Langeard, C. H. Lovelock and J. E. G. Bateson (Eds), *Marketing Consumer Services Report No. 77–115*, Marketing Science Institute, pp. 1–30.

Bauer, R. A. (1967), 'Consumer Behavior as Risk Taking', in Cox, D. F. (Ed.), *Risk Taking and Information Handling in Consumer Behavior*, Harvard University Press, Boston.

Bayton, J. A. (1958), 'Motivation, Cognition and Learning: Basic Factors in Consumer Behavior', in J. F. Engel (Ed.), *Consumer Behavior: Selected Readings*, Richard D. Irwin, Homewood, Ill., 1968, pp. 20–29.

Belk, R. (1995), 'Studies in the New Consumer Behaviour', in D. Miller (Ed.), *Acknowledging Consumption: A Review of New Studies*, Routledge, London, Chapter 2, pp. 58–95.

Berry, L. (1980), 'Services Marketing is Different', in C. H. Lovelock (Ed.), *Services Marketing* (1984), pp .29–37, Prentice-Hall, Englewood Cliffs, NJ.

Bettman J. R. (1979), 'Memory Factors in Consumer Choice: A Review', *Journal of Marketing*, Vol. 43, pp. 37–53.

Betts, E. (1994), 'Understanding the Financial Consumer', in P. J. McGoldrick and S. J. Greenland (Eds), *Retailing of Financial Services*, McGraw-Hill, London, pp. 41–84.

Betts, E. and Yorke, D. A. (1994), 'Direct Marketing: Its "Excesses" and "Expertness" ', in J. Bell *et al.*, (Ed) *Marketing: Unity in Diversity*, Proceedings of The Marketing Education Group Conference, Coleraine, pp. 101–110.

Bonoma, T. V. (1982), 'Major Sales: Who Really Does the Buying?', *Harvard Business Review*, Vol. 60 (May–June), pp. 111–119.

Booz, Allen and Hamilton (1982), *New Product Development for the 1980s*, Booz, Allen and Hamilton Inc, New York.

Bowen, D. E. and Schneider, B. (1988), 'Services Marketing and Management: Implications for Organizational Behaviour', *Research in Organizational Behaviour*, Vol. 10, pp. 43–80.

Bowles, T. (1985), 'Does Classifying People by Lifestyle Really Help the Advertiser?', *Admap*, May, pp. 36–40.

Broadbridge, A. and Marshall, J. (1995), 'Consumer Complaint Behaviour: The Case of Electrical Goods', *International Journal of Retail and Distribution Management*, September, Vol. 23, No. 9, pp. 8–19.

Buck, S. (1990), 'Turning an Old Problem into a New Opportunity', *Admap*, March, pp. 20–22.

Buerger, J. E. and Ulrich, T. A. (1986), 'What's Important to Small Business in Selecting a Financial Institution', *Journal of Commercial Bank Lending*, Vol. 69, February, pp. 3–9.

Burton, D. (1994), *Financial Services and the Consumer*, Routledge, London.

Butler, P. and Durkin, M. (1995), 'Managing Expectations in the Small Business–Bank Relationship', *Irish Marketing Review*, Vol. 8, pp. 53–60.

Butler, P. and Durkin, M. (1998), 'Relationship Intermediaries: Business Advisers in the Small Firm–Bank Relationship', *International Journal of Bank Marketing*, Vol. 16, No. 1, pp. 32–38.

Buttle, F. (Ed.) (1996), *Relationship Marketing: Theory and Practice*, Paul Chapman Publishing, London.

Chan, A. K. K. and Ma, V. S. M. (1990), 'Corporate Banking Behaviour: A Survey in Hong Kong', *International Journal of Bank Marketing*, Vol. 8, No. 2, pp. 25–31.

Chéron, E. J., McTavish, R. and Perrien, J. (1989), 'Segmentation of Bank Commercial Markets', *International Journal of Bank Marketing*, Vol. 7, No. 6, pp. 25–30.

Chisnall, P. M. (1995), *Consumer Behaviour*, Third Edition, McGraw-Hill, London.

Christopher, M., Payne, A. and Ballantyne, D. (1991), *Relationship Marketing: Bringing Quality, Customer Service and Marketing Together*, Butterworth-Heinemann, Oxford.

Christophers, M. and Macmillan, H. (1997), 'Who Is Winning?', in H. Macmillan and M. Christophers (Eds) *Strategic Issues in the Life Assurance Industry*, Butterworth-Heinemann, Oxford, pp. 13–27.

Chu, F. J. (1990), 'The Challenge and the Myth of Global Investment Banking', *Journal of International Securities Markets*, Autumn, pp. 219–223.

Clutterback, D. (1989), 'Developing Customer Care Training Programmes', *Marketing Intelligence and Planning*, Vol. 7, Nos. 1/2, pp. 34–37.

Colgate, M., Stewart, K. and Kinsella, R. (1995), 'Customer Defection: A Study of the Student Market in Ireland', *International Journal of Bank Marketing*, Vol. 14, No. 8, pp. 23–9.

Cornish, P. and Denny, M. (1989), 'Demographics are Dead – Long Live Demographics', *Journal of the Market Research Society*, Vol. 31, No. 3, pp. 363–373.

Cowell, D. (1984), *The Marketing of Services*, Heinemann, Oxford.

Cowell, D. (1988), 'New Service Development', *Journal of Marketing Management*, Vol. 3, No. 3, pp. 296–312.

Cowles, D. L. (1997), 'The Role of Trust in Customer Relationships: Asking the Right Questions', *Management Decisions*, March–April, Vol. 35, No. 3–4, pp. 273–283.

Darby, M. R. and Karni, E. (1973), 'Free Competition and the Optimal Amount of Fraud', *Journal of Law and Economics*, Vol. 16, April, pp. 67–86.

Davies, H. (1998), Financial Services and Markets Bill Conference, Grosvenor House Hotel, 24 September 1998, Chairman, Financial Services Authority.

Davies, H. (1999), 'Building the Financial Services Authority: What's New?', 1999 Travers Lecture, London Guildhall University Business School, Thursday 11 March 1999.

Davison, H., Watkins, T. and Wright, M. (1989), 'Developing New Personal Financial Products – Some Evidence of the Role of Market Research', *International Journal of Bank Marketing*, Vol. 7, No. 1, pp. 8–15.

De Bretani, R. (1993), 'The New Product Process in Financial Services: Strategies for Success', *International Journal of Bank Marketing*, Vol. 11, No. 3, pp. 15–22.

DeSouza, G. (1992), 'Designing a Customer Retention Plan', *Journal of Business Strategy*, March/April, pp. 24–31.

Devlin, J. (1995), 'Technology and Innovation in Retail Banking Distribution', *International Journal of Bank Marketing*, Vol. 13, No. 4, pp. 19–25.

Dibb, S., Simkin, L., Pride, W. M. and Ferrell, O. C. (1997), *Marketing Concepts and Strategies*, Third European Edition, Houghton Mifflin, Boston.

Dick, A. and Basu, K. (1994), 'Customer Loyalty: Toward an Integrated Framework', *Journal of the Academy of Marketing Science*, Vol. 22, No. 2, pp. 99–113.

Donnelly, J. H., Berry, L. L. and Thompson, T. W. (1985), *Marketing Financial Services*, Dow Jones-Irwin, Homewood, Ill.

Douglas, T. (1985), 'New Doubts Hit ACORN's Data', *Marketing Week*, 31 May.

Dowling, G. R. and Uncles, M. (1997), 'Do Customer Loyalty Programmes Really Work?', *Sloan Management Review*, Summer, Vol. 38, No. 4, pp. 71–82.

Doyle, P. (1991), 'Branding', in M. J. Baker (Ed.) *The Marketing Book*, Butterworth-Heinemann, Oxford, pp. 335–347.

Drucker, P. F. (1985), *Innovation and Entrepreneurship*, Heinemann, London.

Dugmore, K. and Reid, E. (1997), 'Share of Wallet: From Theory to Practice', *Journal of Financial Services Marketing*, Vol. 1, No. 3, pp. 269–275.

Easingwood, C. (1986), 'New Product Development for Services Companies', *Journal of Product Innovation Management*, Vol. 3, No. 4, pp. 264–275.

Easingwood, C. and Storey, C. (1991), 'Success Factors for New Consumer Financial Services', *International Journal of Bank Marketing*, Vol. 9, No. 11, pp. 3–10.

Easingwood, C. and Storey, C. (1997), 'Distribution Strategies in the Financial Services Sector', *Journal of Financial Services Marketing*, Vol. 1, No. 3, pp. 211–224.

Edgett, S. (1993), 'Developing New Financial Services within Building Societies', *International Journal of Bank Marketing*, Vol. 11, No. 3, pp. 35–43.

Edgett, S. and Jones, S. (1991), 'New Product Development in the Financial Service Industry: A Case Study', *Journal of Marketing Management*, Vol. 7 pp. 271–284.

Engel, J. F., Kollat, D. T. and Blackwell, R. D. (1968), *Consumer Behaviour*, Holt, Rinehart and Winston, New York.

Ennew, C. and Binks, M. (1996), 'The Impact of Service Quality and Service Characteristics on Customer Retention: Small Businesses and their Banks in the UK', *British Journal of Management*, Vol. 7, pp. 219–230.

File, K. M. and Prince, R. A. (1992), 'Positive Word-of-Mouth: Customer Satisfaction and Buyer Behaviour', *International Journal of Bank Marketing*, Vol. 10, No. 1, pp. 25–29.

Ford, D., Hakansson, H. and Johanson, J. (1986), 'How Do Companies Interact?', *Industrial Marketing and Purchasing*, Vol. 1, No. 1, pp. 26–41.

Foxall, G. (1985), 'Marketing Is Service Marketing', in *Marketing in the Service Industries*, Frank Cass, London.

Foxall, G. R. and Goldsmith, R. E. (1994), *Consumer Psychology for Marketing*, Routledge, London.

Frank, R. E., Massy, W. F. and Wind, Y. (1972), *Market Segmentation*, Prentice Hall, Englewood Cliffs, NJ.

Freeman, D. K. and Turner, L. (1990), 'A Look at Bank Strategies in the Small Business Market', *Journal of Retail Banking*, Vol. 12, Spring, pp. 4–11.

Gabbott, M. and Hogg, G. (1994), 'Consumer Behaviour and Services: A Review', *Journal of Marketing Management*, Vol. 10, pp. 311–324.

Gavaghan, K. (1991), Paper Presented to the Association of Italian Bankers for Automation and Database Management, Milan, March.

George, T. (1996), 'Mondex Welcomes Rival E-Purse Scheme', *Banking Technology*, April, p. 5.

Gerdes, M. (1996), 'How Demographic Shifts and Undercurrents will Mould the Financial Services Market', *Journal of Financial Services Marketing*, Vol. 1, No. 3, pp. 239–248.

Gofton, K. (1995), 'When Loyalty Lies', *Marketing*, 16 February, pp. 25–27.

Green, P. E. (1977), 'A New Approach to Market Segmentation', *Business Horizons*, Vol. 20, pp. 61–73.

Green, P. E. and Krieger, A. M. (1995), 'Alternative Approaches to Cluster-based Market Segmentation', *Journal of the Market Research Society*, July, Vol. 37, No. 3, pp. 221–240.

Greenland, S. J. (1994), 'The Branch Environment', in P. J. McGoldrick and S. J. Greenland (Eds), *Retailing of Financial Services*, McGraw-Hill, London, pp. 163–198.

Greenland, S. J. (1995), 'Network Management and the Branch Distribution Channel', *International Journal of Bank Marketing*, Vol. 13, No. 4, pp. 12–18.

Griffin, J. (1995), *Customer Loyalty: How to Earn it, How to Keep it*, Lexington Books, Lexington, Mass.

Gronroos, C. (1984), 'A Service Quality Model and its Marketing Implications', *European Journal of Marketing*, Vol. 18, No. 4, pp. 36–44.

Gross, A. C., Banting, P. M., Meredith, L. M. and Ford, I. D. (1993), *Business Marketing*, Houghton Mifflin, Boston.

Guirdham, M. (1987), 'How to Market Unit Trusts: A Consumer Behaviour Model', *Marketing Intelligence and Planning*, Vol. 2, No. 6, pp. 15–19.

Hair, J. F. Jr., Anderson, R. E. and Tatham, R. L. (1987), *Multivariate Data Analysis with Readings*, Second Edition, Macmillan, New York.

Haley, R. I. (1968), 'Benefit Segmentation: A Decision-Oriented Research Tool', *Journal of Marketing*, Vol. 32 (July), pp. 30–35.

Harness, D. and Mackay, S. (1997), 'Product Delection: A Financial Services Perspective', *International Journal of Bank Marketing*, Vol. 15, No. 1, pp. 4–12.

Harrison, T. (1996), 'The Meaning of Life Cycles: Marketing Savings', *Chartered Banker*, Vol. 2, No. 5, May, pp. 32–33.

Harrison, T. S. (1994), 'Mapping Customer Segments for Personal Financial Services', *International Journal of Bank Marketing*, Vol. 12, No.8 , pp. 17–25.

Harrison, T. S. (1997a), 'Mapping Customer Segments for Personal Financial Services: Replication and Validation', *Journal of Financial Services Marketing*, Vol. 2, No. 1, pp. 39–54.

Harrison, T. S. (1997b), 'Pigeon-holing Prospects: Market Segmentation for the Insurance Industry', in H. Macmillan and M. Christophers (Eds) *Strategic Issues in the Life Assurance Industry*, Butterworth-Heinemann, Oxford.

Harvey, D. (1997), 'Smart Card-Based Payment Systems in the United Kingdom and France: The Role of Collaboration between Competing Banks and Retailers in Facilitating Market Adoption of New Technology', *Journal of Financial Services Marketing*, Vol. 1, No. 4, pp. 365–373.

Hayes, S. L. III, Spence, A. M. and Marks, D. V. P. (1983), *Competition in the Investment Banking Industry*, Harvard University Press, Cambridge, Mass.

Henley Centre, The (1994), *The Loyalty Paradox*, London.

Hilgard, E. R., Atkinson, R. C. and Atkinson, R. L. (1975), *Introduction to Psychology*, Harcourt Brace Jovanovich, New York.

Hill, D. J. and Gandhi, N. (1992), 'Services Advertising: A Framework to its Effectiveness', *Journal of Services Marketing*, Vol. 8, July, pp. 60–63.

Howard, J. A. and Sheth, J. N. (1969), *The Theory of Buyer Behavior*, John Wiley, New York.

Howcroft, B. (1991), 'Increased Marketing Orientation: UK Bank Branch Networks', *International Journal of Bank Marketing*, Vol. 9, No. 4, pp. 3–9.

Howcroft, B. and Beckett, A. (1993), 'Change in UK Bank Branch Networks: A Customer Perspective', *Service Industries Journal*, Vol. 13, No. 4, pp. 267–288.

Howcroft, B. and Kiely, J. (1995), 'Distribution Channels', in C. Ennew, T. Watkins and M. Wright (Eds), *Marketing Financial Services*, Butterworth-Heinemann, Oxford, pp. 174–192.

Hughes, M. (1994), 'Retail Branch Security', in P. J. McGoldrick and S. J. Greenland (Eds), *Retailing of Financial Services*, McGraw-Hill, London, pp. 154–162.

Johne, A. and Vermaak, L. (1993), 'Head Office Involvement in Financial Product Development', *International Journal of Bank Marketing*, Vol. 11, No. 3, pp. 28–34.

Johnson, P. (1990a), 'Our Ageing Population – The Implications for Business and Government', *Long Range Planning*, Vol. 23, No. 2, pp. 55–62.

Johnson, P. (1990b), 'Economic Trends in Population – Last 25 Years, Next 10 Years', *Admap*, March, pp. 14–16.

Johnston, W. J. and Bonoma, T. V. (1981), 'The Buying Centre: Structure and Interaction Patterns', *Journal of Marketing*, Vol. 45, Summer, pp. 143–165.

Jones, T. O. and Sasser, W. E. Jnr (1995), 'Why Loyal Customers Defect', in Reichheld, F. F. (Ed.), *The Quest for Loyalty: Creating Value through Partnership*, Harvard Business School Publishing, Boston, 1996, pp. 143–164.

Judd, V. C. (1987), 'Differentiate with the 5th P; People', *Industrial Marketing Management*, Vol. 16, pp. 241–247.

Kamakura, W. A., Ramaswami, S. N. and Srivastava, R. K. (1991), 'Applying Latent Trait Analysis in the Evaluation of Prospects for Cross-selling of Financial Services', *International Journal of Research in Marketing*, Vol. 8, No. 4, November, pp. 329–349.

Kantona, G. (1960), *The Powerful Consumer*, McGraw-Hill, New York.

Keaveney, S. (1995), 'Customer Switching Behaviour in Service Industries: An Exploratory Study', *Journal of Marketing*, Vol. 59, April, pp. 71–82.

Key Note (1992), *Personal Finance in the UK*, Key Note Publications, London.

Kirk, Y. (1994), 'Promotion and Advertising', in P. J. McGoldrick and S. J. Greenland (Eds), *Retailing of Financial Services*, McGraw-Hill, Maidenhead, pp. 240–265.

Klein, G. (1995), *Dictionary of Banking*, Second Edition, Financial Times Pitman Publishing, Glasgow.

Kotler, P. (1973), 'Atmospherics as a Marketing Tool', *Journal of Retailing*, Vol. 49, No. 4, pp. 48–64.

Kotler, P. (1984), *Marketing Management: Analysis, Planning and Control*, Fifth Edition, Prentice Hall, Englewood Cliffs, NJ.

Kotler, P., (1994), *Marketing Management: Analysis, Planning, Implementation and Control*, Eighth Edition, Prentice Hall, Englewood Cliffs, NJ.

Kotler, P. (1997), *Marketing Management: Analysis, Planning, Implementation and Control*, Ninth Edition, Prentice Hall, Englewood Cliffs, NJ.

Kotler, P. and Armstrong, G. (1997), *Marketing: An Introduction*, Fourth Edition, Prentice Hall, Englewood Cliffs, NJ.

Kreitzman, L. (1994), 'Quantifying the "Third Age" ', *Admap*, July/August, pp. 19–22.

Leach, C. (1987), 'How Conventional Demographics Distort Marketing Realities', *Admap*, May, pp. 41–45.

Lehtinen, U. and Lehtinen, J. R. (1991), 'Two Approaches to Service Quality Dimensions', *Service Industries Journal*, Vol. 11, No. 3, pp. 287–303.

Lewin, K. (1935), *A Dynamic Theory of Personality*, McGraw-Hill, New York.

Lewis, B. R. (1982a), 'Weekly Cash-Paid Workers: Attitudes and Behaviour with Regard to Banks and Other Financial Institutions', *European Journal of Marketing*, Vol. 16, No. 3, pp. 92–101.

Lewis, B. R. (1982b), 'The Personal Account Sector', *European Journal of Marketing*, Vol. 16, No. 3, pp. 37–53.

Lewis, B. R. (1982c), 'An Investigation into School Savings Schemes and School Banks', *European Journal of Marketing*, Vol. 16, No. 3, pp. 73–82.

Lewis, B. R. and Bingham, G. H. (1991), 'The Youth Market for Financial Services', *International Journal of Bank Marketing*, Vol. 9, No. 2, pp. 3–11.

Lewis, B. R., Orledge, J. and Mitchell, V.-W. (1994), 'Service Quality: Students' Assessment of banks and Building Societies', *International Journal of Bank Marketing*, Vol. 12, No. 4, pp. 3–12.

Lifestyle Pocket Book 1996, NTC Publications/Advertising Association, Henley-on-Thames.

Liswood, L. (1989), 'A New System for Rating Service Quality', *Journal of Business Strategy*, July–August, pp. 42–45.

Llewellyn, D. (1999), 'The Economic Rationale for Financial Regulation', *FSA Occasional Paper*, Financial Services Authority, April 1999.

Lovelock, C. H. (1984), *Services Marketing: Text, Cases and Readings*, Prentice-Hall, Englewood Cliffs, NJ.

McGoldrick, P. J. and Greenland, S. J. (1992), 'Competition Between Banks and Building Societies in the Retailing of Financial Services', *British Journal of Management*, Vol. 3, pp. 169–179.

McGoldrick, P. J. and Greenland, S. J. (1994), *Retailing of Financial Services*, McGraw-Hill, Maidenhead.

McKechnie, S. (1992), 'Consumer Buying Behaviour in Financial Services: An Overview', *International Journal of Bank Marketing*, Vol. 10, No. 5, pp. 4–12.

McKechnie, S. and Harrison, T. (1995), 'Understanding Consumers and Markets', in C. Ennew, T. Watkins and M. Wright (Eds), *Marketing Financial Services*, Second Edition, Butterworth-Heinemann, Oxford, pp. 33–59.

McKechnie, S. and Leather, P. (1998), 'Likeability as a Measure of Advertising Effectiveness: The Case of Financial Services', *Journal of Marketing Communication*, Vol. 4, pp. 63–85.

McKechnie, S., Leather, P. and Ozuygun, S. (1997), 'Viewers' Reactions to Financial Services Commercials', *Journal of Financial Services Marketing*, Vol. 1, No. 4, pp. 375–388.

Marketing Pocket Book 1994, NTC Publications, Henley-on-Thames.

Markin, J. (1977), 'Motivation in Buyer Behaviour Theory: from Mechanism to Cognition', in A. Woodside, J. N. Sheth and P. D. Bennett (Eds), *Consumer and Industrial Buying Behaviour*, North-Holland, Amsterdam.

Marx, W. (1995), 'Smart Marketers are Now Seeing Students with Dollar Signs in their Eyes', *Management Review*, September, Vol. 84, No. 9, pp. 40–44.

Maslow, A. (1970), *Motivation and Personality*, Second Edition, Harper & Row, New York.

Mehrabian, A. and Russell, J. A. (1974), *An Approach to Environmental Psychology*, MIT Press, Cambridge, Mass.

Meidan, A. (1984), *Bank Marketing Management*, Macmillan, London.

Meidan, A. and Chin, A. C. (1995), 'Mortgage-Pricing Determinants: A Comparative

Investigation of National, Regional and Local Building Societies', *International Journal of Bank Marketing*, Vol. 13, No. 3, pp. 3–11.

Mills, P. and Geraghty, M. (1997), 'Remote Relationships', *Journal of Financial Services Marketing*, Vol. 1, No. 4, pp. 347–355.

Mintel (1990), *Inherited Wealth*, Special Report, Mintel Publications, London.

Moriarty, R. T., Kimball, R. C. and Gay, J. H. (1983), 'The Management of Corporate Banking Relationships', *Sloan Management Review*, Spring, pp. 3–15.

Moser, C. A. and Scott, W. (1961), *British Towns*, Oliver and Boyd, Edinburgh.

Murray, K. B. (1991), 'A Test of Services Marketing Theory: Consumer Information Acquisition Activities', *Journal of Marketing*, Vol. 55, January, pp. 10–25.

Nelson, P. (1970), 'Information and Consumer Behaviour', *Journal of Political Economy*, Vol. 78, No. 20, pp. 311–329.

Nicosia, F. M. (1966), *Consumer Decision Processes*, Prentice-Hall, Englewood Cliffs, NJ.

Nielsen, J. F. Terry, C. and Trayler, R. M. (1998), 'Business Banking in Australia: A Comparison of Expectations', *International Journal of Bank Marketing*, Vol. 16, No. 6, pp. 253–263.

O'Brien, M. (1993), 'Altered States', *Marketing Week Customer Loyalty*, 15 October, pp. 15–17.

Parasuraman, A., Zeithaml, V. A. and Berry, L. L. (1985), 'A Conceptual Model of Service Quality and its Implications for Future Research', *Journal of Marketing*, Vol. 49, Fall, pp. 41–50.

Parasuraman, A., Zeithaml, V. A. and Berry, L. L. (1988), 'SERVQUAL: A Multiple Item Scale for Measuring Consumer Perceptions of Service Quality', *Journal of Retailing*, Vol. 64, Spring, pp. 14–40.

Parker, S., Pettijohn, C. and Carner, W. (1993), 'Survey of Bank Sales Training Practice', *Human Resource Development Quarterly*, Vol. 4, No. 2, pp. 171–183.

Peacock, A. T. and Bannock, G. (1995), *The Rational of Financial Services Regulation*, Graham Bannock and Partners Limited.

Peattie, S. and Peattie, K. (1994), 'Promoting Financial Services with Glittering Prizes', *International Journal of Bank Marketing*, Vol. 12, No. 6, pp. 19–29.

Perrier, R. (1997), 'Managing and Measuring the Power of the Brand', *Journal of Financial Services Marketing*, Vol. 1, No. 4, pp. 307–314.

Piesse, J., Peasnell, K. and Ward, C. (1995), *British Financial Markets and Institutions: An International Perspective*, Second Edition, Prentice Hall International (UK), Hemel Hempstead.

Prince, R. A. and Schultz, A. (1990), 'Factors that Attract Small Businesses', *Bank Marketing*, Vol. 22, February, pp. 28–30.

Punj, G. and Stewart, D. W. (1983), 'Cluster Analysis in Marketing Research: Review and Suggestions for Application', *Journal of Marketing Research*, Vol. 20, (May), pp. 134–148.

Quinn, V., Meenaghan, T. and Brannick, T. (1992), 'Fear Appeals: Segmentation is the Way to Go', *International Journal of Advertising*, Vol. 11, pp. 355–366.

Ray, M. L. (1973), 'Marketing Communication and the Hierarchy of Effects', unpublished research paper 180, Stanford University, Stanford, California, August.

Ray, M. L. and Wilkie, W. L. (1970), 'Fear: The Potential of an Appeal Neglected by Marketing', *Journal of Marketing*, Vol. 34, January, pp. 54–62.

Regan, W. J. (1963), 'The Service Revolution' *Journal of Marketing*, Vol. 27 July, pp. 57–62.

Reichheld, F. F. (1993), 'Loyalty-Based Management', *Harvard Business Review*, March–April, pp. 64–73.

Reichheld F. and Kenny, D. (1990), 'The Hidden Advantages of Customer Retention', *Journal of Retail Banking*, Vol. 13, No. 4, pp. 19–23.

Reichheld, F. F. and Sasser, W. E. (1990), 'Zero Defections: Quality Comes to Services', *Harvard Business Review*, Vol. 68, No. 5, September/October, pp. 105–111.

Reidenbach, E. and Moak, D. (1986), 'Exploring Retail Bank Performance and New Product Development: A Profile of Industry Practice', *Journal of Product Innovation Management*, No. 3, pp. 187–194.

Rhind, D. (1983), *A Census User's Handbook*, Methuen, London.

Robertson, T. S. (1971), *Innovative Behavior and Communication*, Holt, Rinehart and Winston, New York.

Robinson, P. J., Faris, C. W. and Wind, Y. (1967), *Industrial Buying and Creative Marketing*, Allyn & Bacon, Boston.

Rogers, E. M. (1962), *Diffusion of Innovations*, Free Press, New York.

Rogers, E. M. (1983), *Diffusion of Innovations*, Third Edition, Free Press, New York.

Rosenblatt, J., Laroche, M., Hochstein, A., McTavish, R. and Sheahan, M. (1988), 'Commercial Banking in Canada: A Study of the Selection Criteria and Service Expectations of Treasury Officers', *International Journal of Bank Marketing*, Vol. 6, No. 4, pp. 19–30.

Saunders, J. and Watters, R. (1993), 'Branding Financial Services', *International Journal of Bank Marketing*, Vol. 11, No. 6, pp. 32–38.

Scheuning, E. E. and Johnson, E. M. (1989), 'New Product Development and Management in Financial Institutions', *International Journal of Bank Marketing*, Vol. 7, No. 2, pp. 17–22.

Schlesinger, L. A. and Heskett, J. L. (1991), 'Breaking the Cycle of Failures in Services', *Sloan Management Review*, Vol. 69, No. 5, Spring, pp. 17–28.

Schlesinger, W. D., Unsal, F. and Zaman, M. R. (1987), 'Attributes of Sound Banking as Perceived by Small Businesses: Results of a Survey', *Journal of Small Business Management*, Vol. 25, October, pp. 47–53.

Shapiro, B. P. and Bonoma, T. V. (1984), 'How to Segment Industrial Markets', *Harvard Business Review*, May–June, pp. 104–110.

Shelton, D. (1995), 'Distribution Strategy in the Life and Pensions Market', *International Journal of Bank Marketing*, Vol. 13, No. 4, pp. 41–44.

Shostack, G. L. (1977), 'Breaking Free from Product Marketing', *Journal of Marketing*, Vol. 41, pp. 73–80.

Silman, R. and Poustie, R. (1994), 'What They Eat, Buy, Read and Watch', *Admap*, July/August, pp. 25–28.

Simpson, D. (1997), 'Regulation', in H. Macmillan and M. Christophers (Eds), *Strategic Issues in the Life Assurance Industry*, Butterworth-Heinemann, Oxford, pp. 28–42.

Sly, F. (1994), 'Mothers in the Labour Market', *Employment Gazette*, November, pp. 403–413.

Social Trends, No. 29, 1999 Edition, Office for National Statistics, The Stationery Office, London.

Sonnenberg, F. (1990), '*Marketing to Win*, Harvard Business School Press, New York.

Speed, R. and Smith, G. (1991), 'Retail Financial Services Segmentation', *Services Industries Journal*, Vol. 12, No. 3, July, pp. 368–383.

Spence, H. and Moinpour, R. (1972), 'Fear Appeals in Marketing – A Social Perspective', *Journal of Marketing*, Vol. 36, July, pp. 39–43.

Stanley, T. O., Ford, J. K. and Richards, S. K. (1985), 'Segmentation of Bank Customers by Age', *International Journal of Bank Marketing*, Vol. 3, No. 3, pp. 56–63.

Stephenson, B. and Kiely, J. (1991), 'Success in Selling – The Current Challenge in Banking', *International Journal of Bank Marketing*, Vol. 9, No. 2, pp. 30–38.

Sternthal, B. and Craig, C. S. (1974), 'Fear Appeals: Revisited and Revised', *Journal of Consumer Behaviour*, Vol. 1, December, pp. 22–34.

Stevenson, B. D. (1989), *Marketing Financial Services to Corporate Clients*, Woodhead, Faulkner, Cambridge.

Stewart, K. (1998), 'An Exploration of Customer Exit in Retail Banking', *International Journal of Bank Marketing*, Vol. 16, No. 1, pp. 6–14.

Stone, M. and Lowrie, R. (1996), 'Relationship Marketing in Consumer Banking – Part 2', *Journal of Financial Services Marketing*, Vol. 1, No. 3, pp. 277–292.

Stone, M. and Woodcock, N. (1997), *Winning New Customers in Financial Services: Using Relationship Marketing and Information Technology in Consumer Financial Services*, Pitman in association with IBM, London.

Storey, C. and Easingwood, C. (1993), 'The Impact of the New Product Development Project on the Success of Financial Services', *The Service Industries Journal*, Vol. 13, No. 3, pp. 40–54.

Stum, D. and Thiry, A. (1991), 'Building customer loyalty', *Training and Development Journal*, Vol. 45, No. 4, pp. 34–6.

Tedlow, R. S. and Jones, G. (Eds) (1993), *The Rise and Fall of Mass Marketing*, Routledge, London.

Thomas, D. R. E. (1978), 'Strategy is Different in Service Businesses', *Harvard Business Review*, July–August, pp. 158–163.

Thomas, M. (1980), 'Market Segmentation', *Quarterly Review of Marketing*, Vol. 6, No. 1, Autumn, pp. 25–28.

Thompson, T. W. (1986), 'Segmentation: The Anchor of Effective Client Banking', Part 1, *United States Banker*, Vol. 97, No. 4, pp. 56–57.

Thwaites, D. and Lee, S. C. I. (1994), 'Direct Marketing in the Financial Services Industry', *Journal of Marketing Management*, Vol. 10, pp. 377–390.

Tufano, P. (1989), 'Financial Innovation and First Mover Advantages', *Journal of Financial Economics*, Vol. 25, pp. 213–240.

Turnbull, P. W. and Gibbs, M. L. (1989), 'The Selection of Banks and Banking Services among Corporate Customers in South Africa', *International Journal of Bank Marketing*, Vol. 7, No. 5, pp. 36–39.

Turnbull, P. W. and Moustakatos, T. (1996), 'Marketing and Investment Banking II: Relationships and Competitive Advantage', *International Journal of Bank Marketing*, Vol. 14, No. 2, pp. 38–49.

Tyler, K. (1996), 'Exchange Relationships in Financial Services: Marketing Equities to Institutions', *International Journal of Bank Marketing*, Vol. 14, No. 2, pp. 50–63.

Vittas, D. and Frazer, P. (1982), *The Retail Banking Revolution*, Lafferty, London.

Wedel, M. (1990), Clusterwise Regression and Market Segmentation Developments and Applications, Wageningen University, Netherlands.

Wells, W. D. (1975), 'Psychographics: A Critical Review', *Journal of Marketing Research*, Vol. 12, (May), pp. 196–213.

Wells, W. D. and Gubar, G. (1966), 'Lifecycle Concept in Marketing Research', *Journal of Marketing Research*, Vol. 3, November, pp. 355–63.

Whitehead, J. (1987), 'Geodemographics – The Bridge between Conventional Demographics and Lifestyles', *Admap*, May, pp. 23–36.

Wills, G. (1985), 'Dividing and Conquering: Strategies for Segmentation', *International Journal of Bank Marketing*, Vol. 3, No. 4, pp. 36–46.

Wilson, A. M. (1992), 'The Changing Nature of the Marketing Function within Retail Banks and Building Societies', *Paper Presented at the Sixth Annual Conference of the British Academy of Management*, September.

Wilson, A. (1994), 'High Street Banking: The Culture Has to Change', *Financial Services Training Journal*, Vol. 2, No. 1, pp. 21–28.

Wind, Y. (1978), 'Issues and Advances in Segmentation Research', *Journal of Marketing Research*, Vol. 15, No. 3, pp. 315–337.

Worthington, S. (1995) 'Credit Cards', in C. Ennew, M. Wright and T. Watkins (Eds), *Marketing Financial Services*, Second Edition, Butterworth-Heinemann, Oxford, pp. 294–306.

Yorke, D. A. (1982), 'The Definition of Market Segments for Banking Services', *European Journal of Marketing*, Vol. 16, No. 3, pp. 14–22.

Zeithaml, V. A. (1981), 'How Consumer Evaluation Processes Differ between Goods and Services', in James H. Donnelly and William R.George (Eds), *Marketing of Services*, American Marketing Association, Chicago.

Zineldin, M. (1996), 'Bank–Corporate Client "Partnership" Relationship: Benefits and Life Cycle', *International Journal of Bank Marketing*, Vol. 14, No. 3, pp. 14–22.

Index

NOTE: Emboldened page numbers refer to a main entry in the financial services marketing in practice box topics.